"Deeply researched, impressively f[ ]
market flooded with books on the
God, Van Dorn provides one of the ~~~ ~~~~~
historical research—with a pastor's heart and a scholar's mind. I used this book
for my own research for my best-selling Bible novel series Chronicles of the
Nephilim."

~ **BRIAN GODAWA**, Hollywood screen writer, author: *Chronicles of the Nephilim, When Giants Were Upon the earth*

"Doug does a masterful job at drawing us back to the original text and context of
the Old Testament and to reveal the truth about the Genesis 6 event, the sons of
God and their progeny. This meticulously researched and impeccably written
book unlocks the supernatural reality and worldview of the Bible and of its authors. This work provides incredible context and shines new light on the storyline
of the biblical account, allowing us to see the work of Jesus in a fresh, necessary,
and revolutionary way. The truths that Doug brings to the surface are paramount
in understanding the past, present, and future from a scriptural paradigm and the
giants are the key to unlocking it."

~ **LUKE RODGERS**, *Blurry Creatures Podcast*

"I have read many books on the Nephilim. Doug Van Dorn's book, *Giants, sons
of the gods* is one of my favorites. I'm grateful for this 10-year anniversary update.
The charts tying together the "family tree" of the descendants of Noah are so important. I have the pages tabbed for frequent reference. It makes the tribal names
we have all passed over come to light with new context. This is a valuable reference for all Old Testament reading and study."

~ **DR. SHERRI TENPENNY**, DO, AOBNMM, ABIHM, Founder, Tenpenny Health
Restoration Centers

"After landing at Heathrow airport, a British man came up to a friend of mine who
was reading *Giants: Sons of the gods* on the plane and said, 'I've read that book. It's
excellent.' And then just walked off! It's been great to see this book have an international influence. I know of several churches here in Ireland that have used this book
almost like tracts. In the land of fairies, leprechauns, and giants Doug's book has
provided a way for Christians to meaningfully talk about the supernatural world.
This book has also been challenging Christians over the past 10 years to be more
biblical and more supernatural in their own understanding of Scripture. Doug has
done an excellent job of demonstrating that the giants of the Bible don't just show
up in one scene and are gone in the next. The Nephilim are part of the very fabric
of the biblical storyline. And Doug aptly shows that even this biblical storyline takes
us directly to Christ."

~ **MICHAEL EMADI**, M.Div, MABL, Lecturer of Biblical Languages, Covenant
Baptist Theological Seminary and Reformed Baptist Seminary

"This intriguing book will shed tremendous light on an often neglected but important biblical subject. By examining ancient records and comparing them with the biblical record, Doug Van Dorn has put together one of the most detailed studies on the subject of giants. Even though I have studied and written at length on the subject, I still found a wealth of new data to mull over."

~ TIM CHAFFEY, MDiv., ThM., apologist, and author of *The Sons of God and the Nephilim*

"As a film producer, one dreams of crossing paths with a subject matter so deep and engaging that it alters your life. Doug Van Dorn's *Giants: Sons of the gods* was that very thing for me. His book became a biblical and theological road map that launched a 2+ year journey into the film Angels & Giants, The Watchers & The Nephilim. Doug's research and insight keeps its feet on the ground when oftentimes, on this subject matter, people sensationalize gratuitously. His book launched an epic film project as well as an amazing and lifelong friendship."

~ RUDY LANDA, Director/Producer *Angels & Giants, The Watchers & The Nephilim*

"What do Buffalo Bill Cody and Katy Perry/Kanye West have in common? They talk and sing about 'giants' and 'aliens.' Maybe they referenced these subjects in ignorance, but now Doug Van Dorn has revealed the light of Biblical Truth on these matters in his book *Giants: Sons of the gods*. About three years ago my studies caused me to become a Berean on the subject of 'sons of god' in Genesis chapter six. I discovered some very helpful works done by extremely capable researchers and scholars, but Doug's work has taken me to another level on what scripture has to say on this matter. In addition, on a practical matter, the Apostle Paul's writing on spiritual warfare as become more than just words. Without a doubt if you've ever wondered if Goliath was only biblical folklore read this book and you will greatly benefit from a scholarly effort and an obvious labor of love from Doug."

~ TOM GRAHAM, NFL Linebacker (1972-78), Denver Broncos (1972-74)

"As an African, living in Africa, the supernatural worldview has always been a part of my life. Unfortunately, the implication of this worldview has been that of superstition and a "fear of the dark." Doug Van Dorn's book, *Giants: Sons of the gods*, which I consider a redemptive historical look at the Serpent's incursion into human history, has been one of the many books that have helped me to gain a Biblical perspective of the supernatural. Whereas others have long proposed the denial of the supernatural as the appropriate response to my African view of the world, an approach that has been most unhelpful, Doug's book has helped to set things right, showing that these enemies of Jesus , which are spoken of in the Scriptures, will ultimately be crushed however powerful they may seem to be right now. I can't recommend the book enough."

~ OLAMIDE BODE FALASE, Dean, Institute of Pastoral and Theological Training, Egbe, Kogi State.

"Doug Van Dorn's *Giants: Sons of the gods* was one of the first books to present a sound biblical framework for the giants mentioned in the Bible, making the information accessible to lay Christians. Yes, giants were real, and yes, they matter even today."

~ **DEREK GILBERT**, author of *The Second Coming of Saturn*, co-author of *Veneration and Giants, Gods & Dragons*

Giants: Sons of the gods is a book like no other. Doug Van Dorn is a Reformed Baptist pastor who is not afraid to look at the passages of Scripture that are often skipped or skimmed by the average Christian. This is not a fanciful tale scripted by a sci-if novelist, but a well-researched biblical, historical, and theological work that is sure to clarify and challenge many of the things you thought you knew. Enter the world of the supernatural with an inquisitive mind, and leave with a more robust worldview that keeps Christ at the center as the Lord of lords."

~ **NICK KENNICOTT**, pastor at Emmanuel Baptist Church in Coconut Creek, Florida and President of the Institute of Pastoral and Theological Training.

"Be warned, for those of us so engrossed in the physical realm, this book stretches the mind to consider what is really possible and what really exists in the spiritual realm. Read the book and draw your own conclusions."

~ **CARL NELSON**, President, Transform Minnesota: The Evangelical Network

"It has been awesome getting to know Doug Van Dorn since we started the *Blurry Creatures* podcast in 2020. I've been more than impressed by Doug's deep knowledge & insight into the stranger bible stories and forbidden history. Doug is willing to tread in places most pastors fear to go but gives context and meaning to the supernatural. If you want more understanding into the harder to understand parts of scripture that perplex most, then Doug is your guy and *Giants* is your book!"

~ **NATE HENRY**, *Blurry Creatures Podcast*

"When I first read this book, I was skeptical. Nearly every theological giant (pun intended) in history has denied the spiritual view of Genesis 6 and the many implications that follow. Augustine, Calvin, and Luther each dismissed it, and nearly every professor and pastor I have ever known has denied this view, or at least minimized it. What Doug demonstrated in this book, using Scripture and a wealth of research from both Jewish and early Christian sources, is that the spiritual view of Genesis 6 is the only view that is consistent with Scripture and what most interpreters believed for most of history. As I have slowly assimilated and adopted this world-view, so many Scriptures that I previously considered difficult or even odd are now beginning to make sense. Above all, Doug's book is no mere book of facts about Sons of God and the giants. It is first and foremost about the Unique Son of God who has triumphed over all other gods and has been given a name above every other name, the Lord, Jesus Christ."

~ **TONY JACKSON**, M.Div., pastor

"This book is simply thrilling. If you're fascinated by UFOs, aliens, ancient civilizations, and lost technologies, and yet only seem to hear them being discussed by wackos and loonies, do I have good news for you. Giants is a biblical, Reformed, and redemptive-historical treatment of these taboo topics among Christians. It was the most fun reading I've had in years."

~ LUKE WALKER, pastor of Redeeming Cross Community Church (Minneapolis) and author of *He Gave Them Judges: Jesus in the Book of Judges*

"Doug Van Dorn's treatment of the world of the giants is comprehensive and engaging. This volume is a valuable edition to the library of any prospective giantologist."

~ DR. JUDD H. BURTON, Institute of Biblical Anthropology

"Do you have the courage to look at Scripture objectively and explore what is actually there with an openness to have truth revealed rather than seeing only what you have always been taught? Doug Van Dorn does. He is deeply committed to the historic Christian faith, and at the same time willing to jettison preconceived notions and let the Scriptures speak for themselves. Read *Giants: Sons of the gods*-- You will be entertained, fascinated, informed, and challenged by Van Dorn's careful and passionate discussion of this largely ignored topic of the Bible. Warning: It could radically change the way you see the world."

~ MONTE J. KING, Th.M., M.A., Professional counselor and author of *The Simple Math Diet*

"This book is wonderfully engaging. The non-sensationalistic approach to the topic of the Watchers and the Nephilim dares us to dig ever deeper into scripture while maintaining our sense of wonder and spiritual discovery. Often-times side-stepped by mainstream Christianity, Van Dorn tackles this topic boldly and with well researched authority."

~DAVID CERULLO, President/Founder Inspiration Ministries

GIANTS

SONS OF THE GODS

(REVISED AND EXPANDED)

GIANTS

SONS OF THE GODS

(REVISED AND EXPANDED)

Douglas Van Dorn

Waters of Creation Publishing
Dacono, Colorado

Unless otherwise noted, references are from the *English Standard Version* (ESV) of the Bible.

Cover Design by Stephen Van Dorn

ISBN-13: 978-1-7350038-5-6 (Waters of Creation Publishing)

Table of Contents

Figures and Tables

Figures

All images are found on in the public domain (*wiki*)
unless otherwise indicated.

Tables

Other Books by Waters of Creation Publishing

Douglas Van Dorn

Waters of Creation: A Biblical-Theological Study of Baptism (2009)
Galatians: A Supernatural Justification (2012)
Giants: Sons of the gods (2013)
Covenant Theology: A Reformed Baptist Primer (2014)
From the Shadows to the Savior: Christ in the Old Testament (2015)
The Unseen Realm: Q & A Companion (2016)
Five Solas of the Reformation (2019)
Conspiracy Theory: A Christian Evaluation of a Taboo Subject (2020)
The Creeds: Christian Faith Essentials (2023)

Douglas Van Dorn and Matt Foreman

The Angel of the LORD: A Biblical, Historical, and Theological Study (2020)

Christ in All Scripture Series

Vol. 1. *Appearances of the Son of God Under the Old Testament* by John Owen (2019)

Vol. 2. *A Dissertation Concerning the Angel Who is Called the Redeemer and Other Select Passages* by Peter Allix (2020)

Vol. 3. *The Worship of the Lord Jesus Christ in the Old Testament* by Gerard De Gols (2020)

Vol. 4. *The Angel of the LORD In Early Jewish, Christian, and Reformation History*, a compilation of Allix, Owen, and De Gols (2020)

Vol. 5. *Christ in the Old Testament: Promised, Patterned, and Present* revised and expanded second edition of the previously titled: *From the Shadows to the Savior: Christ in the Old Testament* by Douglas Van Dorn (2020).

Vol. 6. *Jesus: Who, What, Where, When, Why?* By Douglas Van Dorn (coming soon)

Anne Van Dorn

Fiction: *Full Moon* (2022)

For more information, articles, radio shows, podcasts
go to:
douglasvandorn.com

Dedicated to:

Dr. Michael Heiser
who changed my life

And to all the people in
The Blurryverse

ACKNOWLEDGMENTS

N O BOOK WORTH ITS SALT is the product of a single person. Therefore, I want to thank the following people. First and foremost, thank you to my loving and supportive wife Janelle. You are my strength and joy. You always support me in anything I attempt, be it climbing a crazy mountain or writing on such a strange topic as this. Thank you to Annie, Tim, Janelle, Tony, Marsha, Justin, Jonathan, Monte, Jeff, Rob, Scott and Meg and others who proofread part or all of the original book and/or offered ideas and suggestions. Thanks to my bro Steve for the sweet cover designs. I can only dream of having your talents. Thanks to my mom and dad for being the best parents ever. I treasure you like precious jewels. There is no repaying all that you have done for me, especially being so willing to learn from your son. Thank you to my Bible Study guys who were tolerant enough to let me take you through this material (and its predecessor on the fathers of these giants: *The Sons of God*, a book that may still one day see the light of day in some form, no really, it might). Thanks to the church family who listened patiently in the early days of this study, and continues to do so with enthusiasm and excitement for the word of God. Thanks to my girls—just for being you: Alesha, Breanna, Annika, and Elianna. I love you all so very much. One day, you'll read this. I hope you enjoy it! Thanks to my amazing late friend Tom who called me out of the blue after hearing Tony and I discuss this topic on the radio show. Thanks to his beautiful widow Marilyn, her son Philip, and their pastors Keita and

Ron. *Giants* has opened up some many new and important friendships in my life. Thanks to Luke and Nate and the whole Blurryverse for taking this topic to the next level. Thanks to Rudy for that insane call at 6:00 a.m. and all it has led to. Thanks to Judd, Brian, and Derek for the iron sharpening iron on this and so many other related topics. Thanks to Bacon Brothers for putting up with this crazy Reformed dude. Thanks to Michael for opening up the Emerald Isle and the treasured friendship I now have. Thanks to Dr. Tenpenny for bringing this subject to a wider audience. And special thanks to Dr. Michael Heiser. Because I "accidently" stumbled onto your article on Deuteronomy 32 in preparation for a sermon on Exodus some dozen plus years ago, my life has never been the same. Your work has changed the landscape of Middle Earth. We will all do our best to carry the ring all the way to Mordor in your stead. I've often told others that now, because of you, I know I'm able to actually understand the writers of the Holy Scripture.

2013, 2023.

ABBREVIATIONS

AD   Anno Domini (Year of our Lord)
BC   Before Christ
BBE   Bible in Basic English
CTA   *Corpus tablettes alphabetiques*
ca.   circa
cf.   consult, compare
DDD   *Dictionary of Deities and Demons in the Bible*
DULAT   *A Dictionary of the Ugaritic Language in the Alphabetic Tradition*
ESV   English Standard Version
etc.   et cetera
JPS   Jewish Publication Society (Old Testament)
KJV   King James Version
KTU   *Keilalphabetische Texte aus Ugarit*
LA   Last Accessed (image references)
LXX   Septuagint
NAS   New American Standard
NIV   New International Version
NLT   New Living Translation
NT   New Testament
OT   Old Testament
RSV   Revised Standard Version
TNK   JPS Tanakh

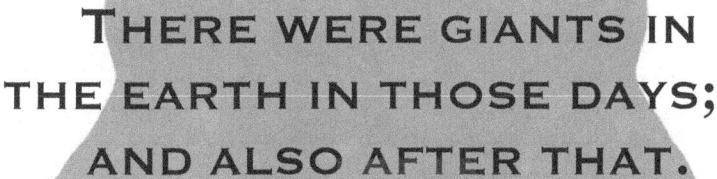

THERE WERE GIANTS IN
THE EARTH IN THOSE DAYS;
AND ALSO AFTER THAT.

GENESIS 6:4 (KJV)

The sons of men, being insensitive to [God, spirits, heavenly armies, Holy Ones, archangels, angels, thrones, and authorities], keep sinning and provoking the anger of the Most High.
(Testament of Levi 3:10)

Preface to the Tenth Anniversary Edition (2023)

TEN YEARS? It can't possibly be that long since I published the book that would change my life? Because of *Giants*, I've been honored to travel to Ireland and Israel to teach and film. Because of *Giants*, I've been interviewed for Podcasts and TV documentaries. Because of *Giants*, I wrote a book (not worthy in the slightest) that the publisher gave the same cover as *The Unseen Realm* (it's the *Q & A Companion*). Because of *Giants*, I've literally met giants—in the field and in the faith. I never could have dreamed of it. God has truly used *Giants* in so many unforeseen ways.

This crazy book began a dozen or so years ago simply as a way for me to try and figure out what this scholar named Heiser was talking about. Back in the day, he didn't have quite the name recognition, except maybe for *Coast to Coast* fans. I stumbled upon the good doctor by

God's Providence, preaching through Exodus. It was a fascinating paper—his research on Deuteronomy 32:7-8, but I had other things to do as a pastor. Then I "stumbled" upon him again for a later sermon in Exodus, and that's when I tracked down his work and fell in love with it. And his mission. Reaching Middle Earth with the Gospel through UFO conferences and crazy radio shows? That's totally what I'm talking about! But no one I knew had ever heard anything about a *divine council* or knew what to do with Nephilim. So I was left to figuring it all out with my keyboard and computer. That's how *Giants* came to be.

This ten-year anniversary edition has given me the opportunity to go over the work I haven't really looked at in detail in a decade. I set out to write a book that told a biblical theology of the war of the seeds (Gen 3:15) that would leave the reader looking squarely at the foot of the cross and the empty tomb of Jesus. The First Coming. And that's how I ended it. Deliberately.

In the intervening years, I've realized that a little more needed to be said, hopefully without destroying that original intent. So, I've gone through the book, thoroughly updating the notes, fixing dead links, adding lots of new and hopefully helpful material to just about every chapter, including two new chapters at the end which give just enough of my thoughts on the Nephilim since the resurrection to tell you what I think. Enough, I hope, to give the reader a much-needed grounding in a day fixated on speculation, while also allowing for such speculation to be, at least to some degree, justifiable, and even necessary. We need to be thinking about the evils in this world so that we don't end up with the Gulag. We need to be thinking about Jesus coming back, because he is King. But we also need sanity through it all, and speculation must be rooted in good hermeneutics and biblical, orthodox theology. If this rediscovery of such an important worldview is going to go anywhere save the dumpster heap of heresy history, we've got to be firmly grounded in *sola scriptura*. Not that we can't read other material, as you will see, but that God's word must be our sole love. It is sufficient.

I hope you will enjoy *Giants* as much as I have thinking and writing about it over the years. May the Lord give you every spiritual blessing as you try to wrap your head around this amazing, daunting, fascinating, and simply imminently fun topic.

Doug Van Dorn
Dacono, Colorado. 2023.

Preface to the Original Edition (2013)

I 'LL BE HONEST.[1] My initial interest in this topic grew out of a lifelong curiosity of our very mysterious human past and a gut-level
feeling that people need to begin to understand it better. As a
youngster, one of my favorite shows was *In Search Of...*, starring Leonard
Nimoy. The show presented conspiracy theories, although they didn't use
that loaded term to sell the series, unorthodox views of history, mysteries
of the paranormal, speculations into the origins of ancient stone monuments, and so on. Since the 1970's, these kinds of shows have flourished.

Yet, even though a part of me—ok, *it's a huge part of me*—enjoys
the speculation about our past and, to some degree about our future,
there is a rational and, frankly, biblical part of me that is very concerned
with books that come out on this topic, using this subject especially to
promote end-times speculations. Though there is always some truth in
these books, these speculations are neither safe nor good. They create
anxiety caused by worrying about the future. They can distract the
reader from what has taken place in Christ's *First* Coming and put the
focus on what has not yet come to pass, often times on things that even
Jesus said he did not know in the flesh, such as the day and hour of his
return. They delve into mysteries that no human being could possibly
know all the answers to, but they claim a kind of authority that some
people take as virtually equal to the Bible itself. This has not changed in
the ten years since this book first came out. If anything, it has increased.

With that in mind, I am writing this *Giants* for the following reasons. First, I am convinced that the biblical topic of giants is little understood. This is changing, slowly. But I doubt we'll ever be able to say
that the vast majority of Christians truly understand why the Bible talks
about this subject. Few dare to tread upon the things about them that
we can know; and those who do dare are far too quick to jump into
things that cannot be known. Because of "guilt by association" with the
latter, it would seem that most everyone else stays away from this topic.

This is bizarre and disconcerting, because the subject of giants is
quite important to understanding the spiritual battle about which the
Bible has so much to say. For example, the basic idea of this battle is

outlined by the Apostle in Ephesians, "We do not wrestle against flesh and blood, but against the rulers, against the authorities, against the cosmic powers over this present darkness, against the spiritual forces of evil in the heavenly places" (Eph 6:12). The giants are not these rulers, authorities, powers, and forces *per se*. But, they were (and in their present form are) related to them in ways that you have probably never dreamed was possible. Their influence continues to be felt, seen, and misunderstood in our world today.

Second, the topic of giants ranges through much more landscape of biblical history than most people are aware, just as the giants themselves do in the land of Canaan and beyond. If for no other reason, the sheer volume alone makes this an important topic. Therefore, it deserves serious attention.

Third, there is a dearth of serious work out there on the subject of giants in the Bible. I have grown weary of books on this subject which cannot be taken seriously because they are poorly sourced, poorly written, and poorly edited, making it difficult to check if what people are saying is true, and harder to accept by people already predisposed to disbelieving it. To give an example of the way this subject is often thought of for these reasons and others, a few years back one of my favorite pastors and authors—a man who received his Ph.D. from Fuller Theological Seminary on the subject of eschatology—took a jab at this whole subject as he aimed his words at the popular book *The Nephilim and the Pyramid of the Apocalypse*[2] in a section of his blog titled, "Just Plain Nutty." He wrote, "So let's see, the Nephilim are the product of human and angelic procreation . . . How would that work? This is theology at the level of the National Enquirer or the Star—but then that explains why it is a best seller."[3] Part of me resonates with this sarcasm, because I have a similar knee-jerk reaction to the same kind of Christian upbringing that this pastor had. This particular book sometimes indulges in bizarre numerology, views Bible codes positively (which is a serious error),[4] and engages in the very speculation I find improper for teachers of the Bible.

But not *everything* in the foresaid book is fit for tabloid magazines, and this goes for other authors who are adding to the corpus of books on giants[5]—books which bring some important contributions to this subject even if they contain some "wacky" things. You can't just click your theological heels three times and make it all just go away. This isn't Oz or Wonderland. Throwing the giant baby out with the nutty eschatological bathwater doesn't help anything.

The giants were real. Their origin, steeped in an almost unimaginable conception, is chilling. Their impact upon our present world continues to be profound ... and dangerous. Pretending that they were not (or are not) here is like ignoring the warning of your neurologist that he found a malignant tumor in your brain. Knowledge of this kind is power. I want to give you well-researched power that you can verify in your own studies.

Finally, and candidly, like so many others who write on this subject, I'm writing this because I find it utterly fascinating and fun. Who doesn't like to figure out a deep mystery or unsolved puzzle, especially one as crazy and interesting as this one? I hope you will share my enthusiasm.

It is the glory of God to conceal things,
but the glory of kings is to search things out.
(Proverbs 25:2 RSV)

> ### *** A PLEA FROM THE AUTHOR***
>
> Please read at least to the break on p. 4 of this Introduction

THIS IS NOT A BOOK ABOUT "slaying the giants in your life." If you want a self-help book, you should probably look elsewhere. This is a book about the slaying of literal historical giants in physical wars with weapons and blood and death; and finally defeating them in the greatest spiritual battle of human history—the War of the Seeds (Gen 3:15). There are strange beings here, and they line the pages of Scripture like Terracotta warriors lining the tomb of the first Emperor of a unified China: Qin Shi Huang (259 BC – 210 BC).[1]

The analogy is fitting in a way. Like the Terracotta, the giants were mighty warriors of prehistory. But unlike them, our warriors are huge and preternatural, having their origin in a story so fantastic, conservatives feel the need to reinterpret it into something tamer and less absurd, while liberals say it proves that the whole Bible must be make-believe. This makes for strange bedfellows indeed.

This story is told succinctly in Genesis 6:1-4, one of the most enigmatic and misinterpreted passages in the Bible. Here is how it reads

FIG. I.1. TERRACOTTA ARMY PIT 1, (XI'AN, CHINA)

in the oldest surviving copy—the Bible that Jesus, the Disciples, and the Church Fathers often quoted—the Greek *Septuagint* (LXX),[2]

> [1] And it came to pass when men began to be numerous upon the earth, and daughters were born to them, [2] that the sons of God [some copies read "angels"] having seen the daughters of men that they were beautiful, took to themselves wives of all whom they chose. [3] And the Lord God said, My Spirit shall certainly not remain among these men for ever, because they are flesh, but their days shall be an hundred and twenty years. [4] Now the giants were upon the earth in those days; and after that when the sons of God [again, some copies read "angels"] were wont to go in to the daughters of men, they bore children to them, those were the giants of old, the men of renown.[3]

Beginning in Chapter 1, we will proceed upon the premise that this passage tells of a time in the remote past when heavenly beings entered the abode of humans, and through our women were able to spawn a race of half-breed children, giants that *all cultures* throughout the world remember as powerful and often wicked, ruthless *demigods*.

It is important to establish at the very beginning that this passage tells the *true* story of bizarre and unthinkable proceedings. It is important to say this because the giants' tale does not stop at the Flood. It does not stop with the Old Testament. In fact, to this day, they have a very real, frightening, and powerful impact upon the world, and that is quite apart from the speculation of some writers on this subject that the giants of the past will return in the flesh in the future.

Were these merely tall people, I would simply invite you to an NBA game where we could share a hotdog and a beer together, I could tell you stories about ancient giants, you could roll your eyes at me, we could get a few autographs of the "real" giants after the game, and then go our separate ways. But this is something altogether different. To paraphrase Gandalf the Grey, "Be on your guard. There are older and fouler things than giants in the deep places of the world." The Bible speaks of dark entities, shades who roam aimlessly, demons that haunt deserts and seek to indwell unsuspecting or uninviting hosts. These and other mysteries cannot be separated from the truth about giants.

Moses tells us, "They sacrificed to demons, not God, to gods they had never known, new gods *that had come along recently* whom your fathers never dreaded" (Deut 32:17). What does this mean: they came along recently? From where did these demons originate? Apparently, they were not here in elder days; but they were here when Moses travelled through their long journey towards the Promised Land. How did they get there? Why weren't they there before this? Are they make-believe, figments of the fertile imaginations of the Jews? Such are the fascinating questions that will occupy our minds as we travel through this ancient land of the giants together.

To arrive at our destination, this Introduction will *exegete* how and why I make the assumption about Genesis 6:1-4 that I do. It will bear the burden of demonstrating why this interpretation is not only a reasonable interpretation, but the only exegetically compelling one. This is a strong claim to say that this is the "only exegetically compelling interpretation." Therefore, let me move through this Introduction like a scientist seeking to validate a hypothesis.

This is going to be semi-technical and if you have never heard any of this before, it might seem overwhelming. If you do not feel the need to have this view proven to you, then feel free to skip the rest of this Introduction. However, I believe you will find it quite fascinating, even if it takes some work on your part as a reader to understand what is being said. If you are a skeptic or hold strongly to one of the other interpretations of this passage, I truly invite you to sit down, grab a warm cup of coffee, perhaps a velvet jacket and pipe if it suits your fancy, and prepare for a little critical thinking and a lot of eye-opening, but very old, ideas.

Preliminary Questions

The first thing to do is ask some basic questions of this text. Who are the different groups of people in Genesis 6:1-4? We have several mentioned: "men," "sons of God," "daughters of men," "giants," "giants of old," and "men of renown"). What was going on between these people and what was the outcome of their interaction? What do these four verses add to our understanding of why God destroyed the world with the Flood? Why was it put here, and in the form that we have it?

History of Interpretation

To make this as simple as possible, the answer to these questions has fallen into two basic categories: the natural and the supernatural. That is, there are two main lines of interpretation proposed for dealing with the characters of this story, its plot, and the outcome of the plot beginning with the Flood, continuing through the conquest of Canaan (the Promised Land), and reaching right into the pages of the New Testament. There are also two major subsets of each view. Over time, each view has seen its fair share of advocates. Take a moment to familiarize yourself with them (see Table 1).

Supernatural Angelic View

The earliest view (ST1) is the *Angelic Procreation Theory*. Now, just because it is the oldest view, this does not necessarily make it correct.

Theory of Genesis 6:1-4	Abb.	Explanation of the Theory
Supernatural Theory 1: Angelic Procreation Theory	(ST1)	Heavenly beings came down from heaven and bred with human women producing hybrid offspring called *nephilim*.
Natural Theory 1: Divine Kingship Theory	(NT1)	The "sons of God" are dynastic rulers who married multiple women (polygamy) and their offspring were powerful, albeit human tyrants of old.
Natural Theory 2: Sethite Antithesis Theory	(NT2)	The "sons of God" are the sons of Seth (Adam's replacement son for Abel) and the "daughters of men" are the daughters of Cain. The two groups intermarried, produced gigantic offspring, and consequently God destroyed the world in a flood.
Supernatural Theory 2: Demonic Infestation Theory	(ST2)	Heavenly beings came down from heaven and genetically manipulated human DNA to create clones or hybrids through human women.

TABLE 1. FOUR THEORIES OF GENESIS 6:1-4 PUT IN TWO MAIN CATEGORIES

However, it does make it something to be carefully examined. This was no fringe, heretical, or Johnny-come-lately to the scene of biblical interpretation. It has never been condemned by any official church council, only ridiculed and mocked. Yet, please understand something. From at least a couple centuries prior to Christ until well after the close of the New Testament (NT) canon and the destruction of the second temple in Jerusalem in 70 A.D., this is *the only* currently attested Jewish view. Jesus and his disciples would have been quite familiar with it. In the Church, this was *the only* known view until the middle of the third century and was virtually the only view for 150 years after that. This is longer than the United States has been a nation! We will return to this view (our view) momentarily.

Naturalistic Dynastic View of the Rabbis

The first non-supernatural view to gain a foothold was NT1—*The Divine Kingship Theory*. Please understand something about this view as well. It originated in *Jewish circles*—among *those who deliberately rejected Christ* as the Messiah—long after ST1 had been established as the standard view among Jews. The history of this view goes something like this. Rabbis, beginning with the *Targums* (Aramaic paraphrases of the Hebrew OT, sort of like The Message Bible or The Living Bible), and especially the writing down of their tradition in the Mishna and Talmud, began to stomp out the supernatural interpretation, due in no small measure to the rapid rise of Christianity and their claims of a man calling himself the Son of God who came down out of heaven in the flesh, something similar—and yet not similar—to the angelic procreation view of Genesis 6:1-4. As a Christian, I cannot think of a more profoundly disturbing motivation for eliminating a long-cherished belief than this.[4]

How did this work itself out in the text? The desupernaturalization begins with the crucial phrase: "sons of God." Who are these persons? *Targum* Neofiti (1st – 4th cent.AD), Targum Onkelos (2nd cent.) and the Greek Symmachus (late 2nd cent.)—all Jewish works—refer to them as natural beings, ordinary humans: "judges," "mighty ones," and "powerful ones" respectively. By the time the *Mishnah* was written (3rd c. AD), it became a matter of importance to condemn the supernatural view in the strongest possible terms.

Earlier, Trypho (believed by some to be Rabbi Tarfon, ca. 135 AD), who was the opponent of Justin Martyr in Justin's defense of Christianity, called the view—*Justin's view*—"contrivances" and "blasphemies" (Justin Martyr, *Dialogue* 79). Even worse, Rabbi Simeon ben Yohai (c.a. 130 – 160 AD) was said to have "cursed all who called them the sons of God."[5] Never mind that "sons of God" is the language the Hebrew and many versions of the LXX use (the rest use "angels"). This Rabbinical condemnation of the original words in favor of *theological* interpretations that smooth out the unthinkable implications that the sons of God are supernatural beings can easily be seen as a reaction against Christ. Jesus is called *The only begotten Son of God*. This refers to his *heavenly* origin (this is also the favorite title demons had for him. "Son of man" was his more earthly, human title). But most Jewish leaders rejected Jesus as the Messiah. If he is a son of God, and there are other heavenly sons of God (though of a very different quality, i.e. they were created by the uncreated Christ; Col 1:16), what implication could this have for this rejection? Sons of God as heavenly beings would be a pillar he could use to support his own claim to deity. Thus, they suppressed the older view.[6]

Naturalistic Sethite View of Christians

In the church, things did not change nearly as fast, but once it did, anathematizing from individuals of the older view hit her with the same fury as it did the Jewish community, though (thankfully) not for the same damnable reasons. From the extant literature, we know that the Church Fathers did not deviate from ST1 until sometime into the third century. It seems to have arisen in Syria, and perhaps because celibacy was starting to dominate of monasticism,[7] though it also seems likely that interaction with Rabbis had a part in its spread. A truly non-supernatural view did not gain a true foothold until the *fifth* century! The first inkling that Christians no longer bought into the idea that the sons of God were heavenly beings is put forth by Julius Africanus (160 – 240 AD), an early Christian traveller and historian who deeply influenced Eusebius' *Histories* book some 50 years later. Africanus writes the following comments on Genesis 6:1-4,

> When men multiplied on earth, the angels of heaven came together with the daughters of men. In some copies I found 'sons of God.' What is meant by the Spirit in my opinion, is that the descendants of Seth are called the sons of God on account of the righteous men and patriarchs who have sprung from him, even down to the Saviour Himself; but that the descendants of Cain are named the seed of man, as having nothing divine in them.
>
> (Julius Africanus, *History of the World* [Fragment])[8]

Here, Julius puts forward a novel view with no known precedent in *church* history, a view which some have labelled the Sethite Antithesis theory. This theory came to dominate Christianity after Augustine, and again after some of the Reformers revived his view put forward in the *City of God* (more on that below). Before we get to that, let us take note of the context in which this citation is found. These "copies" of the Scripture that Africanus refers to are probably the Aramaic Jewish texts discussed above, mostly paraphrases of the Bible, but not actual copies of the Bible. Julius was indigenous to eastern Africa and was a well acquainted traveller to Israel, which by this time was a "Christian-free" zone, thanks to the Rabbis. It is significant to note, however, that Julias immediately goes on to say,

But if it is thought that these refer to angels, we must take them to be
those who deal with magic and jugglery, who taught the women the
motions of the stars and the knowledge of things celestial, by whose
power they conceived the giants as their children, by whom wickedness came to its height on the earth, until God decreed that the whole
race of the living should perish in their impiety by the deluge.

In other words, Julius is not writing a polemical or dogmatic work, but
Christian history. While he comments on his personal agreement with
these Jewish *targumim* concerning their interpretation of the sons of
God, he recognizes that others understand them to refer to angels. (Perhaps Julius was not aware of the virtual unanimity on the ancient understanding of angels, but that is speculation).

The first known dogmatic Christian adherent to the *Sethite View*
will not come along for over 100 years after this, in one Ephrem the
Syrian who wrote around 325 AD. Let that sink in. From the birth of
Christ, this is almost sixty-five years longer than the entire history of our
own beloved United States of America. He stated,

[Moses] called the sons of Seth "sons of God," those who, like the sons
of Seth, had been called "the righteous people of God." The beautiful
daughters of men whom they saw were the daughters of Cain who
adorned themselves and became a snare to the eyes of the sons of Seth.
Then Moses said "they took to wife such of them as they chose," because when "they took" them, they acted very haughtily over those
whom they chose. A poor one would exalt himself over the wife of a
rich man, and an old man would sin with one who was young. The
ugliest of all would act arrogantly over the most beautiful.[9]

After Ephrem, only John Chrysostom (349 – 407 AD) in his *Homily on
Genesis* 22:6-8 holds this view in the church until Augustine who writes
the *City of God* sometime after 410 AD. This means that virtually no
known Christian *until the fifth century* held any other view than the supernatural angelic view.[10]

Again, let that sink in, because it really is a staggering thought,
especially in light of the popularity of the Sethite view ever since. This
view was perpetuated by the following four "giants" of the faith (whom

I personally admire and adore): Chrysostom, Augustine, Martin Luther, and John Calvin. Listen carefully to what they say.

Augustine writes on his denial of the older angelic view saying that because angels are ministering "spirits" (Psalm 104:4), "I could by no means believe that God's holy angels could at that time have so fallen" (Augustine, *City of God 15:23*).[11] *I could by no means believe?* Luther similarly says, "That anything could be born from [the union of a devil and a human being], this " do not believe" and then refers to this as "the silly ideas of the Jews" (Martin Luther, *Genesis 6:2*).[12] *I do not believe?* Calvin is utterly mocking in his tone when he says, "That ancient figment, concerning the intercourse of angels with women, is abundantly refuted by its own absurdity; and it is surprising that learned men should formerly have been fascinated by ravings so gross and prodigious" (John Calvin, *Genesis 6:1*).[13] *That ancient figment?*

To put it in a nutshell, these heroes of mine on so many other doctrines, dismiss with a flick of the wrist and the upturn of the nose, the views of Justin Martyr, Irenaeus, Athenagoras, Pseudo Clement, Clement of Alexandria, Tertullian, Lactantius, Eusebius, Commodian, Ambrose, Jerome, Sulpicius Severus, and many others[14]—not to mention a host of Jewish traditions—on the grounds that it is absurd and because they could not believe it. This is the worst possible form of *exegesis* (it is actually called *eisegesis*) for it understands only what the reader wants the text to say on already biased, presupposed terms. Historically, the Sethite view stands firmly planted in emotional nausea rather than rational logic or exegetical refutation.[15] *Ad Hominem* dominates both early and later rejection of the angelic view.[16] This does not mean decent arguments have not been offered by adherents to the Sethite view (see below), only that its conception and roots are planted on the sandy soil of emotional irritation.

Angelic View Revisited

Until recently, the Sethite view dominated the Protestant church.[17] A few Christians have adopted the old Rabbinical view with modifications, but it has never really caught on like it did in Judaism. This theory is not necessarily incompatible with a supernatural view, since someone like Gilgamesh, one-third human, and two-thirds divine in the stories would fit the bill. But it should still be said that most of its recent adherents believe these kings were quite human.[18]

Then came the (re)discoveries and a newly acquired interest in early Jewish writings that were circulating at the time of Christ. Books like 1 Enoch (which had been lost for a thousand years to the western church), Jubilees, Judith, Sibylline Oracles, Baruch, The Testament of the Twelve Patriarchs, Sirach, Wisdom of Solomon, and the Genesis Apocryphon from the Dead Sea Scrolls could have all been read by the Apostles. In fact, some of them are quoted in the New Testament (cf. 1 Enoch 1:9 in Jude 14-15). Each has a supernatural take on Genesis 6:1-4.

In light of this, most scholars today[19] (including conservative Evangelicals) argue that the supernatural view must have been the view of Peter and Jude, who both comment on this passage (Doedens, Heiser, and others add 1Cor 11:10; 1Pet 3:18-20 [see Ch. 15]. Also probable is Matt 24:38/Luke 17:27). The passages are: "For if God did not spare angels when they sinned, but cast them into hell and committed them to chains of gloomy darkness to be kept until the judgment; if he did not spare the ancient world, but preserved Noah ..." (2 Pet 2:4-5); and "And the angels who did not stay within their own position of authority, but left their proper dwelling, he has kept in eternal chains under gloomy darkness until the judgment of the great day ..." (Jude 1:6). For an exegetical explanation of these verses, see "Appendix: 2 Peter 2:4 and Jude 6."

If our analysis in the Appendix is correct, then critically, this must be *the inspired infallible view* and thus, for anyone who believes in the infallibility of Scripture, a supernatural interpretation is *necessarily* correct. If this is in fact what Jesus' half-brother and the great Apostle Peter are talking about, it is the last nail in the coffin for any non-supernatural view, unless a person wants to say that Jude and Peter were "mad fools." The very conservative John Murray, who does not agree with the angelic view admits as much saying, "Without question, if [Peter] refers to angelic beings, whether exclusively or partially so as to include also the disembodied souls of men, this interpretation would necessarily turn the scales in favour of the view that the sons of God in Genesis 6:1–3 were angelic beings."[20]

Supernatural Genetic Modification View

With the resurfacing of the supernatural view and the rise of modern science (especially the human genome project), a fourth view has become popular in our own day. This view (ST2) is a modification of ST1 and says that the Nephilim were the result of genetic tampering by beings that have existed since God created the heavens and the earth. If we, in just a matter of a few decades, have mapped the entire human genome, are creating living *chimeras*, and are passing (and in some cases, eliminating!) laws outlawing hybridization, these heavenly beings would probably have the intelligence to do the same thing if they so chose (we will talk about some of these things as we make our way through this book). After all, they have been here a *lot* longer than we have.

To me, the historical question really comes back to the two main views (natural vs. supernatural). Variations within each view are not the main point, and it does not particularly matter for our purposes here which view a person holds within these two broader ideas. It is the reason *why* someone would want to reject the original supernatural view in favor of a naturalistic explanation that interests me most. As I have demonstrated, some of the most influential Christians from my own (Protestant) tradition dismissed and made fun of it for emotional reasons. Also, because of even earlier stalwarts, almost the entire church (Eastern, Roman, and Protestant) has come to reject the ancient theory with very little reason other than it seems strange and silly and a waste of time and thought. Yet, today the claim is still made that the Sethite Antithesis View is more exegetically sound than the angelic view. Therefore, let us test this hypothesis by looking at the text and asking some questions.

Sethite Antithesis Argument Explained

Let's see how the Sethite argument proceeds from the text. First, it is noted correctly that Genesis 6:1-4 falls immediately after Genesis 4-5 which traces the genealogies of Cain and Seth, the two named sons of Adam after Abel is murdered. The genealogy of Cain the murderer ends in the seventh generation from Adam with Lamech. This wicked man becomes a polygamist and murderer *par excellence* (Gen 4:19, 23-24). Since Genesis 6:1-4 deals with marriage (perhaps even polygamy in some views), and since Genesis 6:5 and 13 explicitly refer to the terrible violence on the earth, the dots are connected back to Lamech from the line of Cain. This seems a clear hint that the same sin is going on throughout the story, and there is no need to make up ridiculous stories of fallen angels having sex with women.

Meanwhile, as soon as the Cainite line reaches its tragic, wicked apex in Lamech, the Sethite line is immediately picked up and carried for a while. We read that Seth has a descendent named Enosh who "began to call upon the name of the LORD" (Gen 4:26). The seventh descendant on Seth's side is named Enoch who was said to have walked with God and been taken to heaven without dying (Gen 5:22-24). Lamech is the seventh descendant from Adam on Cain's side and Enoch is the seventh on Seth's side. This shows the antithesis between the line of Cain and the line of Seth. The former is wicked. The latter is godly.

When we come to Genesis 6:1-4, it is thus quite natural to read "the sons of God" as being godly Sethites and the "daughters of men" as being ungodly Cainites. Who else could they be in the context? Again, we are told that we have no reason to hold any other view. It fits in perfectly with the genealogies, and acts as a nice transition to God's anger with men. In my own tradition, this is seen as good biblical covenant theology. It is the *plain meaning* of the text.

When we come to the passage itself, we are shown how it explicitly states that God is angry with "men" (Gen 6:3), not "angelic beings." In fact, the passage refers to man (*'adam*) no less than 10 times in the first seven verses, and many more if you add the pronouns. This theory is neat, tidy, and best of all entirely natural. There is no need to see it as mythology or as talking about supernatural beings doing impossible things with human women.

Case closed. Right? Not so fast. There are actually many problems with this *exegesis*.

Sethite Antithesis Argument Deconstructed

Were All Cainites Evil and All Sethites Godly?

First, let's look at the broader context. While it is true that Lamech and Enoch are set apart as opposites, there is no incontrovertible evidence that everyone in the line of Cain was wicked, nor that everyone in the line of Seth was godly. Yet, this is the lynchpin of the entire theory. In fact, it is plausible the text shows us that—almost immediately—*all men* began to become wicked. Shouldn't this necessitate that this include many in the line of Seth (think about the kings of Israel in the line of Christ, they were not all godly). Let us look a little more closely at Genesis 4:26.

The verse concerns the grandson of Adam (if the passage is read without genealogical gaps). Most translations render it something like, "At that time people *began* to call upon the name of the LORD." This is said about the days of Seth's first named descendant: Enosh. The word "began" implies that either, 1. Prior to this time no one called upon God in a worshipful way, or 2. No one knew the personal name of God (Yahweh, i.e. the LORD) until this time. Neither implication is supportable.

Early in Genesis 4, both Cain and Abel went to offer sacrifices (that is "worship") "to the LORD" (Gen 4:3-4). Apparently, people from *both* lines *were* worshiping Yahweh prior to the birth of Enosh. That removes option #1. But maybe they did not know God's name until the days of Enosh? This is clearly not the case either. When Cain was born Eve exclaimed, "I have gotten a man with the help of *the LORD (Yahweh)*" (Gen 4:1). She uses the personal, covenantal name of God. Obviously, God's name was known long before Enosh was born. How then can we make sense of this text?

For these reasons, the Jewish *Targums* (which are not all bad) read the verb *chalal* ("began") as something like "pollute" (a possible meaning). Pseudo-Jonathan paraphrases the idea, "And to Seth also was born a son, and he called his name Enosh. That was the generation in whose days they began to err, and to make themselves idols, and surnamed their idols by the name of the Word (*Memra*) of the Lord." The Onkelos Targum is similar, "To Seth also was born a son, and he called his name Enosh. Then in his days the sons of men desisted (or forbore) from praying in the name of the Lord." The grammar for this idea is not very compelling. Nevertheless, it is obvious that the meaning has been disputed in history, and this ought to give us pause.

No English translation renders the passage like the *targums*. All take it as an act of godly worship. Let's assume that this is correct. What is important to note now is that none of the Hebrew-to-English translations say that *only Sethites* were calling upon God's name.[21] They all use the more generic term "men" or "people."[22] This is important. "Seth" is not equivalent to "man." His name does not mean "Man," that's Adam's name. It means something like "Appointed" or "Substitute." "Man" is a broader term than "Seth" in this verse. This will have implications later on, in Genesis 6:1-4. For now, this means that *the text* gives no indication that only Sethites were godly. That is nothing but speculation, and rather oblivious speculation, if human nature at any time after this is taken into account. To conclude, even though Lamech and Enoch are obviously literary spiritual opposites, the verse in question here does not support the idea that *everyone* in each line followed rank. To import this idea into Genesis 6:1-4 is to go against the very clear teaching of Genesis 4:26. One might be able to argue against this view systematically or using biblical theology, but the text simply can't support the weight of the theology *at this point*.

There is something more subtle going on with this argument of an antithesis between Seth's lineage and Cain's in the Sethite view of Genesis 6. What often goes unnoticed is a switch in the "godliness" of the line of Seth. First, we are told that all of the named descendants of Seth are godly. This is the bait, and we are expected to eat it hook, line, and sinker. This point cannot be proven either way from the genealogy,[23] yet this "fact" creates the justification for reading the passage this way.

Here's the switch. After this has been established, we are then supposed to just accept that in Noah's day, all of this godly line has abandoned true religion for unbridled lust. Huh? *No one* in the line prior to this rebelled. *Everyone* in the line in Noah's day did? This is why it is called the "Sethite" view. We are not just talking about the 10 names mentioned in the genealogy, but everyone who is descended from Seth, presumably millions and millions of men (and I do mean "men"). The entire Sethite interpretation of Genesis 6 hangs on this.

What is strange is that when you stop to think about it from this point of view, it is the godly line—the Sethites—who are committing the wickedness in this passage. *They* are the ones taking ungodly women as their wives. That's hardly what we would expect, given that it is Cain's line that is so degenerate. In fact, it is possible to understand the "taking" of wives in Gen 6:2 to be a violent taking against the will of the women (see chapter 4 n. 3 and context). In the passage, what then are the daughters of Cain even doing wrong? This only compounds the problem. All the good men are suddenly acting wickedly, while all the wicked women are acting innocently? Say what?

Equivocation

The second point, and it is a major one that you should take seriously, has to do with equivocation. *Equivocation* is a logical fallacy. It is the misleading use of a term with more than one meaning or sense. The equivocation occurs with the term "man" (*'adam*) and the term "God" (*'elohim*) in the Sethite view.

"Adam" was the name of the first man. In fact, his name means "Man" (just like Enosh can mean "Man," see above). These two names are equivalent to "man" in Hebrew. "Cain" is not. Cain does not mean "Man." The first equivocation occurs in Genesis 6:1-2. "And it came about, when men (*ha'adam*, literally "the men") began to multiply on the face of the earth, and daughters were born unto them, that the sons of God saw the daughters of men (*ha'adam*) that they were fair..." (KJV). In the Sethite view, in the first instance, "men" means "mankind." Very few dispute this. I certainly don't. In the second instance, however, "men" magically transforms into "daughters of *Cain*."[24] What justification *in these two verses* is there for such a change in meaning? Nowhere are the names "Seth" or "Cain" used in this chapter. They haven't been mentioned for many scores of verses.

In fact, the parallel phrase to the "daughters of *'adam*" would be "sons of *'adam*." "Sons of Adam" occurs later on, at the Tower of Babel, *after the flood* (Gen 11:5). If the phrase refers to Cainites in Genesis 6, and all Cainites were wiped out in the flood, then how would we account for their reappearance at the Tower of Babel? Suddenly, unexpectedly, and necessarily, we will have to change the meaning of *'adam* once more to be something like "sons of Ham" or "sons of Cush." Or I suppose we could just spiritualize the term. If we do this, it needs to be recognized that even in the spiritualization that we are talking about biological family trees, because supposedly God did not choose anyone from these family trees to be saved.

There is another problem. Up to this point, Cain has never been called the son of Adam. It is obviously true that Cain *is* Adam's son (Gen 4:1 explicitly tells us that Adam lay with Eve who gave birth to Cain), but he is never *called* Adam's son, only Eve's son. Why then would "daughters of *'adam*" in Genesis 6:2 suddenly mean "daughters of *Cain*," when we have no grammatical precedent for it? This is not an insurmountable problem, but it is certainly curious that if we are going to argue so stringently for the meaning of a phrase that it would have no actual precedent in the Bible.

Furthermore, Seth *is* referred to as Adam's son (Gen 5:3) as are many sons that he had after Seth (Gen 5:4). If we want to let the text speak, then of the two boys, it is *Sethites* whom we should rightly call the daughters of *'adam*, not Cainites. Thus, while it is true that the genealogies point out some kind of antithesis between the two lineages (in a theological sense, Augustine is correct, there is a "city of man" and a "city of God"), there are many more issues to consider than just the genealogies when determining the meaning of "daughters of men." At the end of the day, "men" appears to be a serious equivocation.

The second equivocation is with the word *'elohim*. This word means "God" or "gods", depending upon the context. This equivocation occurs in Genesis 6:2-3. "The sons of *God* having seen the daughters of men that they were beautiful, took to themselves wives of all whom they chose. And the Lord *God* said ..." In the first instance, we are told that "God" really means "Sethites" (see "Spiritualization" below). But in the second instance it clearly refers to God himself. Again we must ask, what justifies this switching of definitions? Theological systems must have exegetical justification to back them up.

Curiously, as we saw with Cain, so now we see with Seth. Nowhere in the Bible is Seth called the "son of God," just as nowhere was Cain ever called the "son of Adam." But, as we pointed out already, *Seth* is called the "son of man" (*'Adam*) in both the OT and the NT (Luke 3:38).

Spiritualization

The third point has to do with spiritualizing the text. I'm actually not against this, when it is consistently practiced and justified by the context. In this case, I do not think either one is true. The spiritualization occurs when we take the term "sons of God" to mean "godly" Sethites, while "daughters of men" means "wicked" Cainites. Something very tricky is going on here.

Very simply, this is a strange mixture of spiritualizing and physicalizing the text inconsistently, as it suits the interpreter's purposes. While it is theologically conceivable that sons of "God" might refer to "godly" people, it is very difficult to see how daughters of "men" must refer to "wicked" people. "Godly," I suppose, could correspond to "God," but why must "wicked" correspond to "men," or better, "women" (and isn't that inherently sexist)? Are not Sethites also men and their daughters also women? Since all the people involved are human beings, the second case of spiritualizing seems arbitrary and inconsistent with the first.

Only if we presuppose that these daughters of men are Cainites (which as we have seen is logically precarious), *and also* that God did not save *any* Cainites would this even be plausible. But given what we know about God and election, this would be most unlike what he does elsewhere in the Scripture. Throughout the rest of the Bible, he often saves very "unsavable" Gentiles such as Rahab or Ruth (I'm assuming a Reformed view of election here since many or most of the Sethite adherents have been Reformed). Not only does this go against what we know of God's later choice in election, but now we have moved back into the physical realm to justify our spiritualizing. God now chooses all the people he wants saved because of ancestral heritage.

To avoid this problem, we might assume that the "sons of God" and "daughters of men" simply mean "believers" vs. "unbelievers" without any reference to biology (something I'm not aware that anyone does). This would defeat the whole point of the Seth-Cain antithesis. If some (many?) of the daughters of men are actually from the line of Seth, and some (many?) of the sons of God are actually from the line of Cain, what's the point? Spiritualizing these names consistently defeats the whole argument of an antithesis of the family trees.

The inconsistent spiritualization I am claiming is going on in Genesis 6:1-4 is the same problem that regularly occurs in interpretations of Genesis 3:15. The verse reads, "I will put enmity between you (Satan) and the woman, and between your seed and her seed" (NAS). Where is the double standard? Most people will say that the first seed is a *spiritual* seed (i.e., wicked people, those whose spiritual father is the devil; cf. John 8:44), while the second seed is a *biological* seed— Jesus Christ. What justification is there for splicing up the meaning of the two seeds in this way?

I do not have a problem saying that both seeds are spiritual or even that both seeds are at the same time physical. I have a big problem interpreting one seed as spiritual and the other as biological. This is not consistent. In fact, this verse is one of the primary exegetical reasons to understand that Genesis 6:1-4 is in fact talking about heavenly beings. It predicts that Satan will have a "seed." This seed will be of the same kind that the woman is. It will be physical, able to wage war, etc. Without discussing it in full here, I'm sure you can already see a little of why this verse has bearing upon our passage.

Let's return again to Genesis 6:1-4. The inconsistency of spiritualizing the sons of Seth has a very glaring textual problem. The passage tells us that *all mankind* was violent and wicked. In fact, the most "in your face" declaration of total depravity in the Bible occurs in *this* passage, and it does not refer merely to Cainites. "The LORD saw that the wickedness *of man* was great in the earth, and that every intention of the thoughts of his heart was only evil continually. (Gen 6:5). Biology is in view here. "Man" is not "Cainites." Group A sees that Group B is "beautiful." They get "married." They have offspring. All of this occurs because *mankind* was "multiplying." It would seem then, that if there is a way to understand "sons of God" and "daughters of men" biologically, this would be better than the spiritualizing.

Laws about Marriage

A fourth objection is that to assume that Sethites were not allowed to marry Cainites is *anachronistic*. *Anachronism* is an inconsistency in a chronological arrangement. For example, today it would be anachronistic to use a typewriter or to wear a top-hat or to write with a quill. Instead, we write with computers, wear baseball caps, and write with pens. Logical arguments work the same way. What do I mean with this objection?

First, we have no indication anywhere in Genesis 1-6 that it was wrong for Sethites to marry Cainites. This idea comes from the laws of Israel who *millennia* later were not allowed to marry foreigners (Ex 34:16; Ezra 10:3; Mal 2:11; 2 Cor 6:14). This is a reading back into the text what is not there; hence *anachronism*. I would argue that the *principle* of not being yoked with unbelievers or the world is sound and eternal. The problem is, we have no concrete proof that all Cainites were unbelievers, nor that all Sethites were believers. It just isn't in the text.

Other Sons and Daughters

A fifth objection arises from the fact that we are told that Adam had other sons and daughters (see above). If this is true, then why are we only picking out Sethites and Cainites? Let's say, since we do not know their names, that Adam also had sons named Bilbo, Frodo, Samwise, Peregrin, Meriadoc, Gandalf, Aragorn, Boromir, Legolas, and Gimli.[25] Where he got these names, I have no idea. Here's the point. None of these other sons or their descendants would be in either the Sethite or Cainite lines. They are directly descended from Adam, not from Seth or Cain.

Now let's say that Adam's eight other sons all had the same number of sons as Abel and Cain. This would mean that 80% of the people on earth had nothing whatsoever to do with the events of Genesis 6, according to a strict Sethite interpretation. So why were they wiped out in the flood? One could respond that these people were also wicked for other reasons, even if they were not involved in the sins of Genesis 6:1-4. The problem with this reply is that Genesis 6:1-4 explains why there was such violence on the earth. It was a direct result of these marriages and almost certainly, their offspring. The violence and wickedness of *mankind* was so intimately tied to these marriages and children that Moses thought it was critical to put Genesis 6:1-4 at the beginning of his story of the Flood.

How Do Giants Come from Men?

What I want to introduce now is the offspring of these marriages of whomever it was that got married. This final objection to the Sethite view will focus on Genesis 6:4 and the beings referred to in the LXX as "giants." These "giants" are really the focus of the book, but it has been necessary to talk about their fathers until this point, though honestly, their fathers deserve an entire book themselves. The Greek word for giants is *gigantes*. Here is what the *Dictionary of Deities and Demons in the Bible (DDD)* says about them,

> In the strict sense the Gigantes in Greek mythology were the serpent-footed giants who were born from the blood-drops of the castration of Uranus (→Heaven) that had fallen on →Earth (Hesiod *Theogony* 183–186). The term *gigantes* occurs about 40 times in the LXX [Greek *Septuagint*] and refers there respectively to: a) the giant offspring of 'the sons of God' and 'the daughters of mankind' (Gen 6:1–4; Bar 3:26–28; Sir 16:7); b) strong and mighty men, like →Nimrod (Gen 10:8–9); c) several pre-Israelite peoples of tall stature in Canaan and Transjordania. The etymology of the name, which may be pre-Greek, is unknown, but was in Antiquity thought to be *gēgenēs*, or 'born from earth'.[26]

A perusal of ancient Greek art gives a striking visual of these *gigantes* (see Fig. 1.2).

    The significance of the whole world—the *whole world* mind you(!), which supposedly had no interaction with one another until recently—

Villa del Casale   *Gigantomachia*
(Roman Mosaic 3rd C. A.D.)   Istanbul Archaeological Museum, Turkey

FIG. 1.2. SERPENTINE GIANTS OF GREEK MYTHOLOGY

SERAPIS	FUXI AND NŸWA	Kukulkan	Kalïya Daman
(EGYPT)	(CHINA)	(Central & South America)	(India)

FIG. I.3. SERPENTINE GODS OF WORLD MYTHOLOGY

depicting the same creatures (everyone pictured above is considered a god or a giant) the same way must not be ignored. For such a thing to occur by chance is statistically ridiculous. To come to that conclusion would be completely irrational, a faith based in nothing verifiable, nothing objective, nothing but wishful thinking.

Moderns classify the above pictures as *mythology*. While most people relegate myth to the realm of fantasy and fiction (which is why it is the unforgivable sin in many circles to suggest that anything in Scripture is "mythological"), it is increasingly understood by many that these ancient stories, while shrouded in mystery and certain embellishment, nevertheless recollect some token of true events of world history. In fact, speaking of our very text (Genesis 6:1-4), the late Christian apologist Francis Schaeffer wrote,

> More and more we are finding that mythology in general, though greatly contorted, very often has some historic base. And the interesting thing is that one myth that one finds over and over again in many parts of the world is that somewhere a long time ago supernatural beings had sexual intercourse with natural women and produced a special breed of people.[27]

J.R.R. Tolkien and C.S. Lewis were of the same opinion as Schaeffer about mythology.[28] In other words, there is nothing inherently nefarious about mythology, *if* it is a vehicle used to transmit historical information. As Lewis said, the Bible just so happens to be the "True Myth" (that is, it is 100% historically accurate).

Moving on, the Greek word *gigantes* translates the Hebrew word *nephilim*. Nephilim is the word that appears in Genesis 6:4. The ESV leaves it untranslated. It is commonly thought that *nephilim* is related to the Hebrew word *naphal* meaning "to fall." Hebrew was originally written without vowels and viewed in this light the two words are almost identical (*nphlm* and *nphl*). Theologically, "to fall" may fit with either the angelic view (children of those who fell to earth) or a Sethite view (those who fell into sin).[29] If the word derives "to fall," there is an interesting relationship with *nephilim* and *gigantes* or those born from the blood "fallen on earth" from the castrated Uranus (*gigantes* means "born of the earth," and in this context it is easy to see why). Keep in mind that Uranus is a Greek word meaning "heaven," but he was also a god. In other words, perhaps more than any other god of the Greek pantheon, his name shows that he is a *heavenly being*.

A better possibility is that *nephilim* derives from the *Aramaic* word *naphal*.[30] We've already seen how Targums were written in Aramaic, the *lingua franca* of the ANE. Aramaic is a sister tongue of Hebrew. It was also the language of the exiled Jews who returned from Babylon. If this relationship is genuine, then we must consider the transmission of the ancient text to those in the captivity. The Hebrew text was being recopied for each generation as the older copies degraded. Because the course of human events included wars, captivity, the changing of languages etc., sometimes it was necessary to help "modern" people understand what they were reading. An Aramaic speaker might need a special note in a copied manuscript in order to understand the meaning of a particularly important, but now obscure, word. We see this in the NT when a Hebrew or Aramaic word is translated into Greek (cf. John 5:2; 19:13, 19:17; 20:16; Rev 9:11) for the sake of the audience reading the original text. We most likely also see it in Numbers 13:33, the only other time *nephilim* definitely occurs in the Scripture. In this verse, *nephilim* occurs twice, but it is spelled differently. This is tremendously significant.

Verse	Hebrew
Numbers 13:33a	*ne-phy-l-m*
Numbers 13:33b	*ne-ph-l-m*

The first spelling cannot be easily accounted for by the Hebrew verb "to fall." But it is accounted for in the Aramaic word. This word *naphal* means "giant," and makes perfect sense if these people in Canaan were "of great height" (Num 13:32). This is identical to the LXX version of *gigantes*. Importantly, this Aramaic word appears in the Dead Sea Scrolls on several occasions in conjunction with giants.[31] For example, the *Targum* of Job 38:31 uses this word to translate the constellation Orion, which was regarded by Homer (*Odyssey* 5.121) as a gigantic hunter and *demigod*—that is half god and half human.

This leads to the final word study in the group. We have looked at *gigantes* and *nephilim*. Now we want to look at the Hebrew word *gibborim*. Reading the LXX, you would not even know that there was another word in the Hebrew, for the LXX translates both *nephilim* and *gibborim* as *gigantes*. "Now the giants (*nephilim/gigantes*) were upon the earth in those days; and after that when the sons of God were wont to go in to the daughters of men, they bore *children* to them, those were the *giants* (*gibborim/gigantes*) of old, the men of renown." This speaks volumes about the how Jews before Christ interpreted this passage.

In Hebrew to English translations, *gibborim* is usually translated as something like "mighty men," though in the Dead Sea Scrolls its Aramaic equivalent is, as with the Greek, regularly translated as "giants."[32] In Genesis 6:4 it is apparently parallel to *nephilim* and certainly parallel to "men of renown" or more literally "men of the name (*shem*)."[33] The word is next used in the Bible of Nimrod who "was the first on earth [after the Flood] to become a *gibborim*" (Gen 10:8). He was the builder of the Tower of Babel (see Note #33), and as we will see in the first chapter, Nimrod, like Orion, was a hunter (Gen 10:9). In the stories of the ancient near east, he is also identified as a giant.

This also parallels the idea set forth by Hesiod that there were half-god heroes from of old.[34] Thus, the *gibborim* in Genesis 6:4 are said to have been "from of old." This distinguishes them from very human *gibborim* in David's (2 Sam 23:8-39) or Joshua's (cf. Josh 8:3) armies. Instead, the identification "from of old" clearly places them in the "primeval period and not in the recent historical past."[35] Clearly this is the case, since they were destroyed in the Flood. Thus, we can finally see this last objection to the Sethite view. If *nephilim* means "giant," as it so clearly does in Numbers 13:33 and in the LXX of Genesis 6:4, then the obvious question becomes how would marriages of Sethites and Cainites result in gigantic offspring? There has never been a satisfactory answer to this question by anyone in the naturalistic camp.

The Heavenly Interpretation of the "Sons of God"

As you can now see, there are plenty of reasons to be suspicious of the Sethite view. There is no consistent way to understand all Sethites as godly, nor do we have any compelling exegetical reason for interpreting "sons of God" or "daughters of men" as Sethites and Cainites. It seems better, given a choice, not to equivocate on the terms "men" and "God." These words should be interpreted consistently in this passage unless we have some compelling exegetical reason for not doing so. There is no consistent way to spiritualize these phrases, nor is it contextually necessary to do so. Intermarriages between believers and non-believers are both anachronistic and unsubstantiated. Adam had other sons and daughters that are not taken into account. Finally, giants are being born of these unions with no rational explanation for how, if these are just human intermarriages.

There is only one view of this passage that can answer all these objections satisfactorily. This is the supernatural view that the sons of God came down out of heaven and somehow produced gigantic offspring with human women. Whether they did it through semen, genetic manipulation, and if they later became tyrant kings of the earth, it doesn't really matter. The idea is simple if not also bizarre to a culture that worships at the feet of materialism and naturalism. But "bizarre," in itself, is not a good enough justification for jettisoning it. The Trinity, the Virgin Birth, and the Two Natures of Christ are all incredibly difficult ideas to wrap one's mind around, and to unbelievers, they are just as bizarre sounding as this. Christians ought to keep that in mind before mocking the supernatural view of Genesis 6. Do we really want to engage in the same arguments that those who hate our most deeply held convictions engage in against us?

Usage of the "Sons of God"

Thus far, I've tried to show why the arguments against the angelic view are not solid. But what are the exegetical reasons *for* taking a supernatural view? The most important has to do with the term "sons of God" as it is used in the Bible. Chrysostom boldly dares, "Let them demonstrate firstly where angels are called sons of God; they would not, however, be able to show this anywhere. While human beings are called sons of God, angels are nowhere so called."[36] I accept the challenge. This isn't difficult. Not even slightly.

It is undoubtedly the case that Israel is called God's "son" (Ex 4:22-23; Deut 14:1) or his "children" (Ps 73:15; Deut 32:5) in the Bible.[37] But never are they called this using the phrase "*beney ha'elohim*," the Hebrew phrase used in Genesis 6:2 and 4. In fact, Chrysostom could not have been more wrong. In the Bible, this phrase is a technical term for heavenly beings. Let me explain.

First, let's understand the Hebrew. "*Ben*" is a son, as in Benjamin: Son of My Right Hand. "*Beney*" is the plural form of *ben*.[38] *Ha* is the definite article ("the"). Finally, *'elohim* is the generic word for God or gods.[39] So the phrase is literally then, "sons of the God," meaning that it is God and not gods in mind here.

Note that the oldest versions of the LXX read, "the *angels* of God,"[40] where "sons" become "angels." Of course, this is more properly called a translation/interpretation; so it proves nothing more than that our earliest records indicate the angelic view was understood to be the meaning. However, it should be kept in mind, that the LXX was the Bible most often read and cited by the NT evangelists. With that in mind, let us now turn to how this phrase is used in other places.

As noted above, the phrase "sons of God" is a technical term. It is used sparingly in the OT. Below are all of the occurrences:

"SONS OF GOD" PASSAGE	HEBREW PHRASE
Genesis 6:2	
Genesis 6:4	
Job 1:6	*beney ha-'elohim*
Job 2:1	
Job 38:7	
Psalm 29:1	*beney 'elim*
Psalm 89:6	
Psalm 82:6	*beney 'elyon*
Deut 32:8	*aggelōn theou**
Deut 32:43	*uioi theou**
* signifies only found in LXX[41]	

Table 2. Ten Occurrences of "Sons of God"

If we were to study these passages out, we would find that some of them have differing opinions as to who the "sons of God" are. While disagreements will never go away, two things are certain. Each and every instance of the phrase *can be* explained as referring to supernatural referents. In fact, I would argue that this is the best explanation for each, given their contexts. What is equally certain is that some of these references can *only* refer to heavenly beings.

For example, Job 38 is God's great rhetorical question to Job. He asks, "Where were you when I laid the foundation of the earth"? (vs. 4). The next verses explain that what is in mind is the creation week *prior* to day six when Adam was created. However, there were others there watching God do his work. These were "the sons of God" who are also called "morning stars." These beings "sang together" and "shouted for joy" (Job 38:7). It is impossible for this to refer to human beings. Chrysostom is simply mistaken, unless he wants to say that human beings were there watching God create Adam and Eve. Earlier in the book, the sons of God go with Satan into the heavenly throne room of God to present themselves before him (Job 1:6, 2:1). If someone wants to argue that these are human beings, they must explain why Satan is coming with them, how humans are going back and forth between heaven and earth (or why and how God is meeting them on earth, if they aren't in heaven), and how any of this would look in real life.

Importantly—and also never mentioned by those who want to interpret the sons of God as referring to human beings—the phrase is also used in cousin languages of the surrounding nations, particularly Ugaritic. *Ugarit* was an ancient Canaanite city-state located about 45 miles southwest of Antioch in Syria by the coast, in the shadow of Mt. Zaphon or Saphon (5,607 ft.). It became a vassal state of Egypt during the time of the Exodus, and so Moses, the original author of Genesis, trained in the best schools in Egypt, would have been quite familiar with it.[42] Their language and Hebrew are probably akin to comparing the Queen's English to that of "Spanglish," so dubbed by those who border the United States and Mexico because it is a hybrid of the Spanish and English.

Two of the more obviously identifiable phrases in the Ugaritic tablets are *phr bn 'ilm* – "the assembly of the sons of El/the gods," and *mphrt bn 'il* – "the assembly of the gods."[43] Comparing these phrases with ours is instructive:

UGARIT	HEBREW
bn 'il	*beney ha-'elohim*
bn 'ilm	*beney 'elim*

In these ancient tablets, all Old Testament scholars agree that the terms refer to heavenly beings. They make up the seventy sons of El and Asherah, his female consort.[44] El is a name used of Israel's God in the OT.[45] "Seventy" is a number that finds parallels in biblical texts and ancient Jewish and Christian interpretations of sons of God passages.[46] These seventy sons are the pantheon of gods of the Canaanite religion, beings that have real existence in the Scripture,[47] but are created by Yahweh, the only uncreated omnipotent (etc.) God[48] (Hence, perhaps to eliminate confusion, they are translated as "angels" rather than "gods" in some LXX manuscripts).[49]

Curiously, one of the phrases in the chart on "sons of God," refers to God as *'elim*. "*Elim*" is the plural form of *El*, a proper name for God in the OT, and the name just mentioned for the high god *at *Ugarit**.[50] What the findings of Ugarit have done is brought forth compelling corroborating evidence that the phrase "sons of God" in the biblical context refers to heavenly or angelic beings.[51] This evidence was not available prior to their discovery (in 1928), for this information was buried in the desert sands for over 3,000 years. What near-eastern comparisons like this do is show us how others understood the identical phrase in the context of the same name for God. If someone is going to argue against this "sons of God" being supernatural, they must also show why Israel's view would differ from their neighbors to the north, especially when so many elements, including the name of God and the number of the sons of God ("70") overlap. Sethite proponents never deal with Ugarit.

After Their Kind

A second exegetical reason to think these marriages refer to a mixing of species has to do with the oft repeated phrase in Genesis 1-7: "according to its kind" (Gen 1:11, 12 [2x], 21 [2x], 24 [2x], 25 [3x]; 6:20 [3x], and 7:14 [4x]). When reading the Genesis 1 creation story out loud, it is immediately obvious that God is concerned with getting across the point that he made all living things "according to their kinds." If Moses merely wanted you to know this as a piece of trivia, a single mention at the end of the creation would have sufficed. The sheer volume and repetition of the phrase in this chapter (ten of the sixteen occurrences in the Bible) demonstrates that he wants you to notice *and remember it.*

Why is this such a concern to Moses? The most curious thing about this phrase is that it never occurs again anywhere *in the entire Bible* after Genesis 7. This is a clue that whatever the phrase refers to, its main purpose was to point out something important in the world prior to the Flood. When reading the Flood story and the repetition of this same phrase found only in creation, the mind naturally goes back to the *creation* of life on earth.

We are told in Genesis 6:12 that "God saw the earth, and behold, it was corrupt, for all flesh had *corrupted* their *way* on the earth." The word "corrupt" (*shachath*) has many meanings. One meaning, found in the very next verse is "to destroy" (Gen 6:13, 17). Thus, it seems that they destroyed themselves, therefore God will destroy them. But how might they have destroyed themselves?

It is interesting that this word Is used in conjunction with "the way" (*derek*) in other places. For example, the LORD said to Moses, "Go down, for your people, whom you brought up out of the land of Egypt, have *corrupted* themselves. They have turned aside quickly out of the *way*." And what way was that? "They have made for themselves a golden calf and have worshiped it and sacrificed to it and said, 'These are *your gods*'" (Exodus 32:7-8; cf. Deut 9:12; Jdg 2:17-19). In the immortal words of Arte Johnson on *Laugh In* (I'm not really dating myself, as I only saw it in reruns), "Vvvvery interestink."

Sometimes this is referred to as "whoring after the gods" (e.g. Jdg 2:17) where the idolatrous worship is exactly parallel with sexual fornication. In the Old Testament, people "play the whore" with "goat demons" (Lev 17:7), "Molech" (Lev 20:5), and other "foreign gods" (Deut 31:16). They can commit "adultery" with "stone and tree" (Jer 3:9). While we (rightly) spiritualize these kinds of things (it is difficult to conceive how people would literally exchange bodily fluids with non-physical gods and demons, though maybe someone has a guess), it must be recognized that we frankly don't have much idea what takes place in the spiritual realm when people commit idolatry, not to mention the temple prostitution that regularly took place in these places. What is clear is that God uses the idea of sexual immorality, the intimate coming together of a husband and wife, to explain what occurs. Undoubtedly, the mixing of different "kinds" is here *at least* spiritual in these passages, even if no offspring result from the unions.

The word *shachath* can also mean "to spoil" (cf. Jer 13:7). It can mean "to ravage" (cf. 2 Sam 11:1). Both can have similar sexual connotations. Given these word meanings and usage in other places, it is not inconceivable that the people prior to the flood have been "destroyed" through cross-breeding or genetic manipulation, which came about through spiritual beings that transgressed, to use Jude's language, the proper domain.

Let me bring three more points from the Scripture to bear upon this idea of mixing kinds. The first is the language used of Noah in Genesis 6:9. It tells us, "These are the generations of Noah: Noah was a just man and *perfect in his generations*, and Noah walked with God" (KVJ). The opening phrase, "These are the generations" is repeated 10 times in Genesis. It is used the way we use chapter titles to introduce the ten main sections of Genesis. As Meredith Kline notices, "What follows the formula is always an account of the descendants of the person named."[52] The word (*toledoth*) is always concerned, then, with genealogy and *physicality*.

Curiously, a similar word (*dor*) occurs later in the same verse. It is often translated as "generation,"[53] as the KJV puts it, Noah was "*perfect in his generations*." Most English translations understand this phrase as a reference to Noah's *spiritual* estate (notice how much spiritualizing is going on in this passage from conservative scholars). That is, they see this as a continuation of the previous and following phrases about Noah's "righteousness," which is a spiritual thing. A good example is the New Jerusalem Bible, "Noah was a *good* man, an *upright* man among his *contemporaries* (*dor*), and he *walked* with God." The idea is that "good," "upright," and "walked with God" all refer to Noah's *character*. The main problem with this translation is that "generations" has just referred to descendants in the line of Noah ("These are the generations of Noah"). There it was perfectly biological, not ethical. Now it is supposed to refer to contemporaries of a completely different family tree in a totally new way. Though not the identical word, this is perhaps yet another discovery of *equivocation*.

The ESV tries a different translation. "Noah was a righteous man, *blameless* in his *generation*. Noah walked with God." The idea is similar, but "contemporaries" has been changed to "generation." The main problem with this kind of translation is that "generation" in the Hebrew is plural, not singular. The NJB at least saw this (with the plural "contemporaries"). Thus, the KJV has "perfect in his generations." This is a more faithful translation, but what might this mean?

According to Perfectionists like Betty Champion it means we can be morally perfect on earth and Noah is the proof. In her book *Yes We Can Be Perfect In Our Generation* she writes, "If nobody is perfect why does scripture say Noah was a perfect man? See Genesis 6:9."[54] Never mind that almost as soon as Noah gets off the Ark after his miraculous deliverance, he plants a vineyard, gets drunk, and lets his son sleep with his wife.[55] Some sinless perfectionist Noah was.

To understand what Moses might mean by, "perfect in his generations," it will help to see how else the word "perfect" (*tamim*) is used by him (in Genesis – Deuteronomy). Sometimes it is associated with "walking before God," as it is here with Noah and again with Abraham (Gen 17:1). According to a detailed study of this phrase done by a noted scholar, it most properly does not mean "keeping the law," but rather "serve as an emissary" for God.[56] Moses' regular use of this phrase is certainly not a help to the perfectionist point of view.

Other times the word is used in reference to spotless animals. In fact, of the approximately 50 times that Moses uses this word, this is the context over 80% of the time. What is in mind in these passages is that the worshiper must take a *physically* unblemished spotless animal and offer it to the LORD. This has nothing to do with spiritual perfection, but everything to do with physical purity. Thus, if the uses of the words are any indication, It is more than plausible—it is highly probable— that for Noah to be "perfect in his generations" means that he was physically pure, that is, unpolluted, undefiled, and genetically untainted. "In his generations" (plural) would mean that all of his forefathers (that is his lineage including his father Lamech, his grandfather Methuselah and so on) were also physically pure. This is viewed by Moses as an aberration of the way things were in the world in Noah's day. This is a main purpose of Noah's genealogy.

This point seems to have been made in the second century B.C. when the book of Jubilees says, "... [Enoch] bore witness to the Watchers, the ones who sinned with the daughters of men because they began to mingle themselves with the daughters of men *so that they might be polluted*. And Enoch bore witness against all of them" (Jub 4:22). It also seems to appear in 1 Enoch 106 where Lamech begets a son (Noah), who he is deeply concerned is a son of the Watchers rather than himself because his appearance is "like the children of the angels of heaven" (1En 106:5). But Methuselah assures him that the boy is really his son and not a polluted half-breed.

The next point about the significance of "different kinds" regards the practices of the inhabitants of the land of Canaan. This gets us a little ahead of ourselves, so I'll say only what needs to be said here. God was bringing Israel into Canaan. When the 12 spies came back from the land, they carried with them a cluster of grapes so large that Jewish tradition says eight of the 12 spies carried the cluster, one carried a pomegranate, one carried a fig, and Joshua and Caleb carried nothing, because they did not share the plan to discourage the Israelites from attacking Canaan (Num 13:23).[57]

At any rate, it is important to notice a couple of the particular laws that God put in place for Israel, specifically saying that they were not to follow after the practices of these people. The first kind of law refers to bestiality. One says, "You shall not have intercourse with any animal to be defiled with it. . . for by all these the nations which I am casting out before you have become defiled" (Lev 18:23-24 NAS; cf. Lev 20:15-16 and 23). This is the precursor to mixing kinds, whether any offspring can come from such unions is not the point.

The other kind of law involves something we today may find strange and unimportant. "You shall keep my statutes. You shall not let your cattle breed with a different kind. You shall not sow your field with two kinds of seed, nor shall you wear a garment of cloth made of two kinds of material" (Lev 19:19).[58] Amazingly, this verse is at the very center of the center of the center of the Torah![59] A while back, I walked into a discussion on tattoos. The argument was that tattoos are wrong because of a law against them in the Old Testament. When they asked me what I thought, I went over to one of them, lifted up the tag on the back of their shirt, and pointed out that they were wearing a garment made of cotton and wool. This law comes in the middle of the previous set of laws, and thus has in mind the same context of not doing what the inhabitants of Canaan were doing. This conclusion is quite plausible: They were trying to engineer hybrid plants and animals. This isn't even rocket science, for we even see Jacob practicing an early stage of genetic modification when he worked with Laban (Gen 30:31-40).

With this in mind, enter into a speculative thought experiment with me. There are many Christians, and even a few non-Christians, who believe that dinosaurs may not have been as ancient as the theory of evolution teaches. Petroglyphs, small rock paintings, and other ancient artifacts have been uncovered that seem impossible unless people saw them alive. Let's assume that there were dinosaurs on the earth prior to the flood, living side by side with Noah. Why is there so little concrete proof that there have been land-dwelling dinosaurs after the flood? There is an interesting theory that because dinosaurs are believed to have had both avian (bird) and reptilian (lizard) characteristics, they could have been *chimeras* (hybrids). If this is the case, then they could not rightly have been said to be "after their kind." Thus, they were an abomination to God and Noah would not have taken them on the ark.[60] It's an interesting idea at any rate.

The point is, before Genesis 6, right in the middle of Genesis 6, and after Genesis 6 a good deal of time is taken up discussing mixing kinds. Therefore, we have good reason to believe that the origin of this problem occurred sometime prior to the Flood. It made God extremely angry, for he made all things "according to their own kind."[61]

All flesh has corrupted itself

A third argument for the supernatural view of Genesis 6 is that the passage says "all flesh" had corrupted itself (Gen 6:12), therefore God destroyed "all flesh" that was on the earth (Gen 6:13, 17, 7:21, 9:11-17). It is sometimes argued against the supernatural view that God was only angry at *mankind*. These verses obviously fly in the face of that idea.

Clearly, God was angry at birds, reptiles, and crawling things as well as men and women. Did all the critters on the earth "sin"? Can you even apply "sin" to dogs and cats, which clearly are included in "all flesh" (6:7, 20)? If you have one, especially a cat, O.K. you cat lovers, dogs too, it was rhetorical. In my mind, it is a certainty that many animals misbehave on purpose. I owned a dog, which was better behaved than a cat, but still carried certain grudges even though she loved me. It is a difficult question to know whether or not we should call their misbehavior "sin." The farther down the food chain we go, the more difficult this question becomes. But "sin," as I said before, is the usual way that "corruption" is taken in this passage. When we start stretching this to animals, it becomes a thorny theological pursuit.

But what if "all flesh" were corrupt because of the mixing of kinds? What if this refers to *physicality* rather than spirituality and ethics? If this is the case, then the only objection would be one of science: How could they have done it? Most people do not think genetic engineering back then was possible, and yet scientists in our own day are eagerly pursuing the Nazi dream of creating a super race, genetically altered to live forever. We are making such strides in this area that several states have now passed laws making human hybridization a crime.[62]

In the ten years since *Giants* was originally published, this has truly gone off the rails, and some are openly and boldly talking about hacking humans, turning us into hybrid creatures, admitting we have the technology *right now*, and putting into motion a terrifying global plan bring us into their utopian (dystopian!) "Great Reset," which is set to fundamentally destroy human civilization as we've always known it, even as if fundamentally redefines what a human being is through transhumanism, DNA altering gene therapies, and the like.[63] Welcome to the world post-2020. If we can to it today, what makes us so sure they couldn't do it back then? If anything, the last couple of years should only reinforce this point on steroids. It is the theory of evolution (the infection of naturalism again) that makes us think our ancestors were stupid apes. These people lived a lot longer than we do. What about beings that are more ancient, powerful, and intelligent than us?

Nephilim are Giants

Previously I pointed out that the offspring of the unions of the sons of God and daughters of man were giants. Some people deny this to be the case, however. They read the passage as saying something like this: "The Nephilim were on the earth in those days. And after that [that is after the Nephilim were already on the earth], the sons of God came into the daughters of man and bore them children. These were the mighty men, the men of renown." The idea here is that the nephilim are not the product of the union of the sons of God and the daughters of men, for they were already here. Besides being an idea that makes the whole point of the nephilim in the text superfluous and so mysterious that their inclusion makes no sense, I consulted over 30 different English translations and the only one that definitely reads this way is the Bible in Basic English, which is hardly a literal translation.[64]

Though it is possible from the grammar to argue that the Nephilim do not refer to the union in question, it is extremely difficult to find anyone today who will give it a try. If the Nephilim were already on the earth, and if the children born to the sons of God and daughters of men are not Nephilim but Gibborim (totally different people), why mention the *nephilim* at all? But even if this were the case, we still have to deal with who these Nephilim were in the other place they are mentioned in the Bible. In this instance, it is irrefutable that they are literal giants.

The spies told Moses, "... The land, through which we have gone to spy it out, is a land that devours its inhabitants, and all the people that we saw in it are of great height. And there we saw the Nephilim (the sons of Anak, who come from the Nephilim), and we seemed to ourselves like grasshoppers, and so we seemed to them." (Num 13:32-33). We learn from other places that the sons of Anak were extremely tall men (Deut 9:1-2). Therefore, the *nephilim* sons of Anak in Num 13:33 are not some smaller group of people compared with those of "great height" in vs. 32. No. The Anakim are part of a group of giant clans lifted in vv."28-29. If we take "land" here as personification of these tall giants, we learn that the "devouring" going on may very well be a reference to the unthinkable practice of cannibalism (that's how some ancient Jews took it), or if it is not technically correct to call it cannibalism, because the giants were not eating themselves, then to the eating and consumption of human flesh.

On every continent on the planet, the indigenous people tell stories of gods coming down to earth, copulating with human women, who produced very tall offspring that were violent ruthless cannibals. There is nothing inconsistent here with a supernatural interpretation of

Genesis 6:1-4 if "gods" merely means supernatural heavenly created beings. The fact that the Nephilim are here in Genesis 6:4 tells us that they
were part of the reason for the Flood. They were in fact giants. These
giants were not rare genetic abnormalities that could happen to anyone,
but the product of the union in the verse. How can this be if both
groups are perfectly human, especially when it was obviously so common? And why would it only occur from Christians marrying non-
Christians? We don't see that happening today! The Sethite view has no
answer for this.

Angels Before Genesis 6:1-4

Another objection sometimes raised against the supernatural view
is that, if the sons of God are angels (or heavenly beings), this would be
the first instance of such creatures in the Bible. The idea is that such an
introduction here, in the middle of Genesis, is unprecedented and
therefore false (as if God can't introduce a character into his storyline
anytime he feels like it). The use of the cryptic "sons of God" as angels
would make absolutely no sense, since we have no previous referent in
the text to angels.

There are two problems with this theory. The first is that the story
of Job with its three angelic references to the sons of God (see above),
predates the writing of Genesis. Even if the book were not written with
ink on paper until later, the story would have been well known not only
to Moses, but to all of the children of Israel, including the references to
the sons of God.

The second problem is that the objection is patently false. There
are in fact two, and I would argue three, very glaring references to heavenly beings prior to Genesis 6. Genesis 3 tells the story of the fall due to
the temptation of *Satan* (or the *satan*) a heavenly being. Elsewhere Satan
is called "an angel of light" (2 Cor 11:14). He is given the royal title of
a prince (Matt 12:24; Mark 3:22; Luke 11:15; John 12:31; 16:11; Eph 2:2).
Princes are sons of the king. Who is the king? God is the king. Therefore,
Satan is in some sense a son of God, even though that sense is qualitatively different from the only begotten son of God, the Lord Jesus; for
Satan is a *created* "son," and Jesus—who created Satan—is not.[65] The
second instance occurs after God drives our first parents out of Eden.

Outside of the gate of Eden he places two cherubim to guard the way to the tree of life (Gen 3:24). Finally, Christian authors from Theophilus of Antioch to Jerome Zanchi have said that the LORD walking with Adam in the Garden is in fact the Angel of the LORD, yet another supernatural being. These instances prove the assertion false. The angelic idea of the sons of God does not just arrive out of the blue.

Serpent Seed

As mentioned previously, Satan was in the garden with Adam and Eve. After he tempted our parents to sin, he was cursed by God. Part of this curse involves a war that Satan will ultimately lose, "I will put enmity between you and the woman, and between your offspring and her offspring; he shall bruise your head, and you shall bruise his heel" (Gen 3:15). Clearly, the woman will have offspring and the serpent will have offspring. I have already dealt with the inconsistency of seeing one line as biological and the other only as spiritual.

There are some who hold the supernatural view of Genesis 6:1-4 who believe the first son of Satan was Cain; that Satan lay with Eve, and Cain is the first demigod. This "serpent seed" doctrine blatantly contradicts Genesis 4:1, which teaches that Adam is Cain's biological father. This doctrine is false and has been used as early as the Gnostics to undermine biblical theology. Nevertheless, the point I'm making here is that there is compelling exegetical reason from this verse to see that sometime in the future, there would be physical offspring from fallen heavenly beings that would wage war against mankind and try to wipe out the coming seed of the woman. In fact, this is "The Storyline" of the giants in the Bible (see Chapter 1). This was never controversial in the early church.

Here then we have several textual reasons for thinking that the sons of God are angels and that the giants are their half-breed offspring. Whenever the actual phrase "sons of God" occurs in the OT, it can always be read as a reference to heavenly beings. Because of the book/story of Job, the Israelites would have been quite familiar with this as a reference to heavenly beings. The insistence that Noah take with him only animals "after their kind" makes sense if there were lots of mixed animals on the earth. Noah's own physical perfection can easily be read that he is a full-blooded son of Adam with no biological pollution from heavenly beings, but it makes little sense if it refers to something spiritual in Noah's character. God was angry, not just at mankind, but with all flesh on the earth. Nephilim means giant, and it is difficult to see how ordinary marriages of believers to non-believers could regularly and normally produce gigantic offspring. Finally, there are heavenly beings present in the Bible well before Genesis 6 begins. The main figure, Satan, is told that his offspring will make war on Eve's offspring, but that her seed will prevail.

Supernatural Theories Deconstructed?

There have been several charges levelled against the supernatural theories. One resource I found gave no less than 15 arguments against it.[66] I have already dealt with some of these objections, but here they are with brief explanations of why these objections are weightless.

1. The "sons of God" would be the first mention of angels in the Bible. *Answer*: No, Satan and two cherubim (and probably the Angel of the LORD) are mentioned in Genesis 3 and the sons of God story of Job was well known to Moses and Israel.
2. The Bible says that God creates life after its kind. If a hybrid view is correct, then the Nephilim are not after any kind. *Answer*: This is exactly why God became so angry and destroyed the world in the flood.
3. The Flood was a judgment on mankind, not angels. *Answer*: God destroyed "all flesh," not just mankind. All flesh had become corrupt.
4. "And also after that" means that the Nephilim were originally not the children of the sons of God. They were born before that union. This objection goes back at least as far as Augustine (*City of God* 15.23). *Answer*: We have seen the implausibility of this interpretation of Genesis 6:4. It does not explain why the Nephilim would be mentioned, nor does it deal with how the Nephilim were still here at some point. What were they?
5. Angels are not physical beings, but spiritual beings as it says, "Who maketh his angels spirits; his ministers a flaming fire" (Ps 104:4 KJV; Heb 1:7). *Answer*: This objection also has roots in the same section of Augustine's *City of God*. No one doubts that angels are spiritual beings. But in answer to the objection, it can be said that the Psalmist could be talking about human messengers like prophets just as easily as heavenly messengers, for humans also have spirits. This is probably not the case, so the second point is that angels very often take on physicality in the Bible. They can eat, drink, speak, wrestle, grab, and apparently as the men of Sodom thought

... have sex. I make no claim to know how they do it, but I do claim to believe the Bible which says that they do. Besides, the Bible explicitly teaches that angels have bodies (1 Cor 15:40-41), but not all flesh is of the same glory.

6. Angels do not have DNA. *Answer*: How could anyone possibly know that? There is good reason to believe that they knew about DNA a very long time ago. You can Google this idea and up will come thousands of websites. We'll deal with this later in the book.

7. Angels only *appeared* as men in the Bible. *Answer*: The Bible says that they *are* men (Gen 18:2; 19:10; 32:24; Dan 3:25; Luke 24:4 and many others), literally using one of the two main words for "men" (*ish*) in the OT. Undoubtedly, they are a different "kind" of man, but Scripture uses the term "man" to describe angels dozens of times.

8. We have no examples in the Bible of fallen angels appearing as a man. *Answer*: "Angel" means "messenger." Angel is a designation of function not of being. Angels are sent by God to relay messages. Why would God trust fallen angels to send messages to men? We shouldn't expect any fallen angels to come to men. Furthermore, the Bible seems to indicate that the particular beings who sinned at this time in the flood were locked up so that they could not do it again (see 2 Peter 2:4; Jude 6).[67]

9. How can spiritual beings produce physical offspring? Only the Holy Spirit can do this through the virgin, and it was the miraculous birth of the God-man. *Answer*: First of all, comparing Jesus to a Nephilim is heretical. Jesus is not a *demigod*, but very God of very God and fully in every way man. Angels were not able to duplicate this. Nephilim are half heavenly and half human. Angels are not the same species of man as us. Second, if angels can in *some sense* be called men and can manifest themselves physically, then our lack of knowledge about the sexual abilities of heavenly beings is no proof against the supernatural view. Even if it was impossible biologically speaking, genetic manipulation of DNA is theoretically plausible.

10. Christ says angels do not marry. This objection is one of the most common. *Answer*: Christ says angels "in heaven" do not marry. This may seem like a trivial answer, but it isn't. These heavenly beings clearly came down to earth. This was their sin. They were no longer *in heaven*. Marriage seems to be a temporary reality here on earth. In heaven even we will not marry (Luke 20:34-35), though we will be married to Christ as the church. Because we will not marry each other in heaven, it does not follow that we do not marry here. These creatures were fallen out of heaven, willfully rebellious against God, and thus it is entirely feasible that if they could materialize here, they could also marry. If an angel can wrestle with Jacob (by the way, this angel is called "a man;" Gen 32:24), why couldn't they also marry?

11. If Nephilim means "giant," we have Nephilim today. Just watch a pro basketball game. *Answer*: The point of the text is that *whenever* the sons of God had children with the daughters of man, a Nephilim was born. Giants in our day are rare, but this seems to have been an ordinary occurrence.

12. These people are called mighty "men" not angels. If they were angels, why didn't it just say so? *Answer*: It did. It called them Nephilim and Gibborim, words that are both associated with the supernatural. Their fathers are the sons of God, which are also supernatural. Finally, "men" is a term often used to describe supernatural beings.

13. The Nephilim in Numbers 13 are not the children of the sons of God, but of Anak. Therefore, they are not hybrids. Anak was a man not an angel. *Answer*: Anak was himself a giant Nephilim, as were his three sons and his ancestor Arba. Hence, the comparison between Anakim and Nephilim in the passage. The whole point of Genesis 6:4 mentioning that there were Nephilim on the earth after the flood is to point forward to Numbers 13. It directly implies that these later Nephilim are also children of fallen sons of God, even if it is a different group than those who originally descended prior to the flood.

14. Christ offered proof of his resurrection when questioned saying, "Spirits do not have flesh and bone." *Answer*: This question fails to distinguish between angels and spirits. As we will see, spirits are most definitely *not* fallen angels. They are disembodied entities, meaning that at one time they had bodies, which is why they seek to inhabit bodies now. Jesus' point is that he kept his resurrected body, not that he became a demon or ghost or spirit. But just in case an angel decided to pretend that he was Jesus, he tells them to look at the execution marks on his body. Apparently, this cannot be duplicated by an angel ... because they have bodies.

15. If a new race of beings existed, could they be saved? Jesus came to save men not angels. If a Nephilim is a man, he could be saved, but if he is also an angel he could not be saved. This problem is posed not as irrefutable proof against the view, but as a theological danger of the view. *Answer*: A Nephilim is neither an angel nor a man. It is a Nephilim. Nephilim are half-breeds and therefore this tricky dilemma should not be applied to them anymore than to the animal kingdom. Whether or not there will be animals (or Nephilim) in heaven is a question that must be pursued apart from whether they trust that Christ died for them.

As you can see, *every* objection brought against the supernatural view can be answered. The same cannot be said for purely naturalistic views. I believe this is a critical point to come to grips with. All that remains is our individual incredulity and personal offense about the idea. But if we have a preconceived bias against any such ideas from the start, no amount of logic or biblical proof will convince. If someone is simply stuck on "it just couldn't be," then for them, no matter what proof you give, it *never will* be. If this is still your view, I ask you to remember one thing. At the end of the day, Chrysostom, Augustine, Luther, and Calvin did the only thing they could do to attack the older belief. *They made fun of it.* I certainly won't condemn anyone who wants to stick with the Sethite view, but I want to offer a warning about mocking the older view.

Demythologization is a word coined by the late Liberal theologian Rudolf Bultmann (1884-1976). Strictly speaking, demythologization is reinterpreting the message of the New Testament for a time in which people no longer think in the mythological terms of the ancients.[68] The same thing can easily be applied to the OT. The idea is not that we should pursue truth rather than fable (i.e. mythology), but that we no longer need to think about the Bible as an historical document with real people and events. We just need to take the "spiritual" lessons from it. We will still have the core of the faith in doing so. This is the heart and soul, the warp and woof, of liberalism.

In all honesty, while the term may be recent, the idea most certainly is not. When Jesus rose from the dead, the chief priests of Israel practiced *demythologization* by telling the soldiers to spread the news that "his disciples came by night and stole him away while we were asleep" (Matt 28:13). They couldn't deal with the resurrection. Arius practiced *demythologization* by claiming that Jesus was not a divine person, not The Son of God. Thomas Jefferson practiced demythologization by literally taking a pair of scissors and cutting out every instance of a miracle that he could find in his Bible.

I am not the first person to suggest that more recent interpretations of Genesis 6:1-4 are essentially the same thing. It is a "reinterpretation" for "modern" people (even if they lived 1,600 years ago) that the supernatural events of this passage did not—indeed *could* not—occur. Rather, it was a spiritual thing that happened. Godly men sinned with ungodly women, and that's the end of the story. Period.

To put it bluntly, there is no reason to throw out the oldest view known on this passage, other than our own personal disgust for it. But if we do so, we need to remember that atheists refuse to believe in the virgin birth, the deity of Christ, and the resurrection of the dead *for the exact same reasons.* They are silly and absurd to them.

I've given solid exegetical reasons for holding to the ancient view of this passage. The ramifications of this interpretation are literally to be seen in almost every book of the Bible. This is not a time for vain speculation, inferences, and clever theories. The Ancient Ones believed

what they believed for good reasons. The evidence is very strong that
the sons of God, the Nephilim, Gibborim (at least in this passage), and
the correlative Greek translations all point towards the identification of
the giants as demigods—half-breed children of heavenly beings and human women. It really does not matter if this sounds like the *National
Enquirer*, because frankly, it is what the text says. Our choice is to "believe it or not," though I personally think that God is much more reputable than Robert Ripley.

CHAPTER 1

PRE-FLOOD GIANTS

The Nephilim were on the earth in those days (and also after this) when the sons of God were having sexual relations with the daughters of humankind, who gave birth to their children. They were the mighty heroes of old, the famous men.

Genesis 6:4 (NET)

The Story of the Bible

When I tell people about the giants, inevitably one question comes up time and again. It is not a question about whether they really existed or how tall they might have been. The question is pragmatic: How does learning about the giants matter to my life? It is a fair question, though I sometimes get frustrated by it. Learning about the giants does matter to your life; but as I explain how, I want you to be thinking about something else.

Imagine yourself living eighty years ago. You have just come out of the top grossing film of all time. Suddenly a reporter comes up to you with one of those silly hats, a pencil, and paper. He asks, "I'm sure *Gone with the Wind* was a nice movie, but how did that matter to your life?" Wouldn't you think this to be a pretty strange question? I know I would. At the very least, you would probably not think it would be the first question someone would ask you.

We do not ordinarily go to movies because we want to learn some tip for living, though I suppose you might be moved as a by-product of good character development to emulate (or not) a character you liked or hated. In the Bible, Peter and Jude (see Appendix – 2 Peter 2:4 and Jude 6 for *exegesis* of these passages) use the story of the fall of the sons of God in Genesis 6. This includes the abandonment of their preternatural domain, their sexual immorality, and the punishment God inflicted upon them. Peter and Jude use this as part of the overall ethical warning in their letters. Clearly, when we see what they did (not to mention their sons; see Chapter 7: The "Law" of Canaan), we must not copy their ways, even if it is to lesser degrees. As Jude puts it, do not be like the "wandering stars" (Jude 13). I opened the Preface with a little passage I discovered in an ancient Jewish writing, one that I think really gets at this in a thought-provoking way, "The sons of men, being insensitive to [God, spirits, heavenly armies, Holy Ones, archangels, angels, thrones, and authorities], keep sinning and provoking the anger of the most High." That passage comes in the middle of an ancient Jewish testament concerned with teaching people to act rightly in God's world. This is a chief object lesson from the story of the giants.

But the point about being moved by a character in a movie is, to me, more profound, because it works on a deeper level of the human psyche than overt moral instruction. It is able to foster the obedience without a command. You simply see, then get swept away, and after the fact your subconscious says, "That was a really good person to emulate." I think most of us go to movies because we love *to be swept up* in the story. Oh, that people would long to be swept away by God's story once more. If, by the end of this book, I have caused you to be swept up in the invisible story of the Bible, I have accomplished one thing I set out to do.

We love stories. Stories are actually practical, though not in the sense a pragmatist would appreciate. Stories move us at the core of our being. Stories change us as people (including ethically). They help us to imagine, to create, to love, to ponder, to wonder. That's why, long ago, Aesop out his ethical tales in the form of story. Everyone is looking for a story that they can relate to, a story that will move them emotionally, a story that will thrill them, or a story that will scare them, a story they can in some way fantasize and live out as the main or supporting character. God made us this way because human beings take center stage in his drama of creation. Not even angels have this role in the story;

actually, that's one of the reasons Satan took out his revenge on us. Imagine now a story that read like fantasy but was actually true.

It is odd the way the Bible is used today. Some read it as a cookbook, a coaching manual, to gain leadership tips, or to prove scientific theories. This is wrong headed, but also boring. Few people read it as it is supposed to be read—a story. Perhaps they are afraid that if they did that, it would be like saying it is no different than *Gone With the Wind* (just fiction). More likely, they just don't think that would be ... "practical." What a sad way to go through life.

If I were to ask you, "What is the story of the Bible," would you have an answer? What would it be? My answer begins with what many believe is the thesis of the Word of God: Genesis 3:15. "And I will put enmity Between you and the woman, And between your seed and her Seed; He shall bruise your head, And you shall bruise His heel" (NKJV). The reason we have the Bible is so that God might tell you about *this* story and that in the hearing of the story, you might believe in Christ. Often the Bible takes the form of story-telling, especially in the narrative sections. However, even the Psalms, Proverbs, and general Epistles (letters) tell this story in their own unique way.

The whole Bible works out the fulfillment of this promise to Eve and curse to Satan. The New King James demonstrates good theology by capitalizing Eve's Seed, for ultimately Jesus Christ is that Seed. Theologians point out that this verse is the "first gospel" (*proto-evangelium*). It is a *promise* that from the body of the first woman, one will eventually come who will crush the head of the serpent. Yet, some of the same scholars will say that if we view Genesis 6:1-4 as some kind of supernatural angelic intervention in history, then this somehow destroys biblical theology (particularly the thread of the *two kingdoms* first set forth by Augustine in *The City of God*).[1] Nothing could be further from the truth.

This verse contains a prophecy of a war and the ultimate victory of Christ over evil. Good biblical theology is not only about God's people vs. those who are not. It is about good vs. evil and God's absolute sovereignty in both the physical and *spiritual* realms. In the war's final manifestation, Jesus conquers *Satan,* and ushers in his own kingdom, which intrudes upon the kingdoms of the world today through the church and the gospel. But before Jesus arrives on the scene in the flesh, we have wars and stories that foreshadow and precede The Great War and Heavenly Kingdom.[2] War drums of hatred, disdain, and violence thumping steadily in the ears of the people of God; beginning with Cain they resound through the valleys of time, echoing even into the days of Esther.

What many people fail to notice in all this is how a main earthly antagonist throughout this OT war is the giants or people in some way related to them, either through marriage or cultural assimilation (like victims of the Borg in Star Trek). Most are wholly unaware of how many giants there are in the Bible, and why God bothers to tell us about them. Read the "first gospel" again. Eve will have a Seed, *and Satan will have a seed*. As I pointed out in the Introduction, the consistent way to read this is that both seeds are spiritual and/or both seeds are physical. The inconsistent way is that one is physical (Jesus is born literally from a woman), but that the other is spiritual (those who have Satan as their father only have him so in a spiritual sense). There is simply no justification in the text to read it that way. That's an *equivocation*. The verse begs that we interpret the seeds consistently.

Spiritual Giants

If we want to say that both seeds are spiritual, then the first seed of the woman is Abel, while the first seed of the serpent is Cain. Here, we are not viewing either son biologically, but through the prism of faith and faithlessness. This is more than permissible. Other Scripture mandates that we do this. The Bible comments on the spiritual condition of both boys. 1 John 3:12 tells us, "We should not be like Cain, who was of the evil one and murdered his brother."[3] Meanwhile it is said of Abel, "By faith Abel offered to God a more acceptable sacrifice than Cain, through which he was commended as righteous" (Heb 11:4). This spiritual interpretation can consistently be carried out with anyone in the Bible who trusts and obeys God vs. those who do not. This is why believers are called sons of God and unbelievers are called children of the devil. Though I disagree with his interpretation of Genesis 6:1-4, Augustine had this basic theological idea correct.

At its core, this is the doctrine of election. When comparing Israel to the nations, election is corporate. God chose one nation over all the others to be the vessel through which his grace would come to the world. With regard to salvation, however, God chooses individuals who do not deserve to be saved. These people are not good. They are not looking for God. They are not smart or wise by the world's standards. He does it because it pleases him to do so, and because if he didn't, no one would be saved. In both instances, it is the weak, the small, and the foolish in the eyes of the world who are the spiritual giants of the Bible. If, however, we want to read the seed physically, which is also necessary since Christ came *in the flesh*, then who would be the physical seed of the serpent?[4] The answer is: The giants.

PHYSICAL GIANTS

Half Breeds

It would be nice to learn something about these giants before we begin our tour of Scripture. What can we learn about their makeup and character? Genesis 6:1-4 tells us that the giants were born of a union between heavenly beings and earthly women (see Introduction). This makes the giants half-breeds or *demigods*. We do not know how this occurred exactly. Certainly there were conjugal unions or marriages in those days; Jesus affirms as much (Matt 24:38). Angels often take physical form in the Bible, so nothing biblical prevents this as a possibility. Most translations say that the sons of God "took wives."[5] These marriages could have been consensual or not, and the women involved could have been full of passion for them,[6] or not.

However, the term "wife" (*ishshah*) could just mean "women." As such, at least some of these unions could refer to a kind of rape. This is doubtful, because the taking of wives is often a good thing. Believe it or not, the Jews, Greeks, and other ancients believed the sons of God could shape-shift (see note #7), and offered this as a reason for pregnancies.[7] Others suggest some kind of genetic manipulation or other unlawful taking.[8] Though marriages occurred, further details are sketchy. We do know that offspring were brought forth somehow. It really did happen.

Violent Warriors and Heroes of Old

In the Bible you find various tribes of humans fighting against the giants (cf. Gen 14; Deut 2). This is because the giants were fierce, violent warriors. We learn the following things in regard to this. First, Genesis 6:4 calls them *gibborim*. The Greek *Septuagint* (LXX) translated the Hebrew *gibborim* as "giant" (*gigantes*). This word comes straight out of Greek mythology. The Gigantes were the children of heaven (Uranus) and earth (Gaia), just as they are in this verse. Strictly speaking, the Gigantes were serpent-footed giants born after Cronus, the youngest son of Uranus, castrated his father (see Appendix: Th" Stories of the Greeks). This is how the Jewish translators of the Old Testament, 200 years before Jesus was born, understood the Nephilim.

Gibborim is sometimes used to describe brave, though very human, heroes. For example, David had his thirty *gibborim* ("mighty men," cf. 2 Sam 23:17-18). You find the same thing in Joshua's army. They are called *48aphal gibborim* ("valiant warriors;" cf. Josh 10:7). Curiously, both accounts come in the context of these brave warriors fighting and defeating real giants! This makes the use of the term for Israelite warriors ironic; who are the real giants of the story, the literal giants, or the much smaller warriors of God?

The last phrase of Genesis 6:4 refers to these giants as "men of renown" (lit. "men of the name"), for they sought to make a name for themselves. Thus, some translations offer "these were the heroes and warriors of old." The mind cannot help but be drawn to the stories and legends known around the world, stories of *demigods* like Hercules or Orion, Thor or Gilgamesh, Garuda, and many more. But the Bible does not want you to fixate on them here. Instead, we just glance at them, like drivers in a fast-moving car. As quickly as we came upon them, they are, for now, in the rear-view mirror. As we move past and our last gaze of this disturbing image fades from view, we set our sites on what is immediately before us. God wants you to see what their actions brought the LORD to do to the earth.

A Major Reason for the Flood

The LORD was sorry that he made man on earth and was grieved over what we had become (Gen 6:6). For the LORD saw the wickedness of man (6:5), how all flesh had corrupted its way (6:12) and had become full of violence (6:11). Notice how the violence was not just contained with man, but extended to "all flesh." It is interesting that you can actually see the progression of what took place on the earth in the names

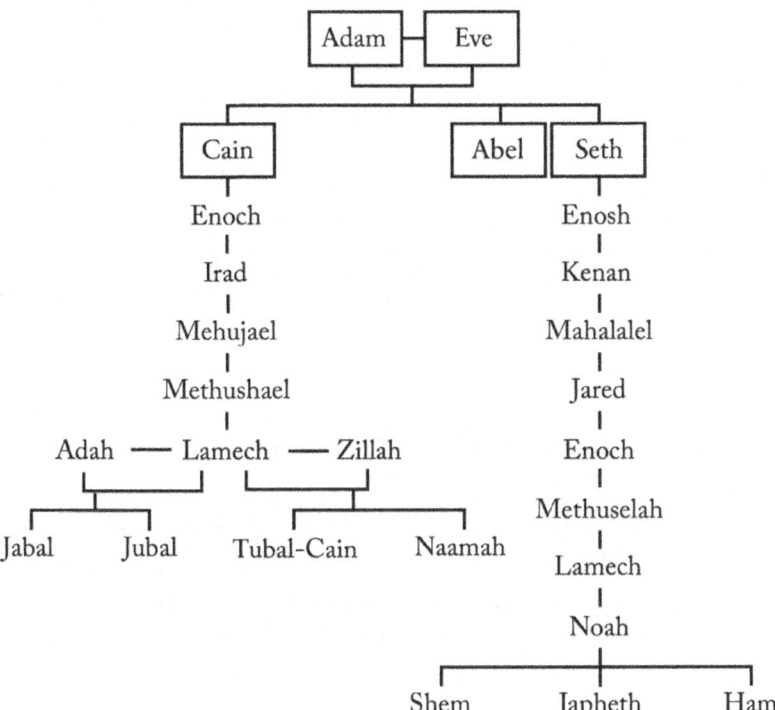

FIG. 1.1. GENESIS 5 GENEALOGIES

of the descendants of Cain and, especially Seth. A person's name is often an important clue into interpreting events or facts in the Bible.

I would like to tell you about some of Seth's descendant's names, not for the purposes of turning them into come kind of cryptic prophecy as some have done,[9] but rather to better see the conditions on the earth prior to the Flood. Beginning with Jared, we will see a possible meaning or two[10] and give a brief comment on how the name tells the story. *Jared* means "descent." The ancient Jewish book called 1 Enoch—a book quoted by Jude as containing the real words of Enoch—comments on this saying that it was in the days of *Jared* that the sons of heaven *descended* upon Mt. Hermon (1 Enoch 6:6). Enoch is using a word play in his retelling of the story.

Jared's son *Enoch* has possible meanings of "initiated" or "teacher." This may have reference to the story told in 1 Enoch, that these heavenly beings began to teach mankind all sorts of hidden knowledge—"the eternal secrets preserved in heaven"—from astronomy and astrology, to aborting a fetus, to warfare (1 Enoch 8:1-3; 9:6; 69:1-13). Whether any of that happened or not, an informed opinion must take into consideration that the same story is told around the world (for example, the Greeks believe Prometheus taught us how to make fire).

Enoch's son *Methuselah*, usually known for being the oldest named person in the Bible, living an incredible 969 years, has a name that can mean "man of the dart," as in an arrow, a javelin, or even a missile of some kind. In other words, from his name we can gather that warfare is being learned. It is also becoming common place. Of course, this is part of the violence that later brings God to destroy the earth in the Flood, so this isn't speculation.

Methuselah's descendant is named *Lamech* which means "powerful/destroyer." The impression is that things have gone from bad to terrible. Lamech then has a son and names him *Noah*. Noah means "rest," because through him the vanity of life, the violence, wickedness and corruption of the earth will come to an end.

For good measure, I should throw in the last few names of the line of Cain, who we get the impression were probably contemporaries with those mentioned here in the line of Seth. *Methusael* means "asking God for death." His son *Lamech*, again, means "destroyer/powerful." This is the Lamech who marries two women, murders a man, and arrogantly defies God to come and kill him. Lamech has three sons all known for their cultural achievements: *Jabal* (father of tent dwellers and livestock), *Jubal* (father of those who play the lyre and pipe), and *Tubal-Cain* (forger of metal, perhaps implying weapons). Curiously, much of this is also said in the book of Enoch to have been taught by a group called the Watchers, who in Enoch and other ancient books are just another name for the sons of God. In the Bible, a Watcher is a heavenly angelic being that looks over the affairs of mankind (cf. Dan 4:13, 23). In the Dead Sea Scrolls they were described as tall and serpentine in appearance.[11]

There is a progression in the names moving from innocence to corruption to violence to death to hope. This is the story of our early history. Reading Genesis 6:4 in conjunction with these names (if that is legitimate) shows that the giants had no special regard for one group of humans over another, but waged war against any of us whom they chose. This idea of violence was also part of the traditions handed down by the Jews in their ancient books.[12]

What else can we learn about the giants before the Flood? Moses did not give us a lot of information, but if we read other passages in the Bible together with the Jewish literature circulating in Israel during the time of Jesus, we may be able to discern a few more things. I'm not suggesting that these books necessarily depict history with 100% accuracy, but knowing what they say does tell us how those in Bible times understood it. (If you have a problem using ancient Jewish literature to determine facts about giants, I would challenge you to read the Appendix: Extra-Biblical Literature at this time).

Time and Place of the Giant's "Arrival"

Targum Pseudo-Jonathan has this for Genesis 6:4, "Schamchazai and Uzziel ['Aza'el], who fell from heaven, were on the earth in those days; and also, after the sons of the Great had gone in with the daughters of men, they bare to them: and these are they who are called men who are of the world, men of names." If you read the Introduction, you will remember that targums are Jewish paraphrases of the Scripture that sometimes elaborate to provide further explanation. Some of this was ancient oral tradition. Who are Schamchazai and Uzziel? According to the even earlier writings, these were the names of two of two hundred sons of God who fell from heaven. 1 Enoch says,

> It came to pass that when the sons of men multiplied, in those days beautiful and fair daughters were born. And the angels, the sons of heaven, saw them and desired them, and said to one another: 'Come! Let us choose for ourselves wives from people, and we will beget for ourselves children.' And *Semiaza* [also written as Shemhazai] who was their ruler, said to them: 'I fear that you will not desire to do this deed, and I alone will be a debtor of a great sin.' Therefore they all answered him: 'Let us swear an oath and let us all anathematize one another, not to turn away from this plan, until we should complete it and do this deed.' Then they all swore together and anathematized one another by it. And these were the two hundred who descended in the days of Jared to the summit of Mount Hermon, and they called the mountain Hermon, because they swore and anathematized one another by it.
>
> (1 Enoch 6:1-6)

If Jude (and 2 Peter) trusts 1 Enoch, quoting him as giving real prophecy and alluding to this very story,[13] then Enoch tells us when the Nephilim first arose on the earth. It says it happened in the day of Jared. There is a word play going on here with "Jared," which as we have seen means "descend." The idea is that his father named him after the incredible events that took place in those days: the descent of the sons of God (also called sons of heaven, angels, and Watchers). Jared was born a minimum of 1,000 years before the flood. This gives plenty of time for the entire earth to become corrupt by the time Noah is called to build the ark.

The location of the descent of these sons of God is Mt. Hermon.[14] Mt. Hermon stands as the highest point in Israel, at 9,320 ft. above sea level. Mt. Hermon is also used in a word play in this passage. Hermon (spelled *khrmn* without the vowels in Hebrew) is almost identical to *khrm*, the word "anathema." On Mt. Hermon the Watchers cursed (anathematized) themselves. There is a fascinating archeological discovery found on Hermon's slopes which confirms that more than two millennia ago, people took this very seriously.[15]

Sir Charles Warren, having become the head of the London Metropolitan Police from 1886-1888, became *infamous* as the Commissioner who botched what remains to this day perhaps the most notorious unsolved serial killer case in history—Jack the Ripper (Warren actually resigned his office to resume his longstanding military career on the day the last murder took place). However, twenty years earlier he commissioned by the Palestinian Exploration Fund to carry out Biblical archaeology "reconnaissance" work throughout the Holy Land. This included the slopes of Mt. Hermon.

Fɪɢ. 1.2. Mᴛ. Hᴇʀᴍᴏɴ

Warren came to Hermon via the Rock of Gibraltar, where a couple years earlier he had become a rather famous surveyor in her majesty's *Corps of Royal Engineers*, creating two 26 ft. long scale models of the city and its famous rock, one of which is still on display in a museum there. High up on Hermon's slopes, he discovered the remains of an ancient Roman temple, built on top of an even earlier Greek temple (which in turn was almost certainly built on even earlier temples).[16] It is known as *Qasr Antar*, and it was the highest temple of the ancient world. Warren explains how in the oldest part, "We found a stone 4ft. by 18in. by 12in. with a Greek inscription on the face very roughly cut ... the inscription does not appear to have been noticed by travelers before."[17] One well-respected scholar dates this inscription to the third century A.D., but as it is stone it could of course be older. It reads,

kata keleusin theou megistou kai agiou oi omnuontes enteuthen
("According to the command of the greatest and holy God,
those who take an oath proceed from here").[18]

It is no coincidence that this inscription and 1 Enoch say almost the same thing. Both are remembering something truly ancient that took place at a time that the Bible places prior to the Flood, at least that's what the ancient Jews believed. But it wasn't just them. This story of Mt. Hermon and the coming down to earth of fallen angels upon its

FIG. 1.3. "OATH" INSCRIPTION, MT. HERMON [19]

summit was known to peoples as diverse as the Israelites, Canaanites, Babylonians, Akkadians, Greeks, Romans, and Christians, even though they were literally thousands of miles apart and sometimes as far from Hermon itself.[20]

The event also seems to be remembered in the name of Hermon (*hrmn*) which means "devote," and is closely related to that Hebrew word (*khrm*, "the ban") used throughout the Bible for OT Holy-War. This is where Israel was to "devote to destruction" all of the men, women, children, animals, and belongings of the inhabitants of Canaan. Guess who they are or are related to? It is the word used whenever Israel "devotes to destruction" certain peoples in the OT who are always in some way associated with the events of those days, particularly through the offspring of the unholy union of angels and women: the Nephilim (Gen 6:4). These same three letters are also the root for the words "sacred" and "forbidden."[21] Again, in Enoch the word means "curse." Obviously, the word Hermon all by itself is telling a story. We will return to Mt. Hermon again in this book, for in the Bible it is the Grand Central Station of the giants of old.

Giants of Great Height

After this Enoch reports,

> The women became pregnant and bore great giants of three thousand cubits, who devoured the labors of people. And when the people were not able to sustain them, the giants dared (to attack) them, and they devoured the people. And they began to sin with birds and wild animals and reptiles and fish, and to devour one another's flesh, and drink blood. Then the earth appealed against the lawless ones.
>
> (1 Enoch 7:2-6)

The text is almost certainly corrupt when it says "three thousand cubits" (or "ells;" some texts say 300) though there are traditions that believe this. In 1999, I was in Israel making a documentary on the giants where we interviewed a rabbi who told us with a straight face that the giants before the flood were 10, 20, 30, even 40 meters high (This was in stunning contrast the archeologist who had been presiding over the dig of Gath, home of Goliath," who just a couple of days previous was insistent that Goliath couldn't have been over six feet tall!). I don't know if he is aware of these traditions of not, but the South African researcher Michael Tellinger insists that he has found thousands of ancient, fossilized hearts, knuckles, ribs, shoulder blades, and so on, that would put the owner at anywhere from 18, 60, even nearly 5,000ft. tall![22] He's an interesting fellow, and his footprint ("the Footprint of God") in the side of a rock in South Africa, seemingly imprinted there when the rock was molten is certainly an interesting find as well.[23] Do with his research what you will, though know he has some new age leanings.

It should be stated that there are other manuscripts of 1En 7:2 that have been reconstructed as saying simply, "They grew in accordance with their greatness."[24] The honest answer is, no one knows how tall they were in the original copy of the book. Clearly, they soared above other men. One passage in Jubilees ("the little Genesis") says that the Rephaim giants who lived after the flood in the land of Gilead were "ten, nine, eight, down to seven cubits tall" (Jub 29:9). That puts them anywhere from 10½ - 15 ft. tall, which is within the range of known height of two of the giants in the Bible who lived after the flood. Amos 2:9 provides partial biblical verification of this saying of the giants after the Flood that their "height was like the height of cedars." The Dead Sea Scroll, echoing Amos, adds that their bodies were like mountains (CD 2:19), perhaps also echoing traditions that the watchers were also giants (TReub 5:7; 2En 1:4; GosPet 40).

Cannibalism

What Enoch then describes is an unthinkable horror, also reported by the spies who entered the land of Canaan who returned so frightened that they did not care that they would be punished to wander in the wilderness for 40 years because of their unbelief in God's ability to save them. It tells us that these giants were cannibals. "They devoured the people." There is a parallel in the book of Jubilees which reads, "They begat sons the Naphidim, and they were all unlike, and they devoured one another" (Jub 7:22).[25] This is not made-up, but is again verified by the biblical text, for this is exactly what the spies report in Numbers 13:32-33, "The land, through which we have gone to spy it out, is *a land that devours its inhabitants*, and all the people that we saw in it are of great height. And there we saw the Nephilim." According to the Enochian tradition, they became so full of blood-lust that they began to eat one another, even drinking the blood. 1 Enoch 7:5 says, "They began to sin with birds and wild animals and reptiles and fish, and to devour one another's flesh, and drink blood."[26]

Vampires and Giants

There is a curious side-note to this blood-drinking by the giants. Some scholars have suggested that this is the origin of vampire myths that go back to ancient Babylon.[27] Most people think that Bram Stoker made up the legend, but nothing could be further from the truth. In China it is called *giang shi*, a demon who drinks blood. In Peru it is the *pumapmicuc* who sucked blood from sleeping victims. In Greece they were the *empusa*, winged demon-women who lured handsome youths to their deaths to drink their blood and eat their flesh. In India they speak of a vampire who hangs upside down from a tree like a bat. The Maya worshiped a giant blood-sucking creature named *Camazotz*—half man, half bat. The Apache and Comanche Indians speak of the giant cannibal owl. Jews called one version the *Lilith*, the female night-roaming monster that drank the blood of babies[28] (in Chapter 13 I will show you that the Lilith comes up in the OT in some very interesting contexts). An ancient Babylonian spell reads,

> Spirits that *minish* heaven and earth, that minish the land, of giant strength, of giant strength and giant tread, demons like raging bulls, great ghosts, ghosts that break through all houses, demons that have no shame, seven are they! They rage against mankind; they spill their blood like rain, devouring their flesh and sucking their veins."
> (Utakki Limnuti Tablet V.Col.IV.10-18, 25-27)[29]

What does each story have in common, besides blood drinking? These vampires are all viewed as *demonic* entities. Vampires are spirits who wander the earth seeking those upon whom they might feed. This is a far cry from the American pop-culture romanticism of the vampire. If you wonder how spirits and demons are related to the giants, keep reading. We will have more to say about this.

Bestiality / Crossbreeding

Finally, as we saw a moment ago, the ancient text tells us that some kind of sin was committed between the giants and animals. While

Enoch probably refers to the *eating* of animal flesh, it cannot be ruled out that this refers to bestiality or even to genetic experiments done upon the brute beasts of the earth. The bestiality idea is definitely connected to the giants in the *Torah* (Law). Leviticus 18:23-24 and 20:15-16 both command Israel not to engage in bestiality.[30] The first begins, "You shall not have intercourse with any animal to be defiled with it, nor shall any woman stand before an animal to mate with it; it is a perversion." The word "perversion" is *tebel*, literally "confusion, violation of nature, or of the divine order,"[31] or an "abominable confusion, contamination."[32] The verse then gives the giant reference (which will be explained more in a coming chapter), "Do not make yourselves unclean by any of these things, for by all these *the nations I am driving out* before you have become unclean [or "defiled]."

Jubilees seems to confirm that this was one ancient view in its expansion of the Genesis story. "Lawlessness increased on the earth and all flesh corrupted its way, alike men and cattle and beasts and birds and everything that walks on the earth—all of them corrupted their ways *and their orders*, and they began to devour each other, and lawlessness increased on the earth and every imagination of the thoughts of all men (was) thus evil continually. And God looked upon the earth, and behold it was corrupt, and all flesh had corrupted *its orders*, and all that were upon the earth had wrought all manner of evil before His eyes" (Jub 5:2-3). Bestiality between the inhabitants and the animals of the land of Canaan is frighteningly similar to the cross-breeding of heavenly men and human women that produced these ogres in the first place.

Here we also find room to run with speculations derived from other ancient stories and depictions that seem to indicate that the ancients understood something about DNA. If you have never come across this idea before, it is stunning. Keep in mind, this is speculation. There is a hint that something strange was going on in the land by the size of the grape cluster carried back to Moses by the 12 spies from the land of Canaan.[33] There is also the strange law referred to in the Introduction about not wearing mixed clothing. The whole verse reads, "You shall keep my statutes. You shall not let your cattle breed with a different kind. You shall not sow your field with two kinds of seed, nor shall you wear a garment of cloth made of two kinds of material" (Lev 19:19). The idea is similar to that of bestiality in that it was an unlawful mixing. The mixing of kinds was obviously a real problem. It was a problem that went against the very core of creation, where God made each after its *own* kind. This law, it should be noted, is found in the middle of the context of the previous laws on bestiality. Therefore, it too is associated with the abominable inhabitants of Canaan.

Confirming that this idea of genetic manipulation is not recent is the Jewish *midrash* *Book of Jasher*, a book taking its name from the book mentioned in Josh 10:13 and 2Sam 1:18. This book probably dates between the 9th -16th centuries and was first published into English in 1625 (well before the advent of modern genetic manipulation). It says, "And every man [...] corrupted the earth, and the earth was filled with violence. And [...] the sons of men in those days took from the cattle of the earth, the beasts of the field and the fowls of the air, and *taught the mixture of animals* of one species with the other, in order therewith to provoke the Lord; and God saw the whole earth and it was corrupt, for all flesh had corrupted its ways upon earth, all men and all animals" (*Jasher* 4:17-18). Along these kinds of highly scientific lines, scholars have noted that the ancient texts even include stories of the taking of an embryo from one womb to another in a kind of ancient alchemy.[34] In modern times, abduction claims made by hundreds of thousands of people say they have been experimented upon and probed. While bizarre, if there is some basis of truth, it could very well be Satanic (probably not alien in the sense we normally think of it) in nature. This would offer rather frightening parallels to more ancient tales.

FIG. 1.4. CADUCEUS

LEFT: *FUXI AND NÛWA* (CHINA). TOP-MIDDLE: *"LIBATION VASE OF GUDEA"* (NINGISHZIDA C. 2100 BC. TOP-RIGHT: *QUETZALCOATL FIGURINE* (PRE-SPANISH CONQUEST). BOTTOM-MIDDLE: *PERUVIAN TEXTILE (LATE PARACAS, 300-200 BC)*. BOTTOM-RIGHT: *"THE SERPENT LORD ENTHRONED" (MESOPOTAMIA, C. 2200 BC)*.

FIG. 1.5. CADUCEUS IN WORLD MYTHOLOGY

I'm not going to press this point. Nevertheless, I have found it most curious that many people, both Christian and non-Christian, have seen a relationship between the ancient symbol of the entwining serpents and the modern DNA strand. The old U.S. Army Medical Core logo is familiar.

The image is called the caduceus. It depicts two serpents entwined around a sacred pole (tree) which has wings like a bird (seraphim?). Its earliest use goes back over 4,000 years to Babylon where a staff surmounted by two serpentine heads represented the supreme sexual powers of the serpent.[35] We have seen a similar depiction already with regard to the half-serpent, half-human first rulers of China, but you find similar ideas in Egypt, Assyria, Scandinavia and other places as well.

Curiously, the modern depiction of the caduceus became the rod or "Wand of Hermes" (Mercury) and was said to depict his "patronage of peace, trade, commerce, and communication."[36] However, two things should be noted. First, Hermes is also the god of healing. Though not a demi-god (e.g., a giant like Hercules; Hermes is the son of an adulterous affair between Zeus and Maia the Nymph, who is technically descended from the gods, although nymphs have a lot in common with demons as well), Hermes is etymologically related to Mt. Hermon and in fact his son Pan had a cult at the foot of Mt. Hermon for untold centuries.[37] Along these lines, one of the main names for the giants in the Bible is a word that can mean "healing."[38] The word is *rapha*. The giants are the *Repha*im. Also remember, Mt. Hermon is where the sons of God were said to have descended in the days of Jared. Second, at least as early as the 3rd cent. A.D., oculists (eye physicians) were using the caduceus as a seal, thus connecting it to medicine,[39] taking us full circle back to Hermes.

When given this kind of a history, it is extremely interesting to compare these figures with the DNA double-helix. In fact, the two depictions are easily found side by side in a search on Google Images. Given the uncanny resemblances and the incredibly bizarre history that is spoken of in Genesis 6 and around the world, it is not difficult to see why some people make such speculations.

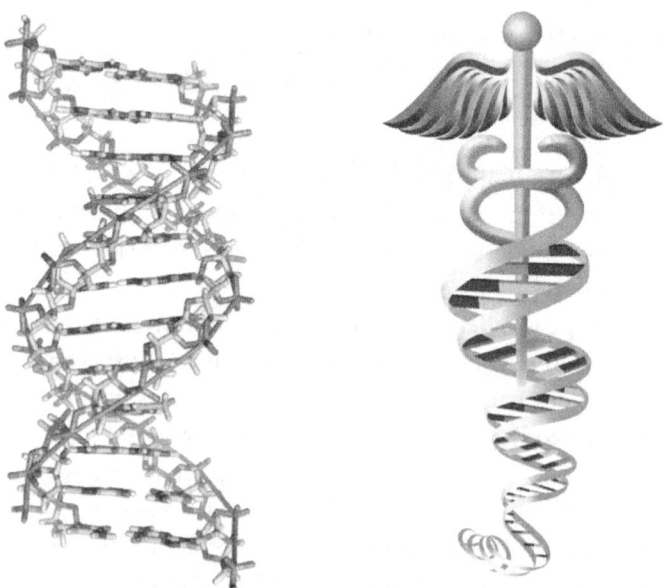

FIG. 1.6. DNA: DOUBLE HELIX.

2

THE GIANT OF BABEL

And Chus [Cush] begot Nebrod [Nimrod]:
He began to be a giant upon the earth.
Genesis 10:8 (LXX)

The Curse of Canaan

ENESIS 6 IS THE GATEWAY, to the story of the Great Flood. Like the tale of the giants, this epic is widely known. In fact, it has been told by at least 270 cultures on every continent and every major

(Chart in Wim van Binsbergen, 2010, 2. Source: Frazer 1918; Dundes 1988; Isaak 2006.)

FIG. 2.1. WORLD FLOOD TRADITIONS

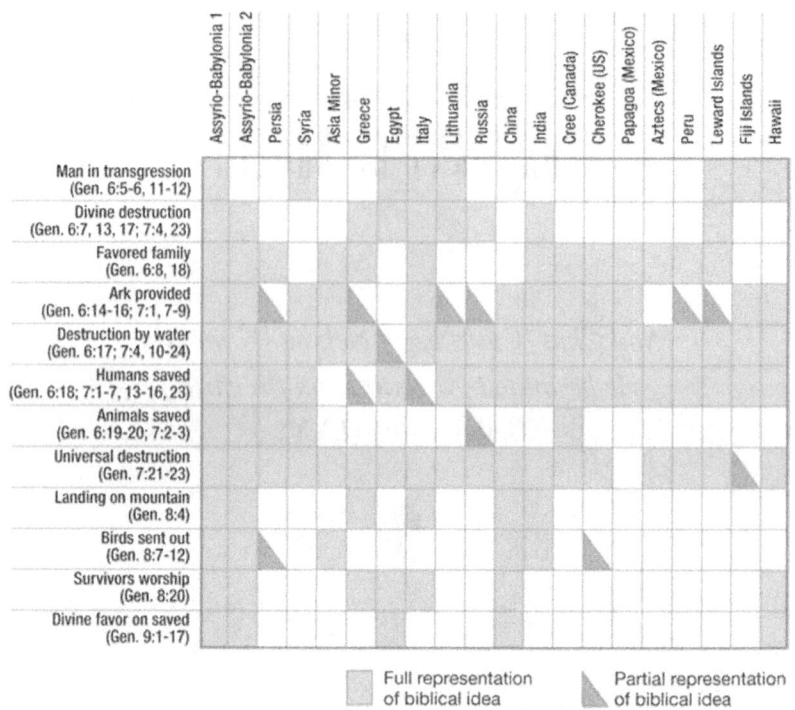

Courtesy: *Answers Magazine* 2:2 (Apr-June 2007).

FIG. 2.2. COMPARISONS OF EVENTS IN FLOOD TRADITIONS

island group on the planet.[1] This isn't a recounting of the Biblical story from Christianized peoples; it is their own primordial memories of the same epic event as remembered by their own cultures.

The Flood was sent to wipe out "all flesh" from the face of the earth. It succeeded. Everything on land and in the air was obliterated, save that which was safe inside the ark where Noah and his family were hidden by God. After the Flood, when Noah leaves the ark behind, we learn very quickly that the Flood did not succeed in eliminating sin. Of course, it was never sent for that purpose. The point I'm about to make is that Noah was most definitely not a perfect man.

The claim is sometimes made that Noah was sinless because, "Noah was perfect in his generations" (Gen 6:9).[2] As we saw in the Introduction, perfection does not refer to Noah's moral quality—God never chooses a person and shows grace to them because they "earned" it. Rather, it refers to his physical purity in the same way that a sacrificial lamb had to be physically perfect. Noah was unblemished. That is, he was fully human, the untainted seed of the woman. Noah walked with God because he had first found grace in God's eyes (Gen 6:8).

Noah was still a sinner. The first (and last) thing we learn about him after leaving the ark and sacrificing to the LORD, is that he builds a vineyard, gets drunk, and allows his son Ham to slip into his tent and have sex with his mother. This last part is often debated, because the passage doesn't say this is so many words. But when we let Scripture interpret itself, we come to see that this is what it has to mean, because the language to "see a father's nakedness" always means to have sex with another man's wife.[3]

The reason I bring this story up is because a strange thing occurs when Noah comes to his senses. It relates directly to the giants. He curses his "son," but it is not Ham. Instead, he curses his grandson ... Canaan. The reason why, in my opinion, is because Canaan was the incestuous child of a union between Noah's wife and Noah's son. Stop right here and notice that there is a similarity to the events of Genesis 6:1-4. Both contain unholy unions and unholy children are born from them. The difference here is that we have little reason to believe that Ham was anything less than fully human. Noah's curse on Canaan becomes the foundation of the hostility that will ensue over the next 2,000 plus years between Israel and the Canaanites who live in the Promised Land. In one form or another, it is still going on to this day.

Noah does something else. He *blesses* his other two sons: Japheth and Shem. In fact, the promised Seed of Eve is narrowed through the line of Shem in Noah's blessing to him. Eventually, Abraham will become the chosen descendant of Shem. He will be blessed by God and become a blessing to all the nations of the earth. Noah's blessing brings a convergence of Shem's descendants and those of Canaan. "Blessed be the LORD, the God of Shem; and let Canaan be his servant" (Gen 9:26). To put this all another way, the hostilities foretold to Eve are being narrowed down to those who come from the line of Canaan and those who come from the line of Shem. By the time of the great exodus out of Egypt, this will become crucial to the overall story of the Bible.

Nimrod the Giant Hunter

Let's go back to Ham for a moment. Ham has several descendants. His sons are named Cush, Egypt, Put, and Canaan (Gen 10:6). We've talked about Canaan; now let's follow the line of Cush. The sons of Cush were Seba, Havilah, Sabtah, Raamah, Sabteca, and a fellow named Nimrod. The information on Nimrod in the Bible is scant. It is found in Genesis 10:8-12.

> [8] Cush fathered Nimrod; he was the first on earth to be a mighty man. [9] He was a mighty hunter before the LORD. Therefore it is said, "Like Nimrod a mighty hunter before the LORD." [10] The beginning of his kingdom was Babel, Erech, Accad, and Calneh, in the land of Shinar. [11] From that land he went into Assyria and built Nineveh, Rehoboth-Ir, Calah, and [12] Resen between Nineveh and Calah; that is the great city.

From this passage we learn that Nimrod is situated in Mesopotamia.[4] His sphere of influence was based in the south (Babylonia), and later extended to the north (Assyria) at least as far as Nineveh, the famous city in the book of Jonah.

One important clue about Nimrod's identity is found in the phrase "a mighty hunter." We have seen the word "mighty" before; it is the word *gibbor* (*gibborim* refers to a group, as "*-im*" is the plural ending of Hebrew words). The ESV translates it "mighty" in both passages. However, the LXX reads "giant" (*gigas*, the singular form of *gigantes*), saying that Nimrod "began to be a *giant* upon the earth." Just like the ESV, the Greek is consistently translating the word in Genesis 6:4 and Genesis 10:9. Since the LXX translated both *gibborim* and *nephilim* as *gigantes* in Genesis 6:4, this is strong evidence that very early on it was thought that Nimrod was a giant. Before we can say any more about this, I would like to see more evidence than just this word.

In Gen 10:9 Nimrod has some kind of a relationship to Yahweh. The question is, what kind? Most translations say something like Nimrod was "a mighty hunter *before* the LORD." What would it mean to be a mighty hunter before the LORD? Many think of it as a positive attribute, that Nimrod was a hero of the chase who hunted wild game and that this was a gift of God's grace.[5] There are several problems with this interpretation.

For one, it does not seem to make a lot of sense. Why would being a good hunter be a gift of God's grace, and why would this trait be something to be singled out in a mere mortal? This is, after all, the only trait of any of the 70 people(s) mentioned in the entire chapter. He could shoot a deer with a bow and arrow? So what?

Next, *gibborim* and "men of renown" seem to be viewed as evil beings in Genesis 6:4. They are one of the reasons God brought the Flood. If that is true, what justification in the text allows us to see Nimrod as a *good* hero? Certainly it is not his lineage, which comes from Ham. Nor is it his association with Babel, the great anti-city of the Bible. Nor is it the fact that he is a city builder, for though cities are not always viewed negatively in the Bible, up to this point the only city builder has been Enoch the son of Cain (Gen 4:17). Nor is one of the popular etymologies of his name helpful. Many people think that Nimrod comes from the word *m-r-d* which means "*rebel.*"

It may be possible to identify Nimrod in the pagan cultures, and this might demonstrate a positive relationship to Yahweh. After all, Moses says that this character was very well known in ancient times, still having a proverbial saying attached to him many centuries later. Because of this, scholars have gone looking to the stories of the Middle East for the identification of this person. The problem is, outside of Israel, the name Nimrod is not known as such. That doesn't stop people from trying.

Throughout the ages, Nimrod has been identified as some pretty remarkable figures: *Zoroaster*, *Marduk* the main god of the Babylonian creation story, Hercules, Orion, and an Assyrian god named Ninurta. The last three heroes are often said to depict the same historic person. Osiris in Egypt, Thor in Scandinavia, and the Hopi Indian god of the underworld Masau'u are also sometimes linked to Orion, which, if also identified with Nimrod, would make him truly world-renown (remembering, of course, that the nations were dispersed *after* Babel).

There is one character in Assyrian mythology that many scholars see as most resembling the little we know about Nimrod: *Ninurta—Lord of Earth*. Some have suggested that Ninurta is derived through this transformation: *$^*nwrt$ > $^*nmrt$ > $nmrd$.*[6] If not his name, it is his extracurricular activities that really fuel the speculation. Like Nimrod, Ninurta was a mighty hunter. His exploits were famous in ancient

Greco-Roman Orion, depicted with club   Osiris with spear-like object and Orion's Belt
(Left: Longdon, constellation cards 1825; Middle: Osirus and Orion's Belt. Right: Theban Tomb 353. Tomb of Senenmut, South Ceiling)

FIG. 2.3. HERCULES AND OSIRIS AS ORION

times. He is said to have gained eleven trophies including a seven-headed serpent, a terrible lion, a buck or stag, the mythological Anzu bird, a large crab, and a bull-man. These stories are so similar to the 12 labors of Hercules, that many scholars think the two figures are the

Left: Hercules wearing the lion skin . Boston 99.538, Attic bilingual amphora, ca. 525-500. Photograph, Museum of Fine Arts, Boston. Right: Ninurta pursues Anzu B.C. Stone sculpture of Ninurta, Nimrud, Iraq. Drawing: Austen Henry Layard (1853)

FIG. 2.4. HERCULES AND NINURTA

same person. Among his quests, Hercules killed the *Hydra*, the *Nemean Lion*, the *Cerynean Hind*, the *Stymphalian Birds*, a crab that assisted the Hydra, and the *Cretan Bull*.[7] (It is curious that Osiris, mentioned above, is son of heaven: Nut, and earth: Geb. He is said to be the god of the heavens and the underworld. When viewed from the 12 constellations, which proceed around the earth night and day, there is a bull: Taurus; a crab: Cancer; a lion: Leo; and other figures that correspond to the labors of Hercules). The thing about these two heroes is that they had positive relationships with their divine fathers (Ninurta to Enil and Hercules to Zeus). Both fathers are the head gods of their respective pantheons. Thus, if Nimrod is related to them, the argument goes, we should see Nimrod in a positive light.

The problem with this "son of a god" interpretation is that Nimrod is said to descend from Cush, not Yahweh. Cush does not appear in any way in the Bible to be a heavenly figure like a god. He is just the son of Ham who was the son of Noah. So why think that Nimrod was a god worshiped by the pagans? Many have taken this argument and run with it the other way, concluding that Nimrod was nothing but a mortal, which of course is possible.

But let us think about this for a moment. As we come to later passages in the Bible, we see that giants are indeed on the earth after the Flood. This is an indisputable fact. They had to get here somehow. Furthermore, these post-Flood giants are not just tall people. They are said to have come from two groups of ancestors, both of which are viewed as semi-divine *in the Bible*. One of these is the Nephilim of Genesis 6:4. The other group are the Rephaim.

How Did Giants Survive the Flood?

Let me insert just here that this is probably the most asked question I have received over the last ten years on giants. *How did giants make it through the Flood?* Given these basic facts, there are all kinds of possibilities that do not contradict the Bible. Here are several to consider. First, we could imagine, as many Jews did, that some of the Nephilim before the Flood actually made it through the Deluge alive. For instance, they say that Og, a famous giant of the Bible, made it through by holding onto Noah's Ark, being fed by the kind patriarch through a hole in the boat.

That's pretty silly and is usually just told as a fairy-tale to children. A more contemporary view that holds a lot of water with OT scholars, is that the Flood was not universal. Problem solved. To my mind, this solution does not do justice to the fact that the Flood destroyed "all flesh" upon the earth. So I personally rule this out as implausible.

Perhaps a better solution is that genetic manipulation was taking place. This could also help explain how the gigantic cluster of grapes brought back to Moses by the 12 spies (Num 13:23) came into being.[8] If such business occurred prior to the Flood, this information could have been known by someone like Ham who then transmitted it to his descendants, especially if he was godless and longed for an earth like it was before God destroyed it. This kind of conjecture is pretty far out there, but given what we can do today, it might be plausible. In fact, the more you learn about the subject of genetic manipulation, the less you realize you want to know about it. This could not be any truer in than in the growing field of transhumanism which has been working diligently on creating every conceivable form of hybrid, not 1,000 years in our future, but this very day. Only if we have a presupposed bias against this kind of a thing from the start (because of a worldview like Darwinism that views are ancestors as little more than apes, or because we have no idea what's actually going on in our own world right now), will we be prevented from at least entertaining its possibility. We will return to this theory momentarily.

A third possibility that is much simpler to fathom is that someone on the ark simply carried the genetic material. Because God chose Noah for the reason that he was genetically untainted (see the Introduction), it is usually assumed that this three sons were also biologically pure. This would leave only their wives left to carry the dormant recessive genes. The usual culprit is thought to be Ham's wife, because, after all, Ham was the evil son after the Flood. Furthermore, it is from Ham's genealogy that most, if not all the biblical giants, originate. Of the views thus far mentioned, this one is the most plausible to me, though we will discover soon enough that we can in fact trace giants very early on to one, if not both of the other two sons.

A fourth solution is that another group of the sons of God fell after the Flood and began doing similar kinds of things that their brothers did prior to it. To my mind, this is the most plausible suggestion and it fits very well with the whole episode that took place at the tower of Babel. If they did, perhaps they thought to themselves, "God swore he would not punish the world by a Flood again, so we're safe." Or, perhaps, they just didn't care. There are plenty of humans in the world like that! If true, as with the first time around, this could have been sexual and/or genetic in nature.

Back to Nimrod

At any rate, if Nimrod's father is human, how could we account for nephilimism (for lack of a better word) in Nimrod? Curiously, some have speculated that genetic manipulation on a living person is exactly what happened to Nimrod. The grammar allows for this translation, "Nimrod began to become a giant."[9] In other words, like Seth Brundle in the 80s horror classic, *The Fly*, Nimrod was a willing participant in a grotesque genetic experiment. While is sounds crazy to some, it is increasingly uncrazy to many more, and the facts are now in that this is precisely what they've begun to do with mRNA technology in living human beings.[10]

A different option could suggest that Nimrod's line is incomplete. In Hebrew there is no word for "grandpa" or "great grandfather." So there could be gaps that would allow for a fall of angelic beings to come to Nimrod's mother, while his ancestor Cush was entirely human. Again, this is speculative, but the ancients who were wrestling with the very same questions didn't seem too troubled by the speculation. The point is that there are ways to conceive of Nimrod's gigantism and demigod status without contradicting the text.

There is quite possibly more information that points to Nimrod being a *demigod*. The first is 2 Kings 19:37. The passage refers to Sennacherib king of Assyria returning to Nineveh (the city built by Nimrod). It says, "It came about as he was worshiping in the house of Nisroch his god..." Nisroch has been identified as another name for Ninurta[11] (like many rulers in history, perhaps Nimrod had several names), and/or as a corruption of the word Nimrod.[12] If this is the case, then it is probable that Nimrod was viewed as at least semi-divine, because ancient peoples did not worship mere mortals.

The second place of interest is Job 38:31, "Can you bind the chains of the Pleiades or loose the cords of Orion"? This verse, which seems so innocuous when you just read it like this, is actually pretty fascinating. The word translated into "Orion" is the Hebrew word *kesil*. *Kesil* was translated by the Jews at the Dead Sea with the Aramaic 70aphal which, as we saw in the Introduction, is a word that means "giant," and itself is probably the root of the Hebrew *nephilim*. This same verse was also translated by the Syriac church to the word *gabbara*, which is that language's equivalent of *gibborim*. There is an *Akkadian* word equivalent to both of these which means "the broad man, giant."[13] So you could translate the verse, "Can you bind the chains of the Pleiades or loose the cords of the giant"?

The Orion/Nimrod association is curious. In Greek culture, Orion was the "hunter ever famed" (Homer, *Odyssey* 11.397) and "The huge Orion" (*Odyssey* 11.721). Odysseus sees him hunting in the underworld with a bronze club, as a great slayer of animals. In other words, he was known as a giant hunter just like Nimrod. Thus, there are traditions that have equated the two throughout the centuries.[14] The idea, according to some is that Job's reference to Orion is one of "a giant who, confiding foolishly in his strength, and defying the Almighty, was, as a punishment for his arrogance, bound for ever in the sky."[15] Is this a cryptic reference to Nimrod, the hero of old?

One more possibility of the meaning of the name Nimrod has associations with Canaanite religion and giants. Though the Bible does not say that Nimrod extended his reign any further west than Nineveh, there are legends aplenty that he came all the way to Lebanon (ancient Phoenicia) where he is said to have built a most remarkable structure called Baalbek and was finally buried in Damascus (in western Syria).

Baalbek is in the heart of Philistine country, about 25 miles east of modern Beirut. Its origins are very old. The complex there has been built and rebuilt by various civilizations. It boasts some of the largest cut stones on earth. Three (known as the trilithon), were set into place midway up a retaining wall which acts to level the entire compound. They weigh around 800 tons each. The two largest stones still sit at the quarry a mile or so away. One weighs an estimated 1,000 tons; the is estimated at an unbelievable 1,200 tons (that's 2.4 million lbs., see Figure 2.5) making it the largest hewn stone on earth.

Upper Left: The Stone of the South (1242 t.); Upper Right: The Stone of the Pregnant Woman (etc. 1,000 t.). Bottom, the Trilithon (est. 800 t. each)

FIG. 2.5. MEGALITHS OF BAALBEK, LEBANON

There was an Arabic manuscript found at Baalbek that reads, "After the flood, when Nimrod reigned over Lebanon, he sent giants to rebuild the fortress of Baalbek, which was so named in honour of Baal, the god of the Moabites and worshipers of the sun."[16] In the legends, Nimrod himself was said to be a giant.[17] These legends surrounding Baalbek and Nimrod may confuse the earlier pre-Roman and Canaanite site with the later Roman reconstruction which was possibly responsible for building and placing the megalithic stones.[18] It is his association with giants and Baal that is our purpose here.

As the name suggests, Baal was a chief god worshiped here. The meaning of Nimrod associated with Baal has been proposed: "Panther of Hadd" (Hadd = Baal).[19] Since we do not have solid evidence that Nimrod's kingdom extended this far, the stories of him in these places remain a mystery. The point of mentioning them is to give you a flavor for the many stories of him in history which say he was a giant.[20]

For these many reasons, it is better to see Nimrod as being a mighty hunter "against" the LORD. Both the Hebrew word and the Greek translation can be interpreted "against."[21] If the *gibborim* of Genesis 6:4 were violent (and it clearly seems that they were), then for Nimrod to be both a *gibbor* and a hunter would almost certainly associate him with violence, at least against animals, but possibly also against humans.

The Tower of Babel

From the passage on Nimrod, we see two important things about his kingdom. First, "The beginning of his kingdom was Babel." Second, this was "in the land of Shinar." This foreshadowing is the reason so many people think that the person behind the building of the Tower of Babel was Nimrod. Babel was *his* city.

The story of Babel occurs immediately after the genealogies of the sons of Noah end (Gen 11:1-9). It tells us that the whole earth had one language. Then as the people migrated from the east, they found a plain in the land of Shinar and settled there. Immediately they sought to build for themselves both "a city" and "a tower" (Gen 11:4). Note, they did not only build a tower, but also a city. Because of the infamous arrogance of this episode where they said, "Let us build a tower with its top in the heavens, and let us make a name for ourselves, lest we be dispersed over the face of the whole earth," God came down and confused their language. Therefore the name of "the city" was Babel (Gen 11:8-9). This means that Nimrod must have been the architect behind the whole sordid affair.

Take notice of the motive for the Tower. "Let us make *a name* for ourselves." Now compare this to the Nephilim of Genesis 6:4. They were the famous "men of renown." "Renown" is literally "the name." "Name" (*shem*) is the same word in both passages, thus linking the

Nephilim, Nimrod, and the Tower of Babel together. Did Nimrod seek to align himself with the Nephilim of old?

The Giants and Babel

Let's look at the legends that exist surrounding the building of this fabled tower. Consider the work of Pseudo-Eupolemus (150 BC) whom Eusebius (the first great Church historian, c. 263-339 AD) quoted.

> The Assyrian city of Babylon was first founded by those who escaped the Flood. They were giants, and they built the tower well known in history. When the tower was destroyed by God's power, these giants were scattered over the whole earth."[22]

The Sibylline Oracle to which Josephus refers[23] has something similar. First, it equates Noah's three sons to the three Titans (giants):[24] Cronos, Titan and Japetus, where Japetus is the Greek equivalent of Japheth. It says they ended up fighting a great war after the Tower fell. The languages were confused. The three sons were given equal realms to rule on the condition that they would not fight one another. But due to the treachery of Cronus (Shem?) against Titan (Ham?)—who had bound him not to have any sons so that he could reign when Cronus died—a war arose between the seventy sons[25] of Titan (who used to kill any male born to Cronus but let the females live) and the sons of Cronus. According to the *Sybil*, the parties were completely destroyed, and soon thereafter the great kingdoms of men rose up (Egypt, Persia, Babylon, etc.).[26]

These stories clearly link giants with the Tower of Babel. Pretty strange, right? Now what if we crossed the ocean? Nestled in the plains a mere 20 miles below the towering heights of the 14,636 ft. La Malinche volcano (also known as Matlalcuéyetl or Malintzin) in Mexico to the NE and the even taller 17,160 ft. Iztaccíhuatl and currently active 17,802 ft Popocatépetl volcanoes to the west (and northwest) stands perhaps the largest monument in the world. Built uncounted centuries ago and topping out at 210 ft., it has a volume of 4.45 million m^3. To put that in perspective, the Great Pyramid at Giza only has 2.5 million m^3. This monument is not really a monument at all, but a sacred structure known as the Cholula Pyramid.

FIG. 2.6. THE CHOLULA PYRAMID

James George Frazier in his book *Folk-Lore in the Old Testament* writes,

> A legend concerning the foundation of this huge monument is recorded by the Dominican friar Pedro de los Rios. It runs as follows. Before the great flood, which took place four thousand years after the creation of the world, this country was inhabited by giants. All who did not perish in the inundation were turned into fishes, except seven who took refuge in caves. When the waters had retired, one of the seven, by name Xelhua, surnamed the Architect, came to Cholula, where, in memory of the mountain of Tlaloc, on which he and his six brothers had found safety, he built an artificial hill in the shape of a pyramid. He caused the bricks to be made ... It was his purpose to raise the mighty edifice to the clouds, but the gods, offended at his presumption, hurled the fire of heaven down on the pyramid, many of the workmen perished, and the building remained unfinished.[27]

A similar Flood tradition of the Toltecs at another monument[28] states that after the deluge, "[Giants] built a *zacuali* of great height, and by this is meant a very high tower, in which to take refuge when the world should be a second time destroyed. After this their tongue became confused, and, not understanding each other, they went to different parts of the world."[29] Frazer says, "In th[ese] legend[s] the coincidences with the Biblical narratives of the flood, ... the tower of Babel, and the confusion of tongues seem too numerous to be accidental."[30] How interesting that, like Pseudo-Eupolemus and the Sybil, giants are involved.

All the way around the world in Tibet/Burma, the Mikir tribe have the following story:

> They say that in days of old the descendants of Ram were mighty men, and growing dissatisfied with the mastery of the earth they aspired to conquer heaven. So they began to build a tower which should reach up to the skies. Higher and higher rose the building, till at last the gods and demons feared lest these giants should become the masters of heaven, as they already were of earth. So they confounded their speech, and scattered them to the four corners of the world. Hence arise all the tongues of mankind.[31]

Next, we move down to India. The Hindus remember the Asuras, evil beings variously translated as demons or giants.[32] They seek to imitate the great fire altar of heaven and "ascend to the sky." This altar is said to rise from the earth to Heaven. These enemies of the heavenly gods, tried to imitate it, but their undertaking came to nothing, as the gods overthrew it by taking away the foundation of bricks.[33] As you can see, not only is the Tower of Babel story told around the world, so is the association of it *with giants*.

Let us stop for a moment and catch our breath. I want you to think about something. I have long been intrigued how many Christians are quick to use the plethora of Flood stories throughout the world as arguments against *uniformitarian* science to demonstrate that there really was a Great Deluge. Yet, many of these same people scoff at any idea that the equally widespread stories of the giants could ever be taken seriously. This is even more ironic when we consider that these stories of the Flood and/or Tower include stories of the giants, and still more ironic since there is significant reason from the Bible itself to see that this is in fact quite plausible in a biblical worldview.

Why did they build this thing? Was it simply because they wanted to see how high they could get? Are modern skyscrapers the equivalent of the Tower of Babel? Maybe they were so close to Neanderthals that they actually thought if they could go high enough they could somehow build their way into heaven? I know a lot of children have this idea in mind when they are told about this story. In fact, neither one of these is the truth. What was taking place at the tower was deeply religious. It was based upon an age-old idea that through this tower, they would be able to interact with heavenly beings.

The Ziggurat of Babel

To understand this, you need to know what the Tower of Babel was. It was not a skyscraper like the Empire State Building. The Tower of Babel was an ancient *ziggurat*. Ziggurats are temples made to look like mountains. They are found all over the world. When you understand what is going on here, it will blow your mind.

"Ziggurat" can be defined very simply as "a staged tower for which the stages were consciously constructed."[34] To reach the top, you would walk up the *simmiltu* or "stairway." Recall the language of the Tower of Babel, the most famous ziggurat of history. "Let us build ourselves a ... tower with its top in the heavens" (Gen 11:4). Not coincidentally, the *Akkadian* word *ziqqurat* means "to be high."[35] Here are a few examples of ziggurats from around the world.

FIG. 2.7. ARTISTIC RENDITION: TOWER OF BABEL

Top: Ur-Nammu (2,100 B.C.?) in Ur, Iraq Oldest Reconstructed Ziggurat in the World;
Bottom: Ziggurat of Chogha-Zanbil (1,250 B.C.?). Model: Rijksmuseum van Oudheden, Leiden (Holland).

Above: Pyramid of the Sun Teotihuacán, Mexico; **Below:** Pyramid of the Moon, Teotihuacán, Mexico Models: Wolfgang Sauber

FIG. 2.8. ZIGGURATS OF THE MIDDLE EAST AND SOUTH AMERICA

Above: Temple of Kukulkan, Summer Solstice Note: shadow of the serpent (left) only occurs on the solstice. Chichen Itza, Yucatan. **Upper Right:** Temple from Google Earth; Serpent Head at the base of the Temple; **Lower Left:** Pyramid of the Niches (66ft. high), El Tajin. **Lower Right:** Tikal (Temple of the Jaguar), Chichen Itza.

FIG. 2.9. ZIGGURATS OF SOUTH AMERICA

Monks Mound (Cahokia Mounds State Historic Site), Collinsville, Illinois

FIG. 2.10. ZIGGURAT OF NORTH AMERICA

Left: Pyramid of Djoser (Step Pyramid) 2630-2611 B.C. Photo by hiro008; Right: Goguryeo's Pyramid Korea, 500 A.D. Photo by Auws

FIG. 2.11. ZIGGURATS OF ASIA

Plans of the Modern Day "Ziggurat Project," Dubai, UAE.

FIG. 2.12. ZIGGURATS OF THE FUTURE

Ziggurat Name	Ziggurat Location
Temple of the Foundation of Heaven and Earth	Babylon
Temple of the Wielder of the 7 Decrees of Heaven and Earth	Borsippa
Temple of the Mountain Breeze	Nippur
Temple of the Stairway to Pure Heaven	Sippar
Temple of the Exalted Mountain	Ehursagkalamma
Temple of the Foundation of Heaven and Earth	Dilbat
Temple which Links Heaven and Earth	Larsa
Temple of the Ziggurat, Exalted Dwelling Place	Kish
Temple of Exalted Splendor	Enlil
Temple of the god Nanna	Kutha
Temple of the god Dadia	Akkad

TABLE 3. ZIGGURATS OF BABYLON: NAMES[36]

What did the *ziggurat* signify? The only truly objective way to know is to study the names given to them (see Fig. 2.10). The oldest ziggurats of Syria and Iraq still have the names recorded on tablets. In these names we can clearly identify the idea of a mountain, a mirror, a stairway between heaven and earth, and the home of the god(s).

Think for a moment about where the gods were said to live in pagan mythology. It was upon Mt. Olympus that Zeus would hold council with the twelve Olympian gods (see Fig. 2.11). The Titans, the adversaries of the Olympians, lived on Mt. Othrys until Zeus overthrew them.

Like the Flood, the Tower story, and the giants, this theme is also replicated around the world. In China, two gods (Holy Shu and Yü Lü) live upon a beautiful mountain called *Tu-shuo*.[37] Another mountain called Kun-Lun is the "mountain abode of the celestial lords."[38] In Egypt, upon *Ta-tenen* the Ennead (the nine) gods meet and hold court.[39] In India it was upon Mount Meru that Lord Brahma and the Devas[40] (these are not attention starved American pop stars, but *demigods* or angels) would hold council. In Scandinavia, Heimdall would regularly gather with the gods in his hall called *Himinbjörg* ("Sky Mountain")[41] where they would drink delicious honey-mead. Day after day he would sit there guarding the bridge from Hill-Giants. Even in North America you find *Nunne Chaha*, the Great Hill upon which the god Esaugetuh Emissee ("Master of Breath") resided.[42]

Mt. Olympus

FIG. 2.13. MTS. OLYMPUS AND OTHRYS, GREECE

We find a similar idea in the Bible. Zion and Sinai are both referred to as the mountain or abode of God, his temple and his house (cf. Ex 3:1; Ps 68:15-17; Isa 2:2-3; Joel 3:17; Micah 3:12; Heb 12:22). It was from Mt. Sinai that God met with Moses and gave him his law. Curiously, the Bible also says that there were angels there too (Deut 33:2-4; Acts 7:53; Gal 3:19). These "angels" (technically, they are the "sons of God") are referred to as the *divine council* (Ps 82:1).

The idea of the *ziggurat* as a mirror is also significant. What is it a mirror of? Heaven. Jesus himself taught us to pray "on earth as it is in heaven" (Matt 6:10). Jesus has the correct take on a very old, but often twisted, idea. It is not up to man to replicate heaven in an attempt to reach up to it. It is up to God to bring heaven down to you. Nevertheless, you can get an idea of how the ancients also understood the basic premise by looking at the layout of some ancient complexes and how they seem to mimic the constellations.

The picture (above right) of the pyramid complex at Giza is particularly of interest, since the complex seems to be a mirror of Orion (Osiris) the Hunter.[43] Along the same lines, there are other interesting hypo-

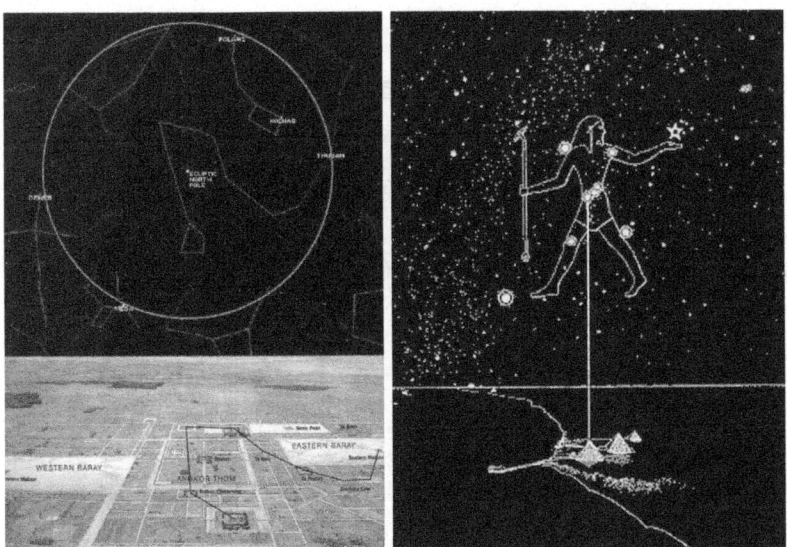

Left: Ankor Thom, Cambodia (Jim Alison); **Right:** Pyramids of Egypt Reflecting Orion the Hunter (The Nile is the Milky Way)

FIG. 2.14. EARTHLY MIRRORS OF THE HEAVENS

theses that on the other side of the world, the ancestors of the Hopi Indians and Mexican builders did the same thing.[44] Speculation about ancient complexes is one thing, but we know that ancient peoples tried to replicate heaven in their earthly temples from their own words. The *Enuma Elish* (6.113) describes *Marduk's* temple, "He shall make on earth the counterpart of what he has brought to pass in heaven." Similarly, Pharaoh Ramses III (1195-1164) wrote about his god, "I made for thee an august house in Nubia … the likeness of the heavens." He also said, "I made for thee an august palace … like the great house of [the god] Atum which is in heaven."[45]

The idea of a *ziggurat*, that it is a holy residence for God, has some similarities with the design of Solomon's Temple, which has several corresponding architectural traits in common with Ziggurats, including the tiered levels and stairways.

The idea of a stairway is important. The Hebrew word for a stairway is *sullam*. It is related to the word *simmiltu*.[46] It occurs only one time in the Bible, in Genesis 28:12. Unfortunately, it often gets translated as "ladder." It refers to something that Jacob saw in a dream. He says, "The top of it reached to heaven. And behold, the angels of God were ascending and descending on it! And behold, the LORD stood above it …

Screenshot: Messages of Christ, Solomon's Temple Explained (Youtube)

FIG. 2.15. SOLOMON'S TEMPLE

FIG. 2.16. STAIRWAY TO HEAVEN, ZIGGURAT AT UR

This is none other than the house of God, and this is the gate of heaven"
(Gen 28:12-13, 17). Notice in the picture of the famous *ziggurat* in
Iraq (Fig. 2.14) how it appears to be a stairway to heaven (Led Zeppelin
didn't invent the idea).

Like Mt. Sinai, angels are here also ascending and descending upon
this stairway that Jacob saw in his dream. Like Sinai, this too is the
"house of God." This was none other than a gateway, a place where the
visible and invisible worlds meet. Thus, all of the signs point to this
idea—what Jacob saw was a kind of *ziggurat*.[47]

The purpose of the Tower of Babel thus seems to have been to
make some kind of forbidden contact with the invisible world, with the
sons of God who had previously descended upon another mountain,
Mt. Hermon. Here, then, is our link between Nimrod and the sons of
God, which seems to further oblige us to relate him to the Nephilim.
Through sacred astronomy and ancient astrology, through the architecture and the principle of the mirror of heaven, we can now see the
Tower story in a much more dubious light. This was not about seeing
how tall they could make a skyscraper. Neither were these people

metaphorically trying to "work" their way to heaven. They were trying to bring heaven down through powerful occult magic. They knew well the ancient Genesis 6 story. They wanted to reestablish contact with the gods of old.

Curiously, in the story, God comes down,[48] and sees what they are doing (Gen 11:7). In an ironic way, their attempt worked. But they did not bargain for what they received, which was not power or fame, but a curse, a dispersion, and the end of their unified attempts at trying to breach the heavenly domain, to force an intersection between heaven and earth on their terms. What we will find after Babel, are scattered, fragmented, incomplete attempts to contact the other world (to reach up to heaven), and while those attempts still rest upon ancient knowledge, nothing like the concerted power of all people together takes place again, at least not until the very end of time.

Returning to the beginning of our chapter, long prior to this end of time, something foreshadowing its culmination occurs in God's statement to Shem. Shem, as we have seen, is the word "name," but it is also the name of a son of Noah. God tells Shem in the story immediately preceding the Tower of Babel that Canaan will be his servant and that he would be the one through whom the promises to Eve would come (Gen 9:26-27). Indeed, it will not be the people of Babel who will make a name for themselves, but God who will make a name for himself through Shem—the Name.

3

Abram and the Giant Wars

They made war.
Genesis 14:2

The Line of Canaan

ABEL DOES NOT STOP the spread of the giants or their desire for world domination. Very quickly we see them spread from one person (Nimrod) to entire clans that are waging wars throughout the Middle East. In fact, it only takes three chapters for them to come back into view. Genesis 14 preserves for us an ancient story of the wars of the giants. The groundwork for these wars is laid in the chapter before Babel, in Genesis 10.

Genesis 10 is the famous "Table of Nations." When you don't know what's going on here, it makes for a long boring list. It gives seventy names,[1] many of which are not individuals but people groups.[2] We spent an entire chapter on just one of these names: Nimrod. Now we need to take note of a few more. If you spend the time to look into this, you will be rewarded with great understanding of coming events.

Like Nimrod, all the names I want to look at here come from the lineage of Ham. Ham is one of three children of Noah. The genealogy gives us four children of Ham: Cush (from whom Nimrod sprang),

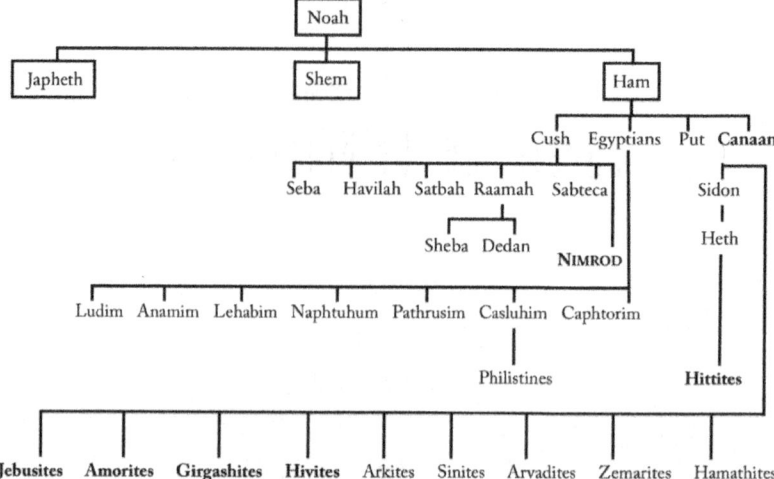

FIG. 3.1. GENEALOGY OF HAM (GENESIS 10)

Mizraim (that is the Egyptians), Put, and Canaan. Canaan, of course, was the son cursed by Noah after the incident in the tent. It is Canaan's line to which we want to pay particular attention.

Canaan is the father of the infamous Canaanites. These are very important people in the Bible. According to Herodotus and other early historians, the Canaanites first lived near the Cushites (from whom Nimrod is descended), their brother race, on the western banks of the Erythraean Sea (Persian Gulf), south of Iraq on the eastern side of Saudi Arabia.[3] Only after long years of war did they flee this land, move west, and settle in *the already inhabited* land we call Canaan. These Canaanites seem to have mixed with the indigenous "peoples" of the land and the place became known as the land of Canaan.

The name "Canaan" tells us something important. It can mean "to be brought low."[4] In a nutshell, this *is* the story of the giants. The name is *apropos*, for Canaan is the ancestor of most of the giants mentioned in Scripture. Another option is a "trafficker" (a harsher term than the possible "trader"). Often we speak of human trafficking as in illegal trading for the purposes of slavery or sexual exploitation. Does this tell us anything about what kind of people these were?

Though there are many descendants of Canaan mentioned in the Table of Nations, only one son is mentioned by name. This is *Sidon*. The city of Sidon was famous throughout biblical history and continues with this name to this day. Strabo called it the oldest city of the Phoenicians (Strabo, XVI, i.22). It is in the ancient land of Canaan. It is located close to Baalbek. It sits on exactly the 33°33' n. latitude. Remarkably, this is the same latitude at Mt. Hermon (which even more remarkably, sits at 33° longitude when going by the older Paris prime meridian), the sites that the watchers chose to come down and the whole Nephilim story began. Mt. Hermon is in Cydonia.

In the myths, Europa was a Sidonian princess. Europa derives from two words. *Eurys* means "wide" and *okw* means "to see." It is literally eyes wide open. Curiously, *ops* in Greek is "eye" (*opsis* is sight) and "serpent" is *ophis*. Recall the words of the serpent to Eve, when you eat of the fruit, "Your eyes will be opened" (Gen 3:5). Europa! Even more bizarre, the fruit of the Garden is often depicted as a very particular kind of fruit. It is a quince, technically a Pyrus *Cydonia*, famous for when you cut it in half at its equator, it makes a pentagram of five stars. We will return and say more about the pentagram and the serpent in a later chapter.

Sidon had a son named Heth. Heth was the father of the Hittites. Both Heth and Hittite mean "dread" or "fear." The Hittite Empire ranged all the way from modern Turkey (the NT Galatia) around and down the Mediterranean Sea to Canaan and the city of Hebron (Gen 23:1-20).

The Table mentions nine more descendants of Canaan, all are groups named after famous sons. Five we know very little about (Arkites, Sinites, Arvadites, Zemarites, Hamathites). Some of their names, however, are illustrative. Arkite can mean "to gnaw" (cannibals?). Arvadite can mean "I shall break loose." Hamathite can mean "fortress" or "furious" or putting them together "enclosure of wrath."

The other four peoples are infamous throughout the Old Testament. These are the Jebusites, Amorites, Girgashites, and Hivites. Along with the Canaanites, Hittites, and a group called the Perizzites, these four are listed together in three different passages (Deut 7:1; Josh 3:10; Josh 24:11). Together they make up seven nations "greater and stronger" than Israel. (You can find at least three of the four listed with the Canaanites and Hittites another 15 times).[5]

Again, let's look at the names. An Amorite is a "talker" or "slayer," and it seems to be a term that can stand in for many of the other tribes.[6] Jebusite means "treading down" (because they were tall?) or "polluted" (an idea we looked at regarding the mixing of species in the Introduction).[7] Girgashite means "driven out." Hivite has the same consonants as a Hebrew word for snake (*chivvi*) and thus may be referred to as the serpent clan,[8] reminding us of the serpentine Gigantes of Greek stories.

It is difficult to know if all the people in various tribes were full-blooded giants. Actually, a giant, by definition, is *not* full-blooded (their blood, at the very most, is half-watcher). And people need to remember this point. It isn't like every single tribal member in latter days were giants. After mixing with humans for generations, you would have many who were basically human, fewer and fewer whose recessive gene(s) game to the forefront. Some of the tribes are clearly associated with giants more than others (Amorites, Anakim), others, not as much (Canaanites, Hittites). Why would this be if there are giants among them? It could be due to some retaining relative blood-line purity, and hence, more giants. It could be because of the leaders associated with them. It could be from fear or fable that grew around the regions. There are lots of reasons that tribes we do not usually think of as giants are put into some of these lists. Nevertheless, if the names tell us anything, these peoples were or had among them ruthless fierce warriors who brought dread with them and trampled down everything in their paths.

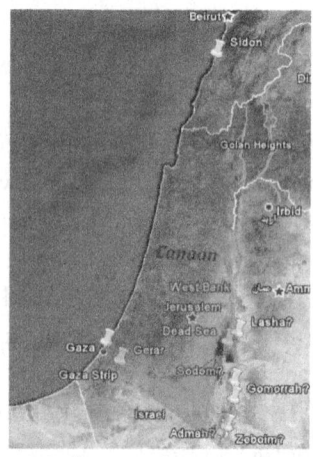

FIG. 3.2. ANCIENT LAND OF CANAAN

After listing these tribes, the Table of Nations subsumes them all under the name Canaanite (Gen 10:18) and then tells us the extent of their territory. It extends to the north into modern Lebanon and moves south, taking up the upper two thirds of ancient Israel. Thus, the Land of Milk and Honey—otherwise known as the Promised Land—was in earlier days called Canaan (cf. Gen 11:31), because this is where the Canaanites settled.

Abraham and the Giants

The Call of Abram

Obviously, if these people settled in Canaan, this is the primary reason why they are singled out in the Table of Nations. They will end up playing a large role in the history of Israel. We first begin to see this in the life of Abraham.

Born "Abram," the most famous Patriarch came from the land of Babylon (called Chaldea, in the middle of southern Iraq), in the city of

FIG. 3.3. ABRAHAM'S ROUTE TO CANAAN

Ur (which today is a vast wasteland in the middle of the Iraqi desert). When his brother Haran died, his father Terah packed up and headed northwest to the modern-day border or Syria and Turkey where they settled and appear to have named a city after the dead boy. Abram was called from this place by the LORD in a vision. He too packed up, and at the age of 75 headed southwest to the land of Canaan and the valley of the giants. A more frightening prospect for a faithful servant of God is difficult to imagine.

Four Great Kings

We pick up the story in Genesis 14.

> [1] In the days of Amraphel king of Shinar, Arioch king of Ellasar, Chedorlaomer king of Elam, and Tidal king of Goiim, [2] these kings made war with Bera king of Sodom, Birsha king of Gomorrah, Shinab king of Admah, Shemeber king of Zeboiim, and the king of Bela (that is, Zoar). [3] And all these joined forces in the Valley of Siddim (that is, the Salt Sea). [4] Twelve years they had served Chedorlaomer, but in the thirteenth year they rebelled. [5] In the fourteenth year Chedorlaomer and the kings who were with him came and defeated the Rephaim in Ashteroth-karnaim, the Zuzim in Ham, the Emim in Shaveh-kiriathaim, [6] and the Horites in their hill country of Seir as far as El-paran on the border of the wilderness. [7] Then they turned back and came to En-mishpat (that is, Kadesh) and defeated all the country of the Amalekites, and also the Amorites who were dwelling in Hazazon-tamar.

This chapter of the Bible is mostly known for what happens later, when Abram meets the king of Salem, a mysterious individual named Melchizedek. What precipitates that joyous encounter is this very strange, very ancient war. Before moving forward, check out how the *Targum* of Genesis 14:1-7 reads,

> [1] And it was in the days of Amraphel,–he is Nimrod, who commanded Abram to be cast into the furnace; he was then king of Pontos; Ariok, (so called) because he was (*arik*) tall among the giants, king of Thalasar, Kedarlaomer, (so called) because he had bound himself (or gone over) among the bondmen of the king of Elam, and Thidal, crafty as a fox, king of the peoples subjected to him, [2] – made war with Bera, whose deeds were evil, king of Sedom, and with Birsha, whose deeds were with the wicked, king of Amora: Shinab, who had hated his father, king of Admah, and Shemebar, who had corrupted himself with fornication,

king of Zeboim; and the king of the city which consumed (Bela) the dwellers thereof, which is Zoar. [3] All these were joined in the vale of the gardens (paredesaia), the place that produced the streamlets of waters that empty themselves into the sea of salt. [4] Twelve years they had served Kedarlaomer; and in the thirteenth year they had rebelled. [5] And in the fourteenth year came Kedarlaomer and the kings who were with him, and smote the Giants (*gibboraia*) which were in Ashtaroth-Karniam, and the Strong who were in Hametha, and the Terrible who were in the plain of Kiriathaim, [6] and the Choraee (dwellers in caverns) who were in the high mountains of Begala, unto the valley of Pharan, which was nigh upon the edge of the desert. [7] And they returned, and came to the place where was rendered the judgment of Mosheh the prophet, to the fountain of the waters of Strife, which is Requam. And they smote all the fields of the Amalkaee, and also the Emoraee, who dwelt in En-gedi.

(Gen 14:1-7 PJE)

Note the strange meeting between Nimrod and Abram. This is clearly a later legend, but it was the attempt of Pseudo-Jonathan to give an ancient interpretation for the events of this passage.[9]

What exactly is going on in this war? We have four powerful kings (suzerains) of the east fighting five petty kings (vassals) of Canaan. These eastern kings appear to have ruled territory from modern day Iran, Iraq, Syria, and Turkey. Let's look at each briefly.

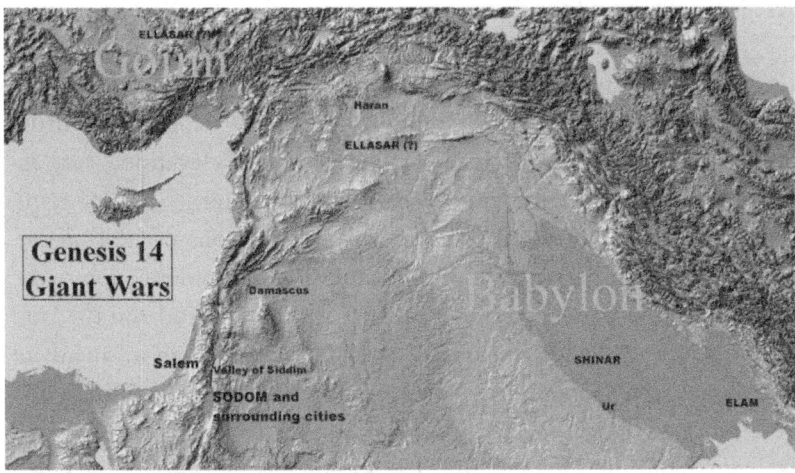

FIG. 3.4. GENESIS 14: GIANT WARS

We'll look at the eastern kings in the order of their territory, moving from east to west. The first is *Chedorlaomer* king of Elam. Elam is Persia (Iran). Chedorlaomer appears to be the most powerful of the four, as he has the major role in the story. The five petty kings had served under him for twelve years, but in the thirteenth year, they rebelled. Chedorlaomer's name has an uncertain meaning. It may be related to the Assyrian underworld god Lagamar so that his name means something like "Protector-No Mercy."[10] It is also probable that the ancient Arabian people knew of him, calling him Codar el Ahmar meaning "the Red."[11] In this light, it is very interesting that throughout the world, the giants are always described as having either blonde or red hair. Could there be a relationship?

The second king is *Amraphel* of Shinar. It is the association with Shinar and a legend of him throwing Abraham into the fire[12] that caused the Jews to associate him with Nimrod. Nimrod was either long gone or long dead, and this king arose after him in the city Nimrod built. Nevertheless, the ancient association between the two is interesting to say the least.[13]

The third king is *Arioch*, king of Ellasar (You may recall that Aragon was given the name Elessar by Galadriel after the elfstone he wore; Tolkien spells the word differently). Ellasar is farther north and west in Syria, probably near the source of the Tigris River.[14] The name can be derived from a word (*'rwk*) meaning "tall." Thus, the *Targum* rendered it "tall among the giants."[15]

The fourth king is *Tidal*, king of Goiim. There are four Hittite kings who bear this name between the 18th and 13th centuries, making it pretty certain that Goiim (literally "the nations") is located in Hittite country in Turkey. Tidal can mean "knowledge of elevation,"[16] or another possibility is "You shall be cast out from heaven," a name reminiscent of the fall of Satan or the descent of the sons of God on Mt. Hermon. To summarize, each of the names has some connection to the other-world, be it to a god of the underworld, to Nimrod and the land of Babel, to great height, or to heaven itself. That does not mean any of these kings *were* giants (plenty of later kings had the same names and were not giants), but it does give us reason for pause, especially when we learn about their ferocity in battle and the people whom they killed in these wars.

Five Lesser Kings

It was because of a rebellion in Canaan that the four mighty kings went to war. The rebellion was localized around the area of the Dead Sea. Five city-lords were responsible for the mutiny. These are Bera, Birsha, Shinab, Admah, and (possibly) Zoar. Let's look at these five kings.

The first two are famous only for the places where they ruled. *Bera* was king of the city of Sodom, which is where Abram's nephew Lot settled. Sodom was later destroyed by God with fire after a particularly horrific incident involving the men of Sodom and the two "strangers" who came to get Lot out of the city. These two strangers are called both "men" and "angels" in Genesis 19.

First, it says, "Two *angels* came to Sodom in the evening" (Gen 19:1). These are two of the three "men" who came to Abram earlier (Gen 18:2), whom Abram instantly recognized by their mere appearance as extraordinary individuals, so much so that he threw a huge feast for them. One of these men ends up being the Angel of the LORD. The other two are his emissaries sent to Sodom. Lot apparently notices the same physical characteristics, for as soon as he sees them, without a word spoken, he "bowed himself with his face to the earth."

Later, when the men of Sodom see these two individuals, they call out to Lot, "Where are the *men* who came to you tonight"? (Gen 19:5). "Bring them out to us so that we can have sex with them" (NET). What many people fail to recognize about this story is that there is more going on here than homosexuality. It is that, but it is also more. These men want to have sex ... *with angels*. Have you ever noticed this before? This is a clear reference back to Genesis 6:1-4, but is an even more wicked perversion of the heavenly/earthly mixing that went on prior to the Flood. Even Calvin, who called our interpretation of Genesis 6:1-4 "absurd" is forced to note that the same kind of "absurd" crime is sought after here.[17]

This story of Sodom is an indication of the kind of evil that was taking place in this city. Not coincidentally, Bera's name foreshadows that evil. His name means "son of evil." *Birsha*–king of the sister city of Gomorrah—does not fare much better. Birsha means "son of wickedness." If the sickening story of Genesis 19 was not an isolated incident, and if these men were aware of the Genesis 6 story, then it is logical to presume that Sodom was at least connected to giants, if not also a city with some of them living there.

Two of the three other kings are also associated with Sodom and Gomorrah. Shinab was king of Admah, and Shemeber was king of Zeboiim. Both of these cities were also overthrown with fire and sulphur from heaven by God in his great wrath against Sodom (Deut 29:23). *Shinab* translates to "sin is my father,"[18] but can also mean "tooth of the father" or "hostile." When I first read this definition, I was amazed. It is probably just a coincidence, but one of the strange physical characteristics of giant remains reported in the Americas are that some have been found with double rows of teeth.[19]

Shemeber has that son of Noah as its root word: *shem*. We have seen it before in the Nephilim, the men of renown, and in Nimrod's towering boast, "Let us make a *name* for ourselves." *Shemeber* means "powerful name."[20] But it can also mean "a winged name of great celebrity" or "soaring on high" or "a winged hero." Does this have anything to do with fallen angels and their offspring of old (not that he is one, but that the name remembers events of ancient days), a name taken in order to incite fear in his enemies?

The fifth name is not known with certainty. The text may not even give us a name, though it is possible that *Zoar* is the name of the king of Bela. Zoar comes from a word meaning "small," but means "bringing low." The common theme of these names is great evil and wickedness. But just as we saw with the four kings, these five hint at something gigantic behind the scenes.

The Giants Defeated

When these five kings of the Levant rebelled, it says that Chedorlaomer gathered his confederation, and within the year was marching upon the peoples immediately to the north and east of the Dead Sea. Here is where things get truly bizarre. First, they defeated a group called the *Rephaim*. As we will see in much more detail later, "Rephaim" becomes the most unsettling generic term for giants. Then they made the *Zuzim* in Ham kneel before them. "Zuzim" means "high standing" or "to buzz." After this they came against the *Emim* ("terrible ones"), the

Horites ("troglodytes" or "cave-dwellers"), the *Amalekites* ("vexation" or "to lick up"), and finally the *Amorites* ("mountain people" or "renowned"). Only after this did the five kings finally engage the battle.

The rebellious kings had figured that they were safe so long as these six clans stood between them and the powerful rulers of the east. They figured this because those six clans *were giants*. Though we cannot be certain that any of the kings—the four or the five—were giants (although from their names and the stories associated with them there are certainly hints that some of them either were giants, or felt themselves greater than giants, or enlisted giants in their armies), one thing is absolutely certain. The clans dispelled by Chedorlaomer in Genesis 14 were giants. They were not just tall warriors. They were ancient tribes, the original inhabitants of the land, peoples associated with dark magic, the underworld, insatiable appetites for human flesh and blood, unthinkable immoral behavior, otherworldly size and proportions, and preternatural lineage. Beginning in the next chapter, we will look at these giant clans individually. Their history and run-ins with Abraham's descendants are fascinating.

For now, there are two passages that demonstrate each of these clans were giants. The first is Numbers 13:21-33. At the end of the text it says, "All the people that we saw are of great height" (13:32). Two of the nations listed in Genesis 14 are listed in Numbers 13. These are the Amalekites and the Amorites (13:29). The other passage is Deuteronomy 2-3. This passage lists the Emim, Zamzummim (Zuzim), Horites, and Amorites which also appear in Genesis 14. It says of each that they were "tall" and were part of the Rephaim. Therefore, there is no question that the six tribes defeated by Chedorlaomer before turning to the rebel vassals of Sodom and Gomorrah were giants.

Gen 6	Gen 14	Gen 15	Num 13	Deut 1-3
Nephilim			Nephilim	
	Rephaim	Rephaim		Rephaim
	Zuzim			Zamzummim (Zumim)
	Emim			Emim
	Horites			Horites
	Amalekites		Amalekites	
	Amorites	Amorites	Amorites	Amorites
		Kenites		
		Kenizzites		
		Kadmonites		
		Hittites	Hittites	
		Perizzites		
		Canaanites	Canaanites	
		Girgashites		
		Jebusites	Jebusites	
			Anakim	Anakim
				Hivites/Avvim

TABLE 4. GIANT CLANS (TEXTUAL COMPARISON)

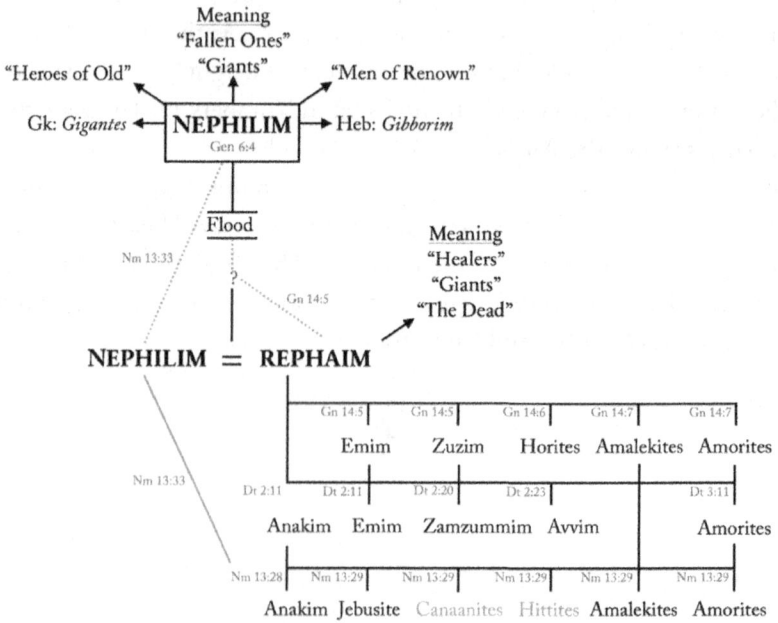

FIG. 3.5. FAMILY TREE OF THE NEPHILIM

4

Patriarchal Giants

And when Shechem the son of Hamor the Hivite,
the prince of the land, saw her, he seized her and
lay with her and humiliated her.
Genesis 34:2

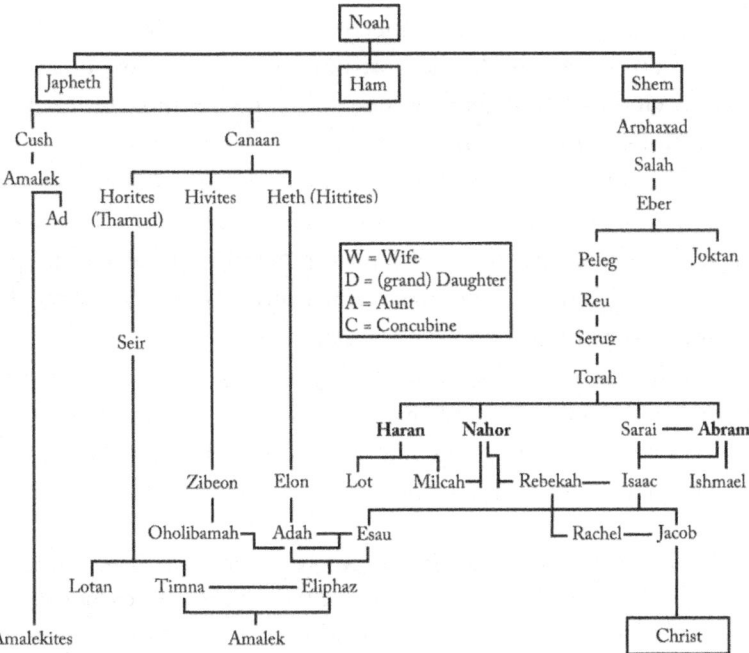

FIG. 4.1. SHEM AND HAM FAMILY TREES

Abraham and the Seed

THE STORY OF ABRAM really begins with Shem. Shem was given the promise: "Blessed be the LORD, the God of Shem, and let Canaan be his servant" (Gen 9:26). Before the Table of Nations, this verse foresees a conflict between Shem and Canaan. This conflict continues the promise given to Eve that there would be a war between two seeds, but that her Seed could win.

Beginning at this curse, the Canaanites become the arch enemies of God. Thus, important clans from the stock of Canaan are traced out, as we saw in the previous chapter. Meanwhile, the genealogy of Shem is the critical lineage for redemptive history, because it traces out the origins of Abram. It is through Abram that Israel, and eventually the Messiah—the Christ—will come. The Giant Wars of Genesis 14 are the first in a seemingly never-ending series of battles between the two seeds. Both seeds are spiritual. Both seeds are physical.

Mamre, Eschol, and Aner

Let's take note of what is happening at this point in the story with the seed of the woman. It is a most intriguing thing. Abram is living near the city of Hebron and has allied himself with three of the Amorites(!) from that area: A man named *Mamre* (after whom the famous Oaks of Mamre were named), and his two brothers *Eschol* and *Aner*. Of these three, Eschol's name is the most interesting. It means "a cluster of grapes," a curious idea that will return in Numbers 13 when the spies return from Eschol's ancient home with a cluster of grapes so large that two men had to carry it on a pole (Num 13:23).

At this point there were peaceful relations between the Amorites and Abram. Soon that would change. God gives Abraham a prophecy. It concerns the coming Exodus and the return to the land of Canaan in the days of Moses/Joshua. God said,

> Know for certain that your offspring will be sojourners in a land that is not theirs and will be servants there, and they will be afflicted for four hundred years ... They shall come back here in the fourth generation, for *the iniquity of the Amorites* is not yet complete ... To your offspring I give this land, from the river of Egypt to the great river, the river

Euphrates, the land of the Kenites, the Kenizzites, the Kadmonites, the
Hittites, the Perizzites, the Rephaim, the Amorites, the Canaanites, the
Girgashites, and the Jebusites.

(Genesis 15:13, 16, 18-21)

Why is Abram hanging out with Amorites? Well, if the land is
filled with giants, perhaps he is trying his best just to stay alive. He has
to befriend someone, because he is not powerful enough to fight them
all by himself (even with his modest army). Also, we can suppose that
not every person in a tribe was a giant. Perhaps the tribes were ruled by
a small group of giants, a giant family as we will see later with the Anakim. Or perhaps, even if all of the Amorites were tall (which is what the
spies told Moses, perhaps exaggerating, perhaps not[1]), their corruption
was not as bad as it would become a couple hundred years later. In fact,
the text says this outright.

Sodom and Gomorrah

As we would expect, if Canaan was filled with giant tribes, the patriarchs (Abraham, Isaac, and Jacob) would have come into contact with
them regularly. There are some really strange stories in Genesis that
seem to confirm this. For instance, we have already looked at the Sodom
and Gomorrah story with two angels coming as men to the city and the
men desiring to have intimate relations with them. This is straight out
of the Genesis 6 worldview, and it offers a glimpse, not only into the
immorality of those places, but to the supernatural worldview they held
as well.

Abimelech

Another interesting character is a king named Abimelech (Genesis
20, 26). Abimelech is said to be "king of the Philistines" (Gen 26:1), who
are descended from the Egyptians (and Ham). Later in the days of David, we run into both giant Egyptians (1 Chron 11:23) as well as giant
Philistines (1 Sam 17:23). It is probable in my mind that the Egyptians
and Philistines enlisted outsider Rephaim giants into their armies, and
so we should not make claims that these *peoples* were giants. There is
little question, however, that they were in league with giants.

At any rate, Abimelech was said to rule in a place called Gerar. In those days, the whole region was known as "Negeb of the Cretans" (Crete being an island in the Mediterranean Sea), and was under the political patronage of Gaza, and later Gath.[2] We have no evidence of Abimelech's size. Yet it is curious that in the Greek stories, Olympus was a *Cretan* giant who mentored Zeus, and Mylinus was a *Cretan* giant slain by Zeus. Also, Gaza and Gath were two of three cities where the giant Anakim lived, and they remained unconquered in the days of Joshua (Josh 11:22). In other words, circumstantial evidence allows for the possibility that Abimelech was a giant.

Consider further the stories told of this great king. Following in the tradition of Pharaoh (Gen 12:10-20), he sees the "beautiful" sister of Abraham (he was told she was his sister) and takes her to be his wife (Gen 20:2). Apparently, taking whichever women sojourning in your land that you liked was perfectly acceptable to this king. The beauty for the "taking" is certainly not put into a positive light, and thus harkens back to the story of Genesis 6:2.[3]

What happens to Abimelech? The first time this happens, God comes to him in a dream and tells him that he is a dead man, because he took another man's wife. Abimelech pleads innocence and God lets him off with a warning, but only after making sure that he knows it was God who kept Abimelech from touching Sarah. Later, Abimelech sees Isaac and Rebekah together, warns his men not to touch her, and eventually tells Isaac to flee because God has made him more powerful than Abimelech. The key point here is that in both stories (as well as the story with Pharaoh), God does not let anyone touch his chosen women. He will not allow the line to be contaminated. I'm not dogmatic that Abimelech was a giant, but the story and the setting have too many coincidences to be completely unrelated to events prior to the Flood.

Shechem and Hamor

Another strange story in Genesis involves two of the sons of Jacob: Levi and Simeon, and a city they destroyed called Shechem (Genesis 34). Shechem was the son of Hamor the Hivite. As we have seen, the Hivites are among the giants listed in the land of Canaan. The story goes that Shechem, the prince of the land, saw Dinah the daughter of Jacob and Leah. So, he "took" her and lay with her by force. Again, a woman in the line of the promise is involved. Again intercourse is in view. Again, echoes of Genesis 6:2 sound off the pages of this story, except this time we are certain that the union was forced. Where this story takes a new spin is in the response of Levi and Simeon to this outrage.

They conceive a plot to utterly destroy every man in Shechem. Shechem decides that he loves Dinah and wants to marry her. He goes to his powerful father Hamor and instructs him to ask Jacob for Dinah's hand in marriage. He proposes mutual "intermarriage" between his people and Jacob's. When the brothers hear it, they demand that all the men of the city be circumcised. Amazingly, Shechem obliges. At the moment all of the men in the city undergo the procedure, the two sons of Jacob swoop in and murder them all, thus defending the honor of their sister. This is the first full scale genocide in the Old Testament, and it is committed against a family which is known to be related to (if not to be) giants.

Jacob was not at all pleased with what his sons had done. At the end of his life, he curses the two boys for it (Gen 49:5-7). In the story he gives his reason. "You have brought trouble on me by making me stink to the inhabitants of the land, the Canaanites and the Perizzites. My numbers are few, and if they gather themselves against me and attack me, I shall be destroyed, both I and my household" (Gen 34:30).

As an addendum to these stories in the latter parts of Genesis, it should be noted that Jewish traditions say that the sons of Israel were fighting with giants on a regular basis. In the *Testament of Judah*, for instance, we read about how Judah killed a king named Achor, "a giant of a man" (Tjud 3:5) and how Jacob killed Belisath, "King of all kings" and a giant "twelve cubits tall" (Tjud 3:7). One scholar takes Sirach 16:7 as only echoing the Genesis 6 storyline, but believes the verse actually has in mind these giant chieftains post-Flood. The verse reads, "He was not propitiated for the ancient giants who revolted in their might. He did not spare the neighbors of Lot, whom he loathed on account of their insolence" (Sir 16:7-8).[4] Obviously, the Jews a long time ago thought that this was a land full of amazing people.

5

Moses Meets Amalek

*Then Amalek came and fought
with Israel at Rephidim*
Exodus 17:8

Esau and the Hivites

HOWEVER YOU VIEW THE STORY Shechem and Hamor, one thing is certain. The actions of Levi and Simeon should be contrasted with those of their uncle, Jacob's twin brother, Esau. One chapter later, the Hivites return again, this time in the genealogy of Esau.

Unlike his brother who retrieved a wife from his own kind, Esau took his wives from the Canaanites. One was named Oholibamah the granddaughter of Zibeon the Hivite; the other was called Adah the daughter of Elon the Hittite (Gen 36:2). "Elon" means "magnificent oak" and is related to the word "God Almighty" (*Elyon*). Given the lineage, the name reminds me of the words of Amos about the Amorites who were "tall like cedars" (Amos 2:9). Esau was wicked because he mixed his line with that of the wicked Canaanites.

What happens to Esau? He moves into the strange land of Seir the Horite who appears to have been a giant (Gen 36:20; Deut 2:12, 22). His mixing with those people makes a lot of sense politically, though it was a godless act. If you live in a land of giants, then do all you can to make alliances with them and to become like them. That is what reason would dictate, even if faith must be discarded to the rubbish bin. There is no better way to do those things than through marriages and children. At any rate, Esau becomes Edom and disappears from the land of Canaan.

The same thing goes for Jacob, though in his case, not by choice. Soon after the story of Shechem, a famine comes to the land, driving him to seek refuge in Egypt. Because God had providentially sent Joseph (his son) before him, Jacob ended up staying in Egypt where he died. Thus, there is no significant interaction between Israel and the giants between the days of Joseph and Moses. This is where we find things at the beginning of the book of Exodus, only now Israel is not a free people living in Egypt. They are slaves that need deliverance and a return to the land of promise, the land of Canaan.

Moses Meets Amalek

Having been in captivity for over 400 years,[1] God was now going to redeem his people out of slavery in Egypt. To put it another way, the sins of the Amorites is nearing completion. Thus, God told Moses, "I have come down to deliver them [the Israelites] out of the land of the Egyptians and to bring them up out of that land to a good and broad land, a land flowing with milk and honey, to the place of the Canaanites, the Hittites, the Amorites, the Perizzites, the Hivites, and the Jebusites" (Ex 3:8). Why does God mention the names of these tribes so often? Because this deliverance will truly be miraculous, for these tribes are made up of giants.

The story goes that Moses comes to Pharaoh with terms of surrender. "Let my people go." Pharaoh is hardened and will not comply. Thus, God sends ten mighty plagues to Egypt to humble Pharaoh and mock his gods. Finally, Pharaoh lets the people go, only to follow them into the wilderness where he surrounds them at a dead end at the coast of the Red Sea. God performs another mighty miracle, opens the sea so that his people can cross on dry land, and then shuts the sea over the Egyptian army that is closing in hot pursuit. Safely on the other side, God leads his people towards the Holy Mountain: Mt. Sinai. Along the way, they are attacked by a fierce tribe of warriors and heroes. They are called Amalekites. This story is the first instance of a tribe of giants attacking God's people in hopes of utterly destroying them. Here is what we read,

> [8] Then Amalek came and fought with Israel at Rephidim. [9] So Moses said to Joshua, "Choose for us men, and go out and fight with Amalek. Tomorrow I will stand on the top of the hill with the staff of God in my hand." [10] So Joshua did as Moses told him, and fought with Amalek, while Moses, Aaron, and Hur went up to the top of the hill. [11] Whenever Moses held up his hand, Israel prevailed, and whenever he lowered his hand, Amalek prevailed. [12] But Moses' hands grew weary, so they took a stone and put it under him, and he sat on it, while Aaron and Hur held up his hands, one on one side, and the other on the other side. So his hands were steady until the going down of the sun. [13] And Joshua overwhelmed Amalek and his people with the sword. [14] Then the LORD said to Moses, "Write this as a memorial in a book and recite it in the ears of Joshua, that I will utterly blot out the memory of Amalek from under heaven." [15] And Moses built an altar and called the name of it, The LORD Is My Banner, [16] saying, "A hand upon the throne of the LORD! The LORD will have war with Amalek from generation to generation."
>
> (Exodus 17:8-16)

When discussing the identity of this Amalek, most dictionaries and commentaries assume it is the grandson of Esau (Gen 36:12). This is one of the reasons I wanted to tell you about him at the beginning of this chapter. This idea is most improbable and has several problems.

Most basically, it assumes that there is only one Amalek in Scripture. This is not true, since Amalekites were there in the Genesis 14 wars with Abram. Obviously, if the Amalekites are there in Abraham's day, then there is more than one group of Amalekites. Also, Moses is told that they are not to despise the descendants of Esau (Deut 23:7) and yet the prophecy says that God will utterly blot out the name of Amalek through his chosen people. If they are the same people, how do these two statements jive? Amalek keeps returning, again and again, to fight against Israel. Israel is told to totally destroy everything associated with these Amalekites. This is what God always commands Israel do to the inhabitants of the land of Canaan, but they are not allowed to do this to the descendants of Esau, because they are his brothers (Deut 2:5-8). Finally, Numbers 14:45 refers to a second encounter with the

Amalekites, who came this time with the Canaanites, and this time won. But Deuteronomy 1:44, referring to this same incident, calls those who fought against Moses "Amorites" who "chased you as bees do and beat you down in Seir as far as Hormah." Nowhere in the Bible are Edomites referred to as Amorites.

For the sake of argument, let's assume for the moment that Moses did fight the sons of Esau. Even if this were true, these people would still be mixed with two giant races. Recall that Esau's wife Adah was a Hittite. It was Adah who bore Esau a child named Eliphaz, and Eliphaz was Amalek's father. His mother was taken by Eliphaz as a concubine *from the Horites*. This woman, a girl named Timna, bore Eliphaz a son named Amalek. Thus, even Esau's grandson Amalek is potentially one-half giant.

Yet, even if Moses did fight these people against every argument I gave above, it still does not explain who the Amalekites were that lost in the Giant Wars to Chedorlaomer. According to the LXX of Genesis 14:7, this Amalek fought in the giant wars. He may have been closely related to Nimrod.[2]

The Bible says some strange things about the Amalekites. Balaam was the infamous pagan prophet who was involved in the favorite Sunday school story of the talking donkey. In Numbers 24, the prophet takes up an oracle where he curses the enemies of God. One of the peoples he cursed was the Amalekites, whom he called "the first among the nations" (Num 24:20). This can hardly refer to the grandson of Esau. Instead, it speaks of a most ancient race of people, the same race smitten (but not exterminated) by the kings of Persia in the days of Abram.[3]

The Arabians speak of an ancient hero they call *Imlāq*, which is their name for Amalek.[4] It should not surprise you to discover that this word means "giant."[5] The form of the word *Imlāq* is clearly related to Amalek. Amalek can mean "vexation," or possibly "to lick up" (more cannibalism or perhaps violence or both?). Here is the true origin of the Amalekites that came out to fight Moses in the wilderness.

These same Arabs also tell of one of Imlāq's famous sons, a behemoth named Ad,[6] who some say made his way down to Egypt, which would certainly fit Israel fighting them so close to Egypt in the wilderness. A tradition told in the famous *Al-Khitat*, a history of Egyptian lore compiled by al-

Maqrizi (1364-1442 AD), recounts the teaching of one master Ibrahim bin
Wasif Shah (d. 1203 AD) who said that King Adim (Ad) was,

> A violent and proud prince, tall in stature. He was he who ordered the
> rocks cut to make the pyramids, as had been done by the ancients. In
> his time there lived two angels cast out of heaven, and who lived in the
> Aftarah well; these two angels taught magic to the Egyptians, and it is
> said that 'Adim, the son of El-Budchir, learned most of their sciences,
> after which the two angels went to Babel. Egyptians, especially the
> Copts, assure us that these were actually two demons named Mahla and
> Bahala, not two angels, and that the two are at Babel in a well, where
> witches meet, and they will remain there until the Day of Judgment.
> Since that time they worshiped idols. It is Satan, they say, who made
> them known to men and raised them for men. According to others, it
> was Badoura who raised the first idol, and the first idol erected was the
> Sun, yet others claim that Nimrod ordered the first idols raised
> and the worship of them.[7]

The Coptic reference is a giveaway that the book of Enoch had at
least some influence on this tradition (for it was the Ethiopian Coptic
Christians who preserved the book during the Dark Ages). However, it
does seem from this citation that this was a common belief held by other
Egyptians as well, including Muslims. Of course, this is not to say that
Ad actually built the pyramids, for the same book says that there is no
agreement on the time or architect(s) of their construction, and it recounts many conflicting legends about them. Nevertheless, a giant
named Ad is one of those legends.

The Adites and the Thamudites (Horites) were contemporaries
who early on dwelt in the same region of western Saudi Arabia, after
the Thamudites were forced to flee their home on the eastern shores of
the Persian Gulf. Like the Thamudites, the Adites are remembered as
"very powerful, that they were giants, and that their king, *Sheddad Ben
Ad* (the son of Ad), reigned over the whole world."[8] The mystical Jewish
Zohar remembers the same tradition of Amalekites being giants.
Beresheet A, 20.224, "There are five races of mixed multitude. These are
the Nefilim (fallen), the Giborim (mighty), the Anakim (giants), the
Refaim (shades) and the Amalekim." Some traditions trace the origin
of Ad and Amalek to Shem,[9] but others trace them to Ham.[10] The later
probably makes the best sense, because of the close proximity of these
giants to those that were certainly spawned from Hamites.

The Amalekites will return in the days of king Saul, and also again in the days of queen Esther. Before we move on, I want you to consider the other side of this story with Amalek. Joshua—the Hebrew form of "Jesus"—is told to listen to the prophecy that God will utterly blot out the memory of Amalek. Given what comes next, this must be viewed as prophetically of the coming work of Christ, as it was seen in the early church.[11]

After the victory over Amalek, it says that Moses built an altar and called it "The LORD Is My Banner" (Ex 17:15). This is a title or name of God: *Jehovah Nissi.* "Banner" reflects the positions of Moses' hands during the battle—outstretched, like Jesus on the cross. Banner is a word (*nes*) used two other times by Moses. One is of the bronze serpent pole (Num 21:8-9), which Jesus says typifies his death (John 3:14). The other is of the earth swallowing up Korah (Num 26:10), which is more language used of Jesus' death (compare Jonah 1:17-2:6 with Matt 12:39-40, 1 Cor 15:54). In this case the banner of Moses is taken up by the prophet Isaiah when he says, "In that day there shall be a root of Jesse, who shall stand as a banner to the people" (Isa 11:10; cf. Gal 3:1). In other words, the story of Moses slaying the giants prefigures the work of Jesus on the cross.

Earlier fights in Genesis between people and giants involved either unbelieving kings or localized warfare with the children of Abraham. This war now takes the prophecy given so long ago to Eve of warfare between two seeds up a notch. It is the first blood bath between a whole army of God's chosen people vs. an entire clan of giants. As such, it is a foreshadowing of the Great Battle to come.

6

Spying Out the Land

There we saw the giants.
Numbers 13:33 LXX

Ten Faithless Spies

I T HAS BEEN DIFFICULT to keep relatively silent about the passages we are looking at in this Chapter. They explain so much about what we have already learned that I have had to allude to them at least a little. Most people do not realize that the stories we have looked at in the previous Chapters are about giants, because we are too far removed historically and culturally from the air that Israel breathed to taste and smell what those ancient people all took for granted. The stories we will look at beginning in this chapter put any doubt about the giants of earlier times to rest.

In Numbers 13, God commands Moses to send twelve spies into the land of Canaan. Everything about this story is strange. The first thing we learn is that they enter the land in the far north, probably near Mt. Hermon.[1] They then travel south through the heart of the land to Hebron. Hebron is 19 miles south of Jerusalem in the hill country.

Hebron is where the oaks of Mamre the Amorite were located. It is where Abraham and Isaac sojourned. Abraham and Sarah, Isaac and Rebekah, and Jacob's wife Leah were all buried there. It is also just south of the very fertile Valley of Eshcol (remember, Eshcol was the brother of Mamre, and his name means "grape cluster"). Moses had asked the spies to bring back some of the produce of the land. All of these facts make Hebron a natural destination to spy.

Hebron was a cyclopean city with walls 10-13 feet thick. One archaeologist wrote that the houses, doors, gates, walls, and other things appear to be "just such dwellings as a race of giants would build."[2] Hebron was also called Kiriath-Arba (cf. Gen 23:2 etc.) after the name of its founder: Arba "the greatest of the Anakim" (Josh 14:15). Arba can mean "perfect stature" (physical size?).[3] I've mentioned these Anakim several times, but this is the first time you run into them in the Bible. Who are they?

A person named Anak is the progenitor of the Anakim. His ancestor was Arba (Josh 15:13, 21:11). Anak originally meant "neck," but came to mean "long-necked," as in a giant.[4]

The very end of the passage gives us one of the most important links to understanding the proliferation of giants after the Flood. "There we saw the Nephilim (the sons of Anak, who come from the Nephilim), and we seemed to ourselves like grasshoppers, and so we seemed to them" (Num 13:33). The verse specifically links the Anakim to the pre-Flood Nephilim, saying that these Anakim *are* Nephilim. In fact, the older versions (LXX) do not have the parenthetical: ("the sons of Anak, who come from the Nephilim").[5] This means that the spies thought everyone in the land was a Nephilim, not just the Anakim. You can gather as much from the previous verse which says that everyone in the entire land was very tall.

Nevertheless, the Anakim are said to be tall in other Scriptures too. "Hear, O Israel: you are to cross over the Jordan today, to go in to dispossess nations [note the plural] greater and mightier than yourselves, cities great and fortified up to heaven [note the size], a people great and tall [note the height], *the sons of the Anakim*, whom you know, and of whom you have heard it said, 'Who can stand before the sons of Anak?'" (Deut 9:1-2; also Deut 1:26). The Egyptians also knew of the Anakim. They called them *Iy'anaq*[6] and *Shasu*.[7] One particular text, a letter viewed as the model for training royal Egyptian scribes, refers to their tremendous height. "The face of the pass is dangerous with Shasu, hidden under the bushes. Some of them are 4 or 5 cubits, nose to foot, with wild faces.[8] This puts them at a range between 7 – 9 feet tall.[9]

Recent archaeological discoveries of skeletons between seven[10] feet and ten feet six inches[11] have been discovered in Palestine. For the record, my present view of the size of these giants in Palestine and also around the world[12] is that they were almost all between 8 feet and probably less than 12 feet tall, for the overwhelming range of giants reported across the world and in Palestine fall in this range. Obviously, these people brought dread and fear to peoples far and wide. In Deut 2:11 they are called Rephaim, and other nations like the Emim, Zamzummim, and Amorites are compared to them.

The first "hing we are told ab"ut the s"ies' visit to Hebron is that they see "Ahiman, Sheshai, and Talmai, the descendants of Anak" (Num 13:22). Rabbinical tradition said that Ahiman was the most feared.[13] Josephus tells us about these "boys" saying that they were a "race of giants, who had bodies so large and countenances so entirely different from humans, that they were amazing to the sight and terrible to the hearing. These bones are still shown to this very day, unlike to any creditable relations of other men" (Josephus, *Antiquities*, 5.2.3). It is possible they were buried in graves which were still around in the days of Micah. The 1st Century record "The Lives of the Prophets" records that Micah was buried "in his own district by himself, near the burial ground of the Anakim" (LivesProph 6:3). Archaeologist J. Jeremias, who wrote a detailed treatment of holy graves in Palestine, said that in 1932, he and a colleague personally discovered the "cemetery of the giants" in a Seleucid graveyard (the eastern Macedonian portion of Alexander's empire), 1.25 miles north of Beit Jibrin (which is 13 miles northwest of Hebron).[14] Quite a story, isn't it? It gets better.

After seeing these three behemoths, the spies travel north to the valley of Eschol where the cut down a single cluster of grapes. The thing is, they have to carry it on a pole between two of them (Num 13:23).[15] Ten of the twelve spies brought the grapes back *in order to discourage the people from going into the land*. The grapes were gigantic and the people who grew them were even larger. Is it any wonder that I speculated about the size of Mamre and Eschol in an earlier chapter?

People often do not realize why the ten spies were so frightened. It is so easy to dismiss the fear we read about them having in the Bible and smugly begin to think, "I would never have acted like that!" Now you are beginning to see that by the looks of things, there is no natural

Newfound mosaic (c. 400 AD). Two spies carrying a cluster of grapes.
(Image credit: Jim Haberman)

FIG. 6.1. SPIES MOSAIC, HUQOQ SYNAGOGUE, NORTHERN ISRAEL

FIG. 6.2. NORTH AFRICAN ROMAN OIL LAMP DEPICTING SPIES (4TH-5TH CENT AD)

reason to believe anyone could have defeated these people. Only the eyes of faith and the trust in the promise of God to Eve could have safely seen them through. It gets better still.

The spies report to Moses that not only are Anakim in the land, so are Hittites, Jebusites, Amorites, and Canaanites. Caleb quieted the people who were obviously frightened saying, "Let us go up at once and occupy it, for we are well able to overcome it." Caleb remembered God's past miraculous deliverances, not the least of which was their victory over the Amalekites. For his faith, Caleb will eventually be given Hebron as his own settlement.

The rest of the spies were not so well inclined. "They brought to the people of Israel a bad report" (Num 13:32). They said the land "devours its inhabitants." Following the ancient tradition, I have suggested that this refers not to the harshness of the land (which produces such great fruit, milk, and honey), but to the inhabitants themselves. The giants killed people and then ate them.

They also said, "All the people that we saw in it are of great height." *All of the people*. It is possible that the spies were exaggerating of course, but the words of Moses (not the spies mind you, but Moses) seem to suggest minimal exaggeration. For instance he says, "Hear, O Israel: you are to cross over the Jordan today, to go in to dispossess nations greater and mightier than yourselves, cities great and fortified up to heaven, a people great and tall, the sons of the Anakim, whom you know, and of whom you have heard it said, 'Who can stand before the sons of Anak?'" (Deut 9:1-2; also Deut 2-3). Apparently, the spies were not completely lying. That was not their problem.

Instead, they were not *trusting*. It really did seem to them like they were grasshoppers. To the giants, they were little edible insects. God had promised to make Israel like hornets (Ex 23:28), not grasshoppers, stinging bees that make much larger men flee in agony and terror. But they would not believe. The whole point of going into the land was to see whether or not the people would trust God to deliver them from the giants.

The people heard the report and took the side of the ten. Joshua and Caleb were in the clear minority. Moses pleaded with the majority to have faith, but they would not trust God. Instead, they grumbled. For their unbelief, God punished that generation with forty years of wandering in the desert, a year for every day the spies were in the land.

7

The "Law" of Canaan

Defile not ye yourselves in any of these things:
For in all these the nations are defiled which
I Cast out before you.
Lev 18:24 KJV

Perversion

I WANT TO TAKE A SHORT BREAK from the history of the giants to look at their lifestyle. Most people never stop to consider the fact that the abominable practices going on in the land of Canaan were directly related to the giants, or that their wickedness becomes the background of God's giving Israel her own laws. Recall how God told Abraham that the sins of the Amorites (giants) had not come to their full fruition in his day (Gen 15:16). Part of the reason for not giving Abraham the land right then and there was that these inhabitants of the Promised Land, no matter who—*or what*—they were, rightly possessed it. God does not just throw people out of a land—much less utterly destroy them—unless there is compelling moral justification for doing so. God is holy, not capricious. It is not until a people reach a point of no return that the "land will vomit" out its inhabitants (Lev 18:28). Until that time, wherever that line is drawn in God's mind, the people have a right to be stewards in the land, apparently, even if they are giants.

Torah: Be Separate

During the forty years of wandering, God gave Moses the *Torah*. *Torah* means "law." Sometimes Torah refers to the first five books of the OT. In this case, I'm thinking of it as those portions of those books that specify law. God gave his laws to this chosen people so that they would be "separate," and unlike the nations they were going to dispossess (Deut 7:8). They had to be righteous people, people that knew and understood what their God was like. As it says, "You shall be holy, for I the LORD your God am holy" (Lev 19:2).

This law, made so famous by Jesus (Matt 5:48), comes at the end of a series of laws wherein Israel is instructed, "You shall not do as they do in the land of Canaan, to which I am bringing you" (Lev 18:3), and "Do not make yourselves unclean by any of these things, for by all these the nations I am driving out before you have become unclean ... and the land vomited out its inhabitants ... for the people of the land, who were before you, did all of these abominations, so that the land became unclean" (Lev 18:24, 25, 27). This same idea is repeated in Deuteronomy as well. "When you come into the land that the LORD your God is giving you, you shall not learn to follow the abominable practices of those nations ... whoever does these things is an abomination to the LORD. And because of these abominations the LORD your God is driving them out before you" (Deut 18:9, 12). Not every law in the Torah has the nations of Canaan as its explicit backdrop, but there are certainly many of them that do.

Before we get to those and for the sake of recollection, in case we forget too quickly, these people are specified time and again in the Torah as, "The Hittites and the Amorites, the Canaanites and the Perizzites, the Hivites and the Jebusites" (cf. Ex 3:8; 23:23; Deut 7:1; 20:17, etc.). Israel was to "utterly destroy" to "devote to complete destruction" these people so that they would not learn their detestable practices" or follow their gods (Deut 20:18; cf. 12:30; Ex 23:33; Josh 23:13, etc.).

The wicked p"actices were done "for their gods" and in order to "serve" them (Deut 12:30-31; 20:18). This is important because it says that their customs (especially religious) were not ends to themselves. There was greater depravity here than you may think. Their gods loved and desired these things. In the case of any people who were actually

FALSE WORSHIP	SEXUAL IMMORALITY	CROSSING OVER	OPPRESSION
Altars, pillars/ poles, carved images	Incest/fornication: mother, mother-in-law, sister, granddaughter, stepsister, aunt, uncle, daughter-in-law, sister-in-law	Necromancy of ghosts or familiar spirits	Neglecting, discriminating against, or otherwise harming the poor
Burn children in fire (to Molech)	Bestiality or other mixing of kinds	Fortune telling	Unfair wages
Groves	Homosexuality	Interpreting omens	Robbery
Sacrifices	Adultery	Sorcery	Slander/gossip
Cutting the body	Prostitution	Charmer	Hate
Tattooing		Medium	Disrespecting the old
Religious prostitution		Eating blood	Unjust weights and measures
		Divination	

TABLE 5. ABOMINATIONS OF THE GIANTS

giants, remember that their gods were their progenitors, fallen created heavenly beings that desired to be worshiped.

This is more easily seen when you understand the kinds of sins that are mentioned when these inhabitants of Canaan are specifically called out like this. As I said before, there are categories of laws that are sandwiched between these calls not to be like those nations. You can divide these sins into four basic groups:

Of course, other nations, *including the Hittites and Canaanites* had legal codes dealing with injustice and sexual practices,[1] though both kinds of laws are different in some important respects from those in the Bible. Sexual practices considered deviant (such as adultery) were not as varied as those delineated in the Bible, nor were they judged as harshly or as fairly. For instance, in the Code of Ur Nammu and the Code of Eshnanna, only the woman was put to death. In the Bible, both parties get the death penalty. Perhaps more striking is a Hittite law against bestiality. The Code of the Nesilim[2] 199 (cf. 1650-1500) says that anyone having intercourse with a pig or a dog shall die, but "if a man has intercourse with a horse or a mule, there is no punishment. But he shall not approach the king, and shall not become a priest."

Laws of social justice (which often overlap those of the Bible) were not divvied out equally either. This is because not all men (let alone women) were created equal in these cultures. For instance, the Sumerians had three distinct social classes: the *amelu* (senior class—government officials, priests, soldiers), the *mushkinu* (citizen class—merchants, shopkeepers, farmers, etc.), and the slave class.[3] A person's tooth was considered more valuable if he was of the senior class (*Hammurabi Code* 200-201). Similarly, the penalty of striking someone on the cheek was more severe if committed by a lower class (*Hammurabi Code* 203-204). Of course, without some basic working of civility and law you can have no society. Anarchy does not build dynasty.

Curiously, these nations have almost no laws regarding contacting the dead, and the few examples we have are themselves littered with superstition. For instance, The Code of Hammurabi 2[4] and the Code of Ur-Nammu 13[5] both refer to a person accused of sorcery. But to find out if they really were a sorcerer, you have to throw them into the river to see if they would float (no, the practice did not begin in the Middle Ages as you might think, if you are familiar with the famous skit by Monty Python).

As far as religious restrictions on temple prostitution (both male and female), idols, groves, sacrifices (including human) etc., well, *there are no laws forbidding any of it*. Combined with the previous set (contacting the dead), this is most revealing. It is religious lawlessness that is especially in mind when God says these things were done "for their gods." To a lesser but related degree, the sexual perversion of these peoples was tied to their religious practices. For example, it is not difficult to get from legal temple prostitution to general prostitution. In the Bible, having other gods and committing idolatry *is* adultery (Ex 34:15-16; Deut 31:16; Ezek 23:37; 1 Cor 6:9, etc.).[6]

The thing to keep in mind about all of this is the origin of the giants. They come from some kind of immoral union between heavenly beings and earthly women. They owe their very existence to sexual rebellion and religious pluralism. Even though these peoples had some sexual, civil, and religious order (even demons have this; cf. Col 2:18; 1 Tim 4:1-3), it was deeply perverted, an affront to God's sovereignty, holiness, and righteousness.

When God gave Moses the Torah, he was making a sharp distinction between himself and the gods of the giants. Because they followed the wickedness of their fathers, and perhaps multiplied it a thousand-fold, God would not let them live in the land any longer. Not only would he not let them live in Canaan, but he gave them over to the other tribes surrounding Canaan, as they too devoted them to complete destruction. It is exactly the same thing we saw prior to the Flood, only this time God's wrath will be carried out through his people. Perhaps this ancient interpretation of Genesis 6:1-4 discovered in the Dead Sea Scrolls serves to illustrate the point best:

> And now, sons, listen to me and I shall open your eyes so that you can see and understand the deeds of God, so that you can choose what he is pleased with and repudiate what he hates, so that you can walk perfectly on all his paths and not allow yourselves to be attracted by the thoughts of a guilty inclination and lascivious eyes. For many have gone astray due to these; brave heroes stumbled on account of them, from ancient times until now. For having walked in the stubbornness of their hearts the Watchers of the heavens fell; on account of it they were caught, for they did not heed the precepts of God. And their sons, whose height was like that of cedars and whose bodies were like mountains, fell. All flesh which there was on the dry earth expired and they became as if they had never been, because they had realized their desires and had failed to keep their creator's precepts, until his wrath flared up against them.
>
> (CD 2.14-21)

In light of this, the biblical warning should be read anew,

> Take care that you be not ensnared to follow them, after they have been destroyed before you, and that you do not inquire about their gods, saying, 'How did these nations serve their gods?—that I also may do the same.' You shall not worship the LORD your God in that way, for every abominable thing that the LORD hates they have done for their gods, for they even burn their sons and their daughters in the fire to their gods.
>
> (Deuteronomy 12:30-31)

8

On the Way to Canaan

*King Og of Bashan was the last survivor of the giant
Rephaites. His bed was made of iron and was more
than thirteen feet long and six feet wide. It can still be
seen in the Ammonite city of Rabbah.*
Deut 3:11 NLT

Dispossession of the Giants by the Nations

NEAR THE END OF THEIR WANDERINGS in the wilderness, as Israel
was preparing to conquer the land, God recapped. At the beginning of Deuteronomy, the history of their wanderings culmi-
nated in two battles east of Canaan. Along the south-eastern corner, in
the land of Edom, the descendants of Esau had already destroyed the
giant Horites of Seir (Deut 2:12). To the north of them, in the land of
Moab, the descendants of Lot had destroyed the Emim (Deut 2:9-10).
Farther north yet, their cousins the Ammonites (not to be confused with
the giant Amorites), also descended from Lot, destroyed the Zamzummim (Deut 2:20-21). Even the Avvim who lived along the Mediterranean in villages as far as Gaza were displaced by the Caphtorim, that
is the Philistines (Deut 2:23). These people were "as tall as the Anakim"
(Deut 2:10, 21), and they were all counted among the Rephaim (Deut
2:11; 20).

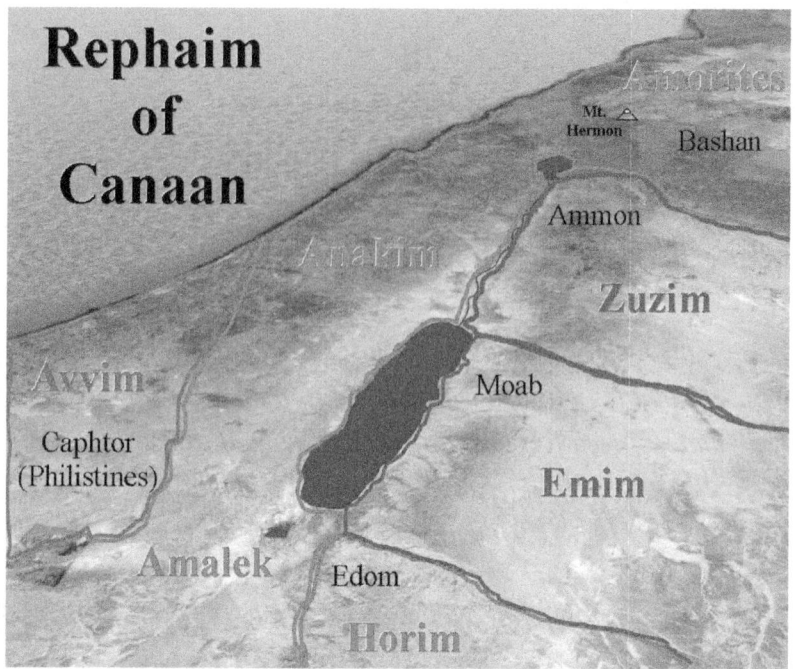

FIG. 8.1. GIANTS IN THE PROMISED LAND

Each of these shorter tribes dispossessed the giants because God was punishing the wicked inhabitants of the entire region. God fought for these distant relatives of Israel and descendants of Abraham (Deut 2:21, 22). Notice that all of the tribes destroyed, even by other nations, were giants. In fact, in the same story, Israel is told in unconditional terms, that they were to leave the descendants of Esau, Moab, and Ammon alone. They could only buy food and water from them (Deut 2:5-6). Why would God be so choosy? This speaks to something about the nature of God that biblical critics completely misunderstand.

The claim is often made that the God of the OT is a capricious, vindictive tyrant. Has anyone ever put it more bluntly than Richard Dawkins when he said, "The [fictional] God of the Old Testament is ... jealous and proud of it; a petty, unjust, unforgiving control-freak; a vindictive, bloodthirsty ethnic cleanser; a misogynistic, homophobic, racist, infanticidal, genocidal, filicidal, pestilential, megalomaniacal, sadomasochistic, capriciously malevolent bully."[1] We can't deal with all of these charges here, but one part we will discuss.

God would not let Israel *touch* many different peoples, let alone utterly destroy them. He promised he would not fight for Israel in a battle like that. But the giants were a different breed (literally). They had become utterly wicked over the centuries, and this is on top of the fact that they were preternatural creatures. Besides this, if the giants were in the land and the people mixed with them, then the promise of the Seed of Eve would be stopped cold. Satan may have greatly desired this, but God would not let anything hinder his prophecy.

Sihon the Amorite

This dispossession of the giants *by other nations* becomes a moral justification for Israel doing likewise. It is also a motivation for them not to fear (which they should not have anyway, since God already fought for them against the Amalekites 40 years earlier). At this point, God recalls for Israel how he commanded them to go and take possession of the Valley of Arnon held by Sihon the Amorite, king of Heshbon (Deut 2:24). Arnon is a river and valley that divides Moab and Ammon, splitting the Dead Sea in half on its eastern shore.

Very little is known from the Bible about Sihon except that God hardened his heart so that he would not let Israel pass through his land (Deut 2:30). The Jews recorded stories about him—exaggerated or historical, it is not always possible to tell. They said that Sihon was born after the Flood to the wife of Ham who committed adultery with Ahiah[2] (the son of Shemhazai the angel[3]) after the deluge. Sihon was a giant "of enormous stature, taller than any tower in all the world."[4] They also said that he was actually the infamous Canaan, Ham's son.[5] This demonstrates that the tradition of Sihon as a giant is ancient.

We also know that Sihon was an Amorite—like Mamre, Eschol, and Aner. It is curious to discover that the Amorites were reported to be, not Semitic peoples, but more like Caucasians, having blonde and red hair and blue eyes, but with elongated heads[6], a practice actually copied in the Egyptian Pharaoh's headdress and by the very painful practice of head-binding. Were they trying to emulate the giants?

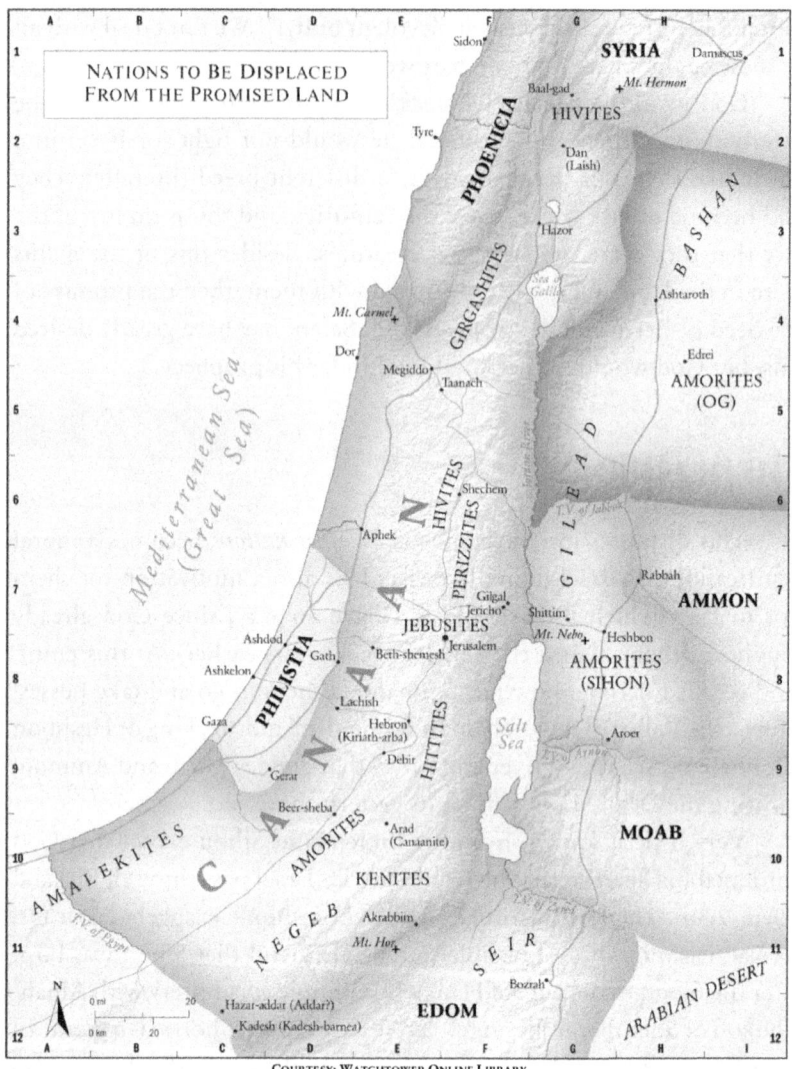

FIG. 8.2. DEUTERONOMY 2-3: NATIONS AND GIANTS

More curious still is that Giants in the Americas are depicted with these same features. The graves of these North American giants, anywhere from 7 to over 12 feet tall,[7] included blondes in Mexico[8] and redheads in Nevada.[9] The Indians tell stories that make the blood run cold (see Appendix – Giants in the Americas). These people were cruel, man-

Pharaoh's "White Crown of Upper Egypt."   **Above left:** Queen Nefertiti – 18ᵗʰ Dynasty (note the head and neck (Anak = 'long necked'). **Above right:** African head-binding. **Lower left:** One of Pharaoh Akhenaten's daughters. **Lower right:** elongated head, Museo De National, Lima Peru.

FIG. 8.3. HEAD BINDING AND ELONGATION

eating monsters. Like their Middle-Eastern counterparts, they were dispossessed from the land.¹⁰ Perhaps these were the same peoples who fled after they were dispossessed in the old world?

Og the Mighty Giant

The Jews also said that Sihon was the younger brother of Og, king of Bashan, whom some believed was born *before* the Flood to the same father.¹¹ Of all the giants in the Bible, Og is by far the most colorful and embellished. The *Targum* tells us, for instance, that Og hitched a ride on Noah's Ark (in other stories he rides on the back of a *Reëm*¹² that was too big to fit into the ark), sustained by food that Noah fed him through a hole, all after promising Noah that he would serve his descendants as a slave forever. God did not spare Og because he was righteous, they said, but so that the world "might see the power of the Lord, and say, 'Were there not giants who in the first times rebelled against the Lord of the world, and perished from the Earth?'"[13]

Only two of the dozens of giants in the Bible have their height recorded. Og is the first. Well, technically it isn't his height, it is his bed,[14] or perhaps sarcophagus (coffin made of stone).[15] It tells us it was 13 ft. long and 6 feet wide (Deut 3:11). This was not a result of Og's penchant for narcissism. If it was a sarcophagus, let's put it into perspective. Robert Earl Hughes (1926 – 1958) became the heaviest person in history, weighing in at an astonishing 1,070 lbs (that's almost as difficult to believe as giants existing). They say that Hughes was buried in a coffin the size of a piano case. I don't know if that was an upright or a grand piano. Let's assume it is medium grand piano called a Parlor Grand, because this piano has the right length dimensions at 6'3". This piano is also 4'10" wide. Og's coffin is twice as long as this and half again as wide, meaning that Og was one seriously large fellow.[16] Finally, it should be noted that the entire region over which Og ruled, Bashan, is one of the larges burial fields on the planet. Filled with uncounted thousands of dolmens, some of which have capstones weighing over 50 tons, this valley of death is truly stunning (see Fig. 8.4).

In the same verse where we learn about his size, the Bible also tells us that Og was all that was left of the remnant of the Rephaim (on the east side of the Jordan River, since the Anakim-Rephaim were still in Canaan). According to the *Ugaritic* tablets which parallel the Biblical record, the Rephaim were considered to be the original inhabitants of their country north of Bashan, specifically in northern Syria, at Mt. Saphon, going all the way down to Mt. Hermon and beyond into Bashan where Og ruled. In our story, now that Sihon was dead, all that stood between Israel and the Promised Land was Og. But like Sihon, God hardened Og's heart too (and God hardened it), and thus Og turned against Israel and fought them at a place called Edrei.

Home Sweet Home

Og was the king of the land of Bashan. Joshua tells us that Og ruled "over Mt. Hermon and Salecah and all Bashan" (Josh 12:5).

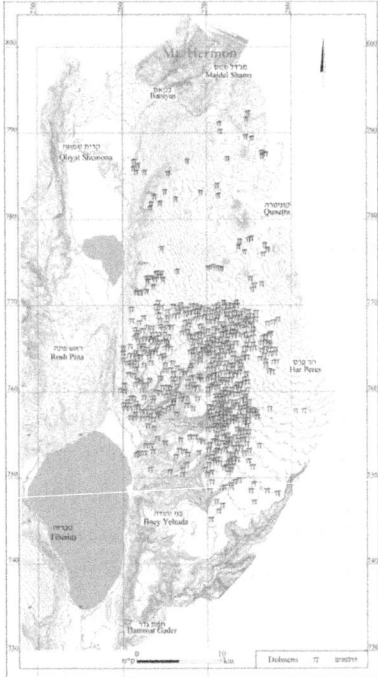

FIG. 8.4. DOLMEN FIELDS OF BASHAN

Somewhere between Og and Sihon is the land of Gilead, which was also part of their territory. Bashan is the region of today's Golan Heights in the upper northwest portion of Israel. At its northern end is Mt. Hermon. Both Bashan and Hermon have absolutely fascinating histories.

Recall that Mt. Hermon is where the Jews believed the fallen heavenly beings (Watchers) first descended upon the earth. The Babylonians tell a very similar story. For them, Hermon was the home of the *Anunnaki*[17] ("the princely blood; royal offspring") gods who lived with men a long time ago. Remember also that Hermon and "anathema" or "devote to destruction" are the same root word. What is God doing to the giants? He is having Israel devote them to complete destruction, just as God himself did in the Flood. Remember also that at the base of Hermon sits Caesarea Philippi or Banias (from the god Pan whose father was Hermes). Pan was a satyr, a half-goat, half-human hybrid in the Greek stories. Jubilees records a bit more detail,

> But formerly the land of Gilead was called "the land of Raphaim" be-
> cause it was the land of the Raphaim. And the Raphaim were born as
> giants whose height was ten cubits, nine cubits, eight cubits, or down
> to seven cubits. And their dwelling was from the land of the Ammonites
> to Mount Hermon and their royal palaces were in Qarnaim, and Ashta-
> roth, and Edrei, and Misur, and Beon.
>
> (Jub 29:9-10)

This puts the height of the Amorites between 10 ½ and 15 feet. This mountain oozes Genesis 6, as does the whole of Bashan.

Bashan has an interesting meaning. It is related to other Semitic words for ... *serpent*.[18] Why is this significant? This deserves a rather interesting detour, one that we just briefly foreshadowed in Ch. 3 when we spoke about Europa, Sidon, Sidonia, and the serpent. In the Garden story where he tells Eve "Your eyes will be opened," Satan is called the serpent (Gen 3:1; Isa 27:1; Rev 20:2). The particular Hebrew word used in Genesis 3:1 is *nachash*.

Nachash is a synonym for a more familiar word: *Seraph* (from whence we get Seraphim or the famous flying angels of Isaiah 6). In Numbers 21:6-9 and Isaiah 14:29, both words are used to describe the same thing. In Numbers, for instance, God sends "fiery serpents" (*seraph*, vs. 6), and the people beg to Moses to have God remove these serpents (*nachash*, vs. 7). God told Moses to make a "fiery serpent" (*seraph*, vs. 8) and set it on a pole. So Moses made a bronze serpent (*nechosheth nachash*, vs. 9). Both words can mean "serpent" and both words can mean "shining" (just like the bronze metal which is from the same root word above). It is also very interesting that *nachash*, when used as a verb, is translated as "divination."[19] The point is, certain angelic beings are identified as having some kind of serpentine shining form, though they are actually angelic beings and not reptiles.[20] The reason there is so much of a relationship between things pertaining to giants and serpents is because these angelic beings were their progenitors.

Bashan is "the settlement of the serpent." In this regard, one of the groups that lived in the region of Bashan, in fact at the very foot of Mt. Hermon (Josh 11:3), and are always associated with giant tribes, are the Hivites. "Hivites" (*chivvi*) has the same consonants as another Hebrew word for snake, and thus some have referred to them as the snake-clan.[21] Later, the tribe of Dan would settle in the same region, and their symbol would become a serpent (Gen 49:17). The Hivites have a curious history in the legends of the Greeks. Samuel Bochart (1599-1667), a French Huguenot divine who knew 18 languages, reported in his book *Geographia Sacra* that the Hivites fled to the Islands of Asian Minor (Cyprus, Rhodes, Samos, Chios, Icaria, etc.) after their defeat at the hands of Joshua.

The Greek Historian Pliny (23 -79 AD) states that Cyprus was originally called Ophiusa, "The place of serpents" (from the word *ophis*). Rhodes was also called Ophiusa. Perhaps the most fascinating is the tiny island of Chios. According to Bochart, "Chios" is derived from *chivia*, the same root of Hivite and serpent. At Chios was a mountain called Pelineus or "The Stupendous Serpent." Under this mountain, according to the Greek historian Claudius Aelianus (175-235 AD), there lived a huge dragon, whose voice was terrible, and no one could approach his cave. The people killed him by setting fire to the mouth of the cavern. Here, on this mountain, the Hivites erected a temple called "AN IMMENSE DRAGON."[22] Satan is also called "the dragon" (Isa 27:1; Rev 20:2). Certainly, the worship of the serpent among the giants was not an accident.

Ten years ago, I began at this point to tell you about a find I discovered in my one "Indiana Jones" moment that is intimately related to our current storyline in the Bible. Now, I want to tell you the story behind this find and what we've discovered in the intervening years. To the best of my recollection, it began as an accidental Google search on "serpent" and "Bashan." My eye was caught by a picture of a ravine, 1.1 miles in length, just north of the Sea of Galilee that researcher David Icke (whose work is a mixed-bag at best) has called a serpent ravine (see Fig. 8.5). The intervening iterations of Google Earth have shown this same feature in very different light, though the current image is almost the same as that original screen shot. I never did look into that ravine, but the picture started an idea percolating in my mind. This is in the land of the Serpent after all. I wonder if anything else might be there?

7.2 miles to the Southwest sits another strange serpentine formation, this time arising out of the earth rather than cut from it. When I first saw it, I was absolutely shocked, for it was a merely .10 mile north of perhaps the oldest megalithic site in Israel, Gilgal-Refaim—the Wheel of Giants (see Fig. 8.6).

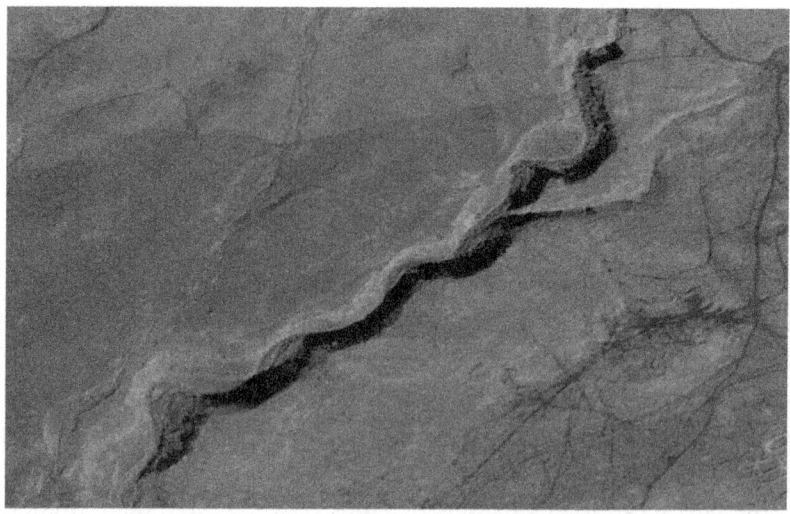

FIG. 8.5. "SERPENT RAVINE" (CIRCA 2012, GOOGLE EARTH)

The Wheel was rediscovered in 1968 in an aerial survey of the Golan. Located 11 miles due east from the point the Jordan River enters the Sea of Galilee, it is an enormous structure consisting of 42,000 basalt rocks weighing over 40,000 tons. It is a circular structure 510 ft. in dia-

Image courtesy *Angels & Giants, The Watchers & the Nephilim*

FIG. 8.6. GILGAL REFAIM (WHEEL OF GIANTS). GOLAN, ISRAEL.

meter with walls 6.5 ft. high. Consisting of five distinct walls, the wheel is aligned to at least the summer solstice.[23] It is dated to a time long before Abraham. Its central tumulus or cairn was perhaps a grave,[24] making it an appropriate GOAT (Greatest Of All Time) burial mound in a region littered with perhaps more dolmens that any other place on earth. In summer of 2019, I was privileged to be able to set feet on and inside this monumental wheel. I do not think it is a coincidence that this was ground zero for Og's territorial dominion. Nor do I think it is accidental this his name can mean "a circle."[25]

This is what makes the following all the more incredible. As I said, sitting just .10 of a mile to the north is a mile-long, 200-340 ft. wide, 15-20 ft. high mound. Using simply a rudimentary investigation from Google Earth, if it is purely man-made, it would have a volume of 15,000,000 ft³ of dirt and rock. Even if it were a natural feature enhanced by men, it would still be an epic undertaking.

When I first saw this feature, I immediately called a friend of mine whom I had been red-pilling in all things giants. "Go to Google Earth. Now."

He said, "OK."

"Go to the wheel."

He said, "OK."

"Now, what else do you see?" He knew about Bashan's name meaning. He knew about the Mt. Hermon event. He had all the necessary background to arrive at his conclusion just a minute or so into his investigation. But I said nothing else.

"It's a serpent mound."

"So I'm not crazy?" I said rhetorically.

"No, you're not crazy," he answered.

Sometime in the intervening years, I decided to call Dr. Heiser's good friend, Dr. Judd Burton, a Ph.D. anthropologist/archologist who has worked on digs at and around Mt. Hermon. I didn't know Judd from Adam, but I thought it was worth a try. Having secured his number, I dialed. As the phone was ringing, I was still certain that I was correct, but I was definitely nervous thinking about how he might take this bit of information from a complete stranger out of the blue.

As we talked and I showed him the feature, he immediately started getting excited. "I think this could be the real deal," he admitted.

Image courtesy *Angels & Giants, The Watchers & the Nephilim*

FIG. 8.7. SERPENT MOUND (GOLAN, ISRAEL)

I was shocked. And yet, not. There's really no question that this thing is manmade or man worked, and it certainly fits with the worldwide phenomena of building serpent mounds (see Fig. 8.8). As Judd and I dug deeper, we decided to write a paper on the mound that we hope to get published. We discovered a couple of truly amazing facts in this search. First, it appears that the serpent is also aligned to the summer

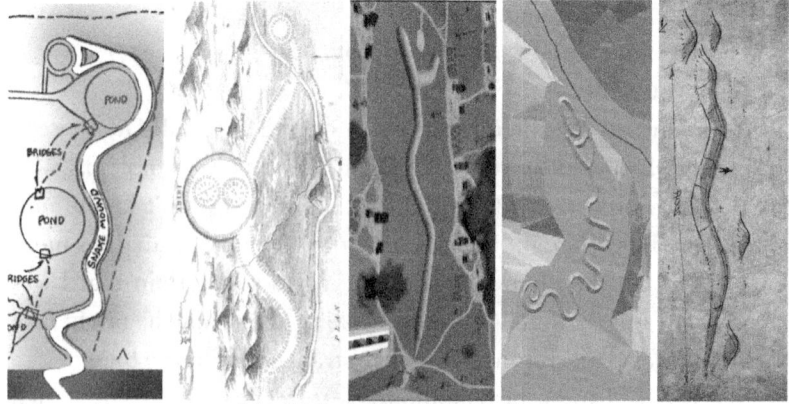

Left to Right: Seattle, England, Florida, Ohio, Ontario

FIG. 8.8. SERPENT MOUNDS OF THE WORLD

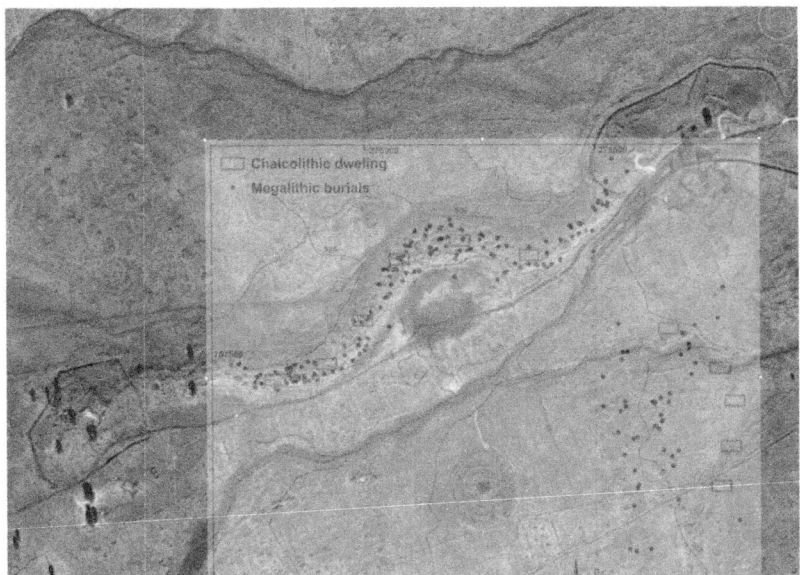

Map: "el-Arba'in Ridge (58)," Map Name/No.: Rujem-el Hiri – 36/2, Site No.: 58, Field No.: 5-7/3, The Archaeological Survey of Israel, *Israel Antiquities Authority*, overlaid on Google Earth

FIG. 8.9. SERPENT MOUNDS OF BASHAN AND MEGALITHIC BURIAL MOUNDS

solstice, making a perfect complement to the Wheel. Second, there are numerous burial cairns littering the top of the mound, but none in the flat lands below it (see Fig. 8.9). In fact, the Israel Antiquities Authority is quite aware of this, as they have done archeological work on this site. The thing is, they simply call this a "ridge," and have no bothered to think beyond that in their surveys.

Moving due north for 28 miles from the Wheel through the center of the serpent mound you will run straight into the summit of Mt. Hermon. It is curious that at this place, the land of the giants, which is so heavily charged with serpentine angelic (Watcher) history, they would build a serpent mound and a "wheel." The prophet Ezekiel once had a vision. In his vision he saw shining heavenly beings. "I looked at the living creatures, I saw a *wheel* on the earth beside the living creatures, one for each of the four of them" (Ezek 1:15). The wheels appeared as "gleaming beryl" (1:16). The wheels ("their bodies") had spokes and rims (Ezek 10:12). Ezekiel also notes that they were "whirring wheels" (Ezek 10:2).

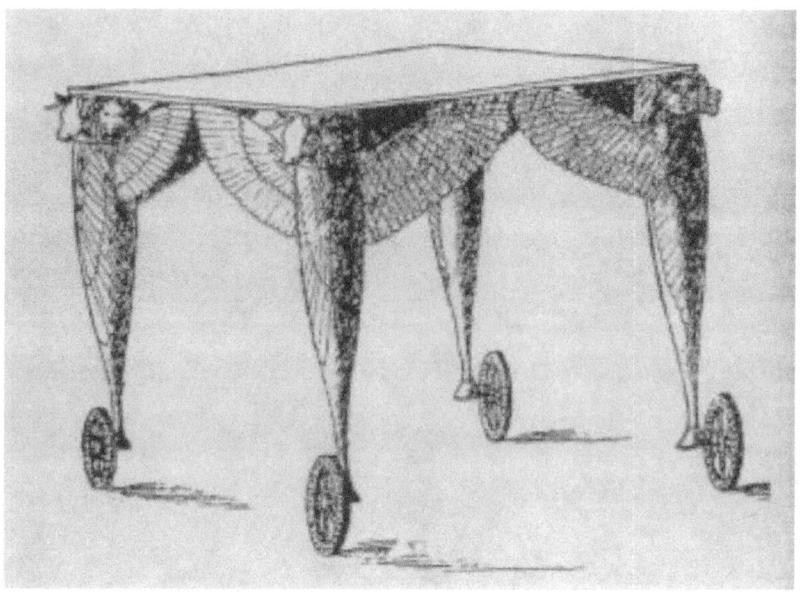

Note: Four seraphim with four hooved legs ending in wheels
Syrio-Palestine[26]

FIG. 8.10. WHEEL THRONE PLATFORM

The word for a "whirring wheel" is related to Gilgal. It is the He-brew: *galgal*. These wheels were not spaceships, but rather Ezekiel is giv-ing a classic description of a Middle Eastern throne platform. Could the giant-wheel be a representation of the house of the god?

Let's recall that the Wheel of Giants is *Gilgal* Refaim. Gilgal means circle. Hence, the place is circular. In Joshua, after they miraculously cross through the Jordan River on dry ground, Joshua commands that twelve stones be erected as a lasting memorial. At the fulfillment we read, "And those twelve stones, which they took out of the Jordan, Joshua set up at Gilgal" (Josh 4:20). No one knows where these stones might be, and they were probably destroyed long ago, but because the word means circle, scholars have suggested that Joshua put them in the form of a stone-stone circle, perhaps as an altar or something.

If so, this would be fascinating. Allow me to speculate a little. It could be a parallel to the idea of Israel camping around the tabernacle in the wilderness. As they did this, God had a very set order for the tribal

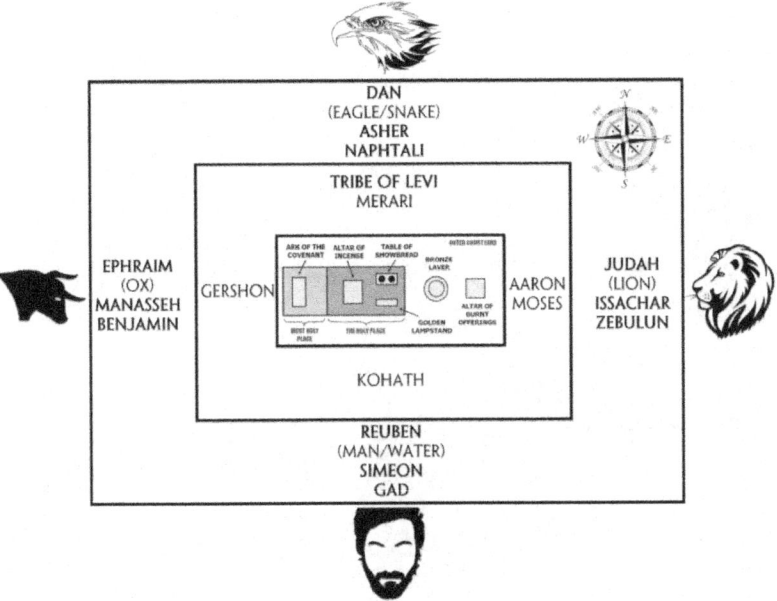

FIG. 8.11. THE CAMP OF ISRAEL

arrangements. Judah was to be on the east, the lion (Gen 49:9). guarding the entrance. Reuben, the man unstable as water (49:3-4) would be south. Dan, whom we have already seen is a serpent, is north. Ephraim, representing Joseph the bull (Gen 49:6 Targum) is west. A lion, a man, a bull, and serpent. Do these ring any bells? Probably, not. But if we were to substitute the serpent for an eagle, you would have the faces of the four living creatures (Ezek 1:10; Rev 4:7), first seen in the same chapter as Ezekiel's wheels. The thing is, if you understand your zodiac, you can see what's going on here. Leo the lion, Aquarius the man holding water, Taurus the bull, and Scorpio the eagle (but in older days a serpent), are the four cardinal points of the zodiac.

What this means is stunning. God is having Israel emulate on earth what the constellations do in heaven. They are, as we saw in a previous chapter with ziggurats, a living mirror of heaven on earth. They are, to put it in Jesus' words, to make things happen "on earth as it is in heaven." They are the kingdom meant to shine God's light on the world. If Joshua's stone are in fact in a circle, it would be doing the same

Beth Alpha Synagogue, Israel (6ᵗʰ Cent.).

FIG. 8.12. JEWISH ZODIAC (TWELVE TRIBES)

thing as the tabernacle camp. Each tribe represents one of the twelve major constellations by which we can determine days, months, seasons, and years. In fact, there are many zodiacs that have been found in ancient synagogues. These zodiacs replace the twelve constellations with the twelve tribes of Israel. God is at the center (in the heavens, the counterpart is Cepheus, the king on the throne).

Curiously, a time lapse of the north star reveals that the heavens circulate and form what Journey sang about, "The Wheel in the sky."

FIG. 8.13. THE WHEEL IN THE SKY

So, now we are back to the wheel theme again. In trying to understand the meaning of Gilgal Refaim, Dr. Burton has suggested that it may represent a kind of stylized ouroboros. Ouroboros is literally "tail (Gk: oura) eater (Gk: boros)." It is an ancient symbol dating back to prehistory and found all over the globe. It is a symbol of life, death, and re-

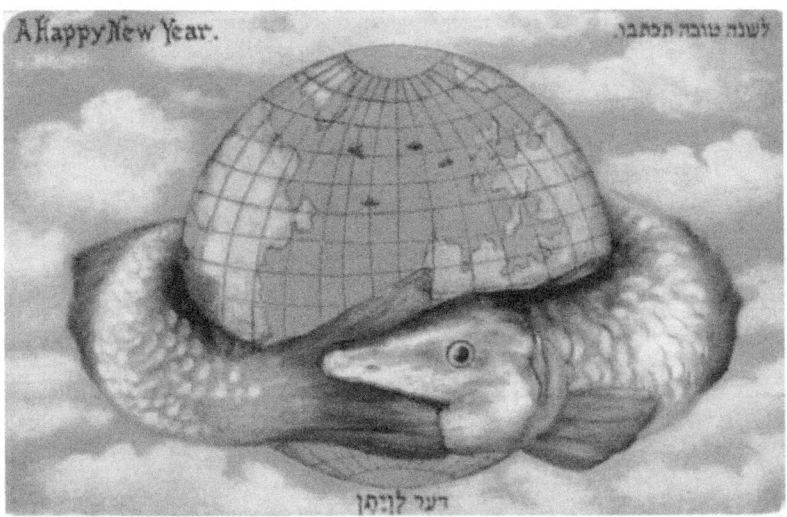

FIG. 8.14. LEVIATHAN TAIL EATER

birth, something we certain find in the dolmen fields and grave cairns of the Wheel and serpent mound.

Most importantly, it is always found as a serpent or dragon eating its tail. Jewish depictions actually call this serpent: *Leviathan* (see Fig. 8.14). This is the name given to Satan in Isaiah 27:1 (cf. Rev 12:9). Now, in esoteric and occult circles, it is common to find a circumscribed up-side-down pentagram. And, of course, this pentagram (the reverse of a regular star) is associated in many minds with the devil. It is also common to find the five points given the letters for Leviathan. Why? There is no question but that they are associating it with Satan, the reasons are not often understood.

Our Milky Way galaxy has always been conceived, by all ancient peoples, as a serpent eating its tail. The center of the galaxy is where this figure can be seen (see Fig. 8.14). Leviathan is a composite word meaning "joined to (Heb: Levi) serpent (Heb: Tan)." So now we are back to the heavens. But more than the heavens.

Let's return to Sidon for a moment. Remember our Sidonia fruit that makes a pentagram? The god Poseidon, brother of Zeus, god of the ocean, and king of Atlantis, is sometimes depicted as an ouroboros. Of the possible meanings of Poseidon, perhaps the most intriguing is "from

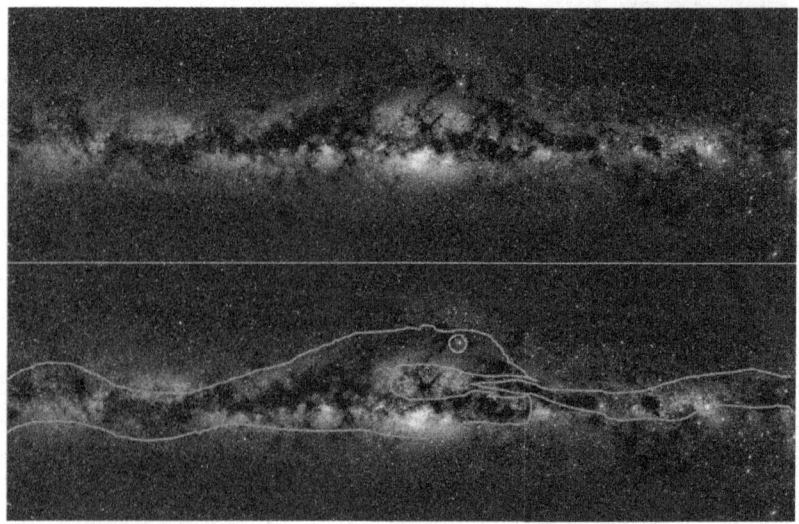

FIG. 8.15. LEVIATHAN OUROBOROS.

Sidon" (Gk: apo Sidon). If so, that takes us back to Sidonia in which we find Mt. Hermon on the exact same parallel as the city Sidon, and upon which the Watchers first came down. All the more reasons to think that the serpent mound, the Wheel of Giants, and the land of Og the giant in the place of serpents (Bashan) are related.

One final point is worth mentioning here. In preparation for our next chapter, after Joshua came into the land and began conquering, he started erecting centers of worship. These centers would be encircled (*gilgal*) by ceremonial stone walls. (Curiously, the plan of the old city of Jericho also resembles a giant right foot). Thing is, these stone walls were erected to look like a giant right foot.[27] Why? God told Joshua, in fulfillment of his promise to Abraham, "Every place that the sole of your foot will tread upon I have given to you, just as I promised to Moses" (Josh 1:3; cf. Gen 13:17). Some think that the foot is symbolic of Yahweh himself. What if it also symbolizes the conquering of the giants in the very land that they had held power over for so many centuries? It is to this conquest that we now turn.

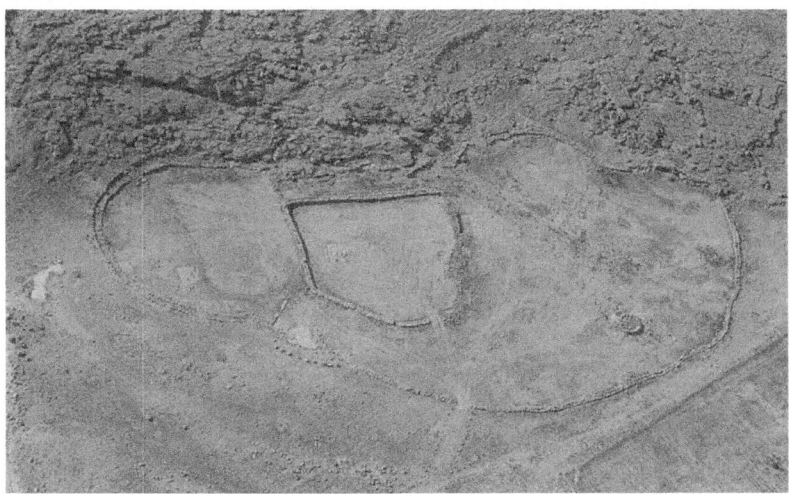

Fɪɢ. 8.16. Gɪᴀɴᴛ Fᴏᴏᴛᴘʀɪɴᴛ Wᴀʟʟ, Gɪʟɢᴀʟ, Isʀᴀᴇʟ

9

Giant Wars, the Sequel

The fear of you has fallen upon us, and all the inhabitants of the land melt away before you.

Joshua 2:9

Preparation for Battle

WITH SIHON AND OG out of the way, the Transjordan (all the land east of the Jordan River) is now cleared of the giant scourge. Israel may safely pursue war without fear of being attacked from behind. Now it is the giants' turn to fear. Whether or not Og survived the Flood, the *Targum* certainly got one thing correct: Giants were allowed to be in the land of Canaan so that all people "might see the power of the Lord" and fall to their knees in terror. If the giants serve any purpose in the Bible, it is to die by God's omnipotent hand.[1] They also show God's steadfast love for his chosen people. As the giants are exterminated from the land, it is because the LORD fights for his people and goes before them, causing the inhabitants to melt away in fear.

The nations began melting with fear when God drowned the Egyptian army in the middle of the Red Sea. Moses sang, "Now are the chiefs of Edom dismayed; trembling seizes the leaders of Moab; all the inhabitants of Canaan have melted away. Terror and dread fall upon them; because of the greatness of your arm" (Ex 15:15-16). This theme is predicted to continue (Ex 23:27; Deut 2:25; 11:25; 28:10). Some forty years later, the prostitute Rahab (who alone was saved in the destruction of Jericho) acknowledged that the prophecy had come true. She told the two spies, "I know that the LORD has given you the land, and that the fear of you has fallen upon us, and that all the inhabitants of the land melt away [in fear] before you" (Josh 2:9).

The opposite of fear is courage. The book of Joshua begins with a saying: "Be strong and courageous." It is easy to find this saying in Evangelical bookstores or to find someone quoting it as their "life verse." But the saying has a context. The first time I read this chapter, not realizing what was going on, I wondered why in the world Joshua would need to be told to be courageous so many times. Yes, he was going into war, but plenty of people have gone into war, including Joshua, during the past forty years.

This is a rare saying, repeated in only three other places in the entire Bible. Yet it is applied *four* times to Joshua in one chapter (Josh 1:6, 7, 9, 18). So what gives? Why does Joshua need to be so courageous? The context is the destruction of the giants from the land of Canaan. Joshua 1 picks up where Deuteronomy 31:3-7, 23 left off.

> [3] The LORD your God himself will go over before you. He will destroy these nations before you, so that you shall dispossess them, and Joshua will go over at your head, as the LORD has spoken. [4] And the LORD will do to them as he did to Sihon and Og, the kings of the Amorites, and to their land, when he destroyed them. [5] And the LORD will give them over to you, and you shall do to them according to the whole commandment that I have commanded you. [6] *Be strong and courageous.* Do not fear or be in dread of them, for it is the LORD your God who goes with you. He will not leave you or forsake you." [7] Then Moses summoned Joshua and said to him in the sight of all Israel, "*Be strong and courageous* ... [23] and the LORD commissioned Joshua the son of Nun and said, "*Be strong and courageous.*"

This passage now makes a total of seven times that the saying is applied to Joshua. "Seven" (the number of completion) makes the perfect repetition for the ultimate fight about to ensue, the battle over the Promised Land, and the outworking of the battle of the two seeds.

The preparation for battle begins in Joshua 1:14 where Joshua commands all the "men of valor" among the tribes of Reuben, Gad, and the half-tribe of Manasseh that they must cross the Jordan and fight with their brothers before they may possess the now empty lands of Og and Sihon. "Men of valor" is the phrase *chayil gibborim*. We have seen this phrase previously. It often comes in the context of Israel fighting literal *gibborim*: Giants. It is an ironic turn of a phrase—the little guys will become giants by defeating the giants of Canaan. It is sort of like when Jesus said, "the last will be first" (Matt 20:16). This makes the giant footprints of Joshua at the end of the previous chapter all the more ironic.

After assembling all Israel together, Joshua gives them a little peptalk before something extraordinary happens. "Come here, and hear the words of the LORD your God. By this you shall know that the living God is among you, and that He will assuredly dispossess from before you the Canaanite, the Hittite, the Hivite, the Perizzite, the Girgashite, the Amorite, and the Jebusite" (Josh 3:9-10). At that moment, the Levites are summoned. They bring the Ark of the Covenant to the shores of the Jordan River and when they step into it, the waters stand and rise up in a heap some miles upstream.

Before devoting the peoples to destruction, we learn two more facts. First, "When all the kings of the Amorites who were beyond the Jordan to the west, and all the kings of the Canaanites who were by the sea, heard how the LORD had dried up the waters of the Jordan before the sons of Israel until they had crossed, their hearts melted, and there was no spirit in them any longer" (Josh 5:1). Again, God's prediction had come true. Second, after circumcising the new generation of Israelites at Gilgal(!) on the day of Passover, the people ate for the first time from the food of Canaan. The manna stopped that same hour. Then, as Joshua was surveying the land, he lifted up his eyes and, "Behold, a man was standing before him with his drawn sword in his hand. And Joshua went to him and said to him, 'Are you for us, or for our adversaries?' And he said, 'No; but I am the commander of the army of the LORD. Now I have come.' And Joshua fell on his face to the earth and worshiped." The captain of the LORD's host said to Joshua, "Take off your sandals from your feet, for the place where you are standing is holy." And Joshua did so (Josh 5:13-15).

This extraordinary story gives Joshua a glimpse of the supernatural battle that will be fought *for* him. This Captain (or prince) is none other than the LORD himself, the LORD in visible form, otherwise known as the Angel of the LORD.[2] This is confirmed by the repetition of the "holy ground" story that Moses hears some 40 years earlier on the side of Mt. Sinai at the burning bush, when the Angel of the LORD appeared to him there (Ex 3:2-5). Also, Joshua worships this person and he accepts Joshua's worship (unfallen created angels never accept worship in the Bible). God will fight for Israel because he promised he would. But he will also fight for Israel because his promise to Eve is on the line. The time of the extermination of the giants from Canaan will now begin.

Jericho

The beginning of the conquest takes place because the inhabitants of Jericho had shut themselves inside the city. God said to Joshua, "I have given Jericho into your hand, with its king and mighty men of valor" (Josh 6:2). The inhabitants of Jericho, including the *gibborim* giants among them, are very afraid.

Like Hebron, Jericho is a city showing, in places, gigantic proportions. For instance,

> An approaching enemy first encountered a stone abutment, eleven feet high, back and up from which sloped a thirty-five degree plastered scarp reaching to the main wall some thirty-five vertical feet above. The steep smooth slope prohibited battering the wall by any effective device or building fires to break it. An army trying to storm the wall found difficulty in climbing the slope, and ladders to scale it could find no satisfactory footing. The normal tactic used by an enemy to take a city so protected was siege, but Israel did not have time for this, if she was to occupy all the land in any reasonable number of months.[3]

Because the walls were unbreachable, because the city was full of giants, and in order to bring great glory to himself and throw even more fear upon the wicked inhabitants of Canaan, God performed an astounding miracle. After marching around the city walls, silently, for seven days,[4] suddenly and without notice, the trumpets blew and walls a dozen feet thick instantly explode *outwards*. The Commander of the heavenly army had struck. Israel rushed in and put everyone who did not flee to the sword, except for Rahab. The Arabs, who have legends that some of the inhabitants of Jericho fled to Africa and became the Berbers, call Jericho "The City of Giants."[5]

Taking Other Cities

The next city taken (though not without difficulty because a man from Israel [Achan] had taken some of the things devoted to destruction) was Ai. Ai was next door to Jericho, to the west, a step closer to Jerusalem (which Joshua would not conquer). It, too, was a strong fortress, though nothing could surpass the glory of Jericho. Was Ai a city of giants? The Bible does not say, but the Jews certainly thought that it was. When Joshua took Ai, they report that he said, "Enter into this town; for God has taken it from the giants, and has given it to you to be your inheritance. But when you pass through the gates, prostrate yourselves, with your heads in the dust, and adore God, saying, *Hittaton, hittaton*, which is by interpretation, Pardon our sins."[6]

After this, the people of the city of Gibeon, the next city in line of the march, become so frightened that they trick Israel into making a covenant of peace with them. The Bible calls these people Hivites and Amorites, and the LXX calls them Horites (who presumably fled here when Esau took over their lands; Josh 9:7). It was a grave mistake to make peace with these people, but because they made a covenant with them, Israel could not go back on its word. Joshua destroyed many cities in the northern part of Israel after this.

From here Joshua set his sights to the south, and the lands filled with Anakim. They conquer Bethel, the ancient home of Jacob. They take Makkedah, Libnah, Lachish and Gezer. Excavations at Gezer and other sites produced skeletons over nine feet tall which, "bear out the unusually tall stature of individuals in ancient Palestine."[7] One city in the vicinity known as Beit Jibrim or "House of the Gibborim" contains "one of the most amazing cave-cities in the world" where you can find labyrinths of caves upwards of eighty feet tall.[8] Guess who the stories say built them? No wonder they call it the House of the Giants.

FIG. 9.1. SIDONIAN TOMBS IN CAVE CITY OF BEIT JIBRIM

Some Giants Remained in Gaza, Gath, and Ashdod

Greatly emboldened by victory after victory, Joshua set his sights on the crown jewel of Canaan—Hebron. Hebron is the headquarters of the giant Anakim and, especially, the three terrifying sons of Anak. They destroy all the Anakim from the hill country, from Hebron, Debir, and Anab (Josh 11:21). "Only in Gaza, Gath, and Ashdod did some remain" (vs. 22).

Ashdod is another city referred to as the "city of giants," this time it is the Egyptians who gave it this name.[9] Gath was said to be the home of an early Christian saint known as St. Christopher. This saint became fabled more than most, his history steeped in the mists of legend. "The legends say that St. Christopher was from the city of Gath; and at this day men who are born there are said to be stronger and more warlike than other men."[10]

As the story goes, Christopher was born Reprobus ("wicked"). They say he was a third century Christian martyred during the reign of

Emperor Decius (249-51). A thirteenth century Italian historian wrote, "Christopher was a Canaanite[11] by birth, a man of prodigious size—he was twelve feet tall—and fearsome of visage."[12] By the time the story got to the British Isles, he belonged to a tribe of dog-headed, cannibalistic giants. The tale is told in the Beowulf manuscript.[13]

This accounting of Christopher bears a remarkable resemblance to one Abominable—a cannibal "with a face like unto that of a dog, four cubits in height with eyes like lamps of fire, teeth like the tusks of a wild boar or of a lion, nails like curved reaping hooks, both awful and terrifying"—who met the disciples Andrew and Alexander, was baptized, and renamed Christianus in the ancient legendary *Contendings of the Apostles*.[14] Christopher is even depicted as dog-faced in early Byzantine art.

Although the legends of Christopher grew into tall-tales, they do tell us one thing. A very long time ago, people made the same kinds of connections of giants coming from Canaan that we are seeing here.[15] The mention of Gaza, Gath, and Ashdod as the remnant of the giants in Canaan is important for what it foreshadows. As we will soon see, Christopher is not the only giant that is said to come from Gath. There is a citizen of Gath much more famous than Christopher. He is found in the Bible. Giants were still in the land. They put up a good fight. But they would have to be destroyed sooner or later.

FIG. 9.2. ST. CHRISTOPHER

Goliath and His Brothers

There was again war at Gath, where there was a man
of great stature, who had six fingers on each hand and
six toes on each foot, twenty-four in number, and he
also was descended from the giants.
1 Chronicles 20:6

He Really Did Slay the Giant in His Life

H E IS UNDOUBTEDLY best-known giant in the Bible. His story is said by some to be pure fantasy, the invention of Jewish sages who needed new bedtime tales to tell their tots. Others think his place in the Bible is that of a fable—a fictional story with a moral at the end. "Have you slain the giants in your life"? I'm talking, of course, about Goliath.

Many Christians have this idea that Goliath is the *only* giant in the Bible and few bother to ask how he even got here. The story of his demise at the hands of a tiny shepherd boy named David is universally known. People are often shocked, however, to discover that there are other giants in the Bible. That is why I waited until now to speak of him. I wanted to talk about Goliath in his own biblical-theological context and moment in history. His story makes so much more sense that way. If you see Goliath in his ancestral milieu as you are now able to do, you can actually process his story and understand why he is in the Bible in the first place. As I mentioned previously, God did not give us the story of Goliath in order to help us slay the "Goliath's in our lives." It is so very much more important than that.

They Did Not Drive Them Out

Before we get to Goliath himself, let's see how it is that David came to fight this monster in the first place. Continuing with the story, we pick it up at the end of the book of Joshua. On the whole, the story of Joshua is positive. Israel obeyed their commander, went from city to city, and destroyed all the giant inhabitants or those who mixed themselves with them. Thus the book concludes, "Not one word has failed of all the good things that the LORD your God promised ... The LORD gave them rest on every side just as he had sworn to their fathers. Not one of all their enemies had withstood them, for the LORD had given all their enemies into their hands" (Josh 23:14-15). This did not mean, however, that Israel had taken all of the land. It means that wherever Joshua went, God routed the giants before him. Israel was able to settle the land, eat from its produce, and live in its houses, all because God had delivered on his word.

Then Joshua died. The story of the book of Judges picks up immediately after the people swear an oath that they will do everything that the LORD has commanded them (Josh 24). Joshua warned them that they could not serve the LORD, because he was holy and they were not. But they thought themselves to be invincible. A subtle pride had crept in and changed their thinking. Perhaps it was they, and not God, who were really responsible for the victories they fought and won?

With Joshua gone, the conquest of other cities not taken earlier began. Judah took the lead, defeated many cities of the Canaanites and Perizzites, and the LORD was with Judah. "But he could not drive out the inhabitants of the plain because they had chariots of iron" (Jdg 1:19). This is a strange verse, because in Joshua's day the chariots did not seem to hinder them at all (Josh 11:4-9). Furthermore, Joshua's promise to another tribe was that they would not hinder them if they were faithful to God (Josh 17:18). Why did Judah not succeed?

From here it only gets worse. It says, "The people of Benjamin did not drive out the Jebusites who lived in Jerusalem" (Jdg 1:21). Manasseh did not drive out the peoples of Bethshean, Taanach, Dor, Ibleam, Megiddo or any of their villages "for the Canaanites persisted in dwelling in that land" (Jdg 1:27). "They put the Canaanites to forced labor, but did not drive them out completely" (vs. 28). Ephraim did not drive out the Canaanites in Gezer (vs. 29). Zebulon left two cities full of Canaanites, but made them slaves (vs. 30). Asher did not drive out Canaanites in seven cities (vs. 31). Naphtali left Canaanites in two cities and turned them into slaves as well (vs. 33). Perhaps worst of all, the Amorites continued to live in the high country in Dan (by Mt. Hermon), but they too were put into labor camps (vs. 34-35).

Slavery was *not* what Israel was supposed to do with these people. They were supposed to utterly destroy them—The Ban, *khrm*, *Hermon*. But it was the LORD who left these nations here "to test Israel by them," "to see if Israel would obey the commandments of the LORD," and "to teach war" and to the generations coming up that had not been involved in the previous victories (Jdg 3:1-5).

But Israel did not obey. They "took their daughters for themselves as wives, and gave their own daughters to their sons, and served their gods" (Jdg 3:6). These things they did with Canaanites, Hittites, Amorites, Perizzites, Hivites, and Jebusites (vs. 5). My thought on this is that perhaps most of the giant Rephaim that lived among these peoples had by now been destroyed, and so Israel figured such mixing would not be such a bad thing now. The problem is, God wanted these nations destroyed because those nations had mixed with the Nephilim of older days and had become utterly corrupted by their vile worship and abominable practices.

The rest of the book of Judges tells the story of a disintegrating cycle. The cycle begins with Israelite apostasy, moves to Israelite captivity at the hands of some group of Canaanites or Philistines etc., then Israel cries out to God for deliverance, and finally the LORD delivers them by giving them a Judge. By the end of the book, the Judge and the people are drifting ships and wandering stars, without morality, without a compass, doing whatever they personally believe is right in their own eyes.

Samson the Giant?

One of the judges is worth spending a little time on. Since writing the first book, it has come to my attention that there are many legends surrounding Samson that say he was a giant.[1] The epicenter of these stories is probably found in a story where he escapes the Philistines. It tells us, "But Samson lay till midnight, and at midnight he arose and took hold of the doors of the gate of the city and the two posts, and pulled them up, bar and all, and put them on his shoulders and carried them to the top of the hill that is in front of Hebron" (Jdg 16:3). Some Rabbis believed that the text here implies that Samson was a giant. "It was taught: R. Simon the Pious said: "The span of Samson's shoulders was sixty cutis, as it says [quotes Judges 16:3] ... and we have a tradition that Gaza's city gates were never less than sixty [about 100 feet] cubits wide" (b. *Sotah* 10a).

Again, gigantic proportions seemed to some to be implied at his death. "And Samson grasped the two middle pillars on which the house rested, and he leaned his weight against them, his right hand on the one and his left hand on the other. And Samson said, 'Let me die with the Philistines.' Then he bowed with all his strength, and the house fell upon the lords and upon all the people who were in it" (Jdg. 16:29-30). Apparently, Samson was large enough to lean on or even grasp the two pillars simultaneously. This was such a tradition that ancient synagogues around the Sea of Galilee depicted Samson as a giant (see Fig. 10.1).

Of course, going with his giant stature would necessitate herculean strength. His strength came from God, but it was his very strange birth story told in Judges 13 that gave rise to speculation that he really got his strength from a god impregnating his mother. Samson's name does recall the sun (Heb: *shemesh*; Samson is *Shimshon*), and there is a solar deity in the ANE named Shamash. His birth is written in a very strange way, with ambiguity over how the boy came to be conceived. The story already resembles that of the demigod Hercules. Thus, legends grew and eventually Samson became a giant.[2] Was he actually a giant? The Scripture does not say that he was, though it is an interesting idea. He could have carried the genetic material, but at the end of the day, it is God who gives him his strength. If anything, this idea that God would use

courtesy of Uzi Leibner

FIG. 10.1. SAMSON THE GIANT, WADI HAMAM SYNAGOGUE, N. ISRAEL (3RD-4TH C)

such a sinful man as Samson to carry out his purposes is really an in-your-face to the Philistines who did have giants in their midst. It is to them that we now turn.

Give Us a King

Thinking about giants is a context in which many do not really consider at the advent of the kings of Israel. We find people finally crying out to Samuel, their last Judge, and to the LORD, "Appoint for us a king to judge us like all the nations" (1 Sam 8:5). This was not a good request but was in effect a rejection of the LORD as their king (8:7). Because the chosen Seed would eventually become King of Israel, the LORD told Samuel to give into the people's demand. Everyone was sent to his home to await the choosing of the new king.

It tells us that there was a man of Benjamin, an Israelite, whose name was Kish. Kish was a wealthy man who had a son named Saul. Including Saul, we are given a genealogy of seven names (1 Sam 9:1), in other words he was a man of perfect generations (remember Noah?) of Israelites. Saul was handsome and more important, "from his shoulders upward he was taller than any of the people" (9:2). Isn't this a strange detail to add? Not really. Israel wanted a king just like the other nations, and in Saul's stature, it looks like they got the best that could be found.

Goliath, the Giant of Gath

Now we are able to pick up the story of Goliath. We read about it in 1 Samuel 17. The Philistines gathered their armies for battle and Saul and his men were gathered and encamped in the Valley of Elah to fight them. The valley is an unremarkable place set between two small hills where the two armies could have set up camp, taunted one another from a distance, and prepared for war. But on this day, the Philistines did not want a war. Rather, they found themselves a champion whom they figured could defeat any Israelite in hand-to-hand combat, and in representative fashion, would win the battle with much less bloodshed. These were civilized people after all. If you've ever seen the movie *Troy*, you've seen virtually what is happening here. Two armies, the Mycenae and the Thessaly, face one another and are poised for all out war, when the generals, Agamemnon and Triopas decide to let their champions fight it out instead. The giant Boagrius comes out and faces Brad Pitt's Achilles, who in the span of about 15 seconds and with one small move, defeats takes down the giant with a single thrust of his sword.

The Philistine champion was "a Philistine" (1 Sam 21:9), Goliath "of Gath" (1 Sam 17:4). Remember that place? "Goliath" is an interesting name. It can mean "soothsayer," which certainly bears affinity to what we know about the giants of Canaan. It can also mean "taken captive." Perhaps Goliath's name was given to him by the Philistines who captured him in their attempt to take the giant fortresses that remained in Gath and Ashdod by the Sea. It needs to be noted again, the Philistines (like many of the other tribes) were probably not, properly speaking, giants. That is, they were not descended from the Rephaim or Nephilim. After all, Goliath is seen here as being much taller than they are too. It is their mixing with the older giants that aroused the wrath of God so that he decided to destroy them from Canaan as well as the giants.

Just how tall was this champion of Gath? There is actually a discrepancy in the Biblical account. The more recent Hebrew Masoretic text says one thing, while the older LXX and Dead Sea Scrolls have a different height. Most English Bibles put his height at 9'9" inches ("six

The "Goliath Shard"
Discovered in 2005 at Tel es-Safi
9th cent. B.C. destruction Level. Gath, Israel[3]

FIG. 10.2. THE GOLIATH SHARD

cubits and a span"), following the Hebrew of 1 Sam 17:4.[4] This view has recently been defended, with a slight modification.[5] Others have argued that the oldest LXX readings of "4 cubits and a span," or a height of 6'9" tall, are correct.[6] Which is right?

When we were filming our documentary in 2019, we not only interviewed a rabbi who said that the Nephilim could have been upwards of 40 meters tall, we also visited this famed city of Gath, which has been excavated now for several decades. We asked the archeologist overseeing the site how tall he thinks Goliath was. He did believe Goliath was real, primarily because he discovered a shard dating to that period of time with Goliath's name on it (see Fig. 10.2). His answer was shocking. He said he could not have been much taller than six feet!

Now, I'm not a giant. I'm about 5'11." Compared to David, who was probably a typical Israelite a little less than 5'6",[7] I might be considered tall, but definitely *not* a giant. My roommate in college was a little over 6'5". To me, that's tall and it is also relatively close to the size Goliath is said to be in the older manuscripts. Curiously, no one, not even my friend's wife—who is 5'0" tall if she stands on a telephone book—ever called my roommate a giant. However, Goliath *is called* a giant.[8]

In a non-scientific experiment, I had my wife measure the length of my head with a ruler. Add in about three inches for my neck, and I have about a foot of length above my shoulders. Saul is said to be taller than the other Israelites starting at his shoulders. Given the average known height of an Israelite at that time, this would put Saul only a few inches shorter than 6'9".

Here's the thing. Once Goliath begins to yell out to the Israelites to fight him, we read that Saul was *deeply afraid* and *terrified* of this monster Philistine (1 Sam 17:11). Now, I would not have liked to have fought my roommate in college, because I would have lost, especially after he gained a hundred pounds of weight and tried out for the Minnesota Vikings and Green Bay Packers and went on to star in the Arena league, playing with the Iowa Barnstormers and Arizona Ratters for six seasons. But even though I would have been more than twice as short to him as Saul (supposedly) was to Goliath, I certainly wouldn't have fled to the hills (along with all the rest of my floor-mates, and in fact the entire school) had he challenged me in a fight.

Next, let's compare Goliath to his armor. We discover that Goliath's armor weighed in at a total of 160 lbs, which was three times as heavy as that worn by a fully armored Greek hoplite soldier who trained their entire lives to fight battles (1 Sam 17:5-6).[9] I'm not saying it is impossible for a man at 6'9" to carry that much armor, but it certainly would have been extremely cumbersome.

Consider also the size of Goliath's spear. The spear would have been thrust at an enemy (as opposed to thrown like his javelin). Its tip alone weighed in excess of 15 lbs. The spear, which was like a weaver's beam (perhaps 2 ½ - 3 inches diameter or the size of the barrel of a baseball bat), must have had a total weight anywhere between 35-65 lbs. Such proportions seem excessive even for a man 6'9" tall, but not for a man almost ten feet tall, especially if he had proper proportions.[10]

The most important thing, however, is Goliath's ancestry. Whereas the Scripture calls Saul a Benjamite, it says of Goliath that he was from Gath (1 Sam 17:4) and descended from the *Rephaim* (2 Sam 21:22)! Goliath was obviously not a Jew. His residence (Gath) and his lineage (Rephaim) tell us exactly who (or what) Goliath really was. If we remember that Og's bed/sarcophagus was thirteen feet long, is it really that inconceivable that the Hebrew manuscript got it so wrong?

With that said, there is a theory that there is no discrepancy at all between the two variants, and that Goliath was in reality somewhere between eight and nine feet tall in *both* the Hebrew and Greek texts.

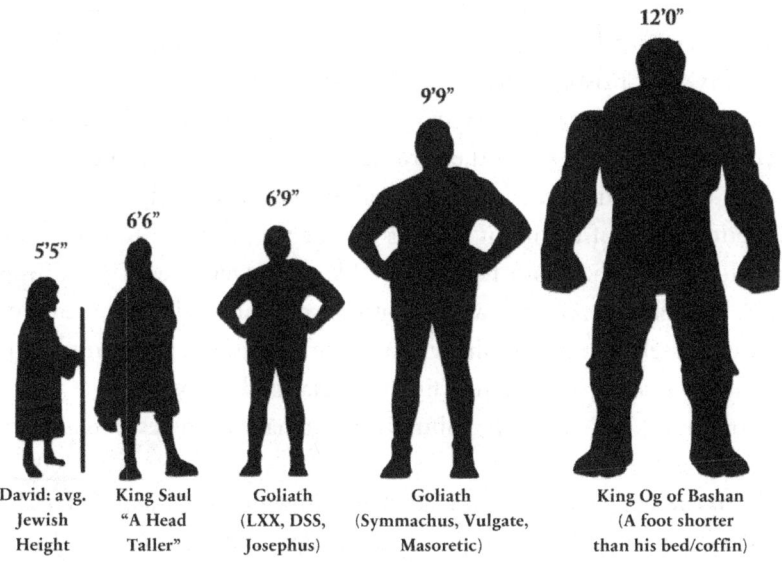

FIG. 10.3. HEIGHTS OF HEROES COMPARED

This argument depends on the LXX using the much longer Egyptian cubit (Egypt is where the LXX was translated), rather than the shorter Hebrew cubit (note the same word for length, but different measurement). The translator would have converted the Hebrew cubit to the correct height in his own unit of measurement.[11] If so, then even the LXX (which itself has a variant reading of 5 cubits), would place Goliath between 7'8" and 9'5". In considering the height of this behemoth, it should be noted that the historian Josephus said that in his day (1,000 years later), there was a "Jewish" man named Eleazar whom Artabanus III of Parthia sent as a gift to Tiberius Caesar. Eleazar was seven cubits or around eleven feet tall.[12] Josephus does not blink when conveying a height taller than the tallest given for Goliath.

Five Stones for Five Giants

One of the other curious facts about the story of Goliath is that there are several other giants who were his contemporaries. Have you ever wondered why David picked up *five* smooth stones (1 Sam 17:40)? These were not his five weapons for spiritual leadership, for pastoral ministry, or Christian faith (wouldn't David have picked up only one stone if the five stones were signs of his faith?). David needed five stones, because Goliath had four other brothers who were all said to be giants.

Goliath had a brother named Lahmi. From the only physical description given of Lahmi, it appears that he was a virtual twin of Goliath, for it says that both had spears "like a weaver's beam" (1 Chron 20:5; cf. 1 Sam 17:7). This would put the spear around 3" diameter, or approximately three times the width of the average spear. Their spear is similar to that of an unnamed Egyptian giant who was 7 ½ feet tall (1 Chron 11:23). Like Goliath, Lahmi is said to have been descended from the Rephaim.

In the same passage you read about three other giants, all slain by David's mighty *gibborim*. Sippai (2 Sam 21:18; 1 Chron 20:4) and Ishbi-benob (2 Sam 21:16) are mentioned by name. Ishbi-benob had a spear-tip that weighed 7 ½ lbs.[13] There is an unnamed giant who had the incredible physical characteristic of having the 24 fingers and toes (2 Sam 21:20). The same kind of genetic defect can be found today among people of quite ordinary stature. However, here we are led to believe that the defect came from the ancestry of this giant freak.

This ancestry is the Rephaim, or in the case of six-fingered giant—the Rapha. Rapha may be a proper name, perhaps the first or a prominent person among the Rephaim. The KJV translates it as "the giant." Thus, these three giants were descended from "the giant" on this interpretation. Since Lahmi is Goliath's brother,[14] the idea is that this is all one clan of giants, among which Goliath is the most famous.

In fact, there is one more giant in the story of David, but you won't see it unless you go the LXX. 2 Samuel 21 is the story of David sparing Mephibosheth, the descendent of king Saul from the Gibeonites who demand revenge for his oppressing them. Then we come to 2 Samuel 21:11 (LXX), "And it was told David what Rizpah the daughter of Aia the concubine of Saul had done, and they were faint and *Dan the son of Joah* of the descendant of the giants overtook them." [17] Dan the son of Joah, was a giant, descended from Rapha (22).

But Brian Godawa makes an important observation here. "Interestingly, the name Dan has a nefarious heritage in Biblical tradition. He was described in Genesis 49:17 as 'a serpent in the way, a viper by the path, that bites the horse's heels so that the rider falls backward.'" We've noted this connection too. Brian continues, "This serpentine connection rings ominously familiar with the Genesis 3:15 prophetic curse on the Serpent's Seed biting the heels of Eve's Seed. Is it mere coincidence that the tribe of Dan lost their apportioned land in Canaan (Josh. 19:47), leading them to take the territory of the city Laish (Judg. 18) in the far north of Bashan, 'place of the serpent,' in the foothills of Mount Hermon, the location of the Watchers' fall and the pagan community of Banias that worshipped [them]."[15]

So why is the story of David vs. Goliath in the Bible? The battle falls within the broader scope of the holy war that began, for Israel, at the fall of Jericho. This is, in a nut-shell, Israel vs. the giants. If you think about it, however, Saul—the tall one—should have been the one to fight Goliath. But Saul was a coward (even though he was supposedly only three inches shorter than the colossus). Saul was also not God's chosen man, nor was he from the royal line through which Messiah would be born.

Long before, in the days of Jacob, Judah his son was promised, "Judah is a lion ... The sceptre shall not depart from Judah, nor the ruler's staff from between his feet, until tribute (lit: *Shiloh*) comes to him; and to him shall be the obedience of the peoples" (Gen 49:10). "Shiloh" is a Messianic title. The *Targum* has a beautiful paraphrase, "Kings shall not cease form the house of Judah ... until the time that the King Meshiha [Messiah] shall come, whose is the kingdom, and to whom all the kingdoms of the earth shall be obedient. How beauteous is the King Meshiha, who is to arise from the house of Judah."

In the larger picture, this is the story of the seed of the serpent mocking, taunting, and battling the seed of the woman. Notice what David says just prior to lopping off the head of the belligerent ogre,

> You come to me with a sword and with a spear and with a javelin, but I come to you in the name of the LORD of hosts, the God of the armies of Israel, whom you have defied. This day the LORD will deliver you into my hand, and I will strike you down and cut off your head. And I will give the dead bodies of the host of the Philistines this day to the birds of the air and to the wild beasts of the earth, that all the earth may know that there is a God in Israel, and that all this assembly may know

that the LORD saves not with sword and spear. For the battle is the
LORD's, and he will give you into our hand.

(1Sa 17:45-47)

David defeats Goliath in anticipation of the greater battle to come between the Messiah and Satan.

11

Agag the Amalekite

Let a gallows fifty cubits high be made, and in the
morning tell the king to have Mordecai hanged upon it.
Esther 5:14

Saul's Failure as King

IN THIS SHORT CHAPTER I want to take you to the end of Old Testament history in order to show you that the theme of giants runs all the way through the story. Simply put, the giants are no minor key or dangling thread. They are one of the major storylines of the Bible. To do this I want to focus in on one group of giants that we ran across earlier: The Amalekites.

Recall that we first encounter the Amalekites in the days of Abraham in the giant wars (Gen 14:7). These Amalekites then come out of nowhere and attack Israel as it is making its way to Mt. Sinai (Exodus 17:8-16). For their crime, Moses tells the people "When the LORD your God has given you rest from all your enemies around you, in the land that the LORD your God is giving you for an inheritance to possess, you shall blot out the memory of Amalek from under heaven; you shall not forget" (Deut 25:19). We do not run into the Amalekites again until the book of Judges, but we cannot be certain that the Amalekites here are the descendants of Esau or the more primitive giant tribe.[1]

It is not until a very important incident in the life of King Saul that we unequivocally come across the people that attacked Moses in the wilderness. This episode also happens to be the event in his life that brought about God's removal of Saul as king of Israel. What did Saul do that was deserving of such great punishment as this? It was not some moral failure such as murder or adultery, but rather his blatant disregard for the command of Samuel to eradicate the giants. This is what brought about Saul's dispossession.

God sends Samuel to the king who tells him, "The LORD sent me to anoint you king over his people Israel; now therefore listen to the words of the LORD. Thus says the LORD of hosts, 'I have noted what Amalek did to Israel in opposing them on the way when they came up out of Egypt. Now go and strike Amalek and devote to destruction all that they have" (1 Sam 15:1-3). Here we see the familiar "ban" which God placed upon all the giants of the land of Canaan. At first it appears as if Saul will comply. He gathers an army and lies in wait in the valley outside the city of Amalek (vs. 5). Saul then chases the Amalekites from Havilah (perhaps in western Arabia) to Shur (east of Egypt; vs. 7).

Next, Saul meets Agag, the king of the Amalekites. Agag means "flaming; to burn; blaze with fire" or "lofty, I will overtop." As an Amalekite, Agag is clearly related to the giants. Perhaps his name hints at his tall stature, especially in light of tall Saul, who was chosen because he was like the other kings of the surrounding nations. There is also a single reference to Agag in Numbers 24:7. The LXX renders "Agag" as "Gog" (which may mean "shining"[2]) of the famed Gog and Magog of Ezekiel 38-39. Both of these names are steeped in sons of God and giant mythology. Some scholars have suggested that they may be supernatural princes, much like the princes of Persia, Greece, and Israel in Daniel 10.[3] Gog's army consists of nations that originate in Genesis 10 (Ezek 38:2-6). In the LXX[B], Gog sometimes replaces Og (Deut 3:1, 13: 4:47), and in one Greek manuscript of Ezekiel 38:2,[4] Gog becomes Og. Finally, according to Josephus, Magog is related to Celtic giants. "Gomer founded those whom the Greeks now call Galatians [Galls], but were then called Gomerites. Magog founded those that from him were named Magogites, but who are by the Greeks called Scythians" (*Antiquities of the Jews* 1.123).

After meeting Agag, Saul commits his fatal blunder. "He took Agag the king of the Amalekites *alive*" (1 Sam 15:8). He spared both Agag and the best of the sheep and oxen, fattened calves and lambs ... "all that was good" (vs. 9) and would not utterly destroy them. Why? Josephus records, "He also took Agag, the enemies' king, captive;--the beauty and tallness of whose body he admired so much, that he thought him worthy of preservation."[5]

God therefore tells Samuel that he regrets making Saul king because he is a worthless fellow who will not obey his commandments. After a long confrontation, Samuel curses Saul and removes the kingship from him (vs. 28). But there is still the messy little detail of what to do with king Agag.

Samuel commands, "Bring here to me Agag the king of the Amalekites." Agag comes cheerfully thinking that death has passed him by (1 Sam 15:32). But when Samuel meets Agag, he curses him and "hacked Agag to pieces before the LORD in Gilgal" (vs. 33). Why such a violent reaction, really, unparalleled in any story in the entire Bible? It is because Agag, a giant by tradition, was descended from and king of the Amalekites whom God swore to blot out from the face of the earth. Like David and Goliath, this too is a story of God vs. the giants. It is the story of the seeds battling it out. The promise must be fulfilled. God must win the war.

You would think that the story of Agag stops here, since he is put to death by Samuel. You would be wrong. Many centuries later, near the very end of the chronological history that is preserved for us in the Bible, we run into him again.

Esther is the last book in the history section (Genesis – Esther) of Protestant Bibles.[6] Really, the only major biblical figures to come after Esther in the OT are Nehemiah and Malachi. In this book, there is a villain named Haman; his nemesis is named Mordecai (Mordecai and Esther are the heroes). The author of the book felt it necessary to give us a genealogy of both men. Why?

It has more to do than with the author simply being a good historically minded Jew. Mordecai is the son of Jair, son of Shimei, son of *Kish*, a *Benjaminite* (Est 2:5). To put it more practically, he is a relative of King Saul. Mordecai has a curious name. It means "little man." Why does this matter? Well, let's look at the genealogy of Haman.

Haman is referred to as the son of Hammedatha an *Agagite*. In fact, it mentions this not once, but *five* times (Est 3:1; 10; 8:3; 5; 9:24). To put this in more practical terms, the story of Esther is, in a sense, a replay of the story of Saul and Agag. Haman was the first Hitler. His goal in life was the complete annihilation of every Jew on earth. This is quite the ironic turn of events for the kindness and mercy that Saul showed to Agag. Haman obviously remembered the deed of Samuel.

In the story, it is Esther who saves the day. The theme of divine providence through "accidental" events that keep happening at just the right time shows that God is orchestrating everything in the book, because this is among the last OT battles between God and Satan. Esther is the Babylonian name given to Hadassah. Esther means "star." Curious, isn't it? A star rises to the throne to defeat Haman?

The story of Haman's death comes at his own hands, though he does not realize it, of course. Haman, who is reveling in his apparent victory over the Jews and his nemesis Mordecai, commands, "Let a gallows *fifty cubits high* be made, and in the morning tell the king to have Mordecai hanged on it" (Est 5:14). That puts the death instrument at 75 ft. These are "giant" gallows. But in the end, just like David and Goliath, the "little man" wins, and Haman the Agagite-Amalekite is strung up on his own gibbet and hanged; a fitting finale to the giants in the OT.

Again we might ask why is the story of Mordecai, Esther, and Haman in the Bible? Among the reasons must certainly be included that this book details for us the battle of the two seeds prophesied so long before to our first mother. In conclusion, I want to return to a prophecy I mentioned earlier. Numbers 24:7 tells us, "Water shall flow from his buckets, and his seed shall be in many waters; his king shall be higher than Agag, and his kingdom shall be exalted." The "seed" here is the seed of Jacob/Israel (vs. 5). But just who is he?

In the very same prophecy, just a few verses later, Balaam uses the same language of the scepter prophesied to Judah. "I see him, but not now; I behold him, but not near: a star shall come out of Jacob, and a scepter shall rise out of Israel; it shall crush the forehead of Moab and break down all the sons of Sheth [Seth]" (Num 24:17). Just a couple verses later, Amalek is brought up, "Amalek was the first among the nations, but its end is utter destruction" (vs. 20). Agag, Amalek, and the Star who rules over them in Israel are all here in such a short span in a book that has its setting a thousand years before Esther. It truly is amazing.

The Targum of Numbers 24:20 reads, "And he looked on the house of *Amalek*, and took up the parable of his prophecy, and said: The *first of the nations* who made war with the house of Israel were those of the house of Amalek; and they at last, in the days of the *King Meshiha*, with all the children of the east, will make war against Israel; but all of them together will have eternal destruction in their end" (Num 24:20 PJE). The Jews saw this as a Messianic prophecy? The Letter of Barnabas, written sometime in the last first century and which is part of our earliest Christian documents after the close of the New Testament says, "For the *Son of God* shall destroy by the roots the whole house of *Amalek* in the end of days" (Barn 12:9).

The star which Esther foreshadows is Messiah, Christ, the Seed of Eve who will ultimately bring about the final demise of Amalek and Agag. He is the Seed that will crush the head of the serpent.

1 2

Demons and Giants

The Rephaim tremble under the waters.
Job 26:5

What is a Demon?

WE ARE GOING TO TAKE A DETOUR from the storyline now. *Or are we?* You may be asking, what is a chapter on demons doing in a book on giants? The answer might surprise you.

The common misconception is that demons are fallen angels. This mistake is illustrated by the discussion between Cyril of Alexandria (376-444 A.D.) and a certain deacon named Tiberius, sometime after the Council of Ephesus in 431. Tiberius asks, "[How shall we respond] to those who say, 'How did the demons, being incorporeal, have intercourse with women?'" Tiberius is confusing demons here with the sons of God, or to use some of the variants of the LXX, fallen angels. Cyril's answer basically follows Augustine's interpretation that the sons of God were Sethites, not demons.[1] This completely misses the point, and shows how an important piece of information had by this time been lost to the catacombs that became Christendom and the Dark Ages.

The earliest Church Fathers would have answered very differently. While some believed that demons were the disembodied spirits of dead people, the most widespread and influential position of the early church was that demons are the disembodied spirits of the giants. There are *not fallen angels.*[2] In their understanding, demons would be the *children* of the fallen angels and human women. Here are some examples:

- "But the angels transgressed this appointment, and were captivated by love of women, and begat children who are those that are called demons" (Justin Martyr, *2 Apology* 5).
- "In my opinion, however, it is certain wicked demons, and, so to speak, of the race of Titans or Giants, who have been guilty of impiety towards the true God, and towards the angels in heaven, and who have fallen from it, and who haunt the denser parts of bodies, and frequent unclean places upon earth, and who, possessing some power of distinguishing future events, because they are without bodies of earthly material, engage in an employment of this kind, and desiring to lead the human race away from the true God" (Origen, *Against Celsus* 4.92).
- "For one might say that these daemons are those giants [Gen 6:4], and that their spirits have been deified by the subsequent generations of men, and that their battles, and their quarrels among themselves, and their wars are the subjects of these legends that are told as of gods" (Eusebius, *Preparation for the Gospel* 5.4).
- "These angels, then, who fell from heaven busy themselves about the air and the earth and are no longer able to rise to the realms above the heavens. The souls of the giants are the demons (*daimones*) who wander about the world" (Athenagoras, *A Plea to Christians* 24).

The Jews were of the same opinion,

- "The demon answered: 'I am called Ornias. . . I am an offspring of an archangel of the power of God...'" "[The demon Asmodeus] I am of an angel, and through the daughter of a man I was born...'" "[another spirit] I am a lecherous spirit of a giant man who died in the slaughter in the time of the giants" (Testament of Solomon 2:1, 5; 5:1, 3, 17:1).
- "And when the angels of God saw the daughters of men that they were beautiful, they took unto themselves wives of all of them whom they chose." Those beings, whom other philosophers call demons, Moses usually calls angels; and they are souls hovering in the air" (Philo, *On Giants* 6).
- "And now, the giants, who are produced from the spirits and flesh, shall be called evil spirits upon the earth, and on the earth shall be their dwelling. Evil spirits have proceeded from their bodies; because they are born from men and from the holy Watchers is their beginning and primal origin; they shall be evil spirits on earth, and evil spirits shall they be called. [As for the spirits of heaven, in heaven shall be their dwelling, but as for the spirits of the earth which were born upon the earth, on

the earth shall be their dwelling.] And the spirits of the giants afflict, oppress, destroy, attack, do battle, and work destruction on the earth, and cause trouble: they take no food, but nevertheless hunger and thirst, and cause offences. And these spirits shall rise up against the children of men and against the women, because they have proceeded from them. From the days of the slaughter and destruction and death of the giants, from the souls of whose flesh the spirits, having gone forth, shall destroy without incurring judgment—thus shall they destroy until the day of the consummation, the great judgment in which the age shall be consummated, over the Watchers and the godless, yea, shall be wholly consummated" (1 Enoch 15:8-16:1).[3]

In fact, this was *the universal belief* of all the earliest Jews until sometime after the destruction of the temple, and all the earliest Christians, basically until 350 AD or so.[4] Where would these Jews and Christians get such an idea? Considering the Greeks had the same concept,[5] perhaps it was handed down to them through oral tradition. Since they were Scripture loving people, perhaps they get it from the Old Testament. This is where we will turn in our investigation.

Keep in mind that the original giants were destroyed in Noah's Flood. One of the more fascinating places where this idea might be found is Job 26:5. "The *rephaim* tremble under the waters." The LXX translates the word as *gigantes*: Giants. It puts it in the form of a question, "Shall giants be born from under the water"? Curiously, we find several English translations rendering the word as "ghosts" (CJB) or "shades" (JPS, TNK, RSV, BBE). Ghosts and shades are usually evil spiritual entities. Thus we seem to have at least a shadowy, ethereal connection between the Rephaim and evil spirits.

To what does this "under the waters" refer? The next verse talks about Sheol, the OT place of the dead. Sheol is often associated with a watery abyss. It is sometimes parallel with "the pit" (*bor*), a word that means a cistern or deep well (Ps 30:3; Prov 1:12; Isa 14:15; 38:18; Ezek 31:16). Likewise, it is parallel with "the deep" (*tehom/abussos*), the watery mass present at creation (Ezek 31:15). As one commentary explains, "Sheol was thought to lie under the ocean and to be a murky, watery abode."[6] In other places the Rephaim are said to be somehow residing in Sheol (Ps 88:10-11; Prov 2:18-19; 9:18; 21:6; Isa 14:9).[7] It should be pointed out here that though they were not considered giants at Ugarit,

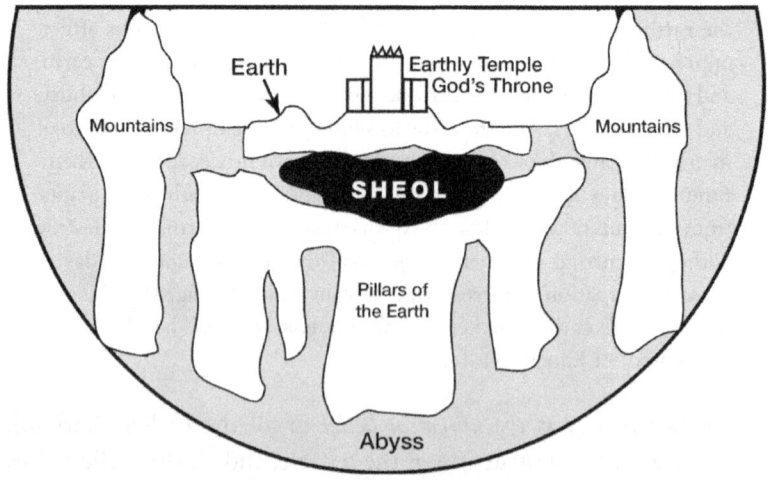

Illustration by Brian Godawa

FIG. 12.1. OLD TESTAMENT CONCEPTION OF THE UNDERWORLD

the counterparts called the *rpum* are parallel with the *ilnym* or "divine ones" and they reside in the netherworld (cf. KTU 1.6 vi:45-46).

It is tempting to read these passages with some commentaries as a reference to the Flood, under which the giants perished in the days of Noah.[8] The broader context seems to fit either the Creation story or the Flood.[9] Verse 12 mentions a being named Rahab (not the woman of Jericho), who appears sparingly in the Bible (Ps 87:4; 89:10; Job 9:13; 26:12; Isa 30:7; 51:9). These texts make it plain that Rahab refers to the mythological sea-monster,[10] the ancient dragon, also called a serpent or leviathan. In fact, words used for Satan are also put in parallelism with Rahab.[11]

The other reference to Rahab in Job mentions "the helpers" of Rahab (Job 9:13). The Babylonian *Enuma Elish*[12] has a monster parallel with Rahab called Tiamat. Tiamat also has helpers. These helpers are called monster serpents, fierce dragons, hairy hero-men, lion monsters, lion men, scorpion men, mighty demons, fish men, and bull men—*chimeras* (half-man half-beast) known in many world mythologies. Similarly, the Canaanites tell of the "Big Ones," monsters who support the sea god Yam (who is eventually destroyed by Baal),[13] and of helper-gods who reside in the netherworld.[14] Curiously, when Tiamat is destroyed by *Marduk*, like the Rephaim under the waters, they "trembled, terrified."[15]

Knowing this background, scholars have argued that these helpers can be translated as "demons." For example, Ps 40:4 could be translated as; "Blessed is the man who makes the LORD his trust, who does not turn to demons (*rehabim*), to those who go astray after a lie."[16] Are the "Rephaim under the waters" similar or even identical to the *rehabim*/demons in the Psalm and other near eastern cultures?[17]

While the OT consistently views the Rephaim as being in Sheol (the point being that they greet wicked men—especially human kings—who go down there, and this is to serve as a kind of deterrent, because you don't want to go to where the Rephaim are), perhaps not all of them were put there,[18] or perhaps they are not bound there (yet).[19] Remember, these are not men we are talking about here, so they may not necessarily be confined to the pit as men would be.[20] Whether this is a consistent theology is a question I'll let someone else figure out, but it may explain something Moses sings about.

Let's turn to the actual use of the word "demon" in the OT. There is no general term for a demon in Hebrew or other ANE languages. The English word appears infrequently. The ESV has it three times (Lev 17:7; Deut 32:17; and Psalm 106:37). It appears no times in the KJV, but they do use "devils" in those three verses as the equivalent, adding also 2Chr 11:15. The LXX adds *daimōn* in Ps 96:5; Isa 13:21; 34:14; and 65:3.[21] As you can see, that isn't very many occurrences.

Shedim

In Moses' famous hymn (recall Deut 32:8-9), Deuteronomy 32:17 says, "They sacrificed to demons (*shedim*), not God (*eloah*), to gods (*elohim*) they had never known, to new gods ("new ones") that had come recently, whom your fathers had never dreaded." Earlier, Moses has said that the older gods (i.e. sons of God) were allotted to the nations and that these nations feared and worshiped them.[22] Who might these newer demons be?

The word used for a demon here is *shedim*. These are strange creatures. Little has been written about them and little is known about them. It is tempting, based on the use of the word which only appears here and Psalm 106:37, and the appearance of the sons of God and host of heaven throughout Deuteronomy and this song, and the demonic "gods of the nations" in Ps 96:5 (LXX) to say that they are the equivalent of the gods of the nations. As such, it seems inexplicable that "demon" would be the word chosen by the LXX to translate them. But a demon could refer to a god in old Greek.[23] Further, many scholars argue that the word is equivalent of the Babylonian word *shedu*, who were territorial entities like the sons of God and so perhaps this rests the case and "demon" is just being used in its broader, more ancient sense.

But let me give you some reasons for thinking that the *shedu* might just be demons as they are described by the Fathers and not those demons parents or some other higher creature. First, let's consider how they seem to be depicted. Google the word and only one kind of image appears. These are winged-bulls or lions with the head of a human, chimerical creatures, like we have seen of the demons of Tiamat or the helpers of Rahab. The sons of God are not chimerical creatures, but demons always are.[24]

Fig. 12.2. Shedu (Lamassu), Iraq

As *HALOT* explains, they can be translated as "malevolent de-mons" or "merciless demons." In this regard, some have said that they are not benevolent at all, but "uniformly sinister."[25] Very few of the gods are regarded as being like this. The Mandaean usage of *šdum* is of a spirit of darkness, a creature that rules in the underworld. Sounds like the Rephaim. The Egyptian equivalent (the divine name *šd*) is an element of *šdrp' Šadrapa*, a god of healing.[26] Again, this reminds us of the re-phaim. Of course, there are other creatures in the underworld (such as Hades, a true son of God), and that heal (such as Hermes), but this at least gets us thinking.

Moses is in the wilderness when he says that these "new gods" have come along lately. In fact, he has defeated the Amalekite giants in the wilderness. If, when a giant dies, its spirit becomes a demon (as we will see in more detail later), then this would certainly qualify as a "new" god. Furthermore, the curious "Valley of Siddim" in our infamous Gen-esis 14 giant wars passage, has been suggested to be translated as "Valley of Demons" (*shedim*).[27] Curiously, at Ugarit we find the following. "Go out into the *plain of the demons*, into the desert of the murderous god" (KTU 1.12).[28]

One final point can be made. The Apostle Paul alludes to this pas-sage in 1 Corinthians 10 when he says, "what pagans sacrifice they offer to demons and not to God. I do not want you to be participants with demons" (1Cor 10:20). While it is logically possible that Paul has in mind the sons of God here, this is clearly not the usual definition of a demon in the New Testament.[29] He usually uses other words for the sons of god: principalities, powers, thrones, dominions, etc.[30]

Unlike, presumably, the shedu-demons, and most people are com-pletely unfamiliar with this, it wasn't until the NT that demons were viewed as exclusively evil (certainly the few OT references do not put them in a good light). For almost all pagan peoples, demons were viewed as morally ambiguous. They could be described as good or evil, and a single demon could bring both good or ill, inflict harm or fulfill your desires when worship and service was rendered, depending upon your piety or fate.

The Greek (and hence English) word "demon" is of unknown origin, but suggestions help show you why the ancients did not neces-sarily view demons as evil. Plato derives it from a Greek word *daémōn* meaning "knowing." Homer derived it from *daimōn* meaning "divinity." Eusebius derived it from *deimainein* meaning "to fear." Modern dictionaries derive it from *daiō* meaning "to divide (destines)," hence the idea of fate or the ability of the spirit to control your fate.[31] None of these definitions are necessarily evil by nature (Eusebius' comes closest).

Augustine has an extensive discussion on demons and the victory Christ won over them *(City of God,* Books 8-10). In it he explains that demons dwell in the air, the space between heaven and earth (9.8.1), and were therefore considered mediators between the gods and mankind (8.23.1). Perhaps this is where the confusion of them as fallen angels (messengers) arises?[32] Or perhaps it also points at their not quite human, not quite heavenly nature.

Because they protected, were powerful to harm or heal (the root word of *rephaim* is *rapha*: "to heal"), interceded, had great knowledge and the like, these beings were revered and venerated. The first time I studied this topic, I was struck by the similarities between the pagan view of demons and the Roman Catholic view of the veneration of the saints. The similarities are uncanny and unnerving. Both may be viewed as spirits of dead people, be they giant or not. Both are guardians and protectors. Both are intercessors. Both can be healers. Both have idols associated with them. The only real difference is that Rome thinks it has eliminated the problem of troublesome evil demons. Yet, the practice of veneration is identical, because the makeup of those being venerated is ... *identical*. It's something to think about anyway.

You will see the word "demon" appear in one or two other OT passages. Leviticus 17:7 talks about goat-demons (the KJV adds 2 Chron 11:15, which is similar). The Hebrew word is a *sair* or *sairim*. It is variously defined as a demon or a satyr. Ever heard of a satyr? These are the strange half-human, half-goat *demigods* of antiquity. If you think the idea that demons are the disembodied spirits of the giants is strange, just wait until you get a load of what is to come.

1 3

Chimeras

The Lord bless you and keep you.
The Lord make His face to shine upon you, & be gracious to you.
The Lord lift up His countenance upon you, and grant you peace.
The Lord bless you in all your deeds, and protect you from the de-
mons of the night, and things that cause terror, and from de-
mons of evening and of the morning, and from evil spirits and
phantoms.

Numbers 6:24 (Targum Pseudo-Jonathan)

Two Strange Passages

I CITED THE LXX the of Isaiah 34:13-14 and 13:21-22 in the last chapter. Now I want to look at them in detail. In light of the helpers of Rahab and Tiamat, these are truly fascinating texts. I will begin this chapter using the ESV's translation as a starting point. The first passage reads, "It shall be the haunt of jackals, an abode for ostriches. And wild animals shall meet with hyenas; the wild goat shall cry to his fellow; indeed, there the night bird settles and finds for herself a resting place." The second is like it, "But wild animals will lie down there, and their houses will be full of howling creatures; there ostriches

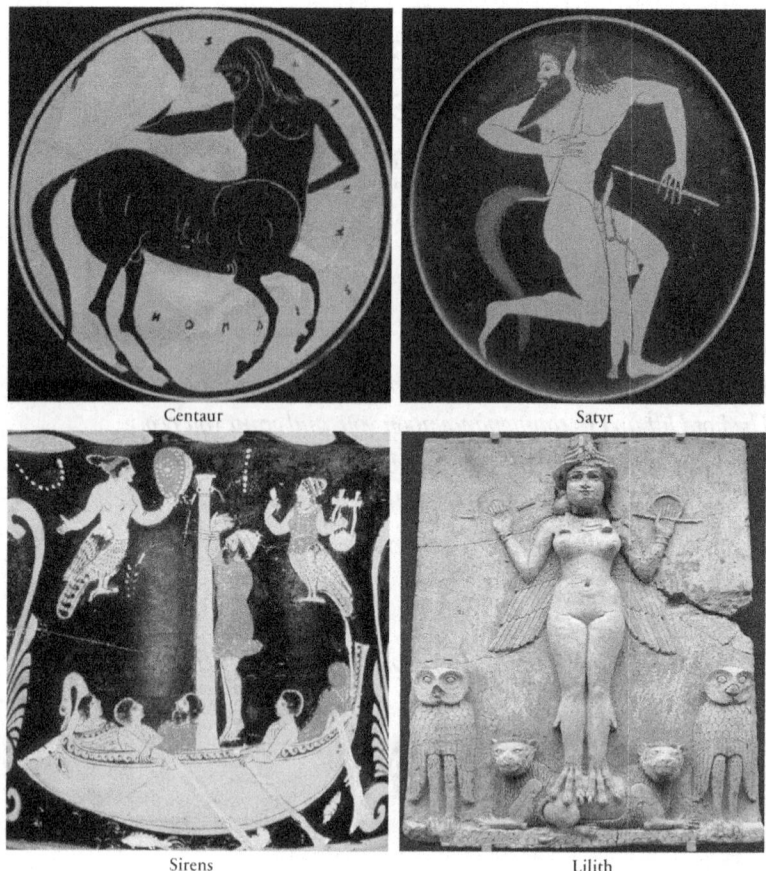

Centaur   Satyr

Sirens   Lilith

FIG. 13.1. DEMONIC CHIMERAS

will dwell, and there wild goats will dance. Hyenas will cry in its towers, and jackals in the pleasant palaces; its time is close at hand and its days will not be prolonged."

You ask, what's so interesting about that? The answer is nothing, particularly, *if* the ESV's translation faithfully captures what is in the prophet's mind. But when we start to look into the Hebrew, the *Septuagint*, and most important, the NT interpretation of this passage, things become very strange, very quickly. The whole thing ends up leading us right back to the giants.

Context

Seir and Babylon

The first pair of verses (Isa 34:13-14) come in a larger context of God cursing Edom, the land of Esau, which in older days was called the land of *Seir* (Gen 32:3). Do you recall how we finished the previous chapter? The goat-demon was called a *sair*. Notice any relationship between those words? You will also run into other related words as we continue the study of this chapter. The second pair of verses (Isa 13:21-22) is God's cursing of Babylon. As we have seen, Babylon was first built by Nimrod the *gibborim* ("giant") hunter. Therefore, in both instances, the lands in view have their most ancient origins with the giants.

Sodom and Gomorrah

Our verses on Babylon are prefaced with these words, "Babylon, the glory of kingdoms, the splendor and pomp of the Chaldeans, will be like *Sodom and Gomorrah* when God overthrew them. It will never be inhabited or lived in for all generations" (Isa 13:19-20). Curiously, Isaiah refers to the destruction of Edom in the same way. Her streams and land are turned into pitch, and her soil into sulfur (Isa 34:9). "Night and day it shall not be quenched; its smoke shall go up forever, from generation to generation it shall lie waste; none shall pass through it forever and ever." (vs. 10). In Genesis 19 we read, "Then the LORD rained on Sodom and Gomorrah *sulfur* and fire from the LORD out of heaven ... and, behold, the *smoke* of the land went up like the smoke of a furnace" (Gen 19:24, 28). Jeremiah reminds us, "When Sodom and Gomorrah and their neighboring cities were overthrown, says the LORD, *no man shall dwell there*, no man shall sojourn in her" (Jer 49:18).

Sodom and Gomorrah were places of unparalleled bounty (Ezek 16:49), but also unspeakable sins, including homosexuality and rape (Gen 19:5, 8), lack of care for the poor and needy (Ezek 16:49), open shameless flaunting of sin (Isa 3:9), and pride (Ezek 16:50), none of which is dissimilar to what we see happening in our own day. One sin that is not often considered, however, is how the men of the city not only wanted to "know" the men who came to Lot's house, the *men* they desired to know were actually ... *angels* (Gen 19:1, 11). This was therefore a distortion of a perversion. The original perversion, of course, is when "sons of God" left their proper abode and married the daughters of men (Gen 6:1-4).

In light of this, remember what we established in the last chapter. The ancient view was that the giant offspring produced by such unions who were destroyed in the flood became "demons." Most of this chapter will be taken up with exploring this idea in our two passages. Sodom and Gomorrah were on the front lines of the "giant wars" of Genesis 14, so their cultural context was smack dab in the middle of this very strange worldview. The intentional comparison between Babylon, Edom, and Sodom and Gomorrah is necessary background to a proper interpretation of at least some of the "animals" that Isaiah has in mind.

NT Inspired Commentary

The most certain proof that Isaiah has something more in mind than unclean desert animals (he has them in mind too, but not exclusively), is John's inspired commentary on the Babylonian passage. He writes, "An angel called out with a mighty voice, 'Fallen, fallen is Babylon the great! She has become a dwelling place for *demons*, a haunt for every *unclean spirit*, a haunt for every unclean bird, a haunt for every unclean and detestable beast" (Rev 18:2). The parallels with Isaiah 13:19-21 are uncanny. This is because, as commentators recognize, John is drawing his language directly from Isaiah.[1] We could properly call this an inspired commentary on that text. Since this is the case, to *not* interpret these passages in light of John's inspired text is to ignore clearer revelation. In these verses then, this makes the ordinarily stellar ESV's translation a travesty of interpretive justice.

Birds

While Sodom and Gomorrah are part of the metaphor used to describe the future judgment of Edom and Babylon, the other metaphor is wild desert creatures. These creatures can be divided into two kinds. The first are birds. The birds described are all "unclean" according to the law (see Lev 11:13-19). John noticed this as well in Revelation 18:2. There is no fundamental problem with the translation of the birds in the ESV in the previous verse that began the list—vs. 11. Hawks, owls, and ravens are perfectly acceptable translations. While various translations identify different birds here, the basic idea is that ravens, owls, vultures and other birds of prey will haunt the new desert wastelands. Here I want you to think back to the beginning of the chapter and take note of the Lilith (see picture above). See how owls are associated with her cult? The thing to note, then, is that from Merlin and his raven, to Lilith and her owls (or owls used in Harry Potter in contemporary use), unclean birds are often associated with *the underworld* and demonic entities.

Mythical Beasts

The second kinds of creatures are desert animals, including a couple that the ESV translates as birds (the "night bird" and "ostrich"), but the oldest translations most certainly do not. This is where we begin to run into problems with the ESV's entirely natural translation. We read about jackals, hyenas, wild goats, and the generic "wild animals." Now, it certainly fits the idea of desolation that these kinds of animals would accompany the unclean birds, for they too feed on dead carcasses in wild places. But there are serious objections to this interpretive decision, not the least of which is that it completely ignores Revelation 18:2, especially in light of the LXX and even certain words in the Hebrew!

The problem is that not one of the "animals" here has an uncontested translation *as a pure animal* (see the Table at the end of the chapter). To put that another way, across the board, the birds are all translated as birds (with the exception of the ostrich and night bird, see below). But the animals are called anything from dragons to satyrs and goat-demons, from devils to night monsters and monsters. Here we find "howlings" and centaurs and sirens in different translations.

These are the demons of Revelation. They are the kinds of beings that accompanied Tiamat in the Babylonian epic. These kinds of translations are also consistent with the way the Jews understood the words Isaiah uses. For example, 2 Baruch 10:8 uses many of the same words. It is translated, "I shall call the Sirens from the sea, and you, Lilin, come from the desert, and you, demons and dragons from the woods."[2] It is to these "animals" that I now wish to turn our attention.

Dragons and Sirens

After a list of four birds (Isa 34:11),[3] the first disputed animal as a supernatural entity is the "jackal." The Hebrew word is a *tan*. *Tan* is the root word for the *tannin*. This is a word sometimes associated with the devil. In Isaiah 51:9, for example, it is parallel with the monster Rahab. The ESV translates it very differently there, "Was it not you who cut Rahab in pieces, who pierced the *dragon*"? In Isaiah 27:1 it is parallel with the Leviathan and the Nachash (the word used for Satan in Genesis 3:1). The *tannin* is basically a monster who lives in the sea. The Greek usually translates it as *drakon* ("dragon"). It is therefore not a coincidence that modern and ancient translations render the ESV's "jackal" as a dragon, which as we have seen, the ESV itself does in other places.

The LXX gives *tannin* the curious translation of *sieren* here. According to the biblical dictionaries, *sieren* are "mythical sisters on the south coast of Italy, who enticed seamen by their songs, and then slew them."[4] We call them sirens. Sirens are properly depicted in movies such as *Harry Potter and the Goblet of Fire* and *Pirates of the Caribbean: On Stranger Tides*. These are not your "Little Mermaids!" And they don't just make a little "Splash!" They are man-destroying demon spawn who starve, drown, or perhaps even eat their victims.

We saw them in the 2 Baruch passage (above). Strangely, we find them appearing in 1 Enoch, where this is what the human wives of the watchers are cursed to become for their part in the otherworldly transgression of Genesis 6:1-4 that started this whole mess in the first place (1En 19:2). In the LXX of Micah 1:8 we read, "Therefore shall she lament and wail, she shall go barefooted, and being naked she shall make lamentation as that of serpents, and mourning as of the daughters of sirens [same Greek word as is found in the LXX of Isa 34:13 and 13:21]." In Jeremiah 27:39 LXX (50:39 English text) they appear in a very similar context to Isaiah. "Therefore shall idols dwell in the islands, and the young of monsters [sirens] shall dwell in it: it shall not be inhabited any more forever." That should give you a flavor for how Jewish interpreters understood the word. So, yes, incredibly, the Bible talks about sirens. I bet you didn't learn that in Sunday School.

As noted above, the LXX also renders the word *yaanah* in Isaiah 13:21 ("ostrich" in the ESV) as *sieren*. *Yaanah* is also found in Isa 34:13.

But here it translates *yaanah* as *strouthion* ("sparrow," or more likely "ostrich") rather than *sieren*. Why the difference? Perhaps it is because in 13:21 the word is prefixed with the strange phrase: *"daughters of* the ostrich." No one knows what a daughter of an ostrich might be, so most leave "daughter" untranslated. Given the context, it must have something to do with monsters (hence, the English translation of the LXX: "monsters"). Seeing it is a female monster that is in mind for the Jewish translators of the LXX, the sirens of mythology seem to fit nicely.

Apparitions and Phantoms

Verse 14 continues the strangeness. The ESV begins with a very tame translation: "wild animals." The Hebrew word is *tsiyiim*. According to one Bible dictionary, "The term is rather a collective designation for demonic desert beings (perhaps 'those that belong to the dry land'")." [5] This is reflected in the Latin Vulgates' *daimonia*. [6] The LXX renders no translation at all, though the same word is found (again) in 13:21 where it calls them *theron* ("wild beasts"). More curious is Jeremiah 50:39 (27:39 LXX), a passage with a similar grouping of animals at Babylon (including the daughters of the ostrich that was translated as sirens). It translates the same word with the fascinating word *indalma* which means "an appearance, form, or apparition." [7] In other words, it means a ghost or a phantom. Yes, the Bible actually talks about such things, and believes them to be real.

Demons, Devils, and Hairy Beasts

The next word in the ESV is the "hyena." Most English translations offer this or some related kind of an animal. The LXX however, gives the view of Jewish scholars before the coming of Christ. It calls them *daimonion*, "demons." [8] This is where John the Revelator (Rev 18:2) gets it. The Hebrew word is poetically related to the *tsiyyim*. The word is *'iyyim*. It is derived from "dog" or the Arabic "jackal" (note the animal translations of some versions: wolves, hyaenas, jackals) or from a word meaning "(ghostly) islander, beach demon, goblin ... The context is demonic." [9] The Douay–Rheims English translation of the Latin Vulgate calls the "monsters" (from *onocentauris*). What might they be?

Since the Babylonian Gilgamesh Epic and the story of Enkidu, people have been told tales of wild hairy men (we saw as much in the later tales of St. Christopher in Ch. 9). Created by the goddess Aruru, Enkidu was "shaggy with hair is his whole body" who lives with wild beasts outside the human population.[10] The story is repeated from culture to culture, across seas and oceans.[11] In keeping with the fabulous flavor of the ancient translation, one specific creature that comes to my mind is the werewolf or lycan.

In the Greek story of Lycaon—the earliest story of the werewolf (popularized in movies like *Underworld*)—Lycaon was the wicked king of Arcadia, who tested Zeus by serving him a dish of a slaughtered and dismembered child in order to see whether Zeus was truly omniscient. In his quest to test Zeus' immortality, Lycaon attempted to murder the god while he slept. In return for these gruesome deeds, Zeus transformed Lycaon into the form of a wolf, and killed Lycaon's fifty sons by lightning bolts. Do you remember what happened to Nebuchadnezzar, king of Babylon? He comes to resemble a lycan during his seven years of punishment by God (Dan 4:23, 33-34). Of course, I'm not saying that Nebuchadnezzar *became* a werewolf. I'm saying that the *idea* of werewolves is ancient, and werewolves were often viewed as demonic. Nebuchadnezzar is likened to a werewolf. Not a very flattering depiction of the king of the world, is it? A similar or perhaps even stranger occurrence of hairy men are the two *ariel* slain by Benaiah in 2 Sam 23:20. Translated "lionlike" by the KJV, some scholars have suggested that they may have been some kind of "mythical figure,"[12] which certainly fits the context of David's valiant warriors killing giants.

Isaiah's demonic context can be seen, not only in noticing the Greek translation and continuing the study of this passage, but by looking at the earlier passage in Isaiah 13 as well. In this text, all three words (*tan*, *tsiyyim*, and *iyyim*) also occur. The LXX translates the "beasts" in Isa 13:21 as "wild beasts," "howling," "monsters," and "devils" (*daimonion* this time translating the Hebrew word *sair*, see below). This all fits the broader context which uses fabulous language as it refers later to the fallen rephaim (variously translated as "shades" and "ghosts" [14:9]), the fall of "Lucifer" (14:12-15), and strange winged seraphim creatures that roam in the desert (14:29). Each adds to the historic fall predicted of this most ancient and pagan of cities in the world: Babylon, whose builder was Nimrod, a mighty giant of old.

Satyrs and Centaurs

The third word in Isaiah 34:14 (ESV) is "wild goat." Here, the ESV is breaking with most English translations by rendering the word as completely natural. Preternatural translations offer up the translation of "goat-demons," "satyrs," or "hairy ones." The LXX gives the translation: *onokentauros*. The Vulgate renders it as *pilosus* (hairy, shaggy, satyr). Look closely at that Greek word and see if you can identify anything from Greek mythology. The definition of this word in the lexicons is a, "Donkey-centaur, mythic creature (a *centaur* resembling a donkey rather than a horse)."[13] The English translation of the LXX renders this word as "satyr." The Hebrew word is *sairim* (remember Seir and Sair at the beginning of the chapter?). Again, the lexicons are clear. They are "wood demons, satyrs, resembling he-goats, inhabiting deserts, Isa 13:21; 34:14."[14]

There is a lot going on with this word which deserves a little more attention. First of all, it is related to the word for a goat associated with the Day of Atonement, where they would place the sins of Israel upon the goat and lead it into the desert to Azazel (see Lev 16). Azazel is the goat-demon. This Azazel has a strange history in Jewish tradition. He is said to have descended upon Mt. Hermon with the 200 Watchers when they viewed the daughters of men as beautiful and wanted to marry them.[15] There has been a shrine to Azazel in Banias, a cave at the foot of Mt. Hermon since time immemorial.[16] For ages it was referred to as Panias (Pan), but in 20 BC Herod Agrippa II built himself a shrine.[17] In Greek mythology, Pan is the demon-god of shepherds and flocks, of mountain wilds, hunting and rustic music. He is associated with the flute. His hindquarters, legs, and horns are those of a goat in the same manner as a faun or a satyr. I remember watching Pan appear on an old episode of *Buck Rogers*. A similar creature to Pan is, of course, to be seen in *Pan's Labyrinth*.

The associations we have already noted with Esau come back into play here in the strange Hebrew midrash called the Book of Jasher (*Sepir Ha Yasher*), not to be confused with a forgery Book of Jasher (Pseudo-Jasher) printed in 1751. Though written sometime long after the close of the NT, and not published until the early 17th century (scholars date it from 9th century on), it purports to tell history of the ancient biblical heroes otherwise unknown. In one story we have Zepho, the grandson of Esau, as the hero. "And Zepho went and he saw and behold there was a large cave at the bottom of the mountain, and there was a great stone there at the entrance of the cave, and Zepho split the stone and he came into the cave and he looked and behold, a large animal was devouring the ox; from *the middle upward it resembled a man, and from the middle downward it resembled an animal*, and Zepho rose up against the animal and slew it with his sword" (Jasher 61:15).

Next, the word for a goat is translated by the LXX as *chimaros* (male) or *chimaira* (female).[18] A *chimera* is "a fire-spouting-monster, with lion's head, serpent's tail, and goat's body, killed by Bellerophon."[19] The LXX does not seem to use the term *chimaros* in any supernatural terms, but *chimera* is today used as a catch-all for all of these strange half-breed creatures.

Though the term is not used supernaturally, perhaps the idea is. Azazel is said by the Jews to be judged by Messiah[20] and cast into the "abyss of complete condemnation," the "burning furnace."[21] Yet, he is said to also be *bound* in a place called Dudael,[22] which could very well be Mt. Hermon.[23] In other words, this goat-demon's end is similar to that of Satan, the one who also roams around like a roaring lion and who hissed wicked temptations at Eve as a serpent. Satan is depicted as a goat, lion, serpent. This is exactly what *chimera* is depicted as being. The idea of sacrificing a goat in the desert to Azazel is definitely wrapped up in God's world-view with the fall of Lucifer.

Finally, there is a word play going on between the satyr (*sairim*) and Edom (*seir*). Seir is another name for Edom (cf. Num 24:18), but refers more specifically to the (giant) Horite ancestor who populated the region there before Esau (Gen 36:20-21). The root of satyr means "hairy," and they are always depicted as hairy creatures. Esau, was of course a "hairy (*sair*) man" (Gen 27:11), who clothed himself in a hairy (*sear*) garment (Gen 25:25), and whose ancestors eventually dispossessed the giant Horites in the days of the Exodus (Deut 2:12). That's a lot of background for one little word, but it helps you see how the word transcends the natural realm, fitting the supernatural worldview of these verses in Isaiah.

FIG. 13.2. CHIMERA (LION, GOAT, SERPENT)

Lilith

The last word in Isaiah 34:14 (ESV) is "night bird." Again, there is discrepancy among the translations. Some refer to it as a "night-monster." The LXX gives the same *onokentauros* as it did for the *sairim* (see above). The Vulgate has *lamia*—a witch who sucks children's blood; in other words, a vampire (Moffatt's 1925 translation also has vampire)! Apparently, they couldn't think of a better word for this unique Hebrew word.

The Hebrew word is *lilith*. The word is similar to the word for "night" (*lilah/layla*). Yes, I'm sure that's where Eric Clapton got it from.

"Lilith" is used only here in the Scripture, but she has a fascinating history in later Jewish tradition like the 2 Baruch passage (above). The *Targum* (Pseudo-Jonathan) refers to Lilith in an addition to the Aaronic blessing, "May the Lord bless you in all your deeds and protect you from the Lilith" ('demons of the night,' Aramaic *lili*).[24] A Jewish *midrash* teaches that Lilith devours her own newborn children if she cannot find other newborn babies to eat.[25] The Talmud says, "It is forbidden to sleep in a room all alone and whoever sleeps in a room all alone—Lilith grabs him."[26]

Lilith was worshiped throughout the ancient near-east. At the beginning of this chapter, you saw a picture of her surrounded by owls. In Babylonian tradition she was associated with Ishtar who plants a tree, later hoping to cut it down and make a bed-throne for herself. But as the tree grows, a snake makes its nest at its roots, the Anzu-bird settles in the top, and in the trunk *lil-la* makes her lair.[27] Also, like the sirens, Lilith is also said to seduce men in order to kill them.

Lilith and the sirens both cause me to think of a third vampiric entity in the OT (sirens certainly have vampiric qualities and Lilith is literally called a vampire in the Latin). It is called the *aluqqah* and is found in Proverbs 30:15. Here is the ESV of this and the next verse. "The leech has two daughters: Give and Give. Three things are never satisfied; four never say, 'Enough': Sheol, the barren womb, the land never satisfied with water, and the fire that never says, 'Enough'" (Prov 30:15-16).

Nothing seems odd about this translation. To see the strangeness, we need to go to the Hebrew and Greek. *Aluqah* is the word for "leech." It is sometimes translated as a horse-leech. Note the blood-sucking idea associated with it. The BBE translation has "night-spirit." This is because it understands that in the ancient world, the aluqah was a vampire or ghoul, sometimes rendered as Jinn in other contexts. Jinn are Genies or the Muslim equivalent of Watchers.

The supernatural flavor of the passage is easily seen in the Greek where the next verse talks about Hades, the wife of Eros (her name is Psyche), Tartaros, and Ge (Gaia). While the English translates these words in the naturalistic sense (the grave, the love of a woman, the earth), it should be pointed out that these are the earliest gods of the Greek pantheon. The previous verses all speak about "the wicked generation" and the whole idea is that the wicked are, like demons and perhaps fallen gods, never satisfied and always doing evil.

Suggested Translation

As you can see, these two passages in Isaiah are far from the plain, natural world that is envisioned by the translators of the ESV. From the very earliest times, these texts were taken to incorporate both the natural world and the *super*natural world. Isaiah is not only saying that the end result of Babylon and Edom will be a desert waste, good for only unclean animals and birds. He is adding that God will give these places over to the demonic entities that roam around our planet, as Jesus said, looking for someplace to inhabit (Matt 12:43-45).

Therefore, if I were to be so bold as to offer a translation of Isaiah 13:20-22 it would be something like this, "Babylon will never be inhabited or lived in from generation to generation; nor will the Arab pitch his tent there, nor will shepherds make their flocks lie down there. But phantoms will crouch down there, and their houses will be full of howling, monsters will live there, and satyrs will dance there. Lycans will howl in fortified towers, and dragons in their pleasant palaces." Similarly, Isaiah 34:11-15 would read, "Hawks and owls shall possess Edom; Great owls and ravens shall dwell there. . . It shall be a home of dragons, an abode of monsters. Phantoms shall meet centaurs, satyrs shall greet each other; there also Lilith shall relax and find herself a resting place. The tree snake shall nest and lay eggs, and shall brood and hatch in its shade. There too the buzzards shall gather with one another."

Could It Be More Than Figurative?

If we recall again that much of the ancient world believed that the demons were the disembodied spirits of the giants who were destroyed in the flood, we can stay grounded to the purpose of our book, which is to think about the giants of old. But why might these creatures be depicted in the Bible?

Isaiah certainly could have just talked only about the generic "demons," and left it at that. But he didn't (neither did several other prophets like Micah and Jeremiah who employ the same terms). It is possible that he is simply utilizing well known mythology to make a scary point about the ruin of Babylon and Edom. Surely, this *is* at least part of what

Isaiah has in mind. But might he have thought there was something more to it than this? Could it have been the case that such creatures were literal, that he *really* believed they *really* existed? I think most Christians will at least admit they believe demons exist, even if they have no real understanding of what they are or what they do.

Traditions across the globe recall the same horrible beings as haunting their own cultures. They talk about giants participating in horrible acts relating to animals. As we have seen even in the Bible, bestiality, for instance, was absolutely forbidden to the Jews because this was the practice of the giants whom God was destroying from before them in Canaan (Lev 18:23-24). We have also looked at how Genesis 6:12 gives the cryptic phrase, "*all flesh* had corrupted their way on the earth," and that included the animal kingdom, which is why God not only destroyed human beings, but all other living creatures on the face of the earth. Could this corruption be more than moral (i.e. animals eating other animals or humans)? Then you have the repeated emphasis found almost exclusively in the creation and the flood on animals (and plants) created "according to their kind" (Gen 1:11; 12, 21, 23, 24, 6:19, 20, 7:14). Why so much obvious repetition about this? I've speculated it had to do with the Nephilim, but perhaps it also had to do with the animal kingdom.

I'm certainly not going to die on this hill but consider the idea that if they were not breeding with the animals (that seems genetically implausible), the sons of God were somehow involved in genetic manipulation of DNA, producing hideous offspring, even as human beings are tinkering with mixing animal DNA with our own for their misguided altruistic or nefarious and dastardly purposes today. I've raised this idea previously. Perhaps now is the best time of all to mention that the word *gigantes*—the Greek giants of Genesis 6:4—is derived from the word *gēgenēs* (see *DDD*, p. 24). *Gēgenēs* is a combination of *gēs* and *genes* or literally, "born from earth." Where this really becomes strange is when we realize that words like "genetics" and "genes" are guilt around the same root word.[28] This has, of course, led some to postulate a linguistic argument for the giants being genetically altered creatures.

Perhaps you are rolling your eyes right now. I wouldn't be completely offended. Yet, consider what is going on today in the real world of modern man and technology. There is a growing scientific movement known as *Transhumanism* which as Wikipedia states, "Affirms the possibility of fundamentally transforming the human condition by developing and making widely available technologies to eliminate aging and to greatly enhance human intellectual, physical, and psychological capacities." Among the ideas are ways of figuring out how, for example, the eyesight of an eagle might be given to a human being through genetic manipulation or crossing of DNA. Is transhumanism merely a platitude, pie-in-the-sky, science fiction?

Consider the following. In 1954, a mad Russian scientist named Vladimir Demikhov performed a successful head transplant, grafting the neck and head of one dog onto the upper torso of another dog?[29] From the 1970's – the 2000's, another scientist named Robert J. White performed Nazi-like experiments, transplanting heads of monkeys onto the bodies of other monkeys? It got to the point where they could live indefinitely, though no one has of yet figured out a way to overcome the paralysis that occurs from such an operation.[30] In 2003 Dr. Hui Zhen Sheng fused human cells with rabbit eggs.[31] In 2004, the Mayo Clinic successfully created pigs with human blood flowing through their bodies.[32] Then there was the bizarre creature that washed ashore on July 13, 2008 on Surfside Beach near Montauk, NY. The creature appeared to have raccoon claws, the beak of a bird, and the body of a dog. Was it a clever hoax or a genetic experiment gone mad? Even Snopes.com cannot determine the answer. OK, reading this comment ten years later I kind of cringe, but I'm keeping it in here because, why not? Coincidentally, there happens to be an "animal disease center" just down the road.

My brother has a good friend, well connected in the political world, who tells the following incredible personal story.

> My life as a professional spy has frequently placed me in a series of harrowing events, one after another. One such example was encountering an entire family of genetically-engineered creatures—or perhaps they were from a different dimension altogether. It was late at night in 1980. I had just been rescued by a colleague (the details of which are also incredible to relate. He drove as I was recovering, and we knew that assassins were on our tail because of the device I had taken from our enemies which was an early stage of the technology which causes the Havana Syndrome. We had been following a coastal road and were on our way

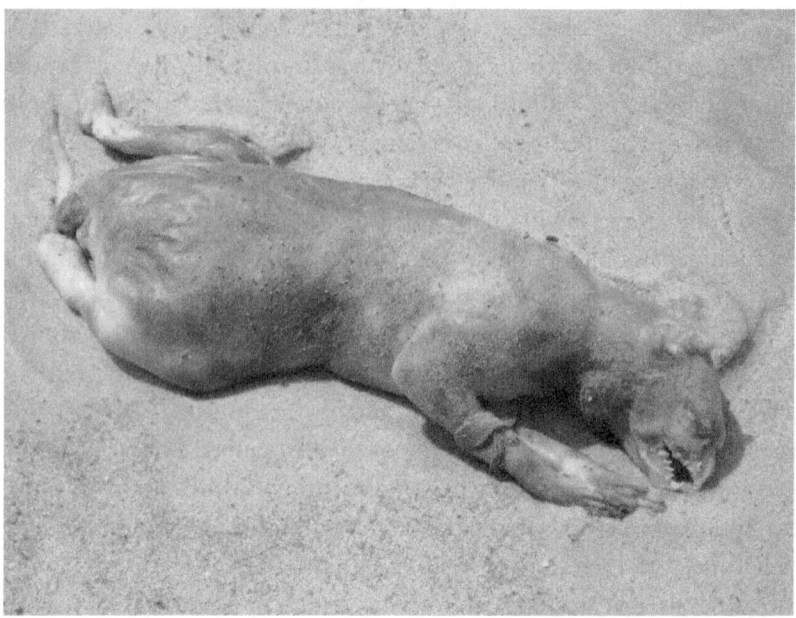

FIG. 13.3. MONTAUK MONSTER

to MIT on a highway which ran near the coast separating the mainland from Plum Island when one team of assassins caught up to us. Before we could react, a creature I can only describe as mixture between wolf, grizzly bear, and bull distracted our attackers. We shortly discovered that there was a family unit: father, mother, and child. As the parents left the child for dead, I took the body for analysis, since we were headed to MIT anyway. As it turned out, the baby was still alive. The DNA revealed by the testing was so unique we could not believe it came anywhere from Earth—it had two chains coiled around each other to form a double helix DNA strand that consisted in the bases of four organisms: Adenine-A, Cytosine-C, Guanine-G, and Thymine-T. I leave it to the reader to decide: extremely advanced DNA splicing in animal genetics; alien beings; or alien DNA spliced into that of terrestrial animals?[33]

It may seem like such an idea as ancient heavenly beings tinkering with human and animal DNA belongs to the world of science fiction, but the Island of Dr. Moreau is real today. Most states and even the nation have or are now passing laws prohibiting human-animal

Breanna Van Dorn, artist; in Julio Antonio del Marmol,
The Lightning and Montauk: Reality vs. Fiction (2021)

FIG. 13.4. THE DEL MARMOL MONSTER

hybridization,[34] not because congress has time to waste or couldn't get their daily fix of Star Trek (obviously, they waste their time in a lot of other ways), but because these are real concerns in the modern world.

In fact, in the last ten years, transhumanism has taken off exponentially. Dr. Thomas R. Horn (Ph.D. astronomy) has spent a lot of time researching and bringing to the public the many current projects that are taking place in labs and schools across our nation and world regarding genetic modification in plants, trees, animals, and humans. We have now created embryos with human and animal (mice and pig that we know about) DNA.[35] The evil scientist sociopath and right-hand man to megalomaniacal dictator wannabe Klaus Schwab, Yuval Noel Harari, openly and proudly boasts that humans are now hackable animals and the goal of such psychopaths is to create Human 2.0, a newly created species hybrid of human, tech, and A.I. that will truly boldly go where no man has gone before. Creating gods in man's image. What could go wrong?

Given that heavenly beings are much smarter than we are and have been around a *lot* longer than any human living today, why would we think that they were incapable of mixing the human genome with other DNA (be it with their own or some animal) in the past? Has a Darwinian worldview so shaped the mindset of Evangelicals that they are unable to entertain the thought that our ancestors, given supernatural help, may have actually been capable of such things? Has naturalism so infected us that we can no longer seriously entertain even the possibility that supernatural beings have interacted with humans in the past? We've seen the caduceus and the double helix. We have plenty of evidence from the Bible and other ancient cultures that such creatures could have been real.

As far as I know, little to nothing in the way of bones of centaurs, *minotaurs*, sirens, or satyrs have ever been found (though there have been reports of giant human skulls having horns).[36] The lack of proof is not proof of the lack. What I do know is this. Isaiah and the prophets employ highly charged mythological language to describe demon infested ruins of various places with roots deep in the giant legends of antiquity. The idea that the Bible speaks about centaurs, sirens, satyrs, werewolves, vampires, Lilith, and *chimeras* is worth taking the time to ponder.

Isaiah 34:12-13 and 13:21-22 Compared

Isaiah	Hebrew	LXX	LXX (trans)	VUL (trans)	Targum	YLT	NAS	ESV	KJV	JPS	TNK
34:11	qaath	ornov	birds	bittern	pelicans	pelican	pelican	hawk	cormorant	pelican	jackdaws
	qippod	echinos	hedgehog	ericius	porcupines	hedge-hog	hedgehog	porcupine	bittern	bittern	owls
	yanshuph	ibis	ibises	Ibis	owls	owl	owl	owl	owl	owl	great owls
	oreb	korak	ravens	raven	ravens	raven	raven	raven	raven	raven	ravens
34:13	tan	seiren	monsters	dragons	jackals	dragons	jackals	jackals	dragons	wild-dogs	jackals
	yaanah	strouthion	ostriches	ostriches	ostriches	ostriches	ostriches	ostriches	owls	ostriches	ostriches
34:14	tsiyyim	daimonion	devils	demons	wild beasts	Ziim	des. creatures	wild animals	wild beasts	wild-cats	wildcats
	'iyyim	ovokentauros	satyrs	monsters	cats	Aiim	wolves	hyenas	wild beasts	jackals	hyenas
	sair	onokentauros	satyrs	hairy ones	demons	goat	hairy goat	wild goat	satyr	satyr	goat-demon
	lilith			vampires	night hags	night-owl	night monster	night bird	screech owl	night-monster	lilith
34:15	qippoz	echinos	hedgehog	ericius	porcupine	bittern	tree snake	owl	great owl	arrowsnake	arrowsnake
	dayyah	elapos	deer	kites	kites	vulture	hawk	hawk	vulture	kite	buzzard
Isaiah	Hebrew	LXX	LXX (trans)	VUL (trans)	Targum	YLT	NAS	ESV	KJV	JPS	TNK
13:21	tsiyyim	theron	wild beasts	wild beasts	wild beasts	ziim	des. creatures	wild animals	wild beasts	wild-cats	beasts
	oach	echos	"howling"	dragons	howling creat.	howlings	owls	hyenas	doleful creat.	ferrets	owls
	yaanah	seiren	monsters	ostriches	ostriches	daut of ostrich	ostriches	ostriches	owls	ostriches	ostriches
	sair	daimonion	devils	hairy ones	demons	goats	shaggy goats	wild goats	satyrs	satyrs	goats
13:22	'iyyim	ovokentauros	satyrs	owls	cats	hyenas	hyenas	hyenas	wild beasts	jackals	jackals
	tan	echos	hedgehogs	sirens	jackals	jackals	jackals	jackals	dragons	wild-dogs	dragons

14

Jesus and the Demons

"What do you want with us, Son of God? ... Have you come
here to torture us before the appointed time"?
Matthew 8:29 (NIV)

Common Mistakes

W E ARE COMING NOW TO THE CLIMAX of our great battle between the two seeds. This will take place in two stages, the
already and the not yet. This and the next chapter deal with
the "already" (at least as far as we are concerned in the 21st century).
This, to me, is to the more important of the two, at least in terms of the
focus of our attention, since the second stage must remain to one degree
or another, speculative. I ask you, the reader, to take the time and ponder the content of these next two chapters.

There are two mistakes that people make when considering what
has happened in this war. One is to obsess. The other is to snub or over-
look. For at least the last couple of centuries, and to a large degree, ever
since Augustine and Chrysostom, the giants seem to have been lost in
the shuffle of cultural shifts and theological systems. People do not
seem to realize that there even were or are giants (in a present physical
form, we will deal with that in a later appendix), let alone know what
function they serve in the story of redemption. This also goes for their
present spiritual form: demons.

Most people have almost no knowledge about what demons are, and how to think properly about them. It is typical in more conservative traditions to never speak of demons (just like the giants). It is almost like a kind of superstition holds us in captivity, so that if we say anything about them, they may come and do mischief or worse. Many Christians are afraid to even bring up the topic or think that to do so is somehow dangerous, ungodly, or unbiblical. Ironically, superstition is often at the heart of those who obsess over demons too. So called "deliverance ministries" (I would not say these are all bad, but some certainly are) that see devils under every rock, and strange doctrines of tongues (to keep demons from understanding what people are saying), are the kinds of theological systems that develop when superstition and incorrect understanding of demons is at play. Each can get a person into spiritual trouble.

It is important to keep in mind that the giants were powerful, intelligent rulers of earth's remote (and perhaps not all that remote) history. If the early view is in fact correct, their spirits, when departed from the body, seem to continue to display the attributes the giants had while in the flesh. The NT has a lot to say about demons, much more than most people are comfortable acknowledging. We'll discover why in a moment.

Demons in the New Testament

For now, consider just a few things we learn about them in the pages of the NT (here we are going to focus on the narrower definition of a demon as an evil spirit and disembodied spirit of a nephilim as opposed to that broader usage that Paul and/or the LXX may or may not be using). 1. Demons love to inhabit or possess. This is not true of angels, because angels are heavenly beings that already have a kind of flesh (cf. 1 Cor 15:40-41) and can take on the appearance of human flesh without possessing a host.[1] This alone ought to tell you that angels and demons are different kinds of beings. If demons were the giants who lost their bodies, it makes sense that they would seek to regain some kind of physical existence, even if it is by proxy.

Jesus talks about this compulsive desire of demons to inhabit. "When the unclean spirit has gone out of a person, it passes through waterless places seeking rest, and finding none it says, 'I will return to my house from which I came.' And when it comes, it finds the house swept and put in order. Then it goes and brings seven other spirits more evil than itself, and they enter and dwell there" (Luke 11:24-26). As we saw with the demons and the desert in Isaiah, notice that Jesus says the demons love "waterless places." Is this because of what happened to them so long ago in the Flood?

This is a theme you find throughout Scripture and it spills over into the surrounding cultures. Think of the time when Jesus commanded an unclean spirit to come out of a man who had been "kept under guard and bound with chains and shackles, but he would break the bonds and be driven by the demon into the desert" (Luke 8:29). This story speaks about a second attribute of demons.

2. Demons are sometimes able to give their host great strength (cf. Mark 5:4). The book of Acts recalls a rather humorous story of seven itinerant Jewish exorcists (exorcism was practiced throughout the ancient world), sons of a Jewish high priest named Sceva, who took it upon themselves to invoke the name of the Lord Jesus over those who had evil spirits. They would say, "I adjure you by the Jesus whom Paul proclaims" (Acts 19:13). Suddenly, an evil spirit answered them and said, "Jesus I know, and Paul I recognize, but who are you"? (vs. 15). These men had never trusted in Christ, but merely used his name like a magic incantation. Then, without warning, "the man in whom was the evil spirit leaped on [the seven men], mastered all of them and overpowered them, so that they fled out of that house naked and wounded" (vs. 16). One might say this man possessed the strength of a giant. Maybe the expression isn't merely figurative.

3. Demons possess great knowledge and the ability to teach that knowledge to human beings, generally through human beings whom they inspire or possess. Paul teaches that in later times men will "devote themselves to deceitful spirits and teachings of demons" (1 Tim 4:1). The repeated warnings of false teachers (1 Cor 10:20-21; Col 2:18, 21; 2 Tim 3:13; 2 Pet 2:12; Jude 8, 12-13, etc.) implies that they are inspired by demons.

4. Demons have a kind of limited power to heal (or make sick). In Revelation 16:14 you have "demonic spirits" performing great signs, and this is in line with a host of verses that tell us about the "signs and

wonders" of antichrists, false prophets, and dreamers (Deut 13:1-2, Matt 24:24; 2 Thess 2:9, etc.). Perhaps a story with Jesus gets at this the best.

Jesus had been teaching the people in the temple at his home in Galilee. His teaching was so astonishing that they began to mutter, "How is it that this man has learning, when he has never studied"? (John 7:15). They began to accuse him of having a demon (vs. 20). Not only do they associate Jesus with a demon because of his knowledge of unknown origin (in many exorcisms, it is common to hear about the possessed having impossible knowledge of people and speaking in languages that otherwise do not know, usually Latin[2]), but because of his *miracles*. Jesus' reply to the accusation is, "I did one work, and you all marvel at it" (John 7:21). He is probably referring to his healing of the invalid at the strange pool of Bethesda in Jerusalem (John 5:2-7).[3] The point being, the people associated Jesus' healing with the work of a demon.

This is curious in light of the fact that the word rephaim comes from the root word *rapha*: "to heal." The LXX even translates two instances of the rephaim in Sheol as "healers" (Isa 26:14; Ps 88:11) and the Samaritan *Targum* translates the living giants of Deut 2:20 and 3:13 the same way. Because of these things, some scholars have argued that "by virtue of their connections with the netherworld, the [Rephaim were] healers *par excellence*."[4] Such is the mindset you enter when you move into the world of NT demonology.

Jesus vs. the Demons

For the remainder of this chapter, let's look at Jesus and the demons as we find it during his ministry in the Gospels. It is strange that "demon" (English) would be mentioned less than a handful of times in the entire OT, and of those it is possible that none refers to the spirits of the giants (as we've argued, words like rephaim and other specific demons do), but in the Gospels alone the word *daimonión* occurs 53x. Couple this with dozens of references to "spirits" and "evil spirits" in the Gospels and you get the sense that this is a major theme in the ministry of Jesus. But why? It is because Jesus' encounters with the demons are the climactic judicial blow to these ancient tormentors of mankind and enemies of God's people. Jesus vs. the demons is the NT equivalent of Israel vs. the giants. It is the beginning of the final battle, as it were, between Eve's Seed and the serpent's seed. In this battle, Jesus shows the demons his power, authority, and ultimate victory.

Jesus' Power over the Demons

The ancient world dealt with demons. Babylonians and Greeks, American Indians and Chinese, Jews and Christians all had their rituals for exorcizing these creatures. You've surely seen some movie where a Roman Catholic priest stands before a demon-possessed person with a book and some holy water. He then carefully and meticulously begins chanting the spells from the book in order to cast the demon out of the person. This often is a long, excruciating ordeal, as it was throughout the ancient world. Sometimes amulets, bowls, rings, or other talismans are used, such as in the case of the strange Jewish book the *Testament of Solomon* where the archangel Michael comes to Solomon with a magic ring whereby he begins to capture and bind demons to help him build the temple. Improbably, Josephus (*Antiquities* 8.2.5) reports on this same magic ring as having basis in real history. In all, you find spells, formulae, incantations, hymns, trinkets, elements (like water), and rituals being used in unison to expel the demons.

Not so with Jesus. Perhaps the most remarkable thing about Jesus' ministry in relation to demons is his power to cast out spirits "with a word" (Matt 8:16). In stark contrast to other exorcists, including even the Disciples (Mark 9:28), it appears as if nothing could be easier for Jesus than to exorcize a demon. And this is exactly what Jesus did. One of the first things we learn about the ministry of Jesus is how he would heal those "oppressed by demons" (Matt 4:24). In fact, it appears that he did this almost everywhere he went.[5]

Jesus' Authority over the Demons

The power that Jesus exercised (and exorcized) over demons was directly related to the authority that he had over them. This was an authority that they instantly recognized and were unable to overcome. The title "Son of God" (there's that idea again ... the son of God; only this son is the Only Begotten Son of the Father, the Creator of all other life in the universe) is most often used on the lips ... *of demons* (Mark 1:24; 3:11; Luke 4:34, etc.). They knew his mission (Mark 5:7) and they knew they had an appointed time to finally perish at his hands (Matt 8:31).

One of the more famous episodes is the story of Legion ("many demons") when Jesus came to the country of the Gerasenes (see Mark 5:1-13). As soon as Jesus steps off the boat, a man who lived in the tombs who had an unclean spirit came upon him. He was exceedingly strong so that not even chains could bind him. He was constantly crying out and cutting himself with stones. But as soon as he saw Jesus, he came running over to him, fell down before him, and yelled, "What have you to do with me, Jesus, Son of the Most High God?" He then laid an oath upon Jesus saying, "I adjure you by God, do not torment me," because Jesus had already begun commanding the demon to come out of the man.

The demon pleaded with Jesus, who asked him his name and it replied, "My name is Legion, for we are many" (Mark 5:9). Then it strangely says, "He begged him earnestly not to send them out of the country" (vs. 10). As the demon(s) quickly scanned the landscape, it spotted a herd of pigs and begged the Lord to be cast into them. "Jesus gave them permission" (vs. 13). Instantly, the herd numbering 2,000(!) rushed down the steep bank and were drowned in the sea.[6] This is a remarkable and funny story, not the least reason being that they ended up being cast out of the pigs (when they died). That Jesus would send them into the pigs knowing that this was someone's livelihood is also fascinating, especially since the townspeople apparently gather to go reproach him, but when they see what has happened all they can do is tell him to get away from them because he is so powerful.

But we can look deeper than this. There are a couple of strange "coincidences" here. First, this incident "just so happens" to have the most demons *by far* of any story in the Bible. These demons "just so happen" to be indwelling this man in the home and epicenter of the ancient giants of the OT—the very place where so many were destroyed in the days of Joshua. This was the old stomping ground of Og and the Amorites. Second, the man is hanging out in the tombs, and this region of Bashan is littered with perhaps more dolmans (megalithic tombs) than any place on earth (see Fig. 8.4). With Jesus' exorcism, it's as if they now have to live out the terrors endured by their older brothers in the days of Noah (assuming that these are not those more primeval giants).

No more dry places. No more habitation. Only suffering under the waters, down to Sheol, where they joined their brothers of old.

Third, this general area on the east side of the Sea of Galilee is the most probable location for the baptism of Jesus. John 1:28 tells us that John the Baptist was baptizing "in Bethany across the Jordan." Since the times of Origen (184-254 AD), there has been vigorous debate over this location, because he traveled to the area and could find no such place called Bethany on the east side of the Jordan (the Bethany where Jesus raised Lazarus is right near Jerusalem). Hence the question, where is this place?

Many proposals have been suggested. The one defended by most scholars today—following old *Targum* spellings of the area and the necessity of a location being in the north given the geographical locations in the story and the short time span for these events to occur—is that "Bethany" refers not to a town, but to a region: Bashan (or Bathan).[7] If Jesus was baptized in Bashan on the east side of the Jordan, north and east of Sea of Galilee, then he symbolically came out of the same water in which the demons would later drown. Even earlier symbolism would be apparent, that he came out of the water ordeal *alive*, whereas the original Nephilim *perished* in the Flood. The fact that his baptism could very well have been very near to the place where this Legion of demons was located would also explain how they knew who he was (demons are not all knowing). Perhaps they saw the same thing John saw at Jesus baptism, when the Spirit descended upon him and the Father spoke of his great pleasure in his beloved Son.

Jesus' authority is seen in other instances as well. One time, demons came out of a certain man crying, "You are the Son of God!" but he rebuked them "and would not allow them to speak, because they knew that he was the Christ" (Luke 4:41). Often times Jesus would not permit the demons to speak any longer (cf. Mark 1:24-25; 34; 3:11-12, etc.). You see, what the demons understood was that the Seed of the woman had come down to earth out of heaven and was born now as a man, as the second Adam. This meant he had come to fulfil the promise, and reclaim the authority abdicated so long before by Adam. This, then, would be the beginning of the end for the demons, and so they worked overtime trying to figure out a way to stop him.

But everywhere Jesus went, he proved they were no match—all while the people kept accusing him of having a demon. Perhaps you remember a time when Jesus had cast out a demon that was making a man mute. All the people marveled, but some of them accused him of casting out the demon by the power of Beelzebub (Luke 11:14-20). Beelzebub is "the prince of demons" and it is probably a title given to Satan himself. Jesus explained that if Satan cast out demons, his kingdom would be divided and could not stand. Such an idea was ludicrous. But instead, Jesus' authority over demons meant that he had ushered in a new kingdom (vs. 20), one over which Satan exercised no authority or dominion.

In this new kingdom, those who had lost authority over Satan and his seed could now reclaim it; not by force, nor by will, but by the grace, power, and authority of Jesus Christ. One of the most important of all the stories regarding demons is when Jesus sends out his seventy[8] disciples and commands them to go before him into every town and place where he was about to go (Luke 10:1). They would be "lambs in the midst of wolves" (vs. 3), a reference, no doubt, to both human and non-human intelligences residing in those places. They could bring "peace" to a house (vv. 5-6) or curses (vv. 11-12), depending upon the reception they received.

What so astonished the disciples is that when they returned to him they said, "Lord, even the demons are subject to us in your name!" (vs. 17). Jesus then tells them, "I saw Satan fall like lightning from heaven" (vs. 18). This is not a reference to the original fall of Satan (what would be the point of mentioning that?), but to his human-earthly battle with the devil in the wilderness temptation. That is, Jesus is talking about a time in the not too distant past when he battled the devil and overcame him, thus securing the fall of Satan's kingdom and the rising up of his own. As he says in another place, I have bound the strongman (who is also called Beelzebub; Matt 12:29). "Now the ruler/prince of this world will be cast out" (John 12:31). "He is judged" (John 16:11).

The next verse mentions a strange group of creatures called scorpions. Jesus explains, "Behold, I have given you authority to tread on serpents and scorpions, and over all the power of the enemy, and nothing shall hurt you" (vs. 19). People have yanked this passage out of context (along with Mark 16:17-18), and all sorts of bizarre serpent cults have sprung up in the exegetical wasteland. It is clear, however, when you understand the cultural background that serpents and scorpions refer to spiritual entities.

Look at the words in the surrounding verses: demons (vs. 17), Satan (vs. 18), spirits (vs. 20). Crawling, slithering animals hardly fits that context. Jesus is not giving the disciples power to be Pied Pipers over rodents and reptiles, except without flutes (interestingly, in the legend of St. Patrick, he goes to Ireland and rids the Emerald Isle of its serpents, a reference not to snakes, but demons; that is, he came with the gospel of Jesus Christ and the powers of darkness fled). The connection of serpents and scorpions probably originates in Deuteronomy 8:15 where God "led you through the great and terrifying wilderness, with its fiery *serpents and scorpions* and thirsty ground where there was no water." In apocalyptic literature, scorpions are given power over the earth (Rev 9:3).

In the Babylonian *Epic of Gilgamesh*, "Scorpion-Beings" act as shedu (demonic guardians) of the Netherworld, and they protect the "assembly of the gods": (*Gilgamesh*, Tablet 9). Then there is the Phoenician god Šadrafa (whose name contains the word *'rafa*) who is likewise a guardian of the underworld.[9] In Jewish literature you have "the guardians of

Šadrafa, Palmyra, Syria, 55AD

FIG. 14.1. SCORPION MAN

the keys of hell, standing by the very large doors, their faces like those of very large snakes."[10] Serpents and scorpions guarding the doors of hell? Its sounds very much like the Rephaim who "greet" the kings down in Sheol.

In a world filled with snake handling cults, such bizarre practices are not primarily (if even secondarily) what Jesus has in mind. He is speaking about overcoming the devil and his minions ("the helpers of Rahab"). This overcoming is first the authority to cast out demons from the demonized. It is not *our* authority, but Christ's; and as the sons of Sceva learned, if you do not have Christ, you do not have the authority of Christ. Also, it is dangerous business to get involved in this kind of a thing. At one point in time, even the disciples came back to Jesus and wondered why they could not cast out a certain demon. Jesus said, "This kind only comes out with prayer" (Mark 9:29).

This authority over demons and the hordes of hell is pronounced in no more powerful way than by Jesus at the foot of Mt. Hermon in that now familiar place called Banias or Caesarea Philippi. Here, where the Watchers of tradition literally came down to earth, Jesus tells Peter (*petros*—The Rock), "On this rock (*petra*) I will build my church, and the gates of hell shall not prevail against it" (Matt 16:18). How much ink has been spilt debating the question of whether or not Jesus is calling Peter the first Pope here? While that question is important, and I take the Protestant position that in one sense "the rock" Jesus refers to is Peter's confession, another rock is almost always overlooked. That rock is quite literally Mt. Hermon. Jesus is saying in a powerful way that here, at epicenter and origin of the Giant Wars, where fallen Watchers left their positions of authority in heavenly places and came down to earth, here is where Jesus will begin to build his church, and those very same gates will be powerless to stop him.[11] Is it a coincidence that immediately after this, Jesus is transfigured (probably at Mt. Hermon) and then he heals a boy possessed by an evil spirit (Mark 9:17-30)?[12]

Ours is certainly not a book on demonology or a how-to manual for casting out demons. I bring these things up only because they show you the power and authority that Christ displayed over these ancient beings in his ministry on the earth. But as I said, the forces of evil were working double shifts trying to figure out a way to stop Christ from gaining the final victory over them. This is what they thought they had accomplished when they put him to death.

15

Victory

*[Christ] went and proclaimed to the spirits in prison, be-
cause they formerly did not obey, when God's patience
waited in the days of Noah.*

1 Peter 3:19-20

Christ's Death and the Victory

Bulls of Bashan

ONE OF THE MOST QUOTED PSALMS in the New Testament is Psalm
22 which begins, "My God, my God, why have you forsaken me?"
These words and several more passages from this Psalm are
quoted or alluded to throughout Jesus' ordeal at Calvary.[1] I believe this
includes Psalm 22:12, "Many bulls encompass me; strong bulls of Bashan surround me." Knowing now that Bashan is Grand Central Station
for ancient giants, "bulls of Bashan" takes on a richer meaning. In this
chapter, we are going to look at Christ's death, descent, and resurrection
in light of the giants and the victory he achieved over them.

It is clearly the case, in the prophecy-fulfillment of the Gospels, that
the bulls of Bashan are viewed as human beings. I submit that in Matthew's reconstruction of the event, he has in mind "the whole battalion"

of Roman soldiers that gathered around Jesus during the mock trial (Matt 27:27). But it is also the case in biblical theology that behind humans there often stand satanic and demonic forces. One thinks, for instance, of David numbering his fighting men (2 Sam 24:1), but also of Satan inciting him to do it (1 Chron 21:1); or of Judas betraying the Lord (Luke 22:48) but Satan entering into him (Luke 22:3); or of Peter denying Christ (John 13:38) but Satan asking to sift him like wheat (Luke 22:31). In the case of the bulls of Bashan, a few scholars have suggested that these are demonic hordes that aligned themselves against Christ.[2] It is certainly a plausible idea, given the demonic geography of Bashan.

Goliath and Golgotha

If this is true, then Jesus' crucifixion has direct bearing upon them. The thing is, at just the point the demons thought they had defeated Christ—surrounding him, mocking him, inspiring men to put him to death—he surprised them and gained the decisive victory. Christ's death was not, ultimately speaking, the doing of men or demons, but God. "It was the will of the LORD to crush him" (Isa 53:10). "Both Herod and Pontius Pilate, along with the Gentiles and the peoples of Israel" did whatever God's hand and plan "had predestined to take place" (Acts 4:27). Apparently, the demons had misread the Scriptures as badly as the Jews and even Jesus' own Disciples who did not understand that Messiah must be put to death in order to win the war. "You will bruise his heel," God had told the serpent (Gen 3:15). Did that really mean he must die in the process?

There is a fascinating possibility surrounding the place that Jesus was put to death that has direct bearing on the giants. In fact, it is on one particular giant, one we have already seen. His name is Goliath. We must remember that this story has as its ultimate context the king of Israel beginning the last stages of the physical reclamation project of Israel from the giants. It is no accident that David will become the king after he slays Goliath. That story typifies the Great King to come.

There are traditions about what happened after David lopped off the behemoth's head (1Sam 17:51) with the giant's own sword. We know that David eventually retained the sword (1Sam 21:9; 22:10). But what happened to the head? 1 Samuel tells us that he took the head of the Philistine and "brought it to Jerusalem" (17:54). What happened to it then? Where exactly did he put it? Did he keep it in a collection in some trophy room? Where did it go?

Recall that Jesus was crucified at a place called "Golgotha" (Matt 27:33; Mark 15:22; John 19:17). Golgotha is an Aramaic term, and so the Gospels tells us it's meaning: "Place of the Skull." You can go today just outside old city Jerusalem to a place called Skull Hill. Right around the corner there is a little Evangelical owned spot called the Garden Tomb. Now, thankfully, the folks there do not say dogmatically that they believe Jesus was buried here (there is virtually no reason to think he was). However, the location of its ancient tomb so close to this Skull Hill makes for a wonderful trip when visiting, to see what the place might have looked like prior to 2,000 years' worth of churches being built on top of it.

Because there is a hill that does (or rather, did until recently) re-semble a skull, many people believe that this is what Golgotha must have been named after—a geographical feature. However, this is most likely not the case. Others have suggested that because the summit of any hill could be called a *rosh* (head) in Hebrew, that maybe this is all it

FIG. 15.1. SKULL HILL, JERUSALEM

refers to. But that doesn't make any sense, because then every hill in Israel would be known as Skull Hill. Instead, we might ask another question. "Whose skull?"

Early Church Fathers, following even older Jewish traditions, had heard and/or believed that Adam was buried on Golgotha. Therefore, the skull must have been his. Jerome said, "I have heard Calvary expounded as the spot in which Adam was buried, as though it had been so called from the head of the old man being buried there. A plausible interpretation, and agreeable to the ears of the people, yet not a true one."[3] A much better option is that it was the head of Goliath. Here's how it works.

It begins by understanding something in Jeremiah 31:39, which speaks of a place near Jerusalem called "Goata" (variously translated as Goah or Goatha; or literally *g'th*). The LXX translates this as "choice stones" (GK: *eklekton lithon*). It translates a different Hebrew phrase in Ezra 5:8 with the exact same two Greek words. In Hebrew those words are "stones of Gelal" (*eben gelal* or literally: stones, huge stone). This huge stone with no vowels is simply *gll*. So *gll* and *g'th* may be the same thought/place. But *gll* also happens to be the root form of *a skull* (which is *glglt*; see the wiki on "Calvary"). Goliath is *glyt*. He is from Gath which is simply *gt*. Golgotha (which is Aramaic) is *gglt*.

The idea is that when David brought the skull to Jerusalem, the place where it was put was then called "Mount Goliath" (*gl glyt; gl* or *gol* is the Aramaic for a mountain), or "heap of Goliath" (the Hebrew *gl* or *gal* means a "heap," meaning that they placed a heap of stones as a memorial of David's victory over the giant). Over time, this begins to get confused with "choice stones," that is Ezra's *gll* and Jeremiah's *g'th*. But they are all talking about the same place so that in the NT it becomes Golgotha (*glgtha*), the place of the skull. Whose skull? Goliath's.[4] Warren Gage summarizes, "While Golgotha is derived from the Hebrew word for skull, this Aramaic name resonates with vocalic sounds reminiscent of the name of Goliath of Gath. Indeed, Golgotha and Goliath of Gath have a similar sound. David, we are told, was a prophet (Acts 2:29–30). The text reporting David's delivery of the head of the giant to Jerusalem seems to have seen in David's triumph over Goliath an even greater triumph of the Son of David that was to come."[5]

Of course, if Goliath is a Rephaim (as we've seen that he is), then at the very least, this spot, chosen in eternity past for the site of Jesus' death, is a symbolic crushing of the head of the spawn of the serpent. Jesus is treading on the demons, even as he hangs on a cross.

1 Peter 3:19 and Christ's Descent and the Proclamation of Victory

Questions on 1 Peter 3:19

Let's now turn to one of the most significant verses in the Bible for understanding Christ's victory over the giants as we think about Christ's "descent into hell." It is a verse found in 1 Peter 3:19-20, "[Christ] went and proclaimed to the spirits in prison." In one way, this verse brings us full circle. Just like Genesis 6:4, the meaning of this passage is disputed among scholars and laymen alike. This may be because the passage is difficult, and surely it is. It could also be, for reasons we've also see in the Genesis counterpart, that the text is controversial and some people simply don't like what it says. Dr. Heiser once told me a story of visiting a church in the Seattle area to which they had just moved. He was excited, because the subject of the sermon was 1 Peter 3. But when the time came to preach about these verses, the pastor promptly just skipped right over them, a lot like people do today with the Nephilim, as if they weren't even there. With his palm in his face, his wife leans over to him and whispers, "We aren't coming back, are we?" She knew the answer. Tough, controversial, and especially inexplicable is no reason to ever skip over God's word.

To understand our verse properly, we need to read the verse preceding and following.

> [18] For Christ also suffered once for sins, the righteous for the unrighteous, that he might bring us to God, being put to death in the flesh but made alive in the spirit, [19] in which he went and proclaimed to the spirits in prison, [20] because they formerly did not obey, when God's patience waited in the days of Noah, while the ark was being prepared, in which a few, that is, eight persons, were brought safely through water."

There are basically four issues that must be addressed in verse 19.

1. To what does the "in which" (at the beginning of vs. 19) refer?
2. Who are these "spirits"?

3. What was the nature of the proclamation?
4. Where was this proclamation made?

Views of 1 Peter 3:19

Before we look at this verse in more detail, I'll give you my view. It has changed a little in the last ten years. I previously said, following the excellent treatment of this passage by Ramsey Michaels in the Word Biblical Commentary,[6] this verse refers to *Christ, proclaiming to demonic spirits, in his new spiritual body, a message of their defeat, wherever they might be.* I've since modified my view to include proclamation to the fallen Watchers imprisoned at the time of the Flood (see Appendix 2), for in places like 1 Enoch and Jubilees, they are called "spirits" (cf. 1En 15:4; Jub 15:31-32).

According to other Scripture, Christ did this during this three-day descent into hell found in passages like Psalm 24's, "Lift up your heads, O gates! And be lifted up, O ancient doors, that the King of glory may come in. Who is this King of glory? The LORD, strong and mighty, the LORD, mighty in battle!" (Ps 24:7-8). Notice, the LORD is coming to the gates to do battle. What gates? The gates of hell (Matt 16:18). It is also found in Psalm 68, referenced in Ephesians 4:8 which says, "Therefore it says, 'When he ascended on high, he led a host of captives, and he gave gifts to men.' (In saying, 'He ascended,' what does it mean but that he had also descended into the lower regions of the earth?)" (Eph 4:8-9). This is a quote from Psalm 68:18, "You ascended on high, leading a host of captives in your train and receiving gifts among men, even among the rebellious, that the LORD God may dwell there."[7]

You will immediately notice there is a big difference in Paul's quotation. The Psalm says the Lord *"received"* gifts "among" men. The Apostle says he *"gave" gifts* "to" men. Does Paul not know his OT? Of course he does. Is this a quote taken badly out of context? Absolutely not. So what is going on? This summary of Ephesians is helpful to understanding Paul's intention:

> Paul's description of God's powerful work on behalf of his Gentile readers in 2:11–22 led him in 3:1–21 to pray that God would give them the power to grasp "the breadth and length and height and depth … of the love of Christ" (3:18–19). This prayer included … Paul's divine commission "to preach to the Gentiles the unfathomable wealth of

Christ" (3:8) and to illumine all people about the mystery that Gentiles and Jews who believe in Christ are one body (3:3–9) ... Paul [then] says that ... Unity and peace should therefore characterize God's ... church (4:1–6).[8]

This is the context into which giving gifts to men arises. Importantly, these gifts are not "things" such as "helps" or "prophecy" or "faith" as they are in a place like 1 Corinthians 12. Rather, these gifts are *people* (prophets, evangelists, shepherds, and teachers; vs. 11). These people-gifts are to help the Ephesians understand better God's incredible power and love and the unfathomable wealth they have in Jesus Christ. He is able to give anything he desires to his people. Where did they come from? How are these people-gifts "gotten" by God to then be distributed among the churches? This is the amazing part. And it is all about their salvation. But how? Through the war described in Psalm 68 which harkens all the way back to Genesis 3:15.

While this Psalm deals with Mt. Hermon (Ps 68:15, 22) and fallen angelic creatures such as Baal and/or Satan, I'm only going to focus on that which is most closely related to our storyline of the giants as we stand here near the end of our book.[9]

The Psalm is "to the Choirmaster" or "For the End" (LXX). The LXX's translation has in mind a prophetic timeline. In this case, it is very much related to the works of Jesus between his death and resurrection, for like Psalm 24, Psalm 68 also a military psalm of conquest and victory.

Looking at the relevant portions, many have observed that Psalm 68:18 is similar in theme to Deborah's Song when it sings, "Awake, awake, Deborah! Awake, awake, break out in a song! Arise, Barak, *lead away your captives*, O son of Abinoam" (Jdg 5:12).[10] So somehow the Psalm verse is harkening back to this great victory and leading captives away in the days of Deborah.

To help us understand this better, we can note that the entire Psalm is a chiasm (a form of literature that parallels itself to a center in an ABCBA format). The parallel on the other side of this verse is, "But God will strike the heads of his enemies, the hairy crown of him who walks in his guilty ways" (Ps 68:21). You may not see a parallel, until you realize that this language also comes from Deborah's song. "She

sent her hand to the tent peg and her right hand to the workmen's mal-
let; she struck Sisera; *she crushed his head*; she shattered and pierced his
temple" (Jdg 5:26). The parallel between Psalm 68:18 and 21 is not linguistic, but conceptual. Both use of the victory in Deborah's song to
illuminate a greater victory sung about in the Psalm. It is a victory won
by Jesus. It is a crushing of the head of the serpent through the imagery
of the "hairy" head, where "hairy" [*sear*] is a word perhaps deliberately
chosen to remind one of Satyrs (*sairim*) like Pan.

We looked at the satyrs in the previous chapter. Eaton comments
on this, "The hairy crown may allude to the warrior's practice of leaving
the hair uncut, while also hinting at the demonic character of the enemy
(sair) ... none of his monstrous allies are suffered to escape; though they
seek refuge in the heights of Bashan or the depths of the sea."[11] So these
psalms establish that in fact Jesus did descend to hell and that while
there, he fought a mighty battle and won. With that, we can turn back
to 1 Peter 3.

In the history of interpretation on this verse, probably the most
popular recent view has been that Christ in his pre-incarnate state,
through Noah, preached to Noah's contemporaries who were alive before the flood. It is a mostly naturalistic interpretation consistent with
the demythologization we've seen with other texts in our study, since
few want to say that the preacher was Christ himself (as the Angel of
the LORD). Another view has been that Christ preached to the souls of
Noah's contemporaries dwelling in the lower world (Sheol) while he
was in the grave before his resurrection. This now moves us into the
descent into hell (found in the Apostle's Creed), but keeps the hearers
perfectly human. Another view, which I have now subsumed under my
own is that Christ preached to the fallen angels in Tartarus (see 2 Pet
2:4; Jude 6) that he defeated them at the cross.[12]

I'm presenting a fourth view, not incompatible with the third and
even the second (though Peter does not have this in mind), which is
certainly not a novel view. In each case above, the nature of the proclamation is all over the map. Some think Christ preached *salvation* in the
first two categories. Some think that Christ only preached salvation to
those who were converted. Others think there was a sort of *second chance
in Sheol* for those who perished in the Flood. Some think Christ proclaimed *condemnation* to these people. Certainly, those taking the

angelic view think the message was one of *judgment* not salvation. The point is, this has been a rather messy passage in church history. For that reason, I certainly do not hang my entire argument upon this single verse of the Bible. If one of these interpretations happens to be the correct view, it does little to change anything we've said in this book. Christ still has the victory, whether Peter talks about it or not.

If the interpretation I present here is correct, however, it means that Christ made a definitive proclamation to the spirits of the giants long ago imprisoned (Jub 10:9, see below) that he now has won the final victory, that the promise given to Eve has been fulfilled, that victory is secure, that he is bringing new citizens into their lands (think about Canaan, the giants, and the conquest), that their time is short, and that they no longer have any authority over anyone that he chooses to bring out of their kingdom and into his own blessed eternal realm. This is a powerful message indeed. It is a reversal of all of redemptive history outside of the nation of Israel, as these beings (along with the sons of God) did have a certain authority to keep the world in darkness, though they did so in rebellion against God. They did have authority over those in their kingdoms. God did not have a *legal* right to take anyone out of their realm (due to his own legal promise to these entities in ancient times past), unless that person transferred allegiance to the nation of Israel. This becomes the whole impetus for the evangelism of the nations, for Paul's proclamation to Gentiles that "today is the day of salvation" (2 Cor 6:2) or that "now God commands all people everywhere to repent" (Acts 17:30).

Proclamation of Victory to the Lystrian Galatians

A particularly interesting combination of these two ideas is found in the people of Lystra in Galatia (Acts 14:8-19) who believed for some reason that Barnabas was Zeus and that Paul was Hermes (Acts 14:12). Why? I think you will enjoy this little excursion.

Galatia is today's modern Turkey. It has a particularly eerie relationship to the giants. It is home to the oldest ceremonial centers known to exist: Göbekli Tepe and Karahan Tepe. It is the more ancient home of the peoples known as the Celts, or their lesser known name, the Gauls. (We normally think of the Celts as being Irish, but Gaul is an

FIG. 15.2. GÖBEKLI TEPE

ancient term that describes France, Luxembourg, Belgium, most of Switzerland, the western part of Northern Italy, and parts of the Netherlands and Germany on the west bank of the Rhine.)[13] "Gaul" is thought by some to derive from a word meaning "powerful."[14] Others suggest that "Celt" and "Gaul" have the same meaning, something like "potent" and "valiant men."[15] Why might they have been so powerful?

Many ancient historians tell us that these Gauls, and especially their princes, were giants. The early 18th Century historian Paul Pezron says these Gauls "exceeded all others in bulk and strength of body; and hence it is that they have been looked upon to be terrible people, and as it were Giants."[16] For example, the Roman historian Julias Florus (2nd Century A.D.) describes one Teutobocchus (a blue eyed, yellow haired Gaul king) as "a man of extraordinary stature" who used to "vault over four or six horses at once" but "could scarcely mount one when he fled." When captured he "was seen above all the trophies or spoils of the enemies, which were carried upon the tops of spears."[17] The Greek historian Polybius (200 – 188 B.C.) laments that thanks to the Celts, the Roman legionaries had become super fighting machines. "Once they had got used to being struck down by Gauls they were incapable of imagining anything worse."[18] This was eventually very bad news for the Greeks. Some of the largest giant remains of the medieval period come from this region.

The Celts across the Rhine were called Germani (*germani* meant "true Celts" according to Strabo [63 B.C. – 24 A.D.; *Geography of Strabo* 7.1.2.]). The Christian historian Hegesippus (110 – 180 A.D.) wrote that the Germans "are superior to other nations by the largeness of their bodies and their contempt of death."[19] The Roman Vegetius (4th – 5th Cent. A.D.) wrote, "What could our undersized men have done against the tall Germans"? Columella (4 – 70 A.D.) says, "Nature has made Germany remarkable for armies of very tall men."[20] Sidonius Apollinaris (430 – 489 A.D.) reports that so many of the people were seven feet tall and up that he could not address them properly.[21] Augustine reports of a German (Goth) woman being paraded around the streets of Rome who "by her gigantic size over-topped all others."[22] As late as the 1500s, a German by the name of Aymon grew to 11 feet tall. The famed Baron Bentenrieder—who was himself eight feet eight inches—"hardly reached up to Arymon's armpits."[23] Still another named Hans Braw was estimated at 12 feet 8 inches tall.[24] So fierce were these Germans that, "The Gauls," reports Julius Caesar (100 – 15 B.C.), "had not been able to endure even the expression on their faces or the glare of their eyes."[25] The Romans called them "Berserkers," and for decades the greatest army on earth was continually slaughtered by these giants in war (and people wonder where Hitler got the idea of a "super-race." He knew the history of these people and he wanted to reclaim it for himself, curiously, through scientific experiments, DNA manipulation, and the like).[26]

Josephus (37 – 100 A.D.), the Jewish historian, relates that Magog, the brother of Gomer and grandson of Noah, was the ancestor of these people.[27] He believed that Gomer settled in Galatia. "Gomer founded those whom the Greeks now call Galatians [Galls], but were then called Gomerites."[28] The name Gomer in *Akkadian* is Gimirru (they called them Gimmerai). Europeans called them Cimmerians or Cimbri. Many of these Cimbri migrated out of Galatia, north and west into Gaul, and became the Celts.

During the centuries long wars with the up and coming Romans (3rd – 1st centuries B.C.), these Celts began to leave Gaul *en masse* (many had undoubtedly continued past Gaul in earlier times). Some went north into Britannia, and there is evidence to suggest some migrated into North America, where they became the tall blonde/red-haired, white-skinned giants sometimes associated with the mysterious Mound-Builders[29] of Ohio (see Appendix: Giants in the Americas). Curiously, Galatia takes its name from the Gauls (Celts). It comes from a Greek word (*gala*) meaning "milk." *Galatea* means "she who is milk-white," as the Celts were the white skinned blonde giants of ancient times, just as we saw was true of the Amorites.

The migration of these ancient peoples seems to have begun in the region of today's Uzbekistan and Kazakhstan around the Jaxartes River which flows into the Aral Sea.[30] Some moved northwest, north of the Black Sea, into Serbia and finally to Germany. Others went southwest, first into Margiana, Hircania, and Bactriana, and then south of the Caspian Sea into Armenia where they continued to migrate south (into Syria and Arabia) and west (into Galatia, Phrygia and beyond).[31] It is curious the southern migrations go right past the ancient region of Babel, where Nimrod built his famous Tower. It also takes you near the regions of the giant-kings mentioned in Genesis 14 (including Shinar, Elasar and Elam, and Goiim which may have been near Galatia).

All of this is to whet your appetite for understanding the references to Hermes and Zeus when Paul went to Lystra. If these people knew their history, they would have been familiar not only with these Greek gods, but also with the giants. They also clearly had had a similar view of spiritual beings that held rule over the people, as Paul makes clear to them when they seek to worship him.

But why did they refer to Paul as Hermes? Hermes is the chief messenger of the gods as well as the chief healer (from his name we get *hermeneutic* which deals with interpreting a text and *hermeticism* which deals with magic and healing). In the story, Paul heals a man crippled from birth after he preaches a sermon to them. Thus, he fits the role of Hermes perfectly. When the people seek to worship him and Barnabas, they shout, "Men, why are you doing these things? We also are men, of like nature with you, and we bring you good news, that you should turn from these vain things to a living God, who made the heaven and the earth and the sea and all that is in them. In past generations he allowed all the nations to walk in their own ways" (Acts 14:15-16).

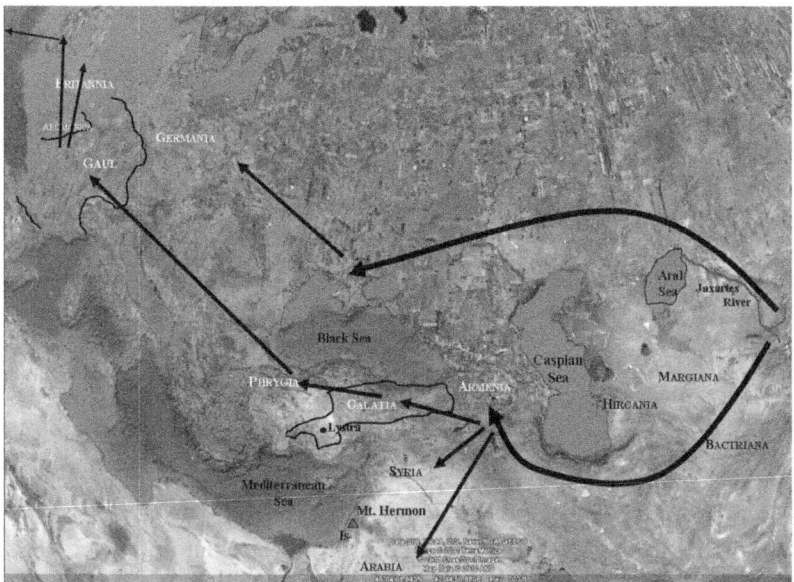

FIG. 15.3. MIGRATIONS OF THE GAULS

The Apostles do not deny that there are other "men" of a different nature. Nor do they say that Zeus and Hermes are figments of the imagination. Rather, they affirm that they (Paul and Barnabas) are men and not gods. Then they say that the worship of Zeus and Hermes is vanity, a chasing after the wind. How interesting is it in this light that Paul near the end of his letter says, "You know it was because of a *bodily ailment* that I preached the gospel to you at first, and though *my condition was a trial to you*, you did not scorn or despise me, but received me as *an angel of God*, as Christ Jesus" (Gal 4:13-14).[32]

In Galatians, Paul adds that these same people were at one time "enslaved" to something called the *stoicheia* (Gal 4:3, 9). These *stoicheia* are "by nature not gods" (vs. 8). Paul is not denying their existence. He is referring to their demonic origin.[33] Thus, the proclamation of the gospel to these people at Lystra is that they must now repent and turn to Christ, for he has defeated the evil rulers of the spirit world, be they "gods" or demons. This is the drastic reversal of human fortune in the Gentile world outside of Israel. Salvation in Christ apart from national identity can now occur.

Who are the "spirits"?

So let's look at Peter's verse. I'll begin by looking at these "spirits" (*pneumasin*, the plural of *pneuma*—"spirit"). Who are they? First, they definitively have their origin "in the days of Noah." This brings us back to Genesis 6 which begins with the story of the Nephilim.

Now, we've already seen that "spirit" is used of the fallen watchers in Enoch and Jubilees. However, when we survey the word in the rest of the New Testament, the plural occurs only one other time for humans (see Heb 12:23). On the other hand, "spirits" refers to demons at least 34 times.[34] In some of these verses, "demon" and "spirit" are used as synonyms in the verse (Luke 4:33; 8:2; 9:42; Rev 18:2). It is rare, if ever, that "spirit" unambiguously means a higher-level evil being such as a fallen watcher. The regular usage of the word is a pretty good indication that we have at least some kind of a proclamation to demonic entities in mind. In 1 Enoch (which almost all scholars today argue influenced both 1 and 2 Peter and Jude) there is a close parallel.

> The giants who are born from the union of the spirits and the flesh shall be called *evil* [or "*mighty*"] *spirits* upon the earth, because their dwelling shall be upon the earth and inside the earth. *Evil spirits* have come out of their bodies. Since they came from the higher places, and from the holy watchers; their first origin is the spiritual foundation. They will become evil upon the earth and shall be called *evil spirits*. The dwelling of the spiritual beings of heaven is heaven; but the dwelling of the spirits of the earth, which are born upon the earth, is in the earth.
>
> (1 Enoch 15:8-10)

It is true that in this passage, the watchers are called "spirits" here. However, as Ramsey writes, "If this passage is brought to bear on 1 Peter, then the 'spirits in refuge' are neither the souls of those who died in the flood nor precisely the angels whose sin brought the flood on the earth, but rather the 'evil spirits' who came from the angels—probably identified in Peter's mind with the 'evil' or 'unclean' spirits of the Gospel tradition. If the authors of 1 Enoch saw the 'evil spirits' of their day as offspring of the angelic 'watchers,' there is no reason why Peter may not have viewed the 'unclean spirits' of his own Christian tradition in a similar light."[35]

Where was the proclamation made?

This likely identification of the spirits as demons or the evil spirits of the gospels helps to inform *the location* of the proclamation. As we've seen, the Rephaim are in Sheol. There are two explanations about how they could also be on the earth. Jubilees gives a very old interpretation that God had not done anything with the evil spirits after the Flood (the bodies of the giants were destroyed in the Flood), and they were leading Noah's descendants astray. So, Noah prays that they might all be locked up to the place of judgment. God answers and commands that they all be "bound up," but Mastema, the chief of spirits, begs God to let a tenth of them remain on the earth, while the rest go down the place of judgment (Jub 10:9). This tradition clearly shows that the demons were bound somewhere in the underworld, though, not all.

The other option is that they do not seem to always reside there. In exorcisms (if they can be trusted to be telling the truth), it is often the case that some demon has come up from the pit (indeed, we find this in Revelation 9 for instance). So perhaps it is better to think of the Rephaim in Sheol as being the guardians, creatures free to move back and forth between the realm of the dead and the realm of the living.

These two explanations provide a good already-not yet balance that we will tease out for the rest of this chapter and the next. If they were those locked up, then Christ proclaimed his message to them. If they were not, then he proclaimed his message to them. This all pivots, however, on where Peter says this proclamation was made.

Sometimes 2 Peter 2:4 is seen as a parallel to 1 Peter 3:19. 2 Peter (along with Jude 6) very clearly has the sons of God, i.e. the fathers of the evil spirits, in view. That verse calls them "angels" rather than "spirits." "For if God did not spare the *angels* when they sinned ..."

Just as there are two different words used for the creatures in mind (spirits vs. angels), so there are two different places named. Very few English translations bring this out properly. In 2 Peter, we often read the translation "... but cast them into *hell* and committed them to chains of gloomy darkness to be kept until the judgment." The normal words for "hell" are *Gehenna* or *Hades*. Hades is the temporary place; Gehenna is the permanent one.

2 Peter uses neither word, but instead opts for the very rare word *tartarus*. This is the only time the word appears in the NT.[36] This should be a signal. If 2 Peter had meant one of the other two places, he would

have said so. Instead, it uses the word that is steeped in Greek mythology. Here is an example from Hesiod,

> Among the foremost Cottus and Briareos and Gyes[37] insatiate for war raised fierce fighting: three hundred rocks, one upon another, they launched from their strong hands and overshadowed the Titans with their missiles, and buried them beneath the wise-pathed earth, and bound them in bitter chains when they had conquered them by their strength for all their great spirit, as far beneath the earth to *Tartarus*.
>
>   (Hesiod, *Theogony* 313-320)

Hesiod has in mind the story which by now is so very familiar. It is the Greek people's equivalent of Genesis 6:1-4. 2 Peter says that Tatarus was where these rebel angels were bound in the days of Noah. But in 1 Peter he does not use Hell or Hades or Tartarus! He says that these spirits are in "prison" (*phulaké*). In light of all we have said about the Rephaim as guardians in the underworld, it is fascinating to learn that this word "refers to the act of guarding or to a place that is guarded."[38] It often refers to a prison, but it does not have to.

As Ramsey points out, guarding can be for the purpose of either confinement or protection. Recall that in the ancient mindset outside of the NT, demons were not viewed as entirely evil. They protected cities. They protected houses. They protected people. The NT tells us, however, that these protectors are not what they appear to be. If these beings protect or guard more than just the gates of Hades/Sheol, then it becomes apparent that Jesus proclaimed his message to them *wherever they might happen to be*. And this is our already/not yet.

Wherever they are happens to be their *phulaké*, their refuge. Think about the demons desiring to indwell people. They seek out their dwellings as homes, refuges. In Revelation 18:2 (a verse which we saw comes directly from Isaiah 34:13), this is quite apparent. Babylon "has become a dwelling place for demons." Some translations say "home" or "lair." Importantly, the word is *phulaké*. In other words, it isn't a prison, but a refuge. Thus, Ramsey prefers the translation, "... to the spirits in refuge" as opposed to "prison." I think this goes too far, because their residence could in fact a prison (i.e. the pit of Hell), and this translation does not allow for the already proclamation that has occurred there.

What was the nature of the proclamation?

The *nature of the proclamation* can help us further. Those who insist that Christ somehow preached the gospel to sinners who lived in Noah's time have very little to go on. The word "proclaim" is *kérussō*. But when Peter refers to the gospel in his letter (1 Pet 1:12, 25; 4:6, 17), he uses a form of the more familiar word *euaggelion* (from which we derive evangelism). This is the only time he uses this particular word for a proclamation.

The word is sometimes used to refer to the gospel, but the problem is, if Jesus is preaching to demons (dead giants), what good would it do to preach the gospel to them? Or, if he is actually preaching to humans, why is Jesus so desperately concerned about those who perished in the Flood? Why wouldn't Peter make it more inclusive of everyone who perished prior to Jesus' coming in the flesh?

So what did Christ proclaim? It is tempting to see it as a proclamation *of judgment*. But it may be better to see it as a proclamation that he has *defeated them* and that they are no longer able to withstand the intrusion of the kingdom of heaven upon their once safe havens. Their kingdoms can now be raided; their captives, freed. It is a message that the Sovereign Lord of the Universe has fulfilled the promise, and crushed the head of the serpent who now staggers from his mortal wound and very soon will be punished with everlasting punishment in the Judgment to come.

When did Christ proclaim his message?

That leaves us with one final question to answer from this passage. *When* did Christ proclaim this message? The verb "went" is actually a passive aorist participle. The exact same verb is used in just a couple verses later in 1 Peter 3:22 where it says that Jesus "*having gone* into heaven" is at the right hand of God, with angels, authorities, and powers having been subjected to him (a verse, by the way, which supports the supernatural interpretation of the "spirits," except that at the ascension it seems that Jesus subjects not the demons, but their fathers and all other angelic beings to his lordship). The verse clearly speaks of something in the past, when Christ ascended into heaven before the eyes of the disciples (Acts 1:9).

It is a good bet that Peter is not using the verb differently in 3:19, and thus it refers to an event of Christ sometime prior to the resurrection. Exactly when that might be, it is impossible to say with certainty. It does seem foreign to the context to think that Jesus did this way back in the days of Noah. Vs. 18 seems to tie it to Christ's death and resurrection. So, it could be in between those two events, or it could be at a time after his resurrection when he was in his new eternal glorified body.

All of this shows an almost intentional ambiguity throughout the verse. It seems that the spirits are most likely the demons, but they could also be the fallen sons of God. It seems that the holding place could be a place of refuge or a place of imprisonment. It seems that the message could be a proclamation of judgment or of victory. And it seems that this happened during Christ's decent to hell, and perhaps after.[39]

Christ's Resurrection and the Victory

This ambiguity teaches an important point. Jesus did something between his death and resurrection where he proclaimed a message of victory and judgment to those fallen spirits (angelic and demonic) who were locked up there. In doing so, he achieved the greatest spiritual victory to date, one that would only be surpassed three days later, when he rose from the dead.

The resurrection. It is the singular event of history, where a man rises of his own power and not that of another man (as spectacularly rare and miraculous as even that is). It is the ultimate event in the life of any sinner doomed to die not just once, but twice; for in the Gospel, this second death along with those creatures that await him on the other side, is escapable through faith in the one who has conquered the evil spirits by his invincible power through perfect obedience to his Father.

But because of the resurrection, Jesus could actually make good on his atoning, demon crushing crucifixion and his proclamation in the netherworld. Those do no good if you are not alive eternally after that, having conquered death itself. And so we learn that at Christ's death, the Apostle tells us that Christ disarmed the rulers and authorities and put them to open shame, by triumphing over them (Col 2:15). But in his resurrection, he is seated "far above all rule and authority and power and dominion, and above every name that is named" (Eph 1:20). These rulers and authorities include all natural and *supernatural* rulers. All those on earth *and in heaven*, visible and *invisible* (Col 1:16; cf. Eph 3:10; 6:12; 1 Pet 3:22). At the name of Jesus "every knee should bow, of those who are in heaven, and on earth, and *under* the earth" (Php 2:10). Truly, Satan bruised Christ's heel, but the Seed of the woman has now "bruised the head" of the seed of the Serpent.

The ambiguity in the language of Jesus' proclamation to the spirits may very signal that he begins or perhaps continues proclaiming his victory after his resurrection as well. We know that he certainly does this through his people, his Body, as the church militant takes this message to the ends of the earth freeing people from their sins and delivering them over form the kingdom of darkness to God's glorious kingdom of light. This will continue until the Second Coming. It is to these thoughts and how they relate especially to the giants, that we will turn our attention in the last two chapters.

16

Conquest

But if it is by the finger of God
that I cast out demons,
then the kingdom of God has come upon you.
(Luke 11:20)

Speculation and the Future

THIS AND THE LAST CHAPTER ARE NEW to the Tenth Anniversary
Edition of *Giants*. We've had quite a bit of new *material* in previous chapters, but I decided against my earlier better judgment that I really do need to say a bit more about the giants and the
future. I need to let you know something here. I originally wrote *Giants*
to be a, hopefully, sane alternative to the many speculations that have
surrounded the Nephilim in recent years. Those speculations have only
increased in the last ten years.

I very much wanted my readers to understand that the most important part of the war of the seeds predicted in Genesis 3:15 in fact
took place at Jesus' *First* Coming. His Second Coming is more like a
mop-up mission in regard to his victory already achieved. Of course,
that Second Coming will reveal Christ to the world to be the King of
kings in ways we cannot yet conceive, and it is terribly important to our
lives. Nevertheless, our Lord has already won. We don't talk about the
First Coming nearly enough, especially with subjects like these, and I'm

not certain the reason for that. Perhaps it is because this is the key to it all, and the enemy wants us to talk about anything but that!

Still, there was certainly a future aspect of this war after the resurrection, and there continues to be one today. In my opinion, even the speculative aspects of this subject with reference to our future deserve some kind of treatment. My goal in this chapter is to help you think about the "already" part of the war in terms of the church's mission of conquest that continues Jesus' work on earth over the demons. The next chapter will deal with the "not yet" part of this war and the potential return of the Nephilim before the return of Christ.

Pentecost and the Nephilim

Let's begin by thinking a little about life in the earliest church, going all the way back to that day when Jesus ascended to heaven. Luke tells us that Jesus told them, "You will be baptized with the Holy Spirit not many days from now" (Acts 1:5). These were nearly his last words to his Disciples before they saw him rise in a cloud and vanish from their sight (9). I cannot help but think about the Holy Spirit as the antithesis to the "evil spirits" that Jesus had been battling with throughout his earthly ministry. God's Holy Spirit will now replace those evil spirits in the hearts of people. This is a kind of "undoing," but we need to unpack this a little.

People get quite confused about the Holy Spirit and Pentecost. What was unheard of about this event? Was the Holy Spirit not present in the OT? First, of course he was. Isaiah said that Israel "grieved [God's] Holy Spirit who was *in the midst of them*" (Isa 63:10-11). David said, "Take not your Holy Spirit from me" (Ps 51:11). The issue is not the Spirit's presence, or even his regenerating activity. All saved individuals in the OT were regenerated by the Holy Spirit of God.

How can this be, if the "new birth" and being "new creations" are not phrases in the OT? If we equate those terms with regeneration, then we will have obvious problems. However, if these phrases describe something more, namely the *indwelling* of the Holy Spirit in our hearts, thereby uniting us with the risen Christ (he had not risen in the OT) and putting us into his new kingdom (it had not come in the same sense in the OT), then we don't have a problem.[1]

OT saints were in fact given new life by God. "Give me life according to your word" (Ps 119:25), the Psalmist says. They were instructed by God's Spirit. "You gave your good Spirit to instruct them and did not withhold your manna from their mouth and gave them water for their thirst" (Neh 9:20). And God circumcised their hearts. "The LORD your God will circumcise *your* heart *and the heart of your offspring*, so that you will love the LORD your God with all your heart and with all your soul, that you may live" (Deut 30:6). As the Psalmists say, many did love God like this, because they were regenerated.

The difference is not that the Holy Spirit didn't *regenerate* OT saints, but that he did not *indwell* them. Rather, as Isaiah said, he dwelt "in their midst," that is, he dwelt in the tabernacle and temple. They could come *near* to the Holy Spirit, through ritual and cleansing, but that's it, because the place of indwelling was different. This was because the people were themselves impure and could do nothing ultimately about it. Of course, even the tabernacle and temple were constantly impure and unclean because of sins and other contaminations. But in his forbearance, God provided a way whereby his Spirit could dwell there, but only if the Law was rigorously obeyed. Of course, it wasn't, and by the days of Ezekiel, God's Glory left the building.

This is a major reason why Jesus, as the new and perfect Temple (John 2:18; Heb 9:24), came and "tabernacled" (John 1:14) among us. God's Spirit rested upon him and then, after he had fully obeyed all his Father's will, he laid down his life having transformed the place of indwelling from the external temple to the temples of our bodies, through his own perfect sacrifice as the Temple of God. This was a singular monumental achievement in human history, and nothing has been the same since that day. (By the way, when David is saying "take not your Holy Spirit from me," he is speaking like a judge of old, who had the Spirit come "upon him" to anoint him as the powerful king; he is not talking about losing the indwelling presence and salvation.)

Because of this, Jesus tells his Disciples just before his ascension that they will soon be baptized with the Holy Spirit. In my view, this is talking about this indwelling presence of God, this new thing that had never happened before. But then something quite expected occurs … *if* you understand human nature that is. Immediately after these words Luke records, "So when they had come together, they asked him, 'Lord, will you at this time restore the kingdom to Israel?' He said to them, 'It is not for you to know times or seasons that the Father has fixed by his own authority. But you will receive power when the Holy Spirit has come upon you, and you will be my witnesses in Jerusalem and in all Judea and Samaria, and to the end of the earth'" (Acts 1:6-8). Notice that they don't seem to care about this work of the Holy Spirit, but are, like so many of us, wanting to know when Jesus will return. Human nature never changes, so, he tells them as he always had, you can't know that, and then instead of speculating, he turns them right back to this amazing work of the Spirit that will begin in just a few days hence. Why? Because of this contrast with spirits. Unless you understand what's taking place, the mission of conquest that Christ is sending his church into will make much less sense.

It is at this point that we want to think about that amazing day of Pentecost. You recall the story. They are all together in one place. Suddenly, out of heaven there came a sound like a mighty rushing wind and the entire house was filled where they were sitting. "And divided *tongues* as of fire appeared to them and rested on each one of them. And they were all filled with the Holy Spirit and began to speak in other *tongues* as the Spirit gave them utterance" (Acts 2:3-4).

This great sound caused a huge commotion in Jerusalem where there were gathered together devout men *"from every nation* under heaven." As they came together, they all heard the disciples speaking in their own native tongue (6). They couldn't figure out how this was possible. Some said they must be drunk, but Peter told them it was only yet morning and then proceeded to give them the first Christian sermon which cut them to the chase and three thousand people became Christians that very hour.

What is going on in this story? It is often missed that there are a number of direct correspondences with *the Tower of Babel*. In fact, from all being gathered in the same place, to opposites Babel and Jerusalem, from one people become many nations to many nations becoming one people, from one tongue to many tongues becoming many tongues each hearing their own tongue, Pentecost is the reversal of Babel (see Table 16.1). This fits with the exchange of spirits. And this is a tremendously important event that relates back to the giants. How so?

Recall that it was Nimrod who built the tower of Babel. Stories of giants and Babel fill the ancient world of mythology. Babel is a story steeped in the ancient world of demons. It has been suggested that Jubilees,

Pentecost (Acts 2):	Babel (Genesis 11):
Pentecost: On that remarkable morning w] are told *"they were all in one place."* (Acts 2:1]	Babel: At Babel we are told that one worl[settled *into one place*, the plain of Shina[(11:1-2)
Pentecost: *Tongues* of fire came to rest o[each of them. (2:2)	Babel: Is the story of confused *tongues*, where God makes one tongue become many. (11:1, 9)
Pentecost: "There were staying in *Jerusa-lem*" (Acts 2:5)	Babel: Took place in *Babylon* [Babel is anti-Jerusalem].
Pentecost: God-fearing Jews from *every na-tion* under heaven" (2:5)	Babel: "From these *the nations* spread out over the earth after the flood." (10:32)
Pentecost: When they heard the sound, they were *bewildered* (6), *utterly amazed* (7), *amazed* (12) and *perplexed* (12). In other words, they were confused.	Babel: When God came down, he con-fused their language and their name be-came Babel, *Confusion*/bewilderment. (11:9)
Pentecost: *Many languages* are all heard as *one*. "How is it that each of us hears them in his own native language?" (2:8)	Babel: *One language* turned into *many*. (1:9)
Pentecost: Building *God's kingdom*.	Babel: Building *their own kingdom*.
Pentecost: The kingdom was established by God himself and *the gateway to heaven* was opened via the Holy Spirit and God's decent to us.	Babel: Their kingdom was trying to open a *gateway to heaven* (this is what Babel meant to them) via their own methods and accent to God.
Pentecost: They are *gathered together* in or-der to be *scattered*.	Babel: Want to *stay together* and are *scat-tered*.

TABLE 6. THE UNDOING OF BABEL

which we saw in the previous chapter regarding 9/10 of demons being locked up, has these demons in mind in its next story—Babel.

> The narrative (Jub 10) relates the persecution of the grandchildren of Noah by impure demons or wicked spirits. Noah appeals to Yahweh for deliverance and receives a partial reprieve [then Mastema manages to be 1/10 of the demons to remain on earth] … The majority of these spirits will be bound and their persecution of humanity will cease. A small, select group, however, will continue. They will serve a necessary function in the on-going divine governance of the world … It is interesting to note that the account of the pollution of the spirits is immediately followed by *Jubilees'* version of Babel. The possibility of a correlation between

these two narratives is present. Or, to put the matter more directly: in *Jubilees* the account of Babel can be read in demonic juxtaposition. Both the thoughts and the actions of the Babelites can now be read in light of demonic influence by the Nephilim.[2]

Many have seen horror movies such as *The Exorcist* or *The Exorcism of Emily Rose* or *Deliver Us From Evil*, where the demon speaks Latin. In fact, people possessed by demonic powers speaking in unknown (to them) tongues is something we've known about for centuries. In Jerome's *Life of Hilarion* (391 AD), he tells the story of an unnamed officer who spoke only Frankish and Latin. He was long possessed by a demon, and he came to St. Hilary who spoke Greek and Aramaic. When he first started talking to the man in Aramaic,

> Immediately on being questioned by the servant of God the man sprang up on tiptoe, so as scarcely to touch the ground with his feet, and with a wild roar replied in Syriac in which language he had been interrogated. Pure Syriac was heard flowing from the lips of a barbarian who knew only French and Latin, and that without the absence of a sibilant, or an aspirate, or an idiom of the speech of Palestine. The demon then confessed by what means he had entered into him. Further, that his interpreters who knew only Greek and Latin might understand, Hilarion questioned him also in Greek, and he gave the same answer in the same words.
>
> (Jerome, *Life of St. Hilarion* 22)

Yuliya Minets points out that the demon spoke two languages previously unknown to the officer, Syriac and Greek. Jerome emphasized that his Syriac was phonetically and idiomatically perfect.[3] She then takes us to the sixth century and John of Ephesus who, in his *Lives of the Eastern Saints*, presented foreign languages as a tool used by demons arbitrarily to deceive God's saints.[4]

We've seen that the OT forbids such practices as divination, omen reading, soothsaying, sorcery, casting spells, conjuring spirits, and the like (cf. Lev 18:10-12). These practices each involve the demonic occult *and* the use of words. Or we might put it this way, special ritual *tongues*. Gardner writes in this regard,

> Babel increased the availability of such practices as it increased the availability of demonic spirits to man and man to demonic spirits. At Babel all the above abominations became the way man conversed with

his gods and discovered the will of the gods. They also gave me the way they could influence the gods to work for them ... the effects of Babel are enormous. The construction of a tower for demonic beings to access the people, the collective efforts of people against the Lord, the organization of man by powerful men, all restarted here and left a legacy for us all. All the national divisions that come from different languages, with all the misunderstandings, and indeed wars that have resulted as a consequence, stem from Babel.[5]

Nietzsche seemed to believe that language is itself "a demon," because it is only through language (so he thought) that we are obliged to have the idea of God (who, of course, he hated so much that he wouldn't believe in him). He believed that grammar by its nature leads us to think that only his existence can make sense of reality, hence, it is a demon. (We can thank the deconstruction of language in our own day in large part, to this fount). Though in a philosophy book discussing Nietzsche and Descartes, Hemati has observed that "the confusion of languages at Babel was a divine judgment for human arrogance. Though that confusion may merely be that the vocabulary and syntax of each language became jumbled,"[6] the confusion from Babel is certainly related to various demonic linguistic product of byproducts of that event.

Now, any linguist will tell you, especially the father back you go, that languages are themselves heavenly, even divine things. As such, I'm not suggesting that demons *created* the languages at Babel. What I am suggesting is that for whatever reason, demons are also closely associated with languages.

Demons take language and confuse it, and that is the very definition of Babel. At Babel, the people were confused because now they all spoke different languages. But the confusion is surely more than just linguistic. It is also spiritual. They are being led into darkness so that, at best, people can only grope about as blind men to perhaps feel their way towards God (Acts 17:27). Demonic entities were certainly present, and God gave the world over to their presence as punishment.

Pentecost is the undoing of their demonic power. Now, all the languages spoken on that day bring the many people to the same conclusion: Jesus is the Christ and he has power over the supernatural powers that enslave people; therefore, we must turn to him in repentance and faith.

When the Apostle speaks of the elemental spirits, the *stoicheia* (e.g. Gal 4:3), he says that we were *slaves* to them. These demonic entities are like others who people devote themselves to, but which are "deceitful spirits" and whisper the "teachings of demons" (1Tim 4:1). The Apostle's great hope and message is that Jesus has conquered these creatures. Jesus, through this proclamation of his church militant, beginning with the Apostles and continuing down through the centuries, leads us all to the same message and hope, that people will "come to their sense and escape from the snare of the devil, after being captured by him to do his will" (2Tim 2:26). This is the great hope of Pentecost. It is a hope that continues until Christ's Return.

I'll just point out one more thing here. The book of Acts is a two-volume work, by Luke's own admission. Amazingly, these two volumes are an inverse parallel that works on multiple levels. The most obvious that scholars have seen is the geography of the two books. Luke begins in the context of the Roman Empire, then narrows down to Galilee, then moves farther south to Samaria and Judea, then it ends in Jerusalem at the cross and resurrection. Inversely, Acts begins in Jerusalem, moves us outward to Judea and Samaria, then out to Galilee of the Gentiles and the larger Gentile world, finally ending in the city of Rome. You can conceive of the whole thing like this:

A.   Jesus' birth in the context of Roman Empire (Luke 1-2)
   B.   Galilee (Luke 3:1-9:50)
      C.   "Journey to Jerusalem" (though Samaria) (Luke 9:51-19:49)
         D.   Jerusalem (Luke 19:41-24:49)
            E.   Ascension (Luke 24:50-51; Acts 1:1-11)
         D'. Jerusalem (Acts 1:12-8:1a)
      C'. Judea and Samaria (Acts 8:1b-11:18)
   B'. Throughout the Gentiles World (Acts 11:18-28:13)
A'. Paul in Rome (8:14-31).

Amazingly, this seems to work on micro levels. For example, at Pentecost, as we have just seen, the disciples are mocked for being drunk. Luke's exact words are, "But others mocking said, 'They are filled with new wine" (Acts 2:13). I think the whole thing is rather humorous, but much more is going on here. This is the only time that

Luke uses the word "wine" in Acts. But there is a parallel at the end of his Gospel, right in the place we would expect it, if we understood that the two books enfold on one another like the structure signals. At the cross, Jesus is being mocked. In fact, the same word is used. And this is what it says, "The soldiers also mocked him, coming up and offering him sour wine" (Luke 23:36).

What is Luke trying to indicate? I would suggest it is this. What happened to Jesus during his life is going to now be paralleled in the life of his Body, the Church. Throughout the book of Acts, we will see many such parallels with Jesus' life (for instance, right after Pentecost, Peter will be arrested, just as Jesus was arrested just before his death; Barnabas will bring money to the Apostles in a reverse of Judas bringing money to the priests; etc.[7]), including the casting out of demons and various sorts of trouble this creates.

But just as Jesus had the power, so now, through the Spirit's indwelling presence making the Christians pure and holy tabernacles, the unclean spirits don't stand a chance. Beginning at Pentecost and going right through to the Return of Christ, the mission will be to take the unclean and make them clean. And if anything happens to be tormenting them, it will be exorcised. As the old Baptismal formulas, said often after exorcisms were carried out by the Bishop say, "I renounce Satan, and his works, and his pomps, and his worships, and his angels, and his inventions, and all things that are under him" (*Apostolic Constitutions* 7.41). And then they are led under the waters and back out to a brand new life, made fit vessels to serve in Christ's church as spiritual warriors until he returns.

17

Return of the Nephilim?

For as were the days of Noah,
so will be the coming of the Son of Man.
For as in those days before the flood they were eating and drink-
ing, marrying and giving in marriage,
until the day when Noah entered the ark, and they were
unaware until the flood came and swept them all away,
so will be the coming of the Son of Man.
(*Matthew 24:37-39*)

Different Eschatologies

T HE PREVIOUS DISCUSSION now leads us to the final chapter and the Return of Jesus. Originally, I did not want to speculate about such things, because my desire was to not interfere with this message of the Gospel and the victory and conquest that has come about because of the First Coming. Quite honestly, people obsessed with the return of the Nephilim would do well to spend more time thinking about what has already happened.

People are speculating more and more these days about this sub-ject, especially as it regards the Nephilim and a possible role they might play in the future (or present). But speculations are not inherently bad things. To get there, it is important that I say a word about my own eschatological leanings and, ironically, penchant for speculation.

Eschatology is literally the "study of last things." Biblically speaking, the last days are already here. Interestingly, this is precisely what Peter tells the crowds at Pentecost. "And in these last days it shall be…" (Acts 2:17; cf. Heb 1:2) and then promptly tells them that they have been ushered in through the *First* Coming. How interesting it is to read this in light of Peter's own question just one chapter earlier about when Jesus might return!

At any rate, I believe that there is an already and not yet aspect to the last days, as do almost all believing Christians. But the way we think about this has been quite different. We usually talk about this in terms of the relation of the (future) millennium (Rev 20:2) to the return of Christ. *Premillennialists* essentially believe that Jesus will return in the Second Coming *before* the millennium and then will rule on earth bodily for 1,000 years. This seems to have been the view of Justin Martyr (110-165 AD) and Irenaeus (130-202 AD), but it should be kept in mind that Justin himself said, "Many belong to the pure and pious faith, and are true Christians, who think otherwise" (*Dialogue* 80).

The other main view is *Postmillennialism*, which basically teaches that Christ will return after the millennium and any bodily rule of Christ will be for an eternity. In recent centuries, Postmillennialism has been subdivided into a recognized third category, which you may have heard about called *Amillennialism* (Augustine is often said to be the father of this view, but it was surely around before him). That term is a misnomer, since it literally means "without a millennium." But Amillennialists *do* believe in a millennium, they just don't believe that it is future, they believe it is a present reality. Hence, the other name you might hear: Realized Millennialism. The difference between Amillennial and Postmillennial is simply that the former believes we are already in the millennium, while the latter (usually) believes that we have not yet made it there. But both are Postmillennial in the sense that they believe any bodily rule of Christ on earth will be after the millennium rather than during it. I'm not going to get into a discussion of these views beyond this, because that would take up a whole book.[1]

I'll just note a couple of things. First, it is interesting to me that in the last couple hundred years that when (at least from the American perspective) times seem to go good, Postmillennialism seems to catch on, but when times seem to get rough, Premillennialism seems to take over. Second, in part because of this, though I grew up a Dispensation-alist Premillennialist, I grew tired of all the date setting (1988, 1989, 1994, 1996, 2000, 2001, 2007, 2012, and they just keep going on), and over the course of the years I eventually found myself firmly in an Amil-lennial camp. After about the third serious one of these in a row, I re-member one moment in my own life when that hit me like a ton of bricks. It was Nov 5, 1995, and I was walking the streets of Denver with a pastor friend. I looked at the headline of the *Rocky Mountain News* where Yitzhak Rabin, the Prime Minister of Israel, was on it. He had just been assassinated. "Jesus is coming back soon," I simply told him.

His response was unexpected, because I thought everyone believed like I did. "You've got to be kidding me, right? You read the newspaper and think Jesus is coming back?"

That story aside, when I recently preached through Revelation, I discovered that I feel like the more I teach that book, the *less* I actually understand. I remain Amillennial, but I think the other two views each bring important contributions to the subject. All that to say, I agree with Justin that this is not an issue of orthodoxy and it should not be made a test of whether one is a true Christian or not.

I tell you where I sit on this issue because as someone who appreci-ates Amillennialism, it is important to understand that it is more prone to see *ideals* present in any age being spoken about by biblical the proph-ecies, especially when their language is so fanciful and symbolic as it often is. It isn't that it doesn't take things "literally," but sometimes "literal" actually means "spiritual," as in the spirit-realm rather than the physical realm. It isn't always an either/or, of course. But for me it helps me not to be as prone to seeing the next Blood Moon as the certain sign that Jesus is returning next week.

So how does all this fit with the Nephilim? Well, the Nephilim have really caught on in the last few years and the speculations about them returning are increasing exponentially. As I try to psychoanalyze myself, curiously, at the same time that I say I like a system that doesn't specu-late, I can't help but look at this world, knowing that every single gen-eration since Jesus has said, "We are the final generation," and wonder. I don't wonder because of similar things that others have thought was so bad in their own lifetimes that Jesus must come back to stop it all. I wonder it because we have truly entered an age that is unprecedented in world history.

We have the capability of utterly obliterating every life-form on the planet if we wanted to. No one else could say that. We live in an age where we are seriously in the process of reinventing what it is to be a human being through genetic modification, DNA manipulation, and transhumanism. No other time in history could say that. Artificial Intelligence is now at the point where you can tell it to write a 1,000 page novel in the style of Mark Twain on the topic of transhumanism is set in the 1800s, and it would spit it out in three seconds ... and you wouldn't know that Twain didn't write it! No one else has ever said that. Are we headed to some kind of dystopian singularity and Terminator-like Judgment Day? We are also, and I know this will date this book by saying it, presently living through one of the most confusing world-wide propaganda deceptions in world history. Indeed, I dare say on the level of the whole planet, this has also never happened before. The things going on post 2020 are truly mind-boggling, especially in the deception and delusion that so many are under—and don't even know it. Truly, the more you look into those things, the stranger they get and I, at least, can't help with all this but to wonder, we are living right at the end? So I get it about the speculation.

But I also want people to know up front, that *I just don't know*. That may or may not be what you want to hear, but it is the truth. My eschatology allows me to say that Jesus could return this afternoon. Or, that he could return in 10,000 years from now (hopefully that's true for each of us). I can handle it if the Nephilim come back physically or if they never do. I'm not wise enough to know what God is doing, how bad he wants things to get, how much worse things can get, how many more people he wants to save, how great he wants things to get before he returns(!), how far he is willing to let us go in any of these self-destructive planet-wide power grabs, or anything else. I have my gut feelings, of course, but those are precisely the things that I do not view as particularly safe. Especially when there has been so much difference of opinion on this topic.

So now that you know all that, I want to look briefly at a few of the common ideas surrounding the Nephilim that people are talking about these days as it pertains to the Return of Christ.

Daniel 2: Mixing of Kinds

The first regards a verse in Daniel 2. "As you saw the iron mixed with soft clay, so they will mix with one another in marriage, but they will not hold together, just as iron does not mix with clay" (43). Daniel 2 is unquestionably a text that deals with his future. Whether or not it still deals with *our* future, this is a question that Preterists (those who believe some or all of such prophecies were fulfilled in 70 AD) and Futurists (those who believe that such prophecies are still to be fulfilled in our own future) can argue over.

King Nebuchadnezzar has a dream of a statue. The statue is made up of various kinds of metal, from gold, to silver, to bronze, to iron. These metals correspond to four world empires (also slightly debated), which are usually thought to be Babylon, Assyria, Greece, and Rome. When he gets to the toes, he gives this strange language of mixing iron and clay. This is brought out better in the KJV: "And whereas thou sawest iron mixed with miry clay, *they shall mingle themselves with the seed of men*: but they shall not cleave one to another, even as iron is not mixed with clay."

The idea has been posited that "they" refers to angels, ala Genesis 6:4. "They" are mixing with the seed of men and therefore Daniel is predicting a return of the Nephilim in the last days.[2] As far as the language goes, the KJV is correct to translate it as "the seed of men." "With one another" is an interpretation. The ESV seems to get the idea of marriage from the word "hold together" which is found in Gen 2:24 and means "clinging" to his wife. The preposition "with" could be translated that way, or it could also be "in" or "amongst," so you could say they "mingle themselves amongst the seed of man," which could be literal or metaphorical. Any way you look at it, this is rather strange language, and the Nephilim interpretation is using that to its advantage. If someone is doing this with the seed of mankind, it must mean "they" are not the seed of mankind.

But there are a couple of problems with this. First, "mankind" is not the word "*adam*" but a more general term. Angels are often called "men." So, importing angels here doesn't really help if they, too, are "men." Maybe green reptilians or something would? Of course, that's the second problem. There are no green reptilians in this chapter or anywhere in the Bible. (This doesn't mean they don't exist. I'm not saying they do or don't, but that's for another book. OK, maybe the idea of a reptilian kind of being like a Watcher might fit. Actually, I think it kind of does!) The question is, how could you even get angels from the context? "Angels" is said to come from the word "they." "*They* shall mingle with…" Pronouns always have an antecedent noun to which they refer. In this case, it would either be part of the toes or part of the feet. But what are those?

The iron clearly refers to either kings or to their kingdoms in the passage. The parts of the idol (head, chest, thighs, legs) are human kingdoms, this is very clear. Interestingly, vs. 44 seems to refer to them as kings. If taken as parallel to vs. 43 it says, "And in the days of those kings …" What kings? Presumably those mixing in the former verse. All of this would seem to be perfectly normal mixing.[3]

But this is Daniel. This image *is* an idol and where there are idols, there are spiritual beings nearby. I am willing to think that this view is picking up on something that most commentators miss, which is that there may in fact be something supernatural here. But I do not think the Nephilim view makes good sense of this passage. I believe that the fulfillment of this passage takes place in the first century and not in our future (I suppose it could be a double-fulfillment),[4] therefore, Nephilim at least in the flesh, are not involved, since there was no "return of the Nephilim" in the first century, save in the form of their disembodied demonic state, which Christ conquered easily. Most likely, if fallen angels are here, it is at best indirectly through the whole image where there is a heavenly mirror of ruling angels over the nations.[5]

Matthew 24:37-29: As in the Days of Noah

A second passage, and I one that I think has a much more probable bearing on the future is found in Jesus' Olivet Discourse. "For as were the days of Noah, so will be the coming of the Son of Man. For as in those days before the flood they were eating and drinking, marrying and giving in marriage, until the day when Noah entered the ark, and they were unaware until the flood came and swept them all away, so will be the coming of the Son of Man" (Matt 24:37-39). To understand my view, we need to back up and look at the overall discourse.

My view of this great sermon on the future, is one of partial-Preterism and partial Futurism. It all begins with Jesus leaving the temple with his disciples when, at some point, they turn around and look at the temple together and Jesus, pointing at it says, "You see all these, do you not? Truly, I say to you, there will not be left here one stone upon another that will not be thrown down" (2). They must have been thinking to themselves that this was going to get very juicy. But silence accompanies them as they cross over the Kidron valley and begin walking up the Mt. of Olives. When they arrive at the top and he still hasn't explained himself they ask him "privately, saying, 'Tell us, when will these things be, and what will be the sign of your coming and of the end of the age?'" (3).

My view is that, whether they understood this or not, Jesus takes this as two separate rather than one all-encompassing question.[6] The first question is, "When will these things be?" What things? The destruction of the temple and the removal of all of its stones. Jesus will immediately address this question and, essentially, through vs. 35, he will answer it with very precise prophetic warnings. He tells them things like, "When you see … flee." Everything in this part of the discourse gives you the impression that Jesus knew exactly when and how it would occur. Looking back on the terrible ordeal that was the Roman slaughter of over a million people in Jerusalem and the obliteration of their temple and how Josephus tells us exactly what happened, there is simply no reason to think that Jesus didn't get it all exactly right. He predicted it perfectly and, in fact, very few Christians were killed, because they all fled when they saw the warning signs.

However, Jesus changes subjects around vs. 36 and begins discussing the second question, "What will be the sign of your coming at the end of the age?" This question refers not to the temple, but to his Second Coming. This is the place where Jesus says no one knows the day or the hour, not even the Son of Man (36). This is a totally different kind of talk than the precise, detailed, explicit language of the previous thirty plus verses. And this is the preface to our verses about Noah.

Now, if Jesus had just said something generic about the days of Noah, I would probably be content with the thought that he's basically just saying that "people are evil, evil will continue until I return, just as it always has." But the fact that Jesus mentions "marrying and giving in marriage," this is what gives me pause, for we know through this study that this was no ordinary kind of marriage.

Why would the Lord single out this time frame and speak about this action, knowing full well that everyone in that day was obsessed with Enochian Watcher stories, if he wasn't alluding to them in some kind of manner? Even in saying this much, I'm probably entering into the kind of speculation that I wanted to avoid, because the facts are, I really don't know. I have heard the stories of giants under tunnels in the earth, whole armies being kept in stasis, held there by the governments of the world. I certainly believe that if the technology was there to create such hybrids or the modern equivalent through genetic engineering that men would have already begun doing everything they could, even with the help of fallen entities if they could contact them, to bring this to pass. I have a very healthy sense of human depravity. And that's what gives me pause and makes me think that perhaps this passage does open the door, even if just a little, for something like the return of the Nephilim to be a possibility in our future. Systems of theology should neither force us into undo speculation or keep us from seeing what seems to be patently obvious.

But even allowing for that, one thing I do know with certainty is that the Nephilim are already here and they never left. And this is something people must never forget. Remember our demons? That's them! Maybe not in physical form, but it's them nonetheless. This means that in one sense, they never left.

Revelation and the Nephilim

Revelation: An Incredibly Brief Overview

This takes me to probably the most difficult of all things to figure out: the book of Revelation. I'm going to focus in on just two passages, because it clearly relates to our giants. These will be Revelation 9 and the strange creatures the come out of the abyss and then Revelation 20:7-10 and the "Final Battle." But before I do this, I need to explain my view of Revelation.

I used to read the book as I would read a history book—as telling us events that unfold one after the other from beginning to end. This is how most people read Revelation. They see it as a chronological out-working of (usually) our future.

However, Revelation is a very special type of literature called *apocalyptic*. Besides being filled with symbols and metaphors and the like, it is also not written like a history book. Scholars have observed that Revelation can be read as a series of cycles (seven to be precise).[7] In these cycles, history repeats itself over and over again. It's as if John is telling us the same story, but from different perspectives. Imagine going up a circular staircase. At some point you come to the very same vertical axis even though you are now many feet above or below where you were. This gives you a different perspective from which to see the same view.

Furthermore, the entire book of Revelation appears to be one massive inverse parallel structure that centers upon the story of Michael and the Dragon. This gives us even more reason to see the two halves as being repetitions of the same themes. To make things even more interesting, just like Luke-Acts, these structures also seem to parallel the Gospel of John (John wrote or edited both books) in such remarkable ways that John 1 and Revelation 1 correspond all the way through to the last chapters of the books; but also John 21 corresponds to Revelation 1, while John 1 corresponds to Revelation 22. What this means seems to be that what happened in Jesus' life on earth is going to be parallel with his body (the church) in the period of time until he returns—again, just like Luke-Acts. In other words, it may very well be that what Revelation predicts is not (or not only) the far distant short span of time right before the return of Christ, but history between the two Advents.[8] All this is to say that what we are about to look at could be something that has already passed or, indeed, it could be something that is yet future. Or even both.

Revelation 9: As in the Days of Noah

Because there is so much to say, even in Revelation 9, we will only look at the first half of the chapter (vv. 1-11; the second half is its literary parallel, and also includes similar kinds of strange creature we will look at here). It begins with a star fallen from heaven to earth (Rev 9:1). This is not to be taken as a giant ball of gas in the sky going supernova, for we would all be dead. Rather, this is some kind of heavenly being falling in a way that parallels the fall of Satan. The parallel of vs. 11 calls him Apollyon or Abaddon.

He is then given the key to the shaft of the bottomless pit. It is worth noting that earlier in Revelation, Jesus is given the keys of Death and Hades, so this means that whatever the fallen being is doing, it is only at the permission of Christ! It is also worth noting that this abyss is the same word found for where Satan is cast during the millennium (Rev 20:1, 3). In the OT, it is the equivalent of Sheol or Hades. To put this another way, this the place that the demon spawn were sent when God judged them in days gone by.

The fallen god then opens the shaft of the bottomless pit. Suddenly, out come "locusts on the earth" (3). But these are no ordinary locusts. They have the "power of scorpions." But they are "like horses prepared for battle" (7). Curiously, in the myths, Apollo was the father of Centaurus, the half-horse, half-man creature. Their faces were human faces, their hair like woman's hair, and their teeth like lion's teeth (7-8). They also had tails like scorpions (10), but apparently also wings (9).

The serpentine (which appears in the next group in 9:19) and scorpion language is associated with demonic evil by Jesus, as we saw in a previous chapter. "Behold, I have given you authority to tread on serpents and scorpions, and over all the power of the enemy, and nothing shall hurt you" (Luke 10:19). Let's now take this idea and read it against a backdrop that we've already seen.

In the *Epic of Gilgamesh*, Gilgamesh travels to the place of the divine council only to find "scorpion-beings" watching and guarding the gate of the Netherworld (*Gilgamesh* Tablet 9). The Phoenician god Šadrafa (see Fig. 14.1) has two symbols: the snake and the scorpion. The word Šadrafa is possibly related to "Master of the Enchained" (*Rab-basire*; think Rev 20 and the chaining of Satan?) and "God of the Underworld" (*Nergal*).[9] Likewise, you have the Egyptian goddess Selkit (or Serqet) who was "friend of the dead," and had seven scorpions who guarded Isis on her journeys.

Where are these creatures in Rev 9 coming from? The pits of hell, the abyss, *abaddon* (interesting that the creature's name matches the place). What's so very strange is that in two places in the OT, Sheol and

Abaddon are immediately preceded by just one verse with the dead *Rephaim giants*. "The *Rephaim* tremble under the waters and their inhabitants. *Sheol* is naked before God, and *Abaddon* has no covering" (Job 26:5-7). Again, "Do you work wonders for the dead? Do the *Rephaim* rise up to praise you? Is your steadfast love declared in the *grave* or your faithfulness in *Abaddon?*" (Ps 88:10-11). In the same chapter that Lucifer and the flying seraphim are found, Isaiah connects these Rephaim to Sheol and calls them "the leaders of the earth" and the "kings of the nations" (Isa 14:9). That's similar to what Genesis 6:4 called them—"The mighty men of old," "the men of renown," "the Nephilim." Many scholars believe that they were kings. One of them, Nimrod, sure was, and some have even identified Apollo with Nimrod.[10] Isaiah is not saying this just for fun. He is warning the king of Babylon that Sheol and the Rephaim are excited to meet you when you go down to hell. This is not a place you want to go because *they* are there (Prov 9:18, "The Rephaim are there, in the deep places Sheol her invited ones!").

Like Revelation 9, the Rephaim looked like men (only a lot bigger). We've seen some of their possible animal-hybrid counterparts, for instance the Ariel or "lionlike" (2Sam 23:20), the two slain by Benaiah, one of David's mighty men. This reminds us of the teeth of these Locupions (locust-scorpions).[11] All of this to say, John isn't describing man-made 21st century helicopters, as Hal Lindsey notoriously said in *There's a New World Coming*.[12] The truth is so much more interesting and terrifying. He is describing a great plague of demonic activity that is unleashed at the command of Apollyon who must in turn obey the Lord Jesus Christ.

How are these demons harming? It talks about the sting like a scorpion. It is in their tail. But as these are demonic entities, we should probably be thinking of less physical harm (though that can obviously occur), and more psychological and spiritual harm, like what happens to people when they are possessed. In this regard, Beale notices that the language here is very similar to Jeremiah 8 (see Table 7).

The Targum of Jer 8:22 refers to the horse invader as a "plague," and the Jews, who expected Antichrist to come from Dan, used this very passage to prove it.[13] The association these plagues have to idol worship in both passages may then help us to understand that the "sting" comes through deception by false teachers, which is precisely the kind of work John associated with antichrists in his letter

Jeremiah 8:16-17, 19	Revelation 9:6-10, 20
Death shall be preferred to life by all the remnant that remains of this evil family in all the places where I have driven them ... The snorting of their *horses is heard from Dan*; at the sound of the neighing of their *stallions* the whole land quakes. They come and devour the land and all that fills it, the city and those who dwell in it. For behold, I am sending among you *serpents*, adders that cannot be charmed, and they shall bite you," declares the LORD ... "Why have they provoked me to anger with their carved images and with their *foreign idols?"*	And in those days *people will seek death* and will not find it. They will long to die, but death will flee from them. In appearance the locusts were like *horses* prepared for battle: on their heads were what looked like crowns of gold; their faces were like human faces, [8] their hair like women's hair, and their teeth like lions' teeth; [9] they had breastplates like breastplates of iron, and the noise of their wings was like the noise of many chariots with *horses rushing into battle.* [10] They have tails and stings like *scorpions*, and their power to hurt people for five months is in their tails ... [did not repent of] *worshiping demons and idols*

TABLE 7. REVELATION 9 AND JEREMIAH

(1Jn 2:18-26; 4:1-3). "This is the antichrist ... I write these things to you about those who are trying to deceive you." Spiritual deception of a direct and demonic kind is of the very worst kind of torment there is. Spiritual deception leads to absolute ruin. In the here and now, it can even lead to physical ruin!

Many will want to figure out a time period for all this. Here I want to give you a flavor for how varied the interpretations have been. There is one time period given here. It is "five months" (Rev 9:5, 10), but that's all it tells us. Five month is simply the normal life cycle of a locust.[14] But Gentry notices this is not as short a time as you might think, for *infestations* of locusts in any one area only last *a few days* before they move on. Here, however, the plague is continuous on everyone for the entire lifetime of the creatures.[15] As a *preterist*, he takes this to parallel the five-month siege of Jerusalem by Titus. Furthermore, those Christians who listened to Jesus were not in the city when it was destroyed and so they escaped final destruction, just as the Christians here cannot be killed or even harmed. No, this trumpet blasts against *unbelievers*.

However, it seems to me that if this is a demonic horde, and if demons do not actually die (they already died once) after five months, then the symbolism can't be contained to merely 70 AD. Rather, God sends out the demons for periods of time to harm unbelievers *throughout the church age*. Has this not proven true for 2,000 years? *Historicists*, for example, see this fulfilled in the Islamic invasion of the West. The five months are 150 years (reading the number symbolically) from 612 to the removal of the Caliphate to Baghdad in 762.[16] But surely there have been many more dark demonic days in history than that. *Futurists* often view this as some kind of literal five-month period of a future judgment before the end of days or the millennium. Hendriksen combines these all and asks, "Can you conceive of a more frightful and horrible and true(!) picture of the operation of the power of darkness in the soul of the wicked during this present age."[17]

Both physical and spiritual torment accompanies demonic activity in the Bible. Rarely does it lead to death. And here, it does not either. It just torments. It causes a soul often to *want* to die. As one possible center of our passage says, "They were allowed to torment them for five months, but not to kill them, and their torment was like the torment of a scorpion when it stings someone. And in those days people will seek death and will not find it. They will long to die, but death will flee from them" (Rev 9:5-6).

Revelation 20:7-10—Gog and Magog

A second and final passage I want to look at deals, at least in the popular mind, with the same things we find in movies like *Return of the Jedi*, *Independence Day*, *V: The Final Battle*, and *Thor: Ragnarök*. From the real Ragnarök of Scandinavian mythology, to Shambhala, to Armageddon, the Last Battle is engrained into human consciousness. Revelation 20:4-7 seems to be an epicenter for this in the Bible. It says,

> [7] And when the thousand years are ended, Satan will be released from his prison [8] and will come out to deceive the nations that are at the four corners of the earth, Gog and Magog, to gather them for battle; their number is like the sand of the sea. [9] And they marched up over the broad plain of the earth and surrounded the camp of the saints and

the beloved city, but fire came down from heaven and consumed them, [10] and the devil who had deceived them was thrown into the lake of fire and sulfur where the beast and the false prophet were, and they will be tormented day and night forever and ever.

While there are differences of opinion among the systems as to when this battle takes place (anywhere from 70 AD to sometime after a still future Millennium), I want to focus in on how this relates to our story-line.[18] There is every reason to believe that what is being described here is a supernatural spiritual battle involving the demonic and satanic realms.

To see this, we need to understand first that this passage is parallel to Ezekiel 38, especially vv. 1-2, 22. Going back to Ezekiel, we find something strange occurring, which we mentioned briefly in a previous chapter. In some translations of Ezekiel 38:2, "Gog" is translated by the LXX as "Og" (in other places, such as Deut 3:1, 13; 4:47 Og is translated as Gog). Remember our giant from the days of Moses? Some scholars believe this is a scribal error (in both places though?),[19] but others see Gog appearing also in Amos 7:1 LXX in relation to, drum roll please, *the locusts* (remember Revelation 9). "This is what the Lord showed me: And, see! A swarm of locusts coming in the morning and See! One locust is Gog, the king."[20]

Furthermore, Gog has been associated with the giants Amalek, Agag, and his descendant Haman who are also associated with this war. The Rabbis associated the several phrases of the prayer in 1Chr 29:11 with a different OT event: Creation, the Exodus, the sun and moon standing still, the fall of Rome, the battle of Arnon, the war of Sisera where the stars fought against him. The last two ("Thine is the kingdom, O Lord and Thou art exalted") are the war of Amalek and Gog and Magog.[21] Most if not all of these are supernaturally charged and the last two go together. In Num 24:7 LXX, Agag is rendered, "His kingdom shall be higher than Gog." Haman the Agagite is rendered "Haman the Gogite" twice (Est 3:1; 9:24 LXX). And of course, Gogmagog (*Goemagot, Goemagog, Goëmagot* and *Gogmagoc*) is a legendary giant in Welsh and later English mythology. The latter says that London is guarded by the two giants: Gog and Magog (see Fig. 17.1). Curiously, Josephus says that Magog is related to the Celtic giants (*Antiquities* 1.123). All this already gives us a potential supernatural flavor to the battle.

Now we need to look at other names listed in Ezekiel 38-39. The names of the armies include *Magog, Tubal,* and *Meshech* which appear as

FIG. 17.1. GOG AND MAGOG LIFT PADDY OUT OF THE MIRE (PUNCH MAG., 1849)

three of the seven immediate sons of Japheth, the son of Noah (Gen 10:2). A fourth son, *Gomer*, appears in vs. 6 along with *Cush* and *Put* (5), two of the immediate sons of Ham (Gen 10:6). *Sheba* and *Dedan*, two of Cush's sons (10:7), appear just a little later along with *Tarshish* (Ezek 38:7), one of the sons of Gomer (Gen 10:4). These are the most ancient of peoples after the Flood, and to have this many names all come from Gen 10 is no accident. Together, they come from the four corners of the ancient world (or as Rev 20 puts it, "like the sand of the sea"; see Table 8).

Text	Nation	Direction from Israel	Text	Nation	Direction from Israel
38:2	Meshech	N	38:6	Gomer	N
38:2	Tubal	N	38:6	Bet Togarmah	N
38:5	Persia	E	38:13	Sheba	S
38:5	Cush	SW	38:13	Tarshish	W
38:5	Put	W	39:6	"The Coastland"	NW

TABLE 8. NATIONS OF THE GOG-MAGOG CRISIS OF EZEKIEL 38-39[22]

In taking us back to this chapter, we are necessarily taken to the Tower of Babel, for it is from there that the seventy nations of this chapter are derived. But it was at the tower of Babel that God put the seventy heavenly "sons of God" to be rulers or princes over the nations (Dt 32:7-8). And of course, let's not forget our old pal, Nimrod.

This takes us to the title of this Gog. He is called, "Chief *prince* of Meshech and Tubal." Chief prince [*nesi' rō'sh*] becomes *archonta Rōs* in the Greek, which could be rendered, "commander of Ros[h]." Hence, the NKJV says, "Gog … the prince of Rosh." Along with him coming from the "north," this is where many get the idea that Gog is Russia and that the End Times battle will pit Moscow against Jerusalem. The problem is, there is no place called Rosh in the ancient world, and it absolutely does not stand for "Russia." That's just Cold War exegesis rooted in fanciful speculation.[23] Rosh simply means head/chief. And *nasi/archonta* means a prince or ruler. The interesting thing is that the LXX calls the supernatural princes of Greece and Persia *archontos* (Dan 10:13, 20). Archons sometimes refer to supernatural beings in the NT as well. Therefore, it is not impossible that Gog is somehow the supernatural power over Meshech and Tubal, which we know are not in Russia, but Turkey, over 1000 miles from Moscow (the fact that they are in Turkey could have "giant" overtones as well, see Ch. 15). Gog therefore very well could be a mythological or supernatural rather than human figure.

A fourth point is related. The passage is that after identifying Gog, God immediately says, "I will put my hooks in your jaws" (Ezek 38:4). This language only appears in Job 41:2, where God asks Job, "Can you put a rope in his nose or pierce his jaw with a hook?" Whose jaw? Leviathan, the Dragon, who in Revelation 20 is Satan. At the very least, the imagery is evocative of the supernatural. However, I think there is more going on.

Isaiah had predicted, "In that day the Lord with his hard and great and strong sword will punish Leviathan the fleeing serpent, Leviathan the twisting serpent, and he will slay the dragon that is in the sea" (Isa 27:1). This is the final defeat of Satan being predicted. He is going to be punished once-for-all. That's precisely what is happening here in this Gog-Magog battle. This is understood in a most remarkable way by understanding that in Ezekiel, Gog is buried in "the Valley of the Travelers" (Ezek 39:11)." What's that? It could refer to the Valley of Hinnom, the place where human sacrifices were offered to Molech. If so, there is a fascinating connection here to the end of Rev 19 where God makes a great supper for the birds—a supper of evil beings that they feast upon. In other words, God is sacrificing evil as a sacrificial meal where the evil one(s) are consumed forevermore, never to return again. Or, it could refer to the passing on from this realm to the next via the river to hell or the lake of fire, as the word "traveler" (*'ōběrîm*) is the word for crossing over to the netherworld, either literally or through witchcraft.[24]

Add now to this a fifth point which is that Gog comes from the far recesses of the *north* to *assemble* around God's people, and one thinks of Isaiah 14:12 where Lucifer seeks to sit on the mount of *assembly* in the far reaches of the *north*. It's all very much the same idea, except Isaiah is past and Ezekiel is talking about the future. Is it starting to make sense that it is *Satan* who is released from the abyss? This seems to be no ordinary war, but one last terrible supernatural attack against God and Christ's church.

In this regard, there is a sixth point that is interesting, even if I don't think it has a much weight as some want to give to it. The ESV says, "They marched up over the broad plain of the earth…" (Rev 20:9). "Marched up" and "broad plain" seem to be theological rather than literal translations. "Broad plain" could just as easily be translated as "the breadth of the land/earth." Though it can be used of military advances,[25] the word *anabainō* simply means "to go up, ascend." The translators have made the decision for us as to what it must mean. Why must it mean "march?"

Anabainō appears 13 times in Revelation. Virtually all of them are to/from supernatural places. John is told to "come up" to heaven (Rev 4:1). In one, an angel "ascends" (7:2). The smoke of incense of the prayers of the saints rises to God (8:4). Etc. Curiously, smoke rises from the pit of the abyss followed by demonic locusts (9:2-3); the beasts rises from the bottomless pit (11:7; 17:8). A second beast rises out of the earth (13:11). And the smoke of the torment of the damned rises up forever and ever (14:11). In other words, there's a lot in Revelation about things rising up from *below* the earth. What lives down there? Demons, Rephaim. And Satan has himself just been released from there.[26] So could it be that rather than marching on the broad plain, the armies are rising up onto the breadth of the earth *from below*?

Just here, it is interesting to note that several scholars have seen the army Satan gathers composed either entirely of demons or at the very least a mixture of demons and their human possessed counterparts.[27] This fits the Locusts-scorpion hybrids as well as other demonic figures in the book such as the frogs[28] and, the beast, and so on in previous final battle scenes in the book. Thus, someone has said, "Since Ezekiel's time, Gog and Magog had been thought of as rulers of a mythical army. For John, the nations of Gog and Magog are an army of demons from the netherworld (cf. 9, 1-11. 16-19). Passages led from 'the four corners of the earth' to the realm of demons below."[29] And another, "Thus vv. 7-10 are to be interpreted as follows: Satan entices the ghostly nations of the dead, and the demons, 'innumerable as the sand of the sea', from the four corners of the earth where the underworld manifests itself, in order to make war on the resurrected ones. The mythical names God and Magog are also quite fitting in this context, since they do not allude here to historical nations, but to the bands of Hell, similar to the armies of Abaddon which ascend from the bowels of the earth (9,1-11), or the hordes of demons in 9,13-19 (note here also the cosmic number 4). Thus at the end there comes the revelation of the unredeemed and their aims (namely the destruction of the church)."[30]

Clearly, this and the other battles are depicted as having human elements. But that goes without saying. And yet, most if not all of those are also depicted as having a supernatural, satanic, and demonic element as well. In fact, this seems to be the larger point! Satan being released to gather an army against the camp of the saints is the obvious part. Now I hope you can see that Gog-Magog is much more than a bunch of people marching into Jerusalem to fight the War to End All Wars. At the end of the day, whether the Nephilim return bodily, that is speculation. What is not is that we do not fight against flesh and blood. This has been, is, and will be the way of it until Christ returns.

The Time That Is Given To Us

Let us return to the Olivet Discourse. In the section that I believe deals with the fall of the temple *in our past*, Jesus says, "False christs and false prophets will arise and perform great signs and wonders, so as to lead astray, if possible, even the elect. (Matt 24:24). This has already happened, and it was at the very minimum, a demonic kind of deception. The Apostle talks about God sending "a strong delusion, so that [people] may believe what is false" (2Thess 2:11). This reminds me very much of a divine council scene in the OT, where the heavenly court is trying to decide what to do with the wicked king of Israel. At one point a "lying spirit" says that he will go into the mouths of the prophets and deceive the people (1Kg 22:22). Then the LORD says, "Go out and do so, you shall succeed." In other words, God works through means, the means of demonic entities, to carry out his bidding.

I believe that such entities usually if not always have very different motives for such things. It is like Joseph when he says, "As for you, you meant evil against me [throwing me into a pit to kill me], but God meant it for good, to bring it about that many people should be kept alive, as they are today" (Gen 50:20). God's reasons for sending people a strong delusion, either in our past or in our future, are always pure. They may have in mind purifying and saving some. They may have in mind just judgment and holy wrath against others. That's his business. But that he uses evil demons to do it, that's a certainty by me.

There's an old Johnny Cash song that goes, "How high's the water, mamma?" "Two feet high and risin'." After a short lament, the narrator continues, "How high's the water, momma?" "*Three* feet high and risin'." "How high's the water, momma?" "She said *four* feet high and risin'." That's how a lot of people feel about the times we live in. And it may be rightly justified. And we could be in the very last of days (remember, we are already in the "last days"). Or we might not be. As for the giants, whether the Nephilim return or not, whether the Second Coming is far away or right on our doorstep, whether there is a great delusion that will deceive the whole world or whether this is a repeating cycle of history, whether we want the times we live in or not, we would do well to consider the words of the wise Grey Wizard, just before he went and fought his own literal giants deep in the mines of Moria. "All we have to decide is what to do with the time that is given to us."

"There are other forces at work in this world besides the will of evil," he continues. Indeed! After achieving his singular victory of sin, death, and the devil, Christ proclaimed a message of his absolute authority over the demonic world, and they no longer have the power to keep people in slavery and bondage when Christ is proclaimed. This will be true until the very second that Jesus Christ returns in his Glory.

I'm not a pragmatist by nature. I don't particularly care about a subject because of what I can get out of it. I seek to know revealed truth because it is an honor to do so. "It is the glory of God to conceal things, but the glory of kings is to search things out" (Prov 25:2). The things we have spoken of here *are* revealed, and they *are* knowable. And they are also super fun and endlessly interesting.

I do, however, also believe that the Bible is God's repository of all the truth I need to live eternally and in obedience to him in this world. What does this study of the giants contribute to that end? I hope that you will be able to give your own answer to this question now that we have come to the end of the book. But let me give you my own answer.

Some people are captivated by this entire subject, because for them it serves as proof of some eschatological end-game that they believe will play out very shortly in modern events.

I've given you little of that kind of speculation here, though I have also not totally naysaid the idea either. Whether the giants in a physical form have anything to do with the end of the world, I honestly have no idea. I think it is fun (and also a bit terrifying) to think about, but then again, hey, they never really left us anyway. My interest in this subject is not so I can sell you a book that will give you the magic key to knowing when Christ will return and how the whole end-of-the-world scenario will play out. Christ will return. There will be an end of the world. It may be soon, but it may also be long after I'm dead and buried.

For me, the giants are so captivating because they show in a unique way that God made a prediction, remembered his promise, took steps to ensure it would be achieved, worked it out in stages in actual redemptive history, always showing himself to be the Master of the seed of Satan through Christ, and then finally delivering the goods, fulfilling the prophecy, conquering the serpents and their wicked spawn, and ruling over them as he is now seated above them. This works on the soul at a profound level. It also works on a more basic level.

I have come to believe that while we still pay lip service to it, many of us really don't take very seriously at all that there is an authentic spiritual war being waged for each of our souls by extremely powerful and intelligent creatures in heavenly places. These creatures not only include Satan, but a host of angelic powers, as well as demonic entities that seek our eternal harm, and want to destroy our joy and delight in God. As with the topic of giants in general, such things are just too weird and bizarre to be taken seriously by educated, intelligent, enlightened, scientific people. Knowledge is power, and you now have the tools to begin appropriating this knowledge into your worldview.

Is anything more practical than knowing the victory is secure, that Christ has won, that such beings hold no power over him or his people, and that no matter what befalls us, God is absolute Sovereign and Lord of this world and the next? If we could ask one of the demonically possessed people freed by Christ himself, I know what they would say. They would tell everyone about the man who set them free with nothing but the power of his word. They would give great glory to God. Then they would live in light of their new freedom by following him and obeying him.

The story of the giants is about glorifying the God of Israel for his holiness, power, foreknowledge, sovereignty, mercy, judgment, truthfulness, faithfulness, love, and grace. Through the story, God has magnanimously displayed these qualities, so that at the name of Jesus every knee *will* bow in heaven and on earth to the glory of God the Father. This is our chief end, to glorify God. Will you do it willingly through faith, or as a one compelled because of his power and wrath? In light of God's sovereignty and victory, how then should you live?

We all come to the Bible with presuppositions, that is, preconceived ideas of what we think it means. As your presuppositions have been challenged, I hope that this "invisible" story of the Bible, the victory and glory of Holy One of Israel will become your sure hope. To this end, I offer up a prayer for you in the form of Psalm 91, retranslated to account for our supernatural worldview.[31]

Psalm 91

He who dwells in the shelter of the MOST High God will abide in the
shadow of Shaddai, "God of the Mountain," "God of the Wilderness."

He will say to the LORD, "My refuge and my fortress, my Elohim in whom I trust."

For he will deliver you from the snare of the fowler and from the deadly pestilence.

He shall overshadow you with his wings, his truth shall cover you with a shield.

You shall not fear the night demon, nor the arrow-shooting Lilith who shoots her arrows in the day.

Nor the diseased ghost that walks in darkness, nor the noon day demon.

A thousand shall fall at your side, ten thousand at your right hand, but it will not come near you.

You will only look with your eyes and see the recompense of the wicked.

Because you have made the LORD your dwelling place—Elyon, the Most High, who is my refuge.

No evil shall be allowed to befall you, no plague come near your tent.

For he will command his angels concerning you to guard you in all your ways.

On their hands they will bear you up, lest you strike your foot against a stone.

You will tread on the lion-headed demons, you shall trample the lion and the dragon.

Because he holds fast to me in love, I will deliver him; I will protect him, because he knows my name.

When he calls to me, I will answer him; I will be with him in trouble; I will rescue him and honor him.

With long life I will satisfy him and show him my salvation.

APPENDICES

APPENDIX I

EXTRA-BIBLICAL LITERATURE

Many Christians do not know how to handle extra-biblical literature, especially Jewish literature, written during the times of the Bible. I've often wondered if maybe this isn't because they are separated into chapter and verse and make people "feel" like they are reading the Bible, and they don't want to be confused. This is understandable, but unfortunate. There are three choices for understanding these books. The first is to ignore them and pretend that they don't exist. Sadly, this is a popular response of many Christians, but it isn't particularly helpful or honest. Ancient peoples from all over the world speak to the issue of giants and heavenly beings.

The second is to deny that they say anything true; "extrabiblical" becomes "fabrication and lies." A softer position is to treat most or everything in them *not quoted in the Bible* as fable and error. This may originate in a strange kind of fundamentalist error having its roots in a misunderstanding of what makes Scripture Scripture.

The books in the canon that make up our Bibles are not Scripture because they are true and everything else is false. For example, Einstein could write the formula: $E = MC^2$. The formula is true, but it is not Scripture. I could give you my wife's recipe for the best chili in the world, which would be a true recipe, but not Scripture. I could have you read a biography of George Washington, which is true history, but not Scripture. While all Scripture is true, is it not the case that everything that is not Scripture is false. It should be obvious as to why the Einstein formula, the recipe for chili, or the Washington biography should not be considered Holy Wit.

A person can get into some tricky spots when they take this approach that everything said in extrabiblical literature is fabrication. For example, as I said above, Jude quotes the book of Enoch verbatim (see Jude 14 and 1 Enoch 1:9) as being the very words of Enoch, a prophecy that he holds to be quite true. How then do we respond? I've heard more than one person say something like this, "Yes, this particular *verse* of Enoch is true, *but none of the rest of it is.*" This incredible unfalsifiable declaration expects us to shut down all critical thinking, to accept that one verse in Enoch is true because Jude says that it is, and then dump the rest of the book that he quotes and alludes to more than once, *because someone outside of the Bible tells you too.* This is called fideism, the belief that you believe for no good reason. Fideism is opposed to everything taught in the Bible, including the idea of faith. Faith rests on truth, not absurdity.

While a couple of Church Fathers believed 1 Enoch was Scripture,[1] and the NT quotes and often alludes to it,[2] I do not regard this book as canonical for several different reasons.[3] This does not mean, of course, that it relates nothing true about history, or more absurdly, that it gives us only one true verse and Jude happened to discover it. While appealing to Enoch's view of the events of Genesis 6:1-4 cannot, of itself, give us certainty that the view is correct, we can be certain from the material that we presently have available to us that everyone in Jude's day has the same view of the Genesis 6 story that 1 Enoch does. Considering that Jude quotes and alludes positively to 1 Enoch many times (see Fig. App. 1.1), it is a good bet that he has the same view as everyone else.[4] Furthermore, neither Jude nor 2 Peter ever says that 1 Enoch is false history. Nor do they hint at it. This is an argument from silence. Rather, Jude says, "The angels who did not stay within their own position of authority, but left their proper dwelling, he has kept in eternal chains under gloomy darkness until the judgment of the great day" (Jude 1:6). 2 Peter is similar. Both clearly have the Enochian tradition of Genesis 6 in view in these verses,[5] as at least Jude does do throughout his little epistle.[6]

This gives us the third option for understanding this kind of literature. We can use these extant books and texts wisely and discerningly, without being afraid that we are therefore asking for them to be included in the canon. Christians cite John Calvin and John Wesley, Max Lucado and Chuck Swindoll, and no one ever claims that by quoting

JUDE		1 ENOCH	
Jude 6	"The angels that did not keep their own position but left their proper dwelling."	"[The angels] have abandoned the high heaven, the holy eternal place."	1 En 12:4
	"Until the judgment of the great day"	"Preserved for the day of suffering"	1 En 45:2 (1 En 10:6)
	"Angels ... kept in eternal chains under gloomy darkness"	"This is the prison of the angels, and here they will be imprisoned forever"	1 En 21:10 (1 En 10:4)
Jude 12	"Waterless clouds"	"Every cloud ... rain shall be withheld"	1 En 100:11
	"Raging waves"	"Ships tossed to and fro by the waves"	1 En 101:2
	"Fruitless trees"	"Fruit of the trees shall be withheld"	1 En 80:3
Jude 13	"Wandering stars"	"Stars that transgress the order"	1 En 80:6
	"The gloom of utter darkness has been reserved forever"	"Darkness shall be their dwelling"	1 En 46:6
Jude 14	"Enoch the seventh from Adam"	"My grandfather [Enoch] ... seventh from Adam"	1 En 60:8

TABLE 9. SOME OF JUDE'S ALLUSIONS TO 1 ENOCH

them or reading them that they are magically turning them into Scripture. The thought never even crosses our minds. The same grace should be extended to these books as well, especially knowing that they were used by the NT and held up as important by the early church. This kind of an attitude is all the more important for those books written prior to the NT by people in the OT community of God that very well could have been trusting in the coming Messiah. The fact is, these books were the popular literature of the day and biblical authors read them just as we would read popular commentaries or other Christian writings in our own day. This doesn't make them true or false. It does make them important.

If these books tell us about the sons of God or giants, we should use wisdom, we should compare them with the biblical data, we should inspect them for exaggeration, but we should also realize that this was the view of that day and that the NT writers have the same worldview, as I have repeatedly demonstrated throughout the book.

APPENDIX II

2 Peter 2:4 and Jude 6

As a Christian who takes biblical inspiration and infallibility seriously, I presuppose that if other parts of the Scripture were to comment upon and explain Genesis 6:1-4, then whatever conclusions they give must be inspired by God and infallibly correct. Most commentators today believe 2 Peter 2:4 and Jude 6 do just that. As all commentators note, these sections of Jude and 2 Peter are interdependent. Either Jude is borrowing from 2 Peter, 2 Peter is borrowing from Jude, and/or one or both are borrowing from a shared tradition.[1] You may want to take

2 PETER 2:4-5	JUDE 5-6	HESIOD THEOGONY 313-320
(4) For if God did not spare angels when they sinned,	(5) Now I desire to remind you [of] ... (6) angels who did not keep their own domain, but abandoned their proper abode,	Among the foremost Cottus and Briareos and *Gyes* insatiate for war raised fierce fighting: three hundred rocks, one upon another, they launched from their strong hands and overshadowed the Titans with their missiles, and buried them beneath the wise-pathed earth, and bound them in bitter chains when they had conquered them by their strength for all their great spirit, as far beneath the earth to *Tartarus*."
but cast them into *Tartarus* and committed them to pits of darkness, reserved for judgment; (5) and did not spare the ancient world, but preserved Noah, a preacher of righteousness. . .	He has kept in eternal bonds under darkness for the judgment of the great day. . .	

TABLE 10. ANGELIC SPIRITS IN PRISON

the time to read these two chapters now, to see what I'm talking about. See also Table App. 2.1. which puts the two passages side by side, and also compares them with an excerpt from Hesiod.

Since the two letters are parallel, they refer to the same episode, and can therefore shed light on one another. The first thing to notice is that 2 Peter refers to the time when "angels" "sinned." Older Protestant commentators thought this must refer to the original fall of Satan and his angels.[2] But Jude explains the time frame of the sin: when the angels "did not keep their own domain, but abandoned their proper abode" (Jude 6). "Domain" is the Greek word *archēn*, and it refers to the heavenly regions of rule these angels had originally been given. But they abandoned this realm, their proper sphere, in favor of inhabiting our own realm, the earth. Peter adds that this took place squarely in the days of Noah. This can therefore refer with certainty to only one episode in biblical history: Genesis 6:1-4.[3]

Though this creates enough certainty all on its own, we may add to the force of it in several ways. First, Jude parallels the sin of Sodom with the sin of the angels by the phrases "just as" and "in the same way" in the next verse (Peter likewise discusses Sodom after this event). Jude 7 talks about the sin of Sodom and Gomorrah saying there was "gross immorality" and "going after strange flesh." This is sexual sin, specifically between human males and the "men"[4] from heaven (Gen 18:3, 19:5, 8), who are also called "angels" (Gen 19:1). Therefore, "just as" and "in the same way," the sin of the angels in Jude 6 must have likewise been sexual, and indeed was, as angels were having relations with women in Genesis 6. There is no better way to put either episode than "going after strange flesh."[5] This is the most definitive, explicit link between the "sons of God" being angelic beings in the Scripture. But we may be even more assured than even this.

A second reason for our certainty on this matter is that 2 Peter says that this sin of the angels caused them to be thrown into *Tartarus* at the same time that God "did not spare the ancient world" of Noah's day (2Pe 2:4-5). Therefore, the sin occurred in the days of Noah. Two more points clarify this. First, the word *tartaroō* is used only here in the NT.[6] It refers to a subterranean region, doleful and dark, which the Greeks viewed as the abode of the wicked dead, where they suffer punishment for their evil deeds.[7] As you can see from the example in Hesiod's

Theogony, this is where the Titans (i.e. gods or giants) were thrown in a previous age. The fact that Peter did not use the typical word for hades or hell demonstrates he is clearly thinking of this elder time that the poets talk about.

A third reason has to do with the interpretation of Genesis 6:1-4 in Judaism and early Christianity. The idea that this passage refers to angels having relations with women and producing giant offspring was the *universal* interpretation among the Jews *at the time these two letters were written*, and these sources include the book of 1 Enoch which Jude not only quotes, but alludes to several times (for more on the interpretation, see Appendix 6).[8] It was also the universal belief of the cultures surrounding Israel, which scholar Amar Annus has extensively documented.[9]

This is relevant because 1 Enoch 6:1-6 and 7:2-3 are near parallels with Genesis 6:1-4, a fact that was lost to Christianity for over a thousand years until the rediscovery of the book late in the 18th century. You can't blame those who didn't have 1 Enoch, but it is inexcusable when we who do are not willing to interact with the material that we now have. These parallels are explicit in their teaching that the events of Genesis 6:1-4 refer to angels. So, if Jude has been quoting and alluding favorably to Enoch throughout his letter (see Appendix 1: Extra-Biblical Literature), it is unthinkable that he would radically disagree with its interpretation on this point unless he explicitly tells us so. It would make no sense that he would continually use other parts of the book to support the rest of his letter, but utterly disagree at this one point, but not tell us. As Thomas Schreiner rightly notes, "If [Jude] does not have the same interpretation in mind as Enoch (and all the other Jewish literature of his day), then he would surely need to make it clear that he is deviating from the tradition, especially since he has Genesis 6 in mind."[10] This is a very powerful argument. Not only does Jude not do this, both he and Peter make it clear that they *accept* the tradition.

Along similar lines, Jude and 2 Peter each have an historical list of events which they are using to make a moral point (that we should not be like those of long-gone days who disobeyed). Jude refers to the wilderness, the angels, and Sodom while Peter refers to angels, the flood, and Sodom. The important thing to learn is that lists of this kind, with the *very same events* (and few others), were commonplace among the

Sirach 16:7-10	CD 2:17-3:12	3 Macc 2:4-7	m. Sanh. 10:3	Jubilees 20:5	T. Naph 3:4-5	Jude 5-7	2 Peter 2:4-8
	Watchers						Watchers
Giants	Giants	Giants		Giants	Sodom	Generation of the Wilderness	
	Generation of the Flood		Generation of the Flood	Sodom	Watchers	Wilderness	Generation of the Flood
	Flood		Flood			Watchers	Flood
	Sons of Noah		Generation of the Dispersion			Sodom	Sodom
Sodom		Sodom	Sodom				
	Sons of Jacob						
Canaanites	Israel in Egypt	Pharaoh & Egyptians	Spies				
Generation of the Wilderness	Israel at Kadesh		Generation of the Wilderness				
			Company of Korah				

TABLE 11. EIGHT MORAL HISTORIES COMPARED

Jews of that day to make *the same ethical points*. Table App. 2.2. is reproduced from Bauckham's commentary which demonstrates the similarity of the literature.[11]

If Jude has Enoch and other traditions in mind (and it is beyond a reasonable doubt that he does), and if both Peter and Jude are compiling the same lists to make the same points as other literature with which they were obviously familiar (which we know with certainty they are), then there is only one interpretation permissible for the Christian who believes that Jude and Peter were infallibly inspired by God. Genesis 6:1-4 refers to angels who left their proper domains, came to earth, married human women, and had gigantic offspring.[12] Any other opinion blatantly contradicts Jude and Peter and throws the infallibility of Scripture out the window.

APPENDIX III

The Stories of the Greeks

Making Sense of Mythology

Were you one of those people that stayed as far away from mythology as you could in High School, thinking, "What's the use of learning a bunch of ancient silly sacrilegious stories"? I was. If one proceeds from the assumption that the ancient stories of the nations—stories which are called "myths"—but which are usually relegated to fantasy, fable, and fairy-tale—are based in some kind of real history, then one naturally begins to wonder how such stories might fit into a biblical chronology. Sometimes, a single story is pretty easy to identify and classify. We've seen how there are over 180 different Flood stories throughout the earth (see pgs. 63-65). Likewise, we have seen widely spread stories that appear very much to resemble the Tower of Babel (see pgs. 75-77). These did not spontaneously arise from accident or coincidence all over the world.

It gets much more difficult very quickly to try and figure out how multiple stories fit into actual history, especially when these stories often contradict the Bible, let alone themselves. One of the problems with myth is that it is its own unique genre, its own distinctive way of telling history. Myth is not as concerned with brute facts as with telling a story. This is why the modern enlightened mind dislikes it so much (though you would never know it from the Hollywood box office). It often places history, allegory, and metaphor side by side. Sometimes, the same story works on all of these levels. Other times, central figures are often telling one story from two different points of view, or better, a single figure can be used to tell two different aspects of the same grand narrative.

A good example of this, in my opinion, is a figure like Zeus (Jupiter). Zeus is depicted as the highest god in the Olympian pantheon, the creator of mankind, in some ways a perverted equivalent of the biblical God. Yet, you can also read about very human and mortal events in Zeus' life: his birth where he is hidden from his father Cronus on the Island of Crete, his continual liaisons with mortal women, and even that he has a tomb on the same Island on which he was born.[1] This mortal-immortal lives prior to the Flood, is the cause of the Flood, and continues on long after the Flood. Taken as a composite, the story of Zeus cannot be reconciled to anything in real history, so it is tempting to think of him entirely as a figment of the fertile imagination of the Greeks.

But if we take threads that make up Greek (and Roman) mythology, unwind them from larger tapestry, and look at them in isolation, I think it is possible to make some sense of the convolutions, additions, and perversions of the history.[2] In this Appendix, I want to attempt this very thing for you, to see if we can't see some correspondences in the pagan remembrances of world events.

Chaos

Let's start at the beginning. In the beginning, the Greeks saw only Chaos. Chaos is at the very top of the Greek pantheon. This "god" is really nothing of the sort. He is really an "it." The Greek word has carried over into English in a way that few of the other names of the gods have. Chaos is an impersonal abstract random meaningless way to get everything from nothing. "He" corresponds perfectly to the modern naturalist/atheist god of chance or the Big Bang. How curious that Greek polytheism would have so much in common with modern atheism. Of course, Chaos is the diametrical opposite of the Biblical God—a personal concrete purposeful God of order, meaning, intelligence, morality, stability, immutability, eternal sovereignty, and power.

For the Greek, Chaos "begot" a pantheon of "children," impersonal entities called the Protogenoi (First Born or Primeval): Tartarus

(Abyss), Nyx (Night), Erebus (Darkness), Eros (Desire/Love), and Gaia (Earth). Of these, it is really only Gaia and Eros who have been personified in any meaningful sense today. Since Chaos begat them, they must be generated; but since Chaos is herself impersonal, it is not really correct to say that they were "created," for creation takes intention and intelligence, of which Chaos has neither.

These "gods" in turn spawned impersonal forces. For instance, Nyx (Night) begat many children: Moros (Fate), Oneiroi (Dreams), Nemesis (Retribution), Momus (Blame), Philotes (Affection), Geras (Aging), Thanatos (Death), Hypnos (Sleep), Eris (Strife), Apate (Deceit), Oizys (Distress), Moirae (Destinies), and Keres (Doom). Here it is possible to see some very perverted reflection of the biblical angelic world, except that angels are viewed in the Bible as persons rather impersonal forces of nature. How then does this reflect anything true?

In Revelation, angels are very often *assigned to* the forces of nature (e.g., they bring floods, they speak through dreams, they guard the abyss etc.; for example Rev 16:2-12). Peter and Paul both use the same word (*stoicheia*) to refer to the elements of nature and personal spiritual beings respectively (2 Peter 3:10-12; Galatians 4:3-11). This shows the close relationship in Scripture between spiritual beings and earthly forces. The former have some kind of power over the later.

Gaia and Uranus

Let's focus in on one specific Protogenoi, the goddess Gaia. Gaia has never really gone away. In fact, today, she is making a comeback as paganism returns to the west with reckless abandon. She simply personifies earth. But more than the big ball we all live on (in the Roman pantheon, Gaia is Terra), she personifies that which lives upon the earth, especially humanity, we who are made from the dust and return to it. Of course, in Gaia worship, as the creation is worshiped rather than the Creator, earth is a living mother, the goddess of all life. Such is the perversion. At any rate, in the myth, Gaia had a son named Uranus. The seventh planet is named after him. Uranus means "heaven" (Gk: *ouranos*). In the Bible, of course, we see that in Genesis 1:1 LXX, "In the beginning God created the *ouranos* and the *ge*."

The Children of Heaven and Earth

In the Greek story, Gaia and Uranus get married and have children. It is at this point that the primeval creation turns into more recognizable history. Think about these children this way—they are the product of a marriage between heaven and earth. When we understand who these children are, it is easily understood that they tell the Genesis 6:1-4 story. The sons of God (personified in Uranus) married the daughters of men (personified by Gaia) and begat children called the Nephilim.

At this point, the story gets very interesting. There are several branches of children that are born from this unholy union. These branches take place at two different periods in history, and through two different means of generation. The first group of children all come from the union between Gaia and Uranus. These consist of the Cyclopes, the Hekatonkheires, and the Titans. One thing unites all of these groups. They are all giants.

There were three great Cyclopes: Brontes, Steropes, and Arges. They were great wielders of metal and weapons. They are often depicted around forges. Though there is no hint that he is a giant, Tubal-Cain, the son of Lamech, is quite similar in terms of what he does and when he does it. There were also three great Hekatonkheires: Briareus, Cottus, and Gyges. The word *hekatonkheire* means "one hundred handed ones." These were hideous monsters, each with fifty heads and a hundred hands. It is possible that they represent a large number of people, or a large number of *large* people.

The third group were the Titans, and there were twelve of them. The youngest and most important is Cronus. His name is of unknown origin. The Romans called him Saturn. His is the sixth planet and we also remember him ever *Satur*day. Some have suggested that his name derives from a word meaning "to cut" (Gk: *keirō*). Others, thinking of the Latin equivalent Sadorn, suggest it means "martial" or "warlike." Both are reminiscent of this figure.

What happened to these children? The Cyclopes and Hekatonkheires were an abomination to Uranus because they were so ugly. So, he bound them up and placed them in Tartarus, or from Gaia's perspective, he threw them back into her own bowels. Their ugliness has a certain fit with the Nephilim (even if those Nephilim happened to be physically beautiful) in terms of their being an unnatural abomination, violent, and wicked creatures on the earth prior to the flood. The Greek story, however, seems to conflate two different biblical stories.

In 2 Peter and Jude, it is the angels (by the NT, this becomes a catch-all term for various heavenly beings), not the giants, who are bound up and thrown into Tartarus. If they were retelling the Greek myth, these two would not have made such an obvious mistake. Still, the similarities are difficult to miss. Similarly, 1 Peter tells us that there are spirits who now reside in prison. 1 Peter does not use the word *tartarus* here, but as I have argued, it does appear that Peter is talking about the giants. The OT equivalent of this is the Rephaim shades who guard the pit. God's question to Job about unbinding Orion (Job 38:31; see pp. 80-81) may be a dim echo of this ancient story. It seems that the Greeks mixed these two stories together in the creation of their own mytho-historical narrative.

At this point in the story, the actions of Uranus make Gaia furious. So she speaks to her Titanic sons and tells them they must to depose their Father. She decides that castration (cutting off heaven?) is the best option. If he hates his sons so much, then perhaps he should not have any more. The only one with nerve enough to do the deed it is Cronus.

The story goes that Gaia set an ambush for Uranus, while Cronus hid with a sickle. At just the right moment, the youngest son of Heaven leapt out of hiding, and with a well-aimed swipe, cut his father off in his prime. From here, Cronus becomes the High God of the pantheon, until he becomes paranoid just like his father, and begins to destroy each of his children in the same way as Uranus. Zeus, who was hidden away by his mother, has a similar story as Cronus, and eventually he too deposes his father after being saved by his mother.

This story seems to be the Greek anti-story to the Biblical account of the Flood. In the Bible, it is God who cuts off the inhabitants of the earth by destroying them. In fact, the Flood is referred to as a "cutting off" (Gen 9:11), echoing metaphorically the castration of Uranus. The difference, however, is substantial. The Greek story is one of rebellion of earth against heaven, where earth wins. In the Bible, it is one of God's anger against sin against heavenly and earthly beings. But in the end, it is God's grace that overcomes all. If this really was the time when God cast angels and giants into dark places, then I believe the Greeks have remembered a portion of the truth, even though their Flood stories are not connected with the Cronus myth.

The second batch of children between Uranus and Gaia take place *during* the castration. It is through the blood (sometimes semen) of Uranus that is thrown into the sea that the second batch of children are born. These are the Meliae, the Erinyes, and most importantly, the Gigantes. The first two are female. The Meliae are nymph-spirits. The Erinyes are deities that dwell in the underworld to punish whoever has sworn a false oath. Underworld deities and spirits? Hmmm.

The final group, the Gigantes, is where the LXX's translation of *nephilim* originates. Remember, the Nephilim are called *gigantes* in the Greek. Thus, the story of the children of Gaia and Uranus seems to be an interesting, albeit perverted memory of the events of antediluvian and early post-diluvian history where the world, full of giants, perished only to be replaced with wicked spirits and more giants that terrorized humanity all around the globe.

APPENDIX IV

Giants in the Americas

"The eyes of that species of extinct giants,
whose bones fill the mounds of America,
have gazed on Niagara [Falls], as ours do now. "

Abraham Lincoln[1]

In this Appendix, I want to give you a flavor for the myriads of reports of giants, especially in the Americas; then I want to conclude with some thoughts on how to interpret them. Much of this information has been compiled in various non-scientific books on the subject.[2] I obviously can't vouch for the historicity of every report. Some are also clearly less credible than others. Due to the staggering amount of dubious information concerning giants on the internet (especially the infamous Photoshopped pictures of giant skeletons that continue to make the rounds in e-mail spam and Youtube), we must tread carefully. I *can* give you some specifics reports that I have verified, which have been passed along in encyclopedias, newspapers (including local and national such as the *New York Times* and *Washington Post*),[3] biographical journals, state historical societies, the Smithsonian, and scientific magazines of yesteryear, in a day when people (including Christians) felt they had nothing to fear from such remarkable historical discoveries.

North America, with its "virgin" soil, is especially prone to archaeological reports of giant skeletons. As the Europeans made their way westward, they found undisturbed mounds built by an ancient civilization. Upon excavation, many of these mounds were found to be graves. The settlers told tales of skeletons which they dug up, skeletons ranging from 7 to over 12 feet in such places as Alaska,[4] California,[5] Connecticut,[6]

Indiana,[7] Massachusetts,[8] Maine,[9] Nevada,[10] New Hampshire,[11] Ohio,[12] Oklahoma,[13] Pennsylvania,[14] Tennessee,[15] West Virginia,[16] Wisconsin,[17] as well as Arizona, the Dakotas, Florida, Illinois, Michigan, Mississippi, Montana, Texas, Utah, Vermont, Mexico, and others.[18]

Of personal interest for me, this includes Warren, Minnesota. This is a small farming town where my wife was raised. Located within a few feet of the old Pembina trail between Warren and Thief River Falls in Viking Township, they called the mound "Lone mound," presumably because it was the only one around. It is still there and I visited it during the Christmas season of 2011.

There is a funny story surrounding this mound. After telling my in-laws about the write-up in the Minnesota Historical Societies Report,[19] I asked my in-laws if they knew anyone who might know anything about this mound. They said, "Yes. In fact, there is a former president of the Society who lives down the street." I was there before they finished giving me the directions.

Upon walking in and telling them my business, they sat me down with some cookies and we began to talk. They were a wonderful couple. "Have you ever heard of a mound around here called Lone Mound, somewhere over by Viking?" I asked.

"Yes, in fact I've done a couple of digs on it. One was back in the 60s." I was speechless. I'd hit the jackpot.

"What did you find?"

"Not a lot. There were some old Indian relics and that's about it."

"You didn't find any giant bones or anything like that?"

He started to laugh. "No. There's no such thing. They had done a a previous dig on it back in the 30s, but they didn't find anything then either," he told me.

"So you haven't heard about the dig they did in 1882 then, where they said they found giant bones?"

"No, I haven't. But I wouldn't believe a story like that."

"You were the president of the Minnesota Historical Society, right?"

"Yes."

"If I told you that they were the ones that reported it, would you believe it?"

He immediately and whole-heartedly said, "Of course." So I proceeded to pull out the article and we read it together. Back in the day, it was 12 ft. high x 60 ft. wide. It was examined by the Honorable J. P. Nelson, one of the original founders of Warren. He and those digging discovered bones of more than ten persons of "gigantic stature" but with no specific estimate of height. These human skeletons were mingled with horses, dogs, and badgers. The skeletons almost all disintegrated on exposure to the air with the exception of a single skull, which was obtained by one Theodore Lewis, who helped write the report.

My new friend was absolutely beside himself. "I can't believe I've never heard of this story," he said rather dejectedly. I was, however, quite pleased that I had made a new convert.

"What do you think they would have done with that skull," I inquired? He told me that he thought for sure that Lewis, who was hired by the Society to document these ancient places and digs, would have taken the skull for the Society rather than his own collection. He told me that he would check, next time he was in the Cities. Unfortunately, the kind old man died before I was able to see him again.

Like those in many other mounds around the country, especially out east, the skull appeared to have standard "Caucasian" features. Given other similar finds throughout Minnesota (see below),[20] assuming they were genuine, the skeletons could have been between 7 and 10 feet tall.[21]

(Special thanks to Ryan and Holly Knutson for taking us to the mound)

FIG. APP.4.1. AUTHOR STANDING ON "LONE MOUND," VIKING TOWNSHIP, MN

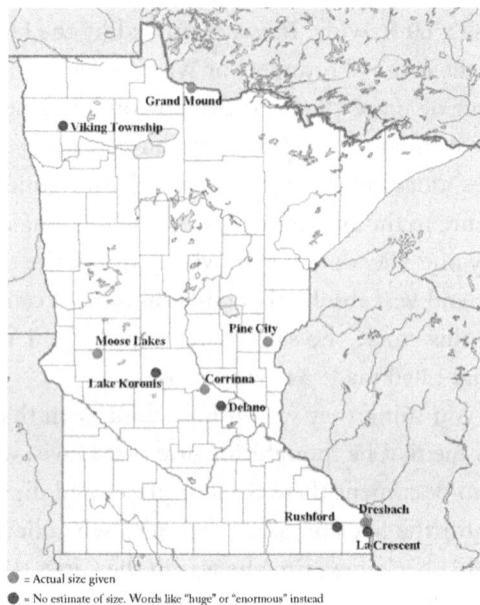

= Actual size given

= No estimate of size. Words like "huge" or "enormous" instead

FIG. APP.4.2. MINNESOTA SKELETONS WITH HEIGHTS ABOVE SEVEN FEET

Other graves of North American giants included blondes in Mexico,[22] and red-heads in Nevada.[23] There are giants with double rows of teeth found throughout the continent.[24] Like the giants of the Bible, as reported by Egyptians, Sumerians, and others, these giants are reported as having Caucasian facial features (which explains the blonde and red hair).

Legends are pervasive. One story is told of no one less than Col. George Washington. During the French and Indian War, Washington was in command of a militia force in Winchester, Virginia. He directed the men to begin digging the foundation of what would become Fort Loudoun. During the dig, the men discovered "Indian" skeletons that Washington reported were seven feet long.[25]

The Indians tell the same kind of history which mostly vanished bones can now only whisper. For example, in her book *Life Among the Paiutes*, Sarah Winnemucca writes,

> Among the traditions of our people is one of a small tribe of barbarians who used to live along the Humboldt River. It was many hundred

years ago. They used to waylay my people and kill and eat them. They would dig large holes in our trails at night, and if any of our people travelled at night, which they did, for they were afraid of these barbarous people, they would oftentimes fall into these holes. That tribe would even eat their own dead— yes, they would even come and dig up our dead after they were buried, and would carry them off and eat them.

Now and then they would come and make war on my people. They would fight, and as fast as they killed one another on either side, the women would carry off those who were killed. My people say they were very brave. When they were fighting they would jump up in the air after the arrows that went over their heads, and shoot the same arrows back again. My people took some of them into their families, but they could not make them like themselves. So at last they made war on them.

This war lasted a long time. Their number was about twenty-six hundred (2600). The war lasted some three years. My people killed them in great numbers, and what few were left went into the thick bush. My people set the bush on fire. This was right above Humboldt Lake. Then they went to work and made tuly or bulrush boats, and went into Humboldt Lake.

They could not live there very long without fire. They were nearly starving. My people were watching them all round the lake, and would kill them as fast as they would come on land. At last one night they all landed on the east side of the lake, and went into a cave near the mountains. It was a most horrible place, for my people watched at the mouth of the cave, and would kill them as they came out to get water. My people would ask them if they would be like us, and not eat people like coyotes or beasts. They talked the same language, but they would not give up.

At last my people were tired, and they went to work and gathered wood, and began to fill up the mouth of the cave. Then the poor fools began to pull the wood inside till the cave was full. At last my people set it on fire; at the same time they cried out to them, "Will you give up and be like men, and not eat people like beasts? Say quick —we will put out the fire." No answer came from them. My people said they thought the cave must be very deep or far into the mountain. They had never seen the cave nor known it was there until then. They called out to them as loud as they could, "Will you give up? Say so, or you will all die." But no answer came.

Then they all left the place. In ten days some went back to see if the fire had gone out. They went back to my third or fifth great-grandfather and told him they must all be dead, there was such a horrible smell. This tribe was called people-eaters, and after my people had killed them all, the people round us called us *Say-do-carah*. It means conqueror; it also means "enemy." I do not know how we came by the name of Piutes. It is not an Indian word. I think it is misinterpreted. Sometimes we are called Pine-nut eaters, for we are the only tribe that lives in the country where Pine-nuts grow. My people say that the tribe we exterminated had reddish hair. I have some of their hair, which has been handed down from father to son.[26]

Incredibly, decades after her book was published and years after she had died, this very cave was excavated in 1911 for its bat guano, a useful fertilizer for the barren desert of Nevada. After digging nearly to the bottom, the men began running across specimens of red hair, human artefacts, and giant bones and skulls. In all, nearly 50 bodies were uncovered.[27] Though many of these have mysteriously vanished, the museum at Winnemucca, NV is still in possession of some of the skulls. (Note: In the intervening years, they too have now "lost" the bones to a University from which, my guess is, they shall never be seen again). The Paiutes claimed that some of these red headed people reached heights up to 12 feet tall. One of the skulls in the museum's possession fit a person over eight feet tall, while skeletons up to ten feet were found in the dried up bottom of the Humbolt Lake.[28]

Another interesting story is told by the legendary Buffalo Bill Cody in his autobiography,

> While we were in the sandhills, scouting the Niobrara country, the Pawnee Indians brought into camp some very large bones, one of which the surgeon of the expedition pronounced to be the thigh bone of a human being. The Indians said the bones were those of a race of people who long ago had lived in that country. They said these people were three times the size of a man of the present day, that they were so swift and strong that they could run by the side of a buffalo, and, taking the animal in one arm, could tear off a leg and eat it as they ran.
>
> These giants, said the Indians, denied the existence of a Great Spirit. When they heard the thunder or saw the lightning, they laughed and declared that they were greater than either. This so displeased the Great Spirit that he caused a deluge. The water rose higher and higher till it drove these proud giants from the low grounds to the hills and thence to the mountains. At last even the mountaintops were submerged and the mammoth men were drowned.
>
> After the flood subsided, the Great Spirit came to the conclusion that he had made men too large and powerful. He therefore corrected his mistake by creating a race of the size and strength of men of the present day. This is the reason, the Indians told us, that the man of modern times is small and not like the giants of old. The story has been handed down among the Pawnees for generations, but what is its origin no man can say."[29]

Cody's story might be chalked up to a Wild West legend knowing how to *spin a yarn* ... though he did say he was in possession of some of these giant bones. Were they animal bones, dinosaur bones, or human bones? It is reported (I cannot verify it) that the bone(s) were given to a museum, many people saw them, but they have since vanished.

The size of the giant bears a striking resemblance to stories told by the Peruvian natives in the 1500s. Half Spanish, half Peruvian, Pedro de Cieza de León was a conquistador and historian of South America. He writes "concerning giants in Peru" who landed on the coast at the point of Santa Elena near the city of Puerto Viejo and were four or five times the height of the native peoples. The entire story is worth citing:

> The natives relate the following tradition, which had been received from their ancestors from very remote times. There arrived on the coast, in boats made of reeds, as big as large ships, a party of men of such size that, *from the knee downwards*, their height was as great as the entire height of an ordinary man, though he might be of good stature. Their limbs were all in proportion to the deformed size of their bodies, and it was a monstrous thing to see their heads, with hair reaching to the shoulders. Their eyes were as large as small plates. They had no beards, and were dressed in the skins of animals, others only in the dress which nature gave them, and they had no women with them.
>
> When they arrived at this point, they made a sort of village, and even now the sites of their houses are pointed out. But as they found no water, in order to remedy the want, they made some very deep wells, works which are truly worthy of remembrance; for such are the magnitude, that they certainly must have been executed by very strong men. They dug these wells in the living rock until they met with water, and then they lined them with masonry from top to bottom in such sort that they will endure for many ages. The water in these wells is very good and wholesome, and always so cold that it is very pleasant to drink it.
>
> Having built their village, and made their wells or cisterns where they could drink, these great men, or giants, consumed all the provisions they could lay their hands upon in the surrounding country; in so much that one of them ate more meat then fifty of the natives of the country could. As all the food they could find was not sufficient to sustain them, they killed many fish in the sea with nets and other gear. They were detested by the natives, because in using their women they killed them, and the men also in another way. But the Indians were not sufficiently numerous to destroy this new people who had come to occupy their lands. They made great leagues against them, but met with no success.
>
> All the natives declare that God our Lord brought upon them a punishment in proportion to the enormity of their offence. While they were

all together, engaged in their accursed . . . a fearful and terrible fire came
down from heaven with a great noise, out of the midst of which there
issued a shining angel with a glittering sword, with which, at one blow,
they were all killed, and the fire consumed them. There only remained
a few bones and skulls, which God allowed to remain without being
consumed by the fire, as a memorial of this punishment. This is what
they say concerning these giants, and we believe the account because in
this neighbourhood they have found, and still find, enormous bones.

I have heard from Spaniards who have seen part of a double tooth,
that they judged the whole tooth would have weighed more than half a
butcher's pound. They also had seen another piece of a shin bone, and it
was marvelous to relate how large it was. These men are witnesses to the
story, and the site of the village may be seen, as well as the wells and
cisterns made by the giants [emphasis and paragraph breaks mine].[30]

Curiously, he goes on to note that "at the point of Santa Elena ... there
are certain wells, or mines, of such excellent tar, that as many ships as
require caulking might be caulked with it." Giants, living near tar-pits,
destroyed by fire from heaven, because of immoral behavior that some
take as sexual in nature?[31] The whole incredible story sounds like Sodom
and Gomorrah.[32] From at least the time of the English translation of de
Leon, these stories have been relegated to cases of mistaken identity,
confusing human bones with those of giant animals,[33] though they were
accepted as true after excavations in 1543 were made of apparently quite
ribs, teeth, and other bones.[34]

There are many very famous explorers who report actually seeing
living giant peoples when Europeans first came to the Americas, though
none are close to the height in the two previous stories. Included are
Capt. John Smith, Hernando De Soto, Francisco Vázquez de Coronado,
Hernando Cortéz, and Ferdinand Magellan.[35] These sightings were all
shocking to them because other Indians were so short. In fact, the entire
region of Patagonia was named by Magellan for the aborigines who
lived there. Patagonia means "Big Feet." As recently as the early 20th
century, an encounter in Greenland was related to the *New York Times*
by Capt. Christian Jensen who had spent a year living with the Eskimos
near Ivigtût Bay. He reports how copper-colored giants ("seven, eight,
and even nine feet tall") who had never been seen by the natives, only
rumored to exist, were encountered. Though they could not speak the
Eskimo language, they made it clear they had been driven from their
homes in the interior by storms and cold weather.[36]

There are also chronicles from around the world (see Fig. App. 4.4). In fact, there are so many stories about giants—and I'm not talking about mythology—it staggers the imagination. The most recent story I've heard was told by an American Military Pilot flying a secret mission out of Afghanistan in 2005. He tells how on this mission he personally flew a dead 12 ft. cannibalistic giant out of the Middle East after it destroyed a Special Forces Op. that was hunting Taliban. This giant was white skinned, had 24 digits, red hair, and weighed perhaps as much as 1,500 lbs. You can listen to the testimony of the actual pilot online[37] or read about it for yourself.[38] Take it for whatever it is worth.

Then there is the Georgian (former Soviet Union) news report by Michael Robakidze for the Russian Channel One from August 6, 2008 (also reported by the Rustavi2 tv-channel, Trend N. Kirtskhalia, and other news outlets). They interview Abesalom Vekua (Ph.D.) of the Academy of Sciences of Georgia who, *while holding up the giant bones*, says that this ancient race (he does not refer to them as the kind of giants we are thinking about in this book), "could be from 2.5 to 3 meters tall."[39] Translated, that's 8.2 – 9.8 feet.

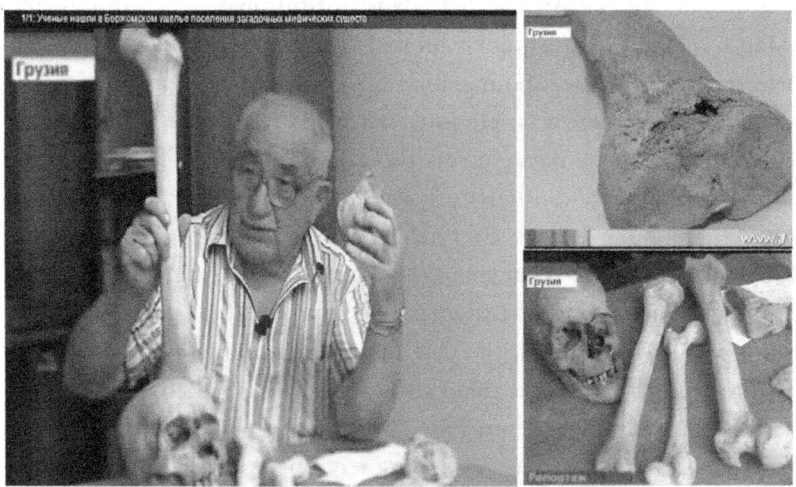

Vidcap of Dr. Abesalom Vekua holding the bones of a 2.5 – 3 meter giant
Lower Right: Normal size femur (middle) next to the giant femur
Courtesy Russian Channel One news

FIG. APP.4.3. GIANT BONES FROM BORJOMI GORGE, GEORGIA (RUSSIA)

What are we to make of such reports? It is common in present day academia, especially in the west, to scoff. This is partly justifiable because there is little hard evidence upon which to conduct empirical analysis. There were also known fakes.[40] We should always keep these things in mind, because they are important factors. On the other hand, many of the reports explain why the evidence is missing: The bones were put into private collections, taken to museums (or seized) and never seen again, they disintegrated upon contact with the air, they were reburied, etc.

To some, this only supports their own conspiracy theory ("of course there are not giants, that's impossible") that those who accept such claims are dishonestly engaging in, supporting, or buying the real conspiracy ("the giants are being suppressed"). Others see here non-falsifiable excuses conveniently offered up at a time when sensational journalism, tall-tales, a need to inspire a new wave of immigration, and a Barnum and Bailey circus like atmosphere dominated *all* western expansion. In other words, nothing that any of these people say about anything extraordinary could ever be taken seriously. The bones of seven, not to mention twelve-foot giants should be treated to the same level of seriousness as Paul Bunyan and Babe, his giant blue ox. When "Caucasian" hair or skeletal features are included in all this, charges of racism and disdain for the American Indian (institutionalized in things like *Manifest Destiny*) are quickly leveled as certain proof that we *must not* believe all of these lies about giants.

Of course, there was certainly racism and ignorance and hucksters all present in those days, just as there are today. People like Joseph Smith took these and other stories and created entirely new religions out of them. But everyone? Everywhere? Talk about a conspiracy theory. Talk about paranoia. What about the reports by the Indians themselves? Certainly, they are not racist against *themselves*? What possible reason could Miss Winnemucca, the daughter of a prominent Indian Chief, have to lie or trick people about stories and personal belongings, especially seeing that her ancestor's memories were reported as fact after she died? And what about the story being seemingly verified decades after she died?

Also (Buffalo Bill excluded), in many cases we are not talking about an odd-ball bone fragment scattered here or there along the ground which can easily become a case of mistaken identity (something which has been all too prevalent in the history of this subject[41]), but of entire skeletons, intricately dressed and laid out in ceremonial fashion in burial mounds. It is irrational, not to mention prejudiced, to conclude that every person who saw them, including trained palaeontologists and biologists, couldn't tell the difference between a human skeleton and one of, say, a dog or a horse. In fact, as we have seen, in some of the sites dogs and horses were buried alongside of the giant human skeletons, *and were reported as such*. Too often, our pioneer ancestors are treated like ignorant, uneducated, superstitious, backwoods hicks who couldn't tell their right hand from their left, or a human skull from that of a wild boar.

What about the missing bones? As I said earlier, this is and should be a factor in making our decision on such stories, but not the *only* factor.[42] Empirical analysis is not the only kind of evidence that is admissible in a court of law. Expert witnesses and eye-witness testimony are a different and significant kind of evidence that should be given its due weight. Often times, doctors were present in the reports. Only if we presuppose that all of these people were *de facto* sinister or out of their minds etc. would we deny their testimony a place as we formulate our own judgments.

In this regard, the similarity and sobriety of the accounts should also be considered. In the reports from North America, not one of them says that 40-foot giants were found, or even 15-foot giants (again Buffalo Bill excluded). None say they had blue hair or one eye socket or other things often associated with giants in mythology.[43] Rather, what we get are mostly the kind of thing we would expect from people digging things up and telling us what they found. It is ordinary, sober, detailed information about some very extraordinary discoveries.

Clearly, some people will take any and every story of a giant that they find and accept it as gospel truth without hesitation or research, even though some of the past discoveries have been discredited. Furthermore, some contemporary writers on this subject do in fact have hidden agendas (e.g. neo-Nazi, new age, or other). Some probably make up or stretch facts and perpetrate them on an unsuspecting public. With this topic, a sucker really may be born every minute (see n. 14). We should be leery of individuals who make incredible claims. Let a matter be heard only on the testimony of "two or three witnesses."

On the other hand, those who take the sceptical position are hardly immune to equally egregious bias such as political correctness, a pre-commitment to naturalism, fear of losing their credibility or even their job, or what have you. Also, it seems to me that the opposite mistake is also often practiced. If some are ultra-gullible, others take none of this seriously, often on the basis that we have no hard evidence. This is patently absurd, predisposed to its own set of biases, and perhaps subject to its own kind of conspiracy theories (i.e., "everyone is lying about this"). As Christians, it is also a double standard. If hard evidence were our only criterion, we could not accept the existence of Goliath, Og, or any giant in the Bible, not to mention *anyone else* in the Bible; for what bones of any of them do we have to do empirical testing (relics found in the crusades not included)?

My own feeling is that somewhere in the middle lies the truth. How close to the edges that truth is, I'm not sure. The majority of credible upper-limit reports seem to taper off at about 12 feet. In the chart below, I offer a sampling of some of these finds, of which as the heights go up, the historical veracity goes down. There are literally hundreds and hundreds of such reports out there on every populated continent and most of the major islands on the planet.

Giant(s)	Description	Date	Place	Height
Christopher Munster	Tomb has a life size picture	d. 1676	Yeoman of the guard, Hanover, England	8 ½ ft.**
Chief Thurourangi	Six ft. tall up to his armpits	1600s	Mokoia Island, New Zealand	9 ft.
John Middleton	Painting preserved in the Library of Brasenose College, Oxford.	b. 1578	Manchester, England	9'3"
Secondilla & Pusio			Keepers of the gardens of Sallust	9 ½ ft.
Calbara		Reign of Claudius Caesar	From Arabia to Rome	10 ft.
Mass grave.		Dec. 17, 1615 (as reported by Jacob le Maire)	Port Desire (near the Straits of Magellan)	10-11 ft.
Aymon		Late 1500s	Germany	11 ft.
Funnam		Reign of Eugene II	Scotland	11 ½ ft.
Hans Braw	The 8 ft. plus Baron Bentenrieder came up to his armpits.	1550s	Austria	12'8"
Guanche Giant	80 teeth		Peak of Teneriffe, Canary Islands (Spain)	15ft.
Ricon de Vallemont	Skull held a bushel of corn, shin bone was 4 ft.	Dug up in 1509	Rouen (France)	17-18 ft.
Ferragus		Slain by Orlande, nephew of Charlemagne		18 ft.
Unnamed	Platerus, a famous physician saw these bones.			19 ft.
Isoret	Rioland, a celebrated anatomist saw the bones.	Reported in 1614	St. Germain (France)	20 ft.
Bucart, tyrant of the Vivarais		Found in 1705	Banks of the Morderi, near Mt. Crussol (France)	22 ½ ft.
Theutobochus Rex	Teeth the size of an ox's foot. Shin bone 4 ft. Tomb was 30 ft. long, 12 ft. wide, 8 ft. high. Entire skeleton found in a grave marking the name.	Jan 11, 1613	Discovered in "The giants field" near a castle in Dauphine (France) at a depth of 18 ft.	25 ½ ft.
Unnamed	Two men together could barely put four arms around its head. Legs still (as of the 1800s) kept in the castle of the city.	758	Totu, Bohemia	26 ft.
Unnamed	Head the size of a hogshead. Teeth: 5 oz.	1516	Mazario, Sicily	30 ft.
Two unnamed skeletons		1548, 1559	Palormo, Sicily in the valley of Mazara	30, 33 ft.
Two unnamed skeletons		Unknown	Athens, Greece	34, 36 ft.

* References are found in Edmund Burke, *The Annual Register: A View of the History, Politicks, and Literature for the Year 1764* (London: J. Dodsley, 1765), 106-07; *Encyclopedia Britannica*, Vol. 9 (Edinburgh: Archibald Constable and Company, 1823), 700; Johann Georg Keyssler, *Travels through Germany, Bohemia, Hungary, Switzerland, Italy, and Lorrain* Vol. 1 (London, G. Keith, 1760), 31, 41-42; George Milbry Gould and Walter Lytle Pyle, *Anomalies and Curiosities of Medicine* (Philadelphia: W.B. Saunders, 1901), 325-26; Edward J. Wood, *Giants and Dwarfs* (London: Bentley, 1868). ** Munster's height is put at "4 Flemish ells (27 inches) 6 inches." That would make him 114+ inches or 9 ½ ft., though *Guinness* puts it at 8 ½ feet.

TABLE 12. A SMALL SAMPLING OF PAST GIANTS

WISCONSIN MOUND OP

**Skeleton Found of a Man Ov
Feet High with an Enormous**

MAPLE CREEK, Wis., Dec. 19.
the three recently discovered moun
town has been opened. In it was f
skeleton of a man of gigantic si
bones measured from head to foot
feet and were in a fair state of
tion. The skull was as large as a ha
measure. Some finely tempered rod
per and other relics were lying
bones.
  The mound from which these re
taken is ten feet high and thirty f
and varies from six to eight feet in
  The two mounds of lesser size wi
cavated soon.

The New York Times
Published: December 20, 1897
Copyright © The New York Times

SKELETON OF A GIANT FOUND.—A
since, some workmen engaged in sub
grounds of Sheriff WICKHAM, at his viney
Wheeling, came across a human skeleton
much decayed, there was little difficulty in
it, by placing the bones, which could n
longed to others than a human body, in t
position. The impression made by the
the earth, and the skeleton itself, were m
the Sheriff and a brother in the craft loc
whom were prepared to swear that it was
inches in length. Its jaws and teeth we
large as those of a horse. The bones are t
the Sheriff's office.—*Wheeling Times.*

The New York Times
Published: November 21, 1856
Copyright © The New York Times

(above) SKELETON OF GIANT FOUND.-
-A day or two since, some workmen engaged
in subsoiling the grounds of Sheriff WICKHAN,
at his vineyard in East Wheeling, came across
a human skeleton. Although much decayed,
there was little difficulty in identifying it, by
placing the bones, which could not have belonged to others than a human body, in their
original position. The impression made by the
skeleton in the earth and the skeleton itself
were measured by the sheriff and a brother of
the craft locale, both of whom were ready to
swear that it was 10 feet nine inches in length.
It's jaws and teeth were almost as large as
those of a horse. The bones are to be seen at
the Sheriff's office. -- *Wheeling Times.*

GIANTS' BONES IN MO

**Scientists Unearth Relics of
Who Lived 700 Years A**
Special to The New York Tim

BINGHAMTON, July 13.—Pr
B. Skinner of the American In
seum, Professor W. K. Mor
Phillips Andover Academy,
George Donohue, Pennsylvan
Historian, who have been condu
searches along the valley of the
hanna, have uncovered an India
at Tioga Point, on the upper p
Queen Esther's Flats, on what
as the Murray farm, a short
from Sayre, Penn., which prom
additions to Indian lore.
  In the mound uncovered we
the bones of sixty-eight men w
believed to have been buried 7
ago. The average height of t
was seven feet, while many we
taller. Further evidence of
gantic size was found in large
axes hewed from stone and t
the grave. On some of the sk
inches above the perfectly form
head, were protuberances of bo
bers of the expedition say that
first discovery of its kind on re
a valuable contribution to the h
the early races.
  The skull and a few bones
one grave were sent to the
Indian Museum.

The New York Times
Published: July 14, 1916
Copyright © The New York Tim

ST. PAUL, 24.—A skull of hero
size and singular formation has ju
been discovered among the relics
the mound builders in the R
River Valley. The mound was
feet in diameter, and 12 feet hig
Near the centre were found th
bones of about a dozen males an
females, mixed with bones of var
ous animals. The skull in questi
was the only perfect one, and ne
it were found some abnormally lar
body bones. The man who bore
was evidently a giant. A thorou
investigation of the mound a
contents will be made by the h
torical society.

These clippings and many more have been posted at one very helpful website:
"Old Newspaper Articles are Serious About Giant Skeletons."
See also Note 3 in this appendix.

FIG. APP.4.4. NEWSPAPER CLIPPINGS OF GIANTS

APPENDIX V

Giants of Monument & Myth

Monument: Giant Intaglios, Effigies and Statues

Before examining oral traditions, I thought a brief display of some of the enormous human intaglios (incised carvings of figures sunk below the surface) from around the world might be fun. These strange figures were hewn, not only with hands and tools, but with oral traditions of giants.

Southwestern United States

Near Yuma, AZ there is a gigantic glyph depicting Kumastamo, the god who created the Colorado River with his magic rod. This deity then plotted the death of Sky-Rattlesnake, an evil spirit and source of dark powers, by cutting off his head. He then turned himself into a fish-eagle and few off into oblivion.[1] If one is open minded to the possibility, it is not difficult to see echoes of the story of Eden (Genesis 3:15) and Noah's flood with its water and birds. It is curious that all around the desert southwest there are gigantic intaglios of giant people and animals, and no one knows their source.[2]

According to the Hopi Indians, Masau'u (another name for Kumastamo) it to be identified with the constellation Orion, which remarkably, be it in the new world or the old, is often drawn as a giant waving a spear or a club.

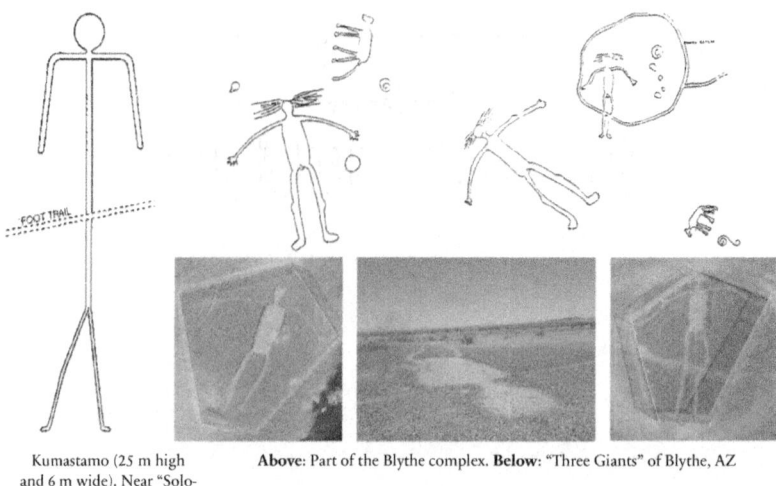

Kumastamo (25 m high and 6 m wide). Near "Solomon's Cross," Yuma, AZ

Above: Part of the Blythe complex. **Below:** "Three Giants" of Blythe, AZ

FIG. APP.5.1. INTAGLIOS OF THE AMERICAN SOUTHWEST

Britain

Around the world in Britain, located near Dorset, England, there stands the 180 ft. high by 167 ft. wide Cerne-Abbas Giant. Visible in Google Earth, this giant is virtually identical to the depictions of Orion, except that in his left hand there was very probably a decapitated head (it has since been destroyed).[3] Some say the Cerne-Abbas Giant is a representation of the demi-god Hercules. But local folklore says that this was a local giant who terrorized the area of Cerne Abbas. On one occasion he got so greedy that he ate a whole flock of sheep, whereupon he fell asleep on the hillside and was killed by the townspeople. One John Gibbons (1670) wrote that this giant took part in a battle on the famed Salisbury plain between King Divitiacus and the Cerngik Giants. Though it may be as recent as the 17th century, this legend puts the origins of the giant back in the 2nd century.[4]

Another giant depiction may be found along the southwest coast of England near Wilmington. Also visible from Google Earth, the so-named "Long Man" giant is 227 ft. and appears to be holding two spears in his hands. Originally, he was portrayed wearing a horned helmet which was destroyed in the 19th century. There is no consistent folklore

Cerne Abbas Giant, Dorset, UK.   Greco-Roman Orion/Hercules   Osiris (Egyptian "Orion")

FIG. APP.5.2. CERNE ABBAS GIANT AND HERCULES/ORION

FIG. APP.5.3. LONGMAN OF WILMINGTON (ENGLAND)

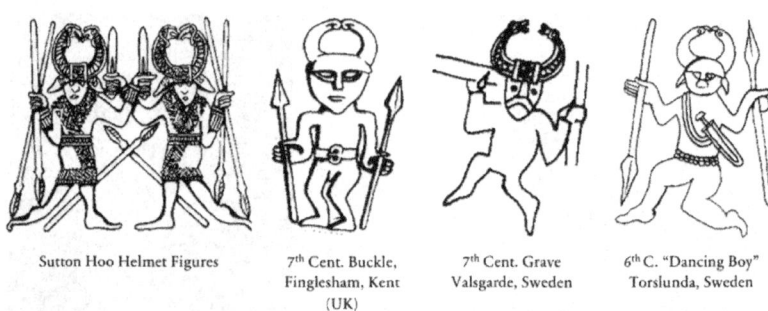

| Sutton Hoo Helmet Figures | 7th Cent. Buckle, Finglesham, Kent (UK) | 7th Cent. Grave Valsgarde, Sweden | 6th C. "Dancing Boy" Torslunda, Sweden |

FIG. APP.5.4. "HORNED MEN" OF NORTHERN EUROPE

pertaining to this giant, though it has been said that he was killed by the Firle Beacon giant, and that the effigy was made before the flood.[5]

Horned Men

There is some reason to see this figure associated with Celtic and Nordic paganism. Throughout Scandinavia, especially in the 6th and 7th centuries, figures like the Long Man have been preserved in tombs and rock carvings.[6] These horned men straddle two continents.

Back in the United States, we travel up to Wisconsin for a most peculiar effigy. It is a 214 ft. long, 48 ft. wide, 3 ft. tall mound called the Man Mound of Baraboo. Actually, there were several "Man Mounds," most of which were destroyed by the early settlers of the area. Some people speculate that these represent the Thunderbird, Waterspirit, or other such creatures.

Frank Joseph suggests that he is Wakt'cexi, the deluge-hero of the Winnebago Indians. In their *Worak* (tribal histories), they speak of the Wolf Clan who came to Turtle Island (North America) after a huge flood destroyed their homeland wearing a horned helmet.[7] A Neolithic rock figure from Rodoy, Norway may depict this same voyage (though my daughter thinks it is a bunny rabbit on skies).

This horned man was known across North America. For instance, a Navaho initiation ceremony for children involved a masked man wearing a red wig (i.e. red hair) and horned helmet. His wife's face was painted white (i.e. a white person). This couple represented the family

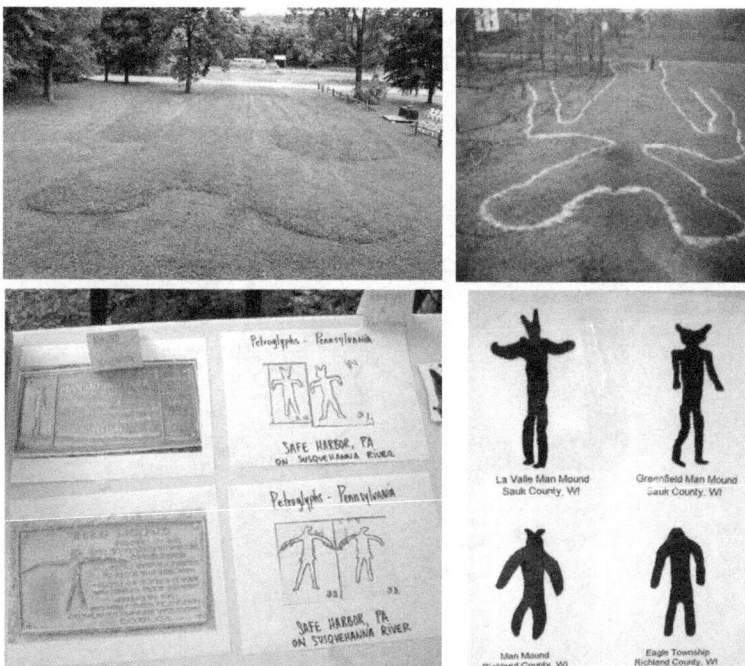

Above: "Man Mound" outlined in chalk. **Below:** Horned & Winged Petroglyphs of the Susquehanna River, PA compared to similar mounds in Wisconsin. Image by Donald Cadzo, Pennsylvania Historical Commission

Above: "Man Mound," Baraboo, WI. **Below:** "Man Mounds" of Wisconsin. Image provided by the Sauk County Historical Society.

Horned Boat-Man. Rodoy, Norway.

FIG. APP.5.5. MAN MOUND AND OTHER RELATED EFFIGIES

that survived the Great Flood as a reminder of the ancient origins of the people.[8] A similar ceremony was performed in the Apache Crown Dance.[9]

In the fall of 2009, I had the opportunity to visit some rock carvings in north-western Colorado. These also depict a horned man, sometimes carrying a rod. These were carved by the Fremont Indians who lived in

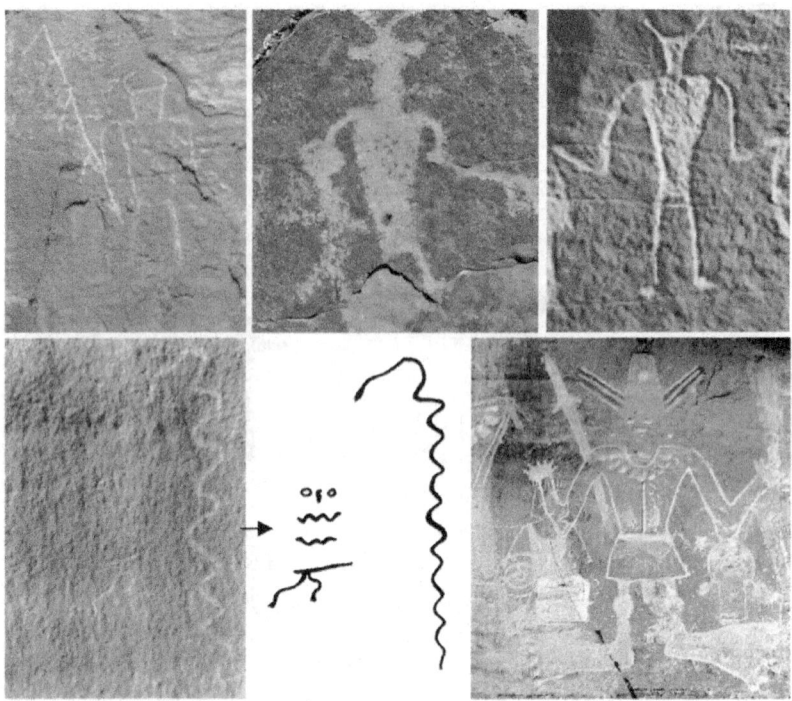

FIG. APP.5.6. FREMONT INDIAN HORNED MEN, COLORADO PLATEAU

the area from 400-1250 AD. As I began searching out other Fremont rock-art on the internet, it became immediately clear that the figure is almost always depicted with horns, often with a family—which usually has many different animals nearby. Some of these figures are clearly depicted as giants. Among the more interesting of this collection are the serpent hovering over the "Owl Man" and the one I dub "Bigfoot" (see if you can spot him).

Much earlier glyphs (called "Barrier Canyon" glyphs), made by an unknown race who lived here between 6,000 B.C.(?) and the turn of the turn of the common era are truly bizarre. They are nothing like the art depicted above. They show giant horned men with elongated proportions. At least one of them even seems to have a beard, which native Americans can't grow. No one knows what they represent.

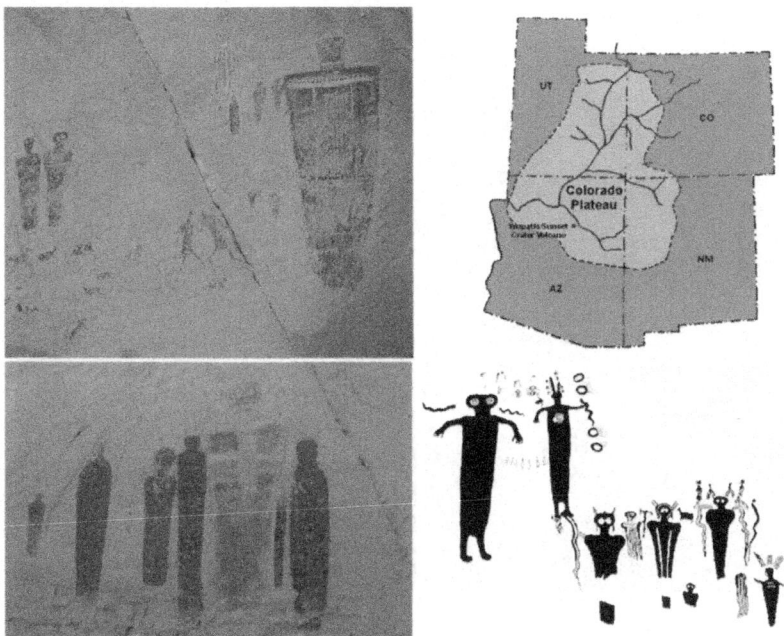

FIG. APP.5.7. BARRIER CANYON HORNED MEN, COLORADO PLATEAU

Meanwhile, sites out east near other horned-men glyphs have yielded bones of giants. A grave containing the supposed remains of Susqehannock Indians (whom Capt. John Smith encountered) were found near Spanish Hill, in Athens, PA. These skeletons ranged between 6 to 8 feet in length, shoulders above other Indians and the Europeans of the time.[10] It was actually reported on Wednesday, July 12, 1916 in a local newspaper that sixty-eight skeletons of men living 700 years ago were unearthed. Among the remains was a seven-foot skeleton of a man with horns protruding from his skull, which was witnessed by several reputable antiquarians.[11] The story seemed to gain a life of its own. In 1983, the *Reader's Digest* did a story on the find.[12]

Japan

If we travel around the world to Japan, we come across more horned giants called the Oni. Like other horned-giants, he also is

Upper Left: Red Oni with his kanabō; Upper Right: Oni Drawing;
Lower Left: Samurai on Horseback, 1878; Lower Right: Oni. Netsuke Carving, 19th Century

FIG. APP.5.8. JAPANESE ONI-HORNED GIANTS (W/ HORNED SAMURAI)

depicted as carrying a large club. The term Oni can mean "Ghost" or "invisible spirit," terminology reminiscent of the Rephaim and other giants of the Bible.

This is all strange, but in accordance with many worldwide stories of giants with horns who terrorized the local inhabitants, such as an African tale of a white horned 24 ft. giant with six fingers and toes (cf. 2 Sam 21:20; 1 Chron 20:6 for giants with six digits) who cannibalized the local people and was carved into a piece of ivory thousands of years ago (see Fig. App. 5.9), or the Celtic horned giant Cernunnos who is often depicted with serpents.

I am not trying to induce belief in such things by mentioning them here. Rather, I am demonstrating that there are common inscriptions, drawings, sightings, and stories around the world that seem to depict a remembrance of the same thing, however distorted it may have become or accurate it may have remained over time.

Giants of Mythology

Rome: Titans

While I have an appendix dealing with understanding myth in light of Scripture, this section will go into more detail about particular

Six fingered giant
African, Ivory
Image provided by
Klaus Dona via Steve
Quayle

Six fingered figurine
Scythian tomb, Altai
Mountains, Russia
Hermitage Museum, St.
Petersburg

Six Fingered Hands, Three Rivers, NM

FIG. APP.5.9. SIX FINGERS

giant myths (I'll try to keep duplication to a minimum, but it is always nice to have things compiled together). Who were the giants according to the myths? There is no better place to start than with the Greeks. It was the poet Hesiod (ca. 8th cent. B.C.) who gave us the following explanation. This is what he writes,

> And great Sky came, bringing night with him; and spreading himself out around Earth in his desire for love he lay outstretched in all directions. Then his son reached out from his ambush with his left hand, and with his right hand he grasped the monstrous sickle, long and jagged-toothed, and eagerly he reaped the genitals from his dear father and threw them behind him to be borne away. But not in vain did they fall from his hand: for Earth received all the bloody drops that short forth, and when the years had revolved she bore the mighty Erinyes and the great Giants, shining in their armor, holding long spears in their hands, and the Nymphs whom they call the Melian ones on the boundless earth.
>
> (Hesiod, *Theogony* 176-186)

The Sky spreading himself around Earth is a sexual euphemism, easily seen in the personification of it in the god Uranus (the sky god), father of the Titan Kronus (Roman: Saturn, who mutilated him) and the goddess Gaia (the earth goddess). These giants possessed a peculiar feature that is related to this union between Heaven and Earth. This feature is the serpentine legs and feet that the giants were often said to possess.

After the Titans lost their epic battle with the gods of Mt. Olympus, Gaia roused her other sons, the Giants, against Zeus. Homer tells us that they tried to storm heaven by building, in effect, a tower. "They threatened to make war with the gods in Olympus, and tried to set Mount Ossa on the top of Mount Olympus, and Mount Pelion on the top of Ossa, that they might scale heaven itself."[13] Some have suggested that this myth belongs to the Tiamat and Rahab cycles of Babylonian origin, which brings the serpents into sharper focus.[14]

Another generation of giants grew up after the first were destroyed by Heracles (Hercules). According to the Roman poet Ovid (43 BC – 18 AD), these giants were "savage, violent, and eager for slaughter, so that you might know they were born from blood." Then, "When Saturn's son, the father of the gods, saw this from his highest citadel, he groaned, and he called the gods to council." "When the gods had taken their seats in the marble council chamber, their king, sitting high above them, leaning on his ivory sceptre spoke saying, 'I was not more troubled than I am now concerning the world's sovereignty than when each of the snake-footed giants prepared to throw his hundred arms around the imprisoned sky. . . Now I must destroy the human race. I swear it by the infernal streams, that glide below the earth."[15] When he had spoken, some gods encouraged him, others sat silently, but all were saddened at this destruction of the human species. Then, after considering destruction with fire, he rethought and finally "sent down rain from the whole sky and drown humanity beneath the waves."[16]

Scandinavia: Frost Giants, Fire Giants, and Mountain Giants

The Nordic Sagas contain a veritable smörgåsbord of giants. They come in three classes: Frost giants (*hrímpursar*), fire giants (*eldjötnar*), and mountain giants (*bergrisar*); while ogres and trolls (so popular as figurines) make up yet another class. Some giants of interest include Ymir (Brimir?) who had a beer-hall in the land of dwarves (men?), a race which was brought forth from his own flesh and blood.[17] There is a curious feature on this hall, "A hall I saw, | far from the sun, On Nas-

Villa del Casale   *Gigantomachia*
(Roman Mosaic 3rd C. A.D.)   Istanbul Archaeological Museum, Turkey

Fig. App.5.10. Serpentine Giants of Greek Mythology

trond it stands, | and the doors face north, Venom drops | through the smoke-vent down, For around the walls | do serpents wind."[18] Völva, the lady of wisdom who sings the *Völuspá* is herself related to the giants,[19] and furthermore, the giants were related to the gods by marriages. Such giants include *Ægir*, *Loki*, *Mimir*, and *Skaði*. At the final battle (*Ragnarök*), the giants will storm Asgard and defeat the gods. Finally, Valhalla (in Asgard) is the place where the spirits of the ancient dead warriors (god-giants) now reside.

North America: Mound Builders

If we recall the Mound Builders in Ohio, we find scholars debating when they were built. There is a peculiar mound near Cincinnati called the Serpent Mound (see below). Some say the Indians built it. However, the Mandan Indians were not in agreement with the professionals of today. For, it was said *by them* to have been built by "powerful, fearsome" beings descended from the "tidal flood."[20] There is evidence that this race may have been quite large.

Many of the mounds built by the Mound Builders were burial mounds. They were excavated in the 19th century, and as we have seen, a good number of them yielded bones of gigantic proportions from 7 ft. – 12ft. in length. A people that archaeologists have dubbed the Adena flourished in this region between 1000 BC – 700 AD. They may or may not have been the builders of the Serpent Mound. But in mounds that they did build, skeletons over 7 ft. were discovered in the 1800s.[21] The legends of the Serpent Mound builders is supported farther south and west in Illinois by the Shawnee Deluge Myth which remember the makers of a now broken 200 mile long stone wall, which they say was built by immigrating giants who survived the Great Flood.[22]

Farther south, along the Mississippi, the Choctaw Indians told of the Nahullo, an ancient race of red and yellow haired, white-skinned giants with tall horns. The folk traditions of the northern Ottawa tell of an alliance with the Ojibwa and Pottawattamic in ancient times to kill "the white giants" called *Yam-Ko-Desh*, and were able to survive *Ron-nong-weto-wanca*, or "Fair-skinned Giant Sorcerers." The Winnebago of Wisconsin have an oral history of their twin heroes, the brothers Red

FIG. APP.5.11. SERPENT MOUND, OHIO

Hair and Yellow Hair, and their crusades with an ancient race of giants.[23] In other words, the stories of the Indians line up with the reports of giant bones dug up during the last three centuries of American expansion to the west.

South America: Bochica

In the farthest southern reaches of South America, in the region of Patagonia, Magellan and his men ran into so many giants that the stories have become legendary, as even the name Patagonia means "big feet." Quetzalcoatl and Viracocha, the bringers of civilization to the Mayan and Aztec peoples, are intimately related to serpent mythology *and giants*. Viracocha was said to be the creator of the giants, but he became furious with them and turned them into stone. It is said that the amazing and impossible megalithic city called Tiahuanaco, which some say is the oldest city on earth, now in a barren wasteland above 13,000 ft, was built by giants called the Huaris. Eventually, Viracocha grew angry with the giants and flooded the earth till all was under water. They say that it rained 60 days and nights, and drown every living thing.[24]

Central America is famous for its fabulous pyramids. Thousands of them dot the jungles. The Cholulu Pyramid is one of the largest structures in the world. Two hundred and ten feet height, it covers forty-five acres. The pre-Conquest Mexican legend about Cholula is very similar to the Biblical account of the Tower of Babel. According to the legend, after the deluge which destroyed the primeval world, seven giants survived, one of whom built the great pyramid of Cholula in order to reach heaven, but the Gods destroyed the pyramid with fire and confounded the language of the builders.[25] "A Flood tradition of the Toltecs mentioned by Ixtlihochitl states that after the Deluge [giants] built a *zacuali* of great height to preserve them in the event of future deluges. After this their tongue became confused, and not understanding each other, they went to different parts of the world."[26]

In South America, throughout coastal Colombia, Venezuela, and Brazil, a white-skinned, long bearded giant named Bochica a once supported the sky on his shoulders, until he dropped it, causing the Great Flood. He later condemns a demon named Chibchacum to hold up the sky after the floods recede, while he takes up residence on the first rainbow. Thus, in *South America*, rainbows are venerated with their association to the Flood.[27]

Middle East: Nimrod

We've discussed Nimrod in detail, but it bears repeating in this Appendix. In legends, giants are said to be the builders of all sorts of cyclopean enigmas throughout the world, from the pyramids in the Americas to Easter Island to Stonehenge to Baalbek in Lebanon. Baalbek has the largest cut stone on earth, weighing in at an unbelievable 1,200 tons (that's 2.4 million pounds, see Figure 16). Michael Alouf writes,

> The Arabs, also, believe that Baalbek is the place where Nimrod built his famous tower… One reads in the Arabic manuscript found at Baalbek that "after the flood, when Nimrod reigned over Lebanon, he sent giants to rebuild the fortress of Baalbek, which was so named in honour of Baal, the god of the Moabites and worshipers of the sun."[28]

Nimrod, according to many legends, was said to be a giant and he used giants to cut the stones and build the temple.[29] While unlikely, as mentioned in an earlier chapter, he was also thought by many to be the builder of the Tower of Babel.

India: Asuras

As for the giants and a tower, variations of the story are recalled throughout the world as well. The Hindus remember the Bakasura, (from *asuras*, meaning "evil" in Sanskrit), red haired, evil beings variously translated as demons or giants,[30] who seek to imitate the great fire altar of heaven and "ascend to the sky." This altar is said to rise from the earth to Heaven. These enemies of the heavenly gods, tried to imitate it, but their undertaking came to nothing, as the gods overthrew it by taking away the foundation of bricks.[31]

New Zealand: Chief Tahourangi

Across the world in New Zealand, many giants appear in Maori legends. One giant is named Ka-whara and was twenty four feet tall. Another, Rau-kawa was over thirty.[32] More plausible (since the Maori also have giants hundreds and thousands of feet tall) are the supposed bones of chief Tahourangi. One person tells his story this way,

> In the Rotorua country, too, there are stories, no doubt based on fact, of huge warriors of the past. There was the chief Tuhourangi, for one; he lived three centuries ago. He was nine feet high, according to tradition, and was about six feet up to his armpits. His bones were buried on the east side of Pukurahi Pa, on Mokoia Island, above the present little settlement on the flat. The old man Tamati Hapimana told me, at Mokoia in 1896, that Tuhourangi's bones were still there, deep in the ground, enclosed in stone slabs. His story was that Sir George Grey, during his first Governorship of New Zealand, visited Mokoia and, hearing about the bones of a man of enormous size, obtained the consent of the chiefs to dig for the skeleton. The men whom he employed purposely dug in the wrong place and so the relics were never brought to light. This long-gone warrior's bones, in olden times, were disinterred at *kumara* planting time and were set up on the edge of the cultivations on Mokoia, while the priest recited the prayers for a bountiful harvest. The presence of the sacred bones was supposed to promote the fertility of the crop.[33]

Ireland: Fomorians and Grendal

The first inhabitants of Ireland were said to be the demonic Fomo-rians, said to be giant sea-people.[34] Their first leader, a giant named Cichol Gricenchos was said to have brought them to the Emerald Isle after the deluge, where they became its first inhabitants.[35] One of their later leaders was said to be a giant Cyclops named Balor, whose evil eye would kill anyone (sometimes turning them into stone like the Medusa) in its line of sight, and in the confusion of the mythology, his eye is even said to have caused the flood that brought them to the Island.[36] Since it is so near, I should probably bring up the great Anglo-Saxon giant named Grendal, a cannibalistic monster who lived in a cave, but finally defeated by the hero Beowulf.

Africa: Balor

On the Gold Coast of West Africa, several deluge myths exist among the Yoruba people. They explain how Olokun, the sea god, be-came angry with sinful human beings and sought to cause their extinc-tion by brining upon them a flood that would drown the whole world. Many nations perished, until a giant hero named Obatala stood in the middle of the waters and through his juju (magical powers) bound Olo-kun in seven chains.[37] David Livingstone, the famous Scottish mission-ary, found similar myths in Africa.[38]

So what are we to make of all these stories and sightings and bones and things? My purpose has not been to convince you that any of them are true. Really, I don't care if you believe them or not. As far as giants in particular are concerned, I have no way of knowing if any individual, nor his reported height, is true. The fact is, scant archaeological evi-dence is available for scientific scrutiny, many of the findings that were present at one time have mysteriously vanished, and so speculation and conspiracy theories abound. This is not *entirely* unjustifiable, since sci-entific proof of giants would throw the precious sacred theory of evolu-tion into a tailspin. They would also do great damage to the myth that the native Indians were the first peoples to settle these lands. There is a great deal of money, power, and politics at stake here; make no mistake about it. There is no doubt that for some people and some theories, the past is very much better left hidden and buried. But this still does not *prove* anything, so we must remain leery.

My point has been to demonstrate that our ancestors from around the world have, in their most ancient memories (and sometimes not so ancient), stories that ring similar to biblical epics like the Flood, the fall of the sons of God, the Tower of Babel, and that the heroes and villains associated with these stories are regularly identified as gigantic. They lived in caves, made horrible sounds, had too many fingers and toes, had strength of a different order of magnitude, were associated with sorcery and witchcraft, were are extremely violent, and ate the dead. That's the data. What will you make of it?

As a kind of postscript to these last two appendices, I want to bring to bring a word of caution that I hope would be self-evident. On one hand, Israel and the surrounding nations (like Moab, Ammon, and Edom) all fought the Rephaim and won great victories. Many accounts say that the surviving remnant of giants fled, settled, and were dispersed again by newer invaders. There is nothing inherently contradictory to the Bible about saying that these giants spread throughout the world and were destroyed by these other cultures.

On the other hand, just because someone is tall, it does not mean they are necessarily descended from Rapha or a Rephaim. This is a patently absurd and dangerous conclusion. Within a fairly broad range, populations can rise taller or fall shorter from quite ordinary causes such as war, diet, or marriage. As an example, the average height of Americans 100 years ago was significantly shorter than today. The height of the French after the Napoleonic wars went down drastically, as all the big tall men were killed off in the front lines of battle.

Other kinds of gigantism are well documented, such as the pituitary gland gone wild. The most famous giant of this kind was Robert Wadlow. Wadlow's growth chart is almost incomprehensible. At age 8 he was over six feet tall. He was 7'4" by 13, 8" by 17, and reached the incredible height of 8'11" at age 22, when he died from complications of his disease.

The tallest man of the 20th century standing next to his father.

Fig. App.5.12. Robert Pershing Wadlow (1918-1940)

Tall populations or improperly functioning organs are *not* what we are talking about in this book, and perhaps some of the giants in the appendices fit into those categories. But some people can pervert just about anything. Hence, the caution. Even if we found incontrovertible proof of living Rephaim today, what should we do about it? The commands of God towards Israel regarding the slaughter of these creatures are not commands given to us today. Israel was a temporary kingdom and her laws in this specific situation no longer obtain. We have not been given the Promised Land. Furthermore, the whole point of the book has been to demonstrate that Christ has defeated these creatures, and it was always and finally his battle to win. Nothing in Scripture gives us reason to commit genocide upon tall people or even Rephaim (assuming we could even figure out the difference).

However, the more general idea of wicked people overrunning a peaceful land to institute unthinkable monstrosities such as human sacrifice, cannibalism, bestiality, and genocide of the native population (as, for instance, the Indians sometimes speak of the giants in North America) is a different story. But of course, this kind of activity is not the sole domain of giants, as all kinds of perfectly human people have engaged in all of them. It seems to me that a civilization has a right to protect itself from such things, and, as we saw in the instance of Allied intervention in the Nazi program, even the obligation to stop its spread. Until such a time as a mass group of cannibalistic head-hunting giants raise their head in the world again, we have no right to or reason to wage war on giants that live among us. Instead, we can go to their basketball games, enjoy the entertainment, collect autographs, and gawk at the amazing physical *human* specimens that stand before our eyes.

APPENDIX VI

Genesis 6:1-4
in Early Jewish and Christian Tradition

This Appendix gives many of the known citations from early Jews and Church Fathers on the supernatural view of Genesis 6:1-4. The dates range from 3rd cent. BC – 4th cent. AD amongst the Jews and the early 2nd cent. – 4th cent. amongst the Christians (it does not include Jude, Peter, or Paul as discussed in the chapter). As noted, in Jewish circles, the Rabbis virtually wiped the only known older (supernatural) view out in the early second century in their circles and the Christians began to adopt the Sethite view (non-supernatural) only around the turn of the fifth century (with Augustine, Chrysostom, and Theodoret). Prior to the middle of the fourth century, the only known view in the church was the supernatural view,

Church Fathers

Papias (Second Century AD)

"PAPIAS SAYS THUS, WORD for word, 'But to some of them—clearly the holy angels of old—he gave authority to give order to the world, and he commanded them to exercise their authority well.' And he says immediately after that, 'But it happened that their order came to nothing.'"

(Papias, *Frag.* 4)

Justin Martyr (100-165 AD)

FOR THE TRUTH SHALL be spoken; since of old these evil demons, effecting apparitions of themselves, both defiled women and corrupted boys, and showed such fearful sights to men, that those who did not use their reason in judging of the actions that were done, were struck with terror; and being carried away by fear, and not knowing that these were demons, they called them gods, and gave to each the name which each of the demons chose for himself.

(Justin Martyr, *1 Apology 5*)

BUT THE ANGELS TRANSGRESSED this appointment, and were captivated by love of women, and begat children who are those that are called demons; and besides, they afterwards subdued the human race to themselves, partly by magical writings, and partly by fears and the punishments they occasioned, and partly by teaching them to offer sacrifices, and incense, and libations, of which things they stood in need after they were enslaved by lustful passions; and among men they sowed murders, wars, adulteries, intemperate deeds, and all wickedness. Whence also the poets and mythologists, not knowing that it was the angels and those demons who had been begotten by them that did these things to men, and women, and cities, and nations, which they related, ascribed them to god himself, and to those who were accounted to be his very offspring, and to the offspring of those who were called his brother), Neptune and Pluto, and to the children again of these their offspring. For whatever name each of the angels had given to himself and his children, by that name they called them.

(Justin, *2 Apology 5*)

Athenagoras (c. 133-190 AD)

SOME, FREE AGENTS, YOU will observe, such as they were created by God, continued in those things for which God had made and over which He had ordained them; but some outraged both the constitution of their nature and the government entrusted to them: namely, this ruler of matter and its various forms, and others of those who were placed about this first firmament (you know that we say nothing without witnesses, but state the things which have been declared by the prophets); these fell into impure love of virgins, and were subjugated by the flesh, and he became negligent and wicked in the management of the things entrusted to him. Of these lovers of virgins, therefore, were begotten those who are called giants. And if something has been said by the poets, too, about the giants, be not surprised at this: worldly Wisdom and divine differ as much from each other as truth and plausibility: the one is of heaven and the other of earth; and indeed, according to the prince of matter, "We know we oft speak lies that look like truths." These angels, then, who fell from heaven busy themselves about the air and the earth and are no longer able to rise to the realms above the heavens. The souls of the giants are the demons who wander about the world. Both angels and demons produce movements—demons movements which are akin to the natures they received, and angels movements which are akin to the lusts with which they were possessed. The prince of matter, as may be seen from what happens, directs and administers things in a manner opposed to God's goodness ... But since the demonic impulses and activities of the hostile spirit bring these wild attacks—indeed we see them move men from within and from without, one man one way and another man another, some individually and some as nations, one at a time and all together, because of our kinship with matter and our affinity with the divine ... But to the extent that it depends on the reason peculiar to each individual and the activity of the ruling prince and his attendant demons, one man is swept along one way, another man another way, even though all have the same rationality within.

(Athenagoras, *A Plea to Christians* 24-25)

Irenaeus (135-202 AD)

ENOCH, TOO, PLEASING GOD, without circumcision, discharged the office of God's legate to the angels although he was a man, and was translated, and is preserved until now as a witness of the just judgment of God, because the angels when they had transgressed fell to the earth for judgment, but the man who pleased [God] was translated for salvation.

(Irenaeus, *Against Heresies* 4.16.2)

IN THE DAYS OF NOAH He justly brought on the deluge for the purpose of extinguishing that most infamous race of men then existent, who could not bring forth fruit to God, since the angels that sinned had commingled with them, and [acted as He did] in order that He might put a check upon the sins of these men.

(Irenaeus, *Against Heresies* 4.36.4)

AND FOR A VERY LONG while wickedness extended and spread, and reached and laid hold upon the whole race of mankind, until a very small seed of righteousness remained among them and illicit unions took place upon the earth, since angels were united with the daughters of the race of mankind; and they bore to them sons who for their exceeding greatness were called giants. And the angels brought as presents to their wives teachings of wickedness, in that they brought them the virtues of roots and herbs, dyeing in colors and cosmetics, the discovery of rare substances, love-potions, aversions, amours, concupiscence, constraints of love, spells of bewitchment, and all sorcery and idolatry hateful to God; by the entry of which things into the world evil extended and spread, while righteousness was diminished and enfeebled.

(Irenaeus, *Demonstration of the Apostolic Preaching* 18)

Clement of Alexandria (150-215 AD)

[CERTAIN ANGELS OF HIGH RANK] having sunk into pleasures, uttered unspeakable things to the women, which had come to their knowledge. Note: This is a quote from 1 Enoch 16:2.

(Clement of Alexandria, *Stromata* 5.1.10.)

Bardaisan of Edessa (154-222 AD)

WE UNDERSTAND THEREFORE, that if angels would not have had their own freedom, they could not have married the daughters of men and could neither have sinned, nor have fallen from their place.

(Bardaisan of Edessa, *Book of the Laws of the Countries* 9)

Pseudo-Clementine Homilies (2ⁿᵈ-3ʳᵈ Cent. AD)

BUT WHEN [ANGELS], having assumed these forms ... they also partook of human lust, and being brought tinder its subjection they fell into cohabitation with women ... And all things, in short, which are for the adornment and delight of women, are the discoveries of these demons bound in flesh. But from their unhallowed intercourse spurious men sprang, ranch greater in stature than ordinary men, whom they afterwards called giants; not those dragon-footed giants who waged war against God, as those blasphemous myths of the Greeks do sing, but wild in manners, and greater than men in size, inasmuch as they were sprung of angels; yet less than angels, as they were born of women ... All things, therefore, going from bad to worse, on account of these brutal demons, God wished to cast them away like an evil leaven, lest each generation from a wicked seed, being like to that before it, and equally impious, should empty the world to come of saved men. And for this purpose, having warned a certain righteous man, with his three sons, together with their wives and their children, to save themselves in an ark, He sent a deluge of water, that all being destroyed, the purified world might be handed over to him who was saved in the ark, in order to a second beginning of life. And thus it came to pass.

(Pseudo Clement, *Homily* 8.13-17)

Tertullian (c. 155-225 AD)

IF (IT IS) ON ACCOUNT OF the angels—those, to wit, whom we read of as having fallen from God and heaven on account of concupiscence after females—who can presume that it was bodies already defiled, and relics of human lust, which such angels yearned after, so as not rather to have been inflamed for virgins, whose bloom pleads an excuse for human lust likewise? For thus does Scripture withal suggest: "And it came to pass," it says, "when men had begun to grow more numerous upon the earth, there were withal daughters born them; but the sons of God, having descried the daughters of men, that they were fair, took to themselves wives of all whom they elected."

(Tertullian, *On the Veiling of Virgins* 7)

FOR INDEED IT IS "on account of the angels" that he saith women must be veiled, because on account of "the daughters of men" angels revolted from God.

(Tertullian, *On Prayer* 22)

The apostle was quite aware that "spiritual wickedness" had been at work in heavenly places, when angels were entrapped into sin by the daughters of men.

(Tertullian, *Against Marcion* 5.18)

Julias Africanus (160-240 AD)

WHEN MEN MULTIPLIED ON EARTH, the angels of heaven came together with the daughters of men. In some copies I found 'sons of God.' What is meant by the Spirit in my opinion, is that the descendants of Seth are called the sons of God on account of the righteous men and patriarchs who have sprung from him, even down to the Saviour Himself; but that the descendants of Cain are named the seed of man, as having nothing divine in them, "But if it is thought that these refer to angels, we must take them to be those who deal with magic and jugglery, who taught the women the motions of the stars and the knowledge of things celestial, by whose power they conceived the giants as their children, by whom wickedness came to its height on the earth, until God decreed that the whole race of the living should perish in their impiety by the deluge."

(Julias Africanus, *History of the World* [Fragment])

Origen (b. 185 AD)

(From 1 Enoch 6:5): BECAUSE HE (JARED) WAS born to Mahalel—as it is written in Enoch (if it pleases one to accept the book as holy)—in the days of the descent of the sons of God to the daughters of men"

(Origen, *Commentary on John* 6:42)

IN MY OPINION, HOWEVER, it is certain wicked demons, and, so to speak, of the race of Titans or Giants, who have been guilty of impiety towards the true God, and towards the angels in heaven, and who have fallen from it, and who haunt the denser parts of bodies, and frequent unclean places upon earth, and who, possessing some power of distinguishing future events, because they are without bodies of earthly material, engage in an employment of this kind, and desiring to lead the human race away from the true God.

(Origen, *Against Celsus* 4.92)

IT IS FROM THIS SOURCE that he [Celsus] might be supposed to have obtained the statement, that "sixty or seventy angels descended at the same time, who fell into a state of wickedness." But, that we may grant to him in a spirit of candour what he has not discovered in the contents of the book of Genesis, that "the sons of God, seeing the daughters of men, that they were fair, took to them wives of all whom they chose," we shall nevertheless even on this point persuade those who are capable of understanding the meaning of the prophet, that even before us there was one who referred this narrative to the doctrine regarding souls, which became possessed with a desire for the corporeal life of men, and this in metaphorical language, he said, was termed "daughters of men." But whatever may be the meaning of the "sons of God desiring to possess the daughters of men," it will not at all contribute to prove that Jesus was not the only one who visited mankind as an angel, and who manifestly became the Saviour and benefactor of all those who depart from the flood of wickedness.

(Origen, *Against Celsus* 5.51-55)

Cyprian (200-258)

SINNING AND APOSTATE ANGELS made all these things known through their arts when they fell down to succumb to earthly and bad influence and gave up their heavenly vitality.

(Cyprian, *On the Dress of Virgins* 14)

Commodian (f. 250 AD)

WHEN GOD, THE ALMIGHTY, beautified the nature of the world
He wanted this earth to be visited by angels
Whose laws they despised as soon as they were sent:
So much was the beauty of women, who turned them aside

That they, being stained, could not return to heaven.

Rebels against God, they uttered words against him.

The Most High therefore uttered his sentence upon them;

From their seed the giants are said to have been born.

Through them on earth arts have been spread;

They taught the dying of wool, and whatever is accomplished.

The mortals erected images for them when they died.

The Almighty, however, because they were of a depraved seed,

did not approve that they, having died, were brought back from death.

In that way wandering now, they ruined many persons:

Especially you who today worship them and pray to them as gods.

(Commodian, *Instructions Against the Gods of the Heathen* 1.3)

Methodius (d. 311)

THAT THIS IS THE NATURE OF ANGELS, that they were created by God with the purpose of caring for the structures created by him" ... The devil, as one of these angels, forfeited this position "similar to the ones who afterwards lusted after bodies and had intercourse with the daughters of men.

(Methodius, *On the Resurrection* 3.7)

Minucius Felix (b. 210 AD)

WHEN ALMIGHTY GOD, to beautify the nature of the world, willed that that earth should be visited by angels, when they were sent down they despised His laws. Such was the beauty of women, that it turned them aside; so that, being contaminated, they could not return to heaven. Rebels from God, they uttered words against Him. Then the Highest uttered His judgment against them; and from their seed giants are said to have been born. By them arts were made known in the earth, and they taught the dyeing of wool, and everything which is done; and to them, when they died, men erected images. But the Almighty, because they were of an evil seed, did not approve that, when dead, they should be brought back from death. Whence wandering they now subvert many bodies, and it is such as these especially that ye this day worship and pray to as gods.

(Minucius Felix, *Instructions of Commodianus* 3)

Lactantius (260-330 AD)

WHEN, THEREFORE, THE NUMBER of men had begun to increase, God in His forethought, lest the devil, to whom from the beginning He had given power over the earth, should by his subtilty either corrupt or destroy men, as he had done at first, sent angels for the protection and improvement of the human race; and inasmuch as He had given these a free will, He enjoined them above all things not to defile themselves with contamination from the earth, and thus lose the dignity of their heavenly nature. He plainly prohibited them from doing that which He knew that they would do, that they might entertain no hope of pardon. Therefore, while they abode among men, that most deceitful ruler of the earth, by his very association, gradually enticed them to vices, and polluted them by intercourse with women. Then, not being admitted into heaven on account of the sins into which they had plunged themselves, they fell to the earth. Thus from angels the devil makes them to become his satellites and attendants. But they who were born from these, because they were neither angels nor men, but bearing a kind of mixed nature, were not admitted into hell, as their fathers were not into heaven. Thus there came to be two kinds of demons; one of heaven, the other of the earth. The latter are the wicked spirits, the authors of all the evils which are done, and the same devil is their prince. Whence Trismegistus calls him the ruler of the demons. But grammarians say that they are called demons, as though *doemones*, that is, skilled and acquainted with matters: for they think that these are gods.

(Lactantius, *Divine Institutes* 2.15)

Alexander of Lycopolis (f. early 4ᵗʰ cent. AD)

WHEN JEWISH HISTORY SAYS that "the angels came together to have sexual intercourse with the daughters of men": such an expression signifies the nourishing powers of the soul which came from above to the things on this earth.

(Alexander of Lycopolis, *On the Teachings of the Manicheans 25*)

Eusebius (260-340 AD)

OF THIS KIND [GIANTS AND TITANS] then perhaps were the statements in the Sacred Scripture concerning the giants before the Mood, and those concerning their progenitors, of whom it is said, 'And when the angels of God saw the daughters of men that they were fair, they took unto them wives of all that they chose,' and of these were born 'the giants the men of renown which were of old.'

For one might say that these daemons are those giants, and that their spirits have been deified by the subsequent generations of men, and that their battles, and their quarrels among themselves, and their wars are the subjects of these legends that are told as of gods.

(Eusebius, *Preparation for the Gospel* 5.4)

Acts of Thomas (200-225 AD)

And he said unto him: I am a reptile of the reptile nature and noxious son of the noxious father: of him that hurt and smote the four brethren which stood upright: I am son to him that sitteth on a throne over all the earth that receiveth back his own from them that borrow: I am son to him that girdeth about the sphere: and I am kin to him that is outside the ocean, whose tail is set in his own mouth: I am he that entered through the barrier (fence) into paradise and spake with Eve the things which my father bade me speak unto her: I am he that kindled and inflamed Cain to kill his own brother, and on mine account did thorns and thistles grow up in the earth: I am he that cast down the angels from above and bound them in lusts after women, that children born of earth might come of them and I might work my will in them: ...

(Acts of Thomas 32)

Cyril of Jerusalem (313-386 AD)

"The giants sinned, and then much lawlessness was poured over the earth, and because of that the deluge had to come."

(Cyril of Jerusalem, *Catechetical Lectures* 8)

Ambrosius (340-397)

THE NARRATOR OF THE DIVINE SCRIPTURE did not want to consider these giants as sons of the earth (*gigas*) in the sense of the poets but asserts that they issued from angels and women.

(Ambrosius, *On Noah and the Ark* 1.3.8)

Finally it is written that angels loved daughters of men.

(Ambrosius, *Exposition on Psalm* 118)

How splendid it is that angels have fallen from heaven into the world because of their intemperance but that virgins have passed from the world to heaven because of their chastity.

(Ambrosius, *Concerning Virgins* 1.8.53)

Sulpicius Severus (363-420 AD)

BY THIS TIME, WHEN THE HUMAN KIND had become abundant, certain angels, whose place was in heaven, were captivated by the beautiful appearance of virgins, and pursued illicit desires; and even degenerated from their own nature and origin, left the higher places they inhabited, and mingled themselves in marriages with mortal women. These angels gradually sowed noxious habits, by which they corrupted the human offspring: from these unions giants are said to have come forth, as the mixing of diverse kinds produces monsters.

(Sulpicius Severus, *Sacred History* 1.2)

Didimus the Blind (310-398 AD)

MANY WONDERED WHETHER ANGELS united themselves physically [... or] that something else is said in the passage.

(Didimus the Blind, *On Genesis*)

Hilary of Poitiers (315-367 AD)

ANGELS, DESIRING THE DAUGHTERS of men, when they descended from heaven, gathered on this mountain Hermon, at its peak.

(Hilary of Poitiers, *Commentary* on Ps 133:3)

Epiphanius of Salamis (315-403 AD)

ACCORDING TO THE TRADITION that has come to us, at that time the practice of evil began to occur in the world. It was also there from the beginning through the transgression of Adam and then through the fratricide of Cain. But now in the times of Jared and thereafter, there was sorcery and magic, debauchery and adultery and iniquity"

(Epiphanius, *Against Heresies* ["Medicine Chest"] 1.1.3)

Ambrose (333-397 AD)

"THE GIANTS (NEPHILIM) WERE on the earth in those days." The author of the divine Scripture does not mean that those giants must be considered, according to the tradition of poets, as sons of the earth but asserts that those whom he defines with such a name because of the extraordinary size of their body were generated by angels and women.

(Ambrose, *On Noah* 4.8)

Jerome (c. 347-420 AD)

THE HEBREW WORD *ELOHIM* is of common number; for both "God" and "gods" are designated in the same way. For this reason Aquila dared to say "sons of the gods," in the plural, understanding "gods" as holy ones or angels. For God stood up in the assembly of the gods: moreover, in the midst of the gods He gives judgment [Psalm 82:1] ... In the Hebrew, it has the following: Falling ones (that is, *annaphilim*) were on the earth in those days ... The name falling ones is indeed fitting both for angels and for offspring of holy ones.

(Jerome, *Hebrew Questions on Genesis 6:2 and 6:4*)

Nemesius of Emesa (Fourth Century AD)

OF THE INCORPOREAL BEINGS, only angels fell away, and not all of them, but some only, that inclined to things below and set their desire on things of earth, withdrawing themselves from their relations with things above, even from God.

(Nemesius of Emesa, *On the Nature of Man* 58)

Jews

Septuagint (Third Century BC)

And Noe was five hundred years old, and he begot three sons, Sem, Cham, and Japheth. And it came to pass when men began to be numerous upon the earth, and daughters were born to them, that the angels of God having seen the daughters of men that they were beautiful, took to themselves wives of all whom they chose. And the Lord God said, My Spirit shall certainly not remain among these men for ever, because they are flesh, but their days shall be an hundred and twenty years. Now the giants were upon the earth in those days; and after that when the sons of God were wont to go in to the daughters of men, they bore *children* to them, those were the giants of old, the men of renown.

(Alexandrinus Codex of the LXX Gen 6:1-4)

1 Enoch (Third-Second Century BC)

NOTE: 1 Enoch contains too much information to justify putting it all into this kind of an appendix. I highly suggest that if you have not read this document, take the time to do so, especially the Book of Watchers (ch. 1-36). Jude quotes from it and says it records the actual words of the patriarch who lived before the flood. Many of the NT books allude to it. It must be remembered that even though its date is the second century BC, it puts down oral traditions that are thousands of years older. Many of the early church fathers believed it to be Scripture, though it contains in some places obvious references that Enoch could not have said, and thus remains suspect as canonized Scripture. Nevertheless, it has obviously impacted the way that Genesis 6 was universally understood in the days of Christ and the Apostles, and you cannot have a truly informed view of this subject without reading this material.

AND IT CAME TO PASS when the children of men had multiplied that in those days were born unto them beautiful and comely daughters. And the angels, the children of the heaven,[1] saw and lusted after them, and said to one another: 'Come, let us choose us wives from among the

---

[1] The Dead Sea Scrolls (4QEnochb Col. ii:3) read, "the Watchers, sons of the sky."

children of men and beget us children.' And Semjaza, who was their leader, said unto them: 'I fear ye will not indeed agree to do this deed, and I alone shall have to pay the penalty of a great sin.' And they all answered him and said: 'Let us all swear an oath, and all bind ourselves by mutual imprecations not to abandon this plan but to do this thing.' Then sware they all together and bound themselves by mutual imprecations upon it. And they were in all two hundred; who descended in the days of Jared on the summit of Mount Hermon, and they called it Mount Hermon, because they had sworn and bound themselves by mutual imprecations upon it. And these are the names of their leaders: Samiazaz, their leader, Arakiba, Rameel, Kokabiel, Tamiel, Ramiel, Danel, Ezeqeel, Baraqijal, Asael, Armaros, Batarel, Ananel, Zaqiel, Samsapeel, Satarel, Turel, Jomjael, Sariel. These are their chiefs of tens.

And all the others together with them took unto themselves wives, and each chose for himself one, and they began to go in unto them and to defile themselves with them, and they taught them charms and enchantments, and the cutting of roots, and made them acquainted with plants. And they became pregnant, and they bare great giants, whose height was three thousand ells: Who consumed all the acquisitions of men. And when men could no longer sustain them, the giants turned against them and devoured mankind. And they began to sin against birds, and beasts, and reptiles, and fish, and to devour one another's flesh, and drink the blood. Then the earth laid accusation against the lawless ones.

(1 Enoch 6:1-7:6)

AND TO GABRIEL SAID THE LORD: 'Proceed against the bastards and the reprobates, and against the children of fornication: and destroy the children of the Watchers from amongst men: send them one against the other that they may destroy each other in battle: for length of days shall they not have. And no request that they (i.e. their fathers) make of thee shall be granted unto their fathers on their behalf; for they hope to live an eternal life, and that each one of them will live five hundred years.' And the Lord said unto Michael: 'Go, bind Semjaza and his associates who have united themselves with women so as to have defiled themselves with them in all their uncleanness. And when their sons have slain one another, and they have seen the destruction of their beloved ones, bind them fast for seventy generations in the valleys of the earth, till the day of their judgement and of their consummation, till the judgement that is for ever and ever is consummated. In those days they shall be led off to the abyss of fire: and to the torment and the prison in which they shall be confined forever. And whosoever shall be condemned and destroyed will from thenceforth be bound together with them to the end of all generations. And destroy all the spirits of the reprobate and the children of the Watchers, because they have wronged mankind.

(1 Enoch 10:9-15)

I, ENOCH, ANSWERED AND SAID unto him: 'The Lord will do a new thing on the earth, and this I have already seen in a vision, and make known to thee that in the generation of my father Jared some, of the angels of heaven transgressed the word of the Lord. And behold they commit sin and transgress the law and have united themselves with women and commit sin with them, and have married some of them, and have begot children by them. Yea, there shall come a great destruction over the whole earth, and there shall be a deluge and a great destruction for one year. And this son who has been born unto you shall be left on the earth, and his three children shall be saved with him: when all mankind that are on the earth shall die [[he and his sons shall be saved]]. And they shall produce on the earth giants not according to the spirit, but according to the flesh, and there shall be a great punishment on the earth, and the earth shall be cleansed from all impurity.

(1 Enoch 106:13-17)

Jubilees (Second Century BC)

AND IN THE SECOND WEEK of the tenth jubilee Mahalalel took unto him to wife Dinah, the daughter of Barakiel the daughter of his father's brother, and she bare him a son in the third week in the sixth year, and he called his name Jared; for in his days the angels of the Lord descended on the earth, those who are named the Watchers, that they should instruct the children of men, and that they should do judgment and uprightness on the earth. . . And he testified to the Watchers, who had

sinned with the daughters of men; for these had begun to unite themselves, so as to be defiled, with the daughters of men, and Enoch testified against (them) all.

And it came to pass when the children of men began to multiply on the face of the earth and daughters were born unto them, that
the angels of God saw them on a certain year of this jubilee, that they
were beautiful to look upon; and they took themselves wives of all
whom they chose, and they bare unto them sons and they were giants
... And lawlessness increased on the earth and all flesh corrupted its
way, alike men and cattle and beasts and birds and everything that walks
on the earth--all of them corrupted their ways and their orders, and they
began to eat one another, and lawlessness increased on the earth and
every imagination of the thoughts of all men (was) thus evil continually
... And against the angels whom He had sent upon the earth, He was
exceedingly wroth, and He gave commandment to root them out of all
their dominion, and He bade us to bind them in the depths of the earth,
and behold they are bound in the midst of them, and are (kept) separate.

(Jubilees 4:15, 22; 5:1-2, 5-6)

Testament of Reuben (Second Century BC)

FOR THUS [LEWD WOMEN] ALLURED the Watchers who were before
the flood; As they continued looking at the women, they lusted after
them, and they conceived the act in their mind; for they changed themselves into the shape of men, and appeared to them when they were
with their husbands. And the women lusting in their minds after their
forms, gave birth to giants, for the Watchers appeared to them as reaching even unto heaven.

(Testament of Reuben 5:6-7)

Testament of Naphtali (Second Century BC)

IN LIKE MANNER THE WATCHERS also changed the order of their
nature, whom the Lord cursed at the flood, on whose account He made
the earth without inhabitants and fruitless.

(Testament of Naphtali 3:5)

Sirach (Second Century BC)

HE [GOD] WAS NOT PROPITIATED for the ancient giants who revolted in their might.

(Sirach 16:7)

3 Maccabees (First Century BC)

IT WAS YOU WHO DESTROYED the former workers of unrighteousness, among whom were the giants, who trusted in their strength and hardihood, by covering them with a measureless flood.

(3 Maccabees 2:4)

Damascus Document (Dead Sea Scrolls) (1st Cent. BC)

FOR MANY HAVE GONE ASTRAY due to these; brave heroes stumbled on account of them, from ancient times until now. For having walked in the stubbornness of their hearts the Watchers of the heavens fell; on account of it they were caught, for they did not heed the precepts of God. And their sons, whose height was like that of cedars and whose bodies were like mountains, fell.

(4Q266 2 ii:16-19)

Genesis Apocryphon (Dead Sea Scrolls) (1st Cent. BC)

THEN I, LAMECH, WAS FRIGHTENED and turned to Bitenosh, my wife, and said: ... Swear to me by the Most High, by the Great Lord, by the King of the Universe, ... the sons of heaven, that you will in truth let me know everything, if ... you will in truth and without lies let me know whether this ... Swear to me by the King of all the Universe that you are speaking to me frankly and without lies ... Then Bitenosh, my bride, spoke to me very harshly. She wept . . . and said: Oh my brother and lord! Remember my pleasure . . . the time of love, the gasping of my breath in my breast. I shall tell you everything accurately ... I swear to you by the Great Holy One, by the King of the heavens ... that this seed comes from you, that this pregnancy comes from you, that the planting of this fruit comes from you, and not from any foreigner or watcher or son of heaven ... Then I, Lamech, ran to my father, Methuselah, and told him everything, so that he would go and ask Enoch, his father, and would know everything for certain from him, since he (Enoch) is liked and well liked ... (This having been done, Enoch responds:) "Go tell Lamech, your son ..."

(Genesis Apocryphon 2)

Philo (20 BC – 50 AD)

"AND WHEN THE ANGELS of God saw the daughters of men that they were beautiful, they took unto themselves wives of all of them whom they chose." Those beings, whom other philosophers call demons, Moses usually calls angels; and they are souls hovering in the air.

(Philo, *On Giants* 6)

Pseudo-Philo (First Century AD)

And he went away and worked with his magic tricks and gave orders to the angels who were in charge of magicians, for he had been sacrificing to them for a long time. Because in that time before they were condemned, magic was revealed by angels and they would have destroyed the age without measure; and because they had transgressed, it happened that the angels did not have the power; and when they were judged, then the power was not given over to others. And they do these things by means of those men, the magicians who minister to men, until the age without measure comes.

(Pseudo-Philo 34:2-3)

2 Enoch (First Century AD)

AND THOSE MEN TOOK ME and led me up on to the second heaven, and showed me darkness, greater than earthly darkness, and there I saw prisoners hanging, watched, awaiting the great and boundless judgment, and these angels (spirits) were dark-looking, more than earthly darkness, and incessantly making weeping through all hours. And I said to the men who were with me: Wherefore are these incessantly tortured? They answered me: These are God's apostates, who obeyed not God's commands, but took counsel with their own will, and turned away with their prince, who also is fastened on the fifth heaven.

(2 Enoch 7:1-2)

THE MEN TOOK ME on to the fifth heaven and placed me, and there I saw many and countless soldiers, called Grigori, of human appearance, and their size (was) greater than that of great giants and their faces withered, and the silence of their mouths perpetual, and their was no service on the fifth heaven, and I said to the men who were with me: Wherefore are these very withered and their faces melancholy, and their mouths silent, and (wherefore) is there no service on this heaven? And they said to me: These are the Grigori, who with their prince Satanail (Satan) rejected the Lord of light, and after them are those who are held in great darkness on the second heaven, and three of them went down on to earth from the Lord's throne, to the place Ermon, and broke through their vows on the shoulder of the hill Ermon and saw the daughters of men how good they are, and took to themselves wives, and befouled the earth with their deeds, who in all times of their age made lawlessness and mixing, and giants are born and marvelous big men and great enmity. And therefore God judged them with great judgment, and they weep for their brethren and they will be punished on the Lord's great day.

(2 Enoch 18:1-4)

3 Baruch (First Century AD)

AND THE ANGEL SAID, "Rightly you ask; when God caused the Deluge upon earth, and destroyed all flesh, and 409,000 giants, and the water rose fifteen cubits above the highest [mountains, then] the water entered into paradise and destroyed every flower; but it removed wholly without the bounds the shoot of the vine and cast it outside."

(3 Baruch 4:10)

Josephus (37-100 AD)

NOW THIS POSTERITY OF SETH continued to esteem God as the Lord of the universe, and to have an entire regard to virtue, for seven generations; but in process of time they were perverted, and forsook the practices of their forefathers, and did neither pay those honors to God which were appointed them, nor had they any concern to do justice towards men. But for what degree of zeal they had formerly shown for virtue, they now showed by their actions a double degree of wickedness; whereby they made God to be their enemy, for many angels of God accompanied with women, and begat sons that proved unjust, and despisers of all that was good, on account of the confidence they had in their own strength; for the tradition is, That these men did what resembled the acts of those whom the Grecians call giants. But Noah was very uneasy at what they did; and, being displeased at their conduct, persuaded them to change their dispositions and their acts for the better;—but, seeing that they did not yield to him, but were slaves to their wicked pleasures, he was afraid they would kill him, together with his wife and children, and those they had married; so he departed out of that land.

(Josephus, *Antiquities* 1.3.1.)

Sibylline Oracle (Pre-150 AD)

DIFFERENT ONES DEVISED THAT with which they were each concerned, enterprising Watchers, who received this appellation because they had a sleepless mind in their hearts and an insatiable personality. They were mighty, of great form, but nevertheless they went under the dread house of Tartarus guarded by unbreakable bonds, to make retribution, to Gehenna of terrible, raging, undying fire. . . [other men] were insolent, much more than those Giants, crooked ones, abominably pouring forth slander. Noah alone among all was most upright and true.

(Sibylline Oracle 1:97-103; 123-125)

2 Baruch (Early Second Century AD)

FOR HE BECAME A DANGER to his own soul: even to the angels became he a danger. For, moreover, at that time when he was created, they enjoyed liberty. And some of them descended, and mingled with the women. And then those who did so were tormented in chains. But the rest of the multitude of the angels, of which there is no number, restrained themselves. And those who dwelt on the earth perished together (with them) through the waters of the deluge.

(2 Baruch 56:10-15)

Targum Pseudo-Jonathan (4th Cent. AD or later)

And it was when the sons of men began to multiply upon the face of the earth, and fair daughters were born to them; and the sons of the great saw that the daughters of men were beautiful, and painted, and curled, walking with revelation of the flesh, and with imaginations of wickedness; that they took them wives of all who pleased them. And the Lord said by His Word, All the generations of the wicked which are to arise shall not be purged after the order of the judgments of the generation of the deluge, which shall be destroyed and exterminated from the midst of the world. Have I not imparted My Holy Spirit to them, (or, placed My Holy Spirit in them,) that they may work good works? And, behold, their works are wicked. Behold, I will give them a prolongment of a hundred and twenty years, that they may work repentance, and not perish. Schamchazai and Uzziel, who fell from heaven, were on the earth in those days; and also, after the sons of the Great had gone in with the daughters of men, they bare to them: and these are they who are called men who are of the world, men of names.

(Pseudo-Jonathan Genesis 6:1-4)

NOTES

NOTES FOR PREFACE (Pgs. i-iv)

[1] My friend called this the "earliest note I've ever seen in a book." I love footnotes and *despise* endnotes. Nevertheless, this book has endnotes. I've come to discover that not everyone shares my love of footnotes. I completely believe that endnotes are put in books deliberately to keep you from reading them! For sake of readability and those of you who want to follow the main argument without all those nasty interruptions, I have endnotes for you. Many are references, not really worth the time unless you want to search something out for yourself. But some notes offer further reflections and insights. Some of these, which I think you may find particularly helpful or interesting, I will alert you to in the book with boldface and underline of the number. For example, instead of [1] it will be **[1]**.

[2] Patrick Heron, *The Nephilim and the Pyramid of the Apocalypse* (New York, NY: Citadel Press, 2004).

[3] Kim Riddlebarger, "Just Plain Nutty," *The Riddleblog*.

[4] See for example, **Michael S. Heiser**, *The Bible Code Myth* (Acid Test Press, 2001).

[5] Some in my own collection include **Timothy Green Beckley**, *Giants on the Earth* (New Brunswick, NJ: Global Communications/Conspiracy Journal, 2009); **Judd Burton**, *Interview With The Giant: Ethnohistorical Notes on the Nephilim* (Burton Beyond Press, 2009); **Charles DeLoach**, *Giants: A Reference Guide from History, the Bible, and Recorded Legend* (Metuchen, NJ: Scarecrow Press, 1995); **Brian Godawa**, *When Giants Were Upon the Earth: The Watchers, the Nephilim, and the Biblical Cosmic War of the Seed* (TX: Warrior Poet Publishing, 2014, 2021); **Jonathan Gray**, *Lost World of the Giants* (Brushton, NY: TEACH Services, Inc. 2006); **Michael S. Heiser**, *The Unseen Realm: Recovering the Supernatural Worldview of the Bible* (Bellingham, WA: Lexham Press, 2015); **Ryan Pitterson**, *Judgment of the Nephilim* (NY: Days of Noe Publishing, 2017); **Stephen Quayle**, *Genesis 6 Giants* (Bozeman, MT: End Time Thunder Publishers, 2002); **Laura Sanger**, *The Roots of the Federal Reserve: Tracing the Nephilim from Noah to the US Dollar* (Dallas, TX: Relentlessly Creative Books, 2020); I highly recommend Godawa and Burton.

NOTES FOR INTRODUCTION (Pgs. 1-41)

[1] In 1974 some local farmers discovered this remarkable find of 8,000 life-sized army figures along with hundreds of other figures including warriors, horses, chariots, officials, acrobats, strongmen and musicians near the Mausoleum of Emperor Qin in the Lintong District of Xi'an China, which also just so happens to be home of perhaps the largest concentration of ancient pyramids in the world. The terracotta were made famous in the third *Mummy* movie (*The Mummy: Tomb of the Dragon Emperor*, 2008; Directed by Rob Cohen).

[2] Words denoted with a *___* can be found in the Glossary at the end of the book.

[3] This is the English translation by Sir Lancelot C. L. Brenton, *The Septuagint with Apocrypha* (London: Samuel Bagster & Sons, 1851).

[4] For more on why Jews changed their earlier supernatural theology after the arrival of Christ, see Alan Segal, *Two Powers in Heaven: Early Rabbinic Reports about Christianity and Gnosticism* (Boston, Brill Academic Pub, 2002).

[5] *Genesis Rabbah* 26:5. Curiously, in the translation provided in the link, they says, "sons of divine beings," even though the actual Hebrew is "sons of God." See *Bereishit Rabbah* 26.5 (Gen 6:2), Sefaria.org.

[6] In fact, Jesus seems to make this very point to the Pharisees, and they understood it perfectly (these Rabbis in the NT era had not yet squashed the supernatural view). In John 10:34 Jesus cites Psalm 82:6 in support of his claim that he has come from heaven. In citing the verse that says, "I said 'You are gods, *sons of the Most High,*'" it is best not to see this as a reference to human beings, but to heavenly beings of the heavenly divine council (see Ps 82:1 ESV). It makes no sense that Jesus would be telling the Pharisees that they are gods in some limited judicial earthly sense (see note #39 "A note on the word '*elohim*"), and that he is simply claiming to be like them, as it is often interpreted, because the Pharisees still want to stone Jesus for blasphemy (John 10:36, 39). Instead, it is better to see this as a reference to the heavenly beings, of which Jesus says he is greater even than they, as he is one with the Father. See Michael Heiser, "You've Seen One Elohim, You've Seen Them All? A Critique of Mormonism's Use of Psalm 82," *FARMS Review* 19/1 (2007): 221–266.

[7] Jacob J. T. Doedens, "The Indecent Descent of the Sethites: The Provenance of the Sethites-Interpretation of Genesis 6:1-4." *Sárospataki Füzetek* 16:3–4 (2012): 47–57.

[8] A. Roberts, J. Donaldson, A. C. Coxe and A. Menzies, *The Ante-Nicene Fathers* (Buffalo: Christian Literature, 1886), 6.131.

[9] Catholic University of America, *Fathers of the Church: A New Translation*. Washington, D.C.: Catholic University of America Press, 1947, 91:134-35. Ephrem is discussed by Arie van der Kooij in, "Peshitta Genesis 6: 'Sons of God' – Angels of Judges?' in *Journal of Northwest Semitic Languages* 23/1 (1997): 43-51. The concluding paragraph of this article states, "The time and circumstances of this anti-angelological revision in Gen 6 are not known to us. One might think here of criticism of the dualistic ideas of Mani and his followers by 'orthodox' circles in Edessa in the second half of the third century. If so, these circles would have done so by drawing on a rendering/interpretation which had a Jewish (Targumic) background." But see Doedens, "The Indecent Descent" for newer work on this.

[10] Two excellent resources are Robert C. Newman, "The Ancient Exegesis of Genesis 6:2, 4." *Grace Theological Journal* 5.1 (1984): 13-36; and Jacob J. T. Doedens, "The Sons of God in Genesis 6:1-4," Ph.D. Dissertation Theologische Universiteit Kampen (2013), 89-167.

[11] Philip Schaff, *The Nicene and Post-Nicene Fathers Vol. II* (Oak Harbor: Logos Research Systems, 1997), 303.

[12] Martin Luther, vol. 2, *Luther's Works, Vol. 2 : Lectures on Genesis: Chapters 6-14*, ed. Jaroslav Jan Pelikan, Hilton C. Oswald and Helmut T. Lehmann, Luther's Works (Saint Louis: Concordia Publishing House, 1999), Gen 6:2.

[13] John Calvin and John King, *Commentary on the First Book of Moses Called Genesis* (Bellingham, WA: Logos Research Systems, Inc., 2010), Gen 6:1.

[14] Doeden's Dissertation provides an exhaustive list, but See Appendix 6

[15] William van Gemeren concurs and puts the question forcefully, "Why does the theology in which creation, miracles, the miraculous birth and resurrection of Jesus have a place, prefer a rational explanation of Genesis 6:1–4? … What concerns me is a seeming inconsistency. Normally, the goal of interpretation has been the elucidation of the Word of God so the community of faith may know what to believe and what to do. When, however, the object of interpretation becomes the removal of apparent obstacles to which the passage may give rise, reinterpretation is introduced, and one may wonder how this differs from demythologization. It is granted that it is hard to imagine how preternatural (angelic, supernatural, demonic) beings have sexual relations with women of the human race and father offspring. But is the difficulty so great that it *must* be removed as something offensive? Is it possible that theology has taken the place of exegesis?" See W. A. van Gemeren, "The Sons of God in Genesis 6:1–4 (An Example of Evangelical Demythologization?)," *Westminster Theological Journal* 43 (1981): 320.

[16] Besides Luther and Calvin, Theodoret, a contemporary of Augustine, calls anyone who holds the angelic view "mad fools" (Theodoret, *Questions on Genesis: XLVII*). Chrysostom may be the harshest of all, throwing the whole tradition not only out the window, but right into the pit of hell when he says, "There is need to make a careful study of this passage and confute the fanciful interpretations of those people whose every remark is made rashly … by demonstrating the absurdity of what is said by them … so that you will not lend your ears idly to people uttering those blasphemies and presuming to speak in a way that brings their own persons into jeopardy" (Chrysostom, *Homilies on Genesis 22.6*). Incredible!

[17] A few, including commentaries on Genesis that do not deal with 2 Peter 2:4, Jude 6, and other biblical texts, still hold to the Sethite view. Cf. K. A. Mathews, vol. 1A, *Genesis 1-11:26*, The New American Commentary (Nashville: Broadman & Holman Publishers, 2001), 322-32; Harold G. Stigers, *A Commentary on Genesis* (Grand Rapids: Zondervan, 1967).

[18] See **Meredith G. Kline**, "Divine Kingship and Genesis 6:1-4," *Westminster Theological Journal* 24.2 (1962): 187-204. See also **E. Kraeling**, "The Significance and Origin of Gen. 6:1-4," *Journal of Near Eastern Studies* 6 (1947): 193-208; **A. R. Millard**, "A New Babylonian 'Genesis' Story," *Tyndale Bulletin* 18 (1967): 12 and notes 27-29. A variation of this view combines it with ST1 so that these rulers are also divine like Gilgamesh. See **D. J. A. Clines**, "The Significance of the 'Sons of God' Episode (Genesis 6:1–4) in the Context of the 'Primeval History' (Genesis 1–11)," *Journal for the Study of the Old Testament* 13 (1979): 33–46. To me, this kind of a merging is plausible and perhaps even correct.

[19] Cf. **Clinton E. Arnold**, *Zondervan Illustrated Bible Backgrounds Commentary Volume 4: Hebrews to Revelation* (Grand Rapids, MI: Zondervan, 2002), 236; **Richard J. Bauckham**, *Jude 2 Peter*, Word Biblical Commentary (Waco, TX: Word Books, 1983), 50-53; **Edwin A. Blum**, *Jude*, The Expositors Bible Commentary Vol. 12 (Grand Rapids, MI: Zondervan, 1981), 390; **Peter H. Davids**, *The Letters of 2 Peter and Jude*, Pillar New Testament Commentary (Grand Rapids, MI: Eerdmans, 2006), 48-51; **Gene L. Green**, *Jude & 2 Peter*, Baker Exegetical Commentary on the New Testament (Grand Rapids, MI: Baker Academic, 2008), 66-70; **Michael Green**, *2 Peter and Jude*, Tyndale New Testament Commentaries (Downers Grove, IL: InterVarsity, 1987), 191-92; **Douglas J. Moo**, *2 Peter, Jude*, NIV Application Commentary (Grand Rapids, MI: Zondervan, 1996), 241-42; **Thomas R. Schreiner**, *1, 2 Peter, Jude*, New American Commentary (Nashville, TN: Broadman & Holman, 2003), 447-51; **Robert L. Webb**, "The Use of 'Story' in the Letter of Jude: Rhetorical Strategies of Jude's Narrative Episodes," *Journal for the Study of the New Testament* 31 (2008): 56-57.

Agreement with this interpretation with or without reference to Jude and Peter include: **Lamar Eugene Cooper**, Sr., *Ezekiel*, New American Commentary (Nashville: Broadman and Holman, 1994), 267; **Nahum M. Sarna**, *Genesis*, The JPS Torah Commentary (Philadelphia: Jewish Publication Society, 1989), 45-46; **W. A. van Gemeren**, "The Sons of God in Genesis 6:1–4 (An Example of Evangelical Demythologization?)," *WTJ* 43 (1981): 320–48; **Michael S. Heiser**, "The Divine Council in Late Canonical and Non-Canonical Second Temple Jewish Literature," A Dissertation at the University of Wisconsin-Madison, 2004: 217-228; ___, *The Unseen Realm: Recovering the Supernatural Worldview of the Bible*, First Edition (Bellingham, WA: Lexham Press, 2015), **Gordon J. Wenham**, vol. 1, *Word Biblical Commentary : Genesis 1-15*, Word Biblical Commentary (Dallas: Word, Incorporated, 2002), 139-43; **Archie T. Wright**, *The Origin of Evil Spirits: The Reception of Genesis 6.1-4 in Early Jewish Literature* (Tübingen: Mohr Siebeck, 2004), 73. Theologians include: **James M. Boice**, *Foundations of the Christian Faith* (Downers Grove, IL: InterVarsity, 1986), 173; **Robert Duncan Culver**, *Systematic Theology* (Great Britain: Mentor, 2005), 178; **Millard Erickson**, *Christian Theology* (Grand Rapids, MI: Baker, 1998), 659; **Charles Feinberg**, *The Prophecy of Ezekiel* (Chicago: Moody Press, 1969), **Arthur W. Pink**, *Gleanings in Genesis* (Bellingham, WA: Logos Research Systems, Inc., 2005), 92-95; 161; **Robert L. Reymond**, *A New Systematic Theology of the Christian Faith* (Nashville: Thomas Nelson, 1998), 659; **Francis Schaeffer**, "Genesis in Space and Time," in *The Complete Works of Francis A. Schaeffer: A Christian Worldview* (Westchester, IL: Crossway Books, 1996), p. 89; **Merrill F. Unger**, "The Old Testament Revelation Concerning Eternity Past," *Bibliotheca Sacra* 114:454 (Apr '57): 135-41; and many others.

[20] John Murray, *Principles of Conduct* (Grand Rapids: Wm. B. Eerdmans, 1957), 246.

[21] The Septuagint does read that Seth "called his name Enosh: he hoped to call on the name of the Lord God." But this translation also has problems, for it seems to imply that he did not think he had much hope in doing so. Why would he think this given the grace that God showed to Adam, Eve, and Cain?

[22] The name Enosh can mean either frailty/mortality or "man" (cf. Deut 32:26; Job 4:17; Ps 8:4 etc). The idea seems to be that there is a word play going on between Enosh (a man's name) and *enosh* (mankind).

[23] It could be argued that not all of these men were godly. Methuselah, for instance, has the possible meaning "Man of the Dart," as in a kind of weapon. Also, his son is named Lamech, who as we have seen was the archetypal polygamist-murderer in the line of Cain. His name means "Powerful/Destroyer."

[24] The equivocation continues in vs. 3, "The Lord God said, My Spirit shall certainly not remain among these men forever." Obviously, God is referring to all mankind, for he destroys everyone but Noah and his family. Yet, the previous meaning was Sethites. Then again in vs. 4 the "daughters of men" return and we are back to Sethites. Thus, back and forth we go with our interpretation of the word *'adam*.

[25] The ancient Jewish work *The Life of Adam and Eve* actually says that Adam had 30 sons and 30 daughters. VitaAE 24:3.

[26] G. Mussies, "Giants," in *Dictionary of Deities and Demons in the Bible DDD*, 2nd extensively rev. ed., ed. K. van der Toorn, Bob Becking and Pieter Willem van der Horst (Leiden; Boston; Grand Rapids, Mich.: Brill; Eerdmans, 1999), 343.

[27] Francis Schaeffer, "Genesis in Space and Time," in *The Complete Works of Francis A. Schaeffer: A Christian Worldview* (Westchester, IL: Crossway Books, 1996), p. 89.

[28] C. S. Lewis, "Autobiography: The Letters of C. S. Lewis to Arthur Greeves," in *The Essential C.S. Lewis*. ed. Lyle W. Dorsett (New York: Touchstone, 1996), 56; J. R. R. Tolkien, "A Letter to Milton Waldman," reprinted in *The Simarillion* (New York: Houghton Mifflin Co, 2001), p. xv; J. R. R. Tolkien, *The Tolkien Reader* (New York: Del Rey, 1968), 88-89.

[29] Nephilim does not, however, refer *to* the heavenly beings, as if they *are* the heavenly beings, as some want to make them.

[30] This view is proposed by H. Gunkel, *Genesis* (Göttingen, 1910), 58-59, and elaborated on by Michael Heiser, *The Unseen Realm*, 105-07. Ronald Hendel ("Of Demigods and the Deluge: Toward an Interpretation of Genesis 6:1–4," *Journal of Biblical Literature* 106 [1987]: 22 n. 46) sees the word as being a something like a qaṭil passive adjective of *naphal*, but this does not explain the alternate spelling. See the discussion below.

[31] A good discussion of this is found in John C. Reeves, *Jewish Lore in Manichaean Cosmogony: Studies in the Book of Giants Traditions* (Cincinnati: Hebrew Union College Press, 1992), 69-72.

[32] For example, in the aptly titled "Book of Giants" it appears in 1Q23 Frag. 9; 4Q530 col. ii:13, 15; 4Q530 Frag. 6 col. i:8 and many other places. Remarkably, it is combined with *nephilim/nephylin* in 4Q531 Frag. 5:2; cf. 4Q530 col. ii:20.

[33] Shem, of course, is the name of Noah's youngest son. The Bible takes this word *shem* and begins to make a word-play beginning in Genesis 11 and the Tower of Babel. Nimrod, the giant (*gibborim*; Gen 10:9) who built the tower (Gen 10:10) wanted to make a "name" (*shem*) for himself (Gen 11:4). But by the end of the story, it is God who makes the name for himself, first by dispersing the people and scattering them over the face of the earth, and then by choosing Abraham who would come from the line of Shem, of whom the promise was given of the coming Messiah (Gen 9:26-27; 11:10-30).

[34] "...Zeus, son of Kronos, created yet another fourth generation on the fertile earth, and these were better and nobler, the wonderful generation of hero-men, who are also called half-gods, the generation before our own on this vast earth. But of these too, evil war and the terrible carnage took some ..." Hesiod, *The Works and Days*, trans. Richmond Lattimore (Ann Arbor: University of Michigan, 1959), 37.

[35] P. W. Coxen, "Gibborim," in *Dictionary of Deities and Demons in the Bible DDD*, 2nd extensively rev. ed., ed. K. van der Toorn, Bob Becking and Pieter Willem van der Horst (Leiden; Boston; Grand Rapids, Mich.: Brill; Eerdmans, 1999), p. 345.

[36] Chrysostom, Homilies on Genesis 22.6.

[37] Keil and Delitzsch refer to Hosea 1:10 "sons of the living God" as proof of their Sethite view. However, this verse is a prophecy which is fulfilled in the NT (cf. John 1:12; Rom 8:14-23; Gen 3:26 etc). See Carl Friedrich Keil and Franz Delitzsch, *Commentary on the Old Testament* (Peabody, MA: Hendrickson, 2002), Gen 6:1.

[38] That is, when it is in the construct form as this is. The normal plural for ben in *benim*.

[39] A note on the word *'elohim*. Despite arguments to the contrary, it has never been demonstrated that this word *incontrovertibly* means a human being in *any* verse in the Bible. The closest is probably 1 Sam 28:13 where the dead spirit of Samuel is described by this term, but importantly, this refers to the dead Samuel's spirit, not to Samuel when alive. Often Psalm 82:6 is referred to as proof that humans can be gods. A quick search of any good Study Bible's notes here shows that it is far from certain that these *'elohim* refer to human beings. Michael Heiser has done the best work on Psalm 82:6 to date. For a synopsis see Michael Heiser, "You've Seen One Elohim, You've Seen Them All? A Critique of Mormonism's Use of Psalm 82," *FARMS Review* 19/1 (2007): 221-266. Other references sometimes cited in support of the idea that "gods" in this Psalm refer to humans include Ex 21:6; 22:8, 9, 20. This understanding is also far from certain, and has been severely criticized by Cyrus Gordon, "אלהים (Elohim) in Its Reputed Meaning of *Rulers, Judges*," *Journal of Biblical Literature* 54 (1935): 139-144.

[40] John William Wevers, vol. I, *Genesis*, Vetus Testamentum Graecum. Auctoritate Academiae Scientiarum Gottingensis editum (Göttingen: Vandenhoeck & Ruprecht, 1974), 109.

[41] The LXX reading is almost certainly the original. See Michael S. Heiser, "Deuteronomy 32:8 and the Sons of God," *Bibliotheca Sacra*: 158:629 (Jan-Mar, 2001): 52-74.

[42] Gordon Douglas Young, *Ugarit in Retrospect* (Winona Lake, IN: Eisenbrauns, 1981), 16.

[43] Some terms found in Ugarit are as follows: pḫr 'ilm -- "the assembly of El / the gods" (A Dictionary of the Ugaritic Language in the Alphabetic Tradition [DULAT] 2:669; Keilalphabetische Texte aus Ugarit [KTU] 1.47:29; 1.118:28; 1.148:9); pḫr bn'ilm – "the assembly of the sons of El/the gods" (DULAT 2:669; KTU 1.4.III:14); pḫr kkbm – "the assembly of the stars" (DULAT 2:670; KTU 1.10.I:4) (parallel to bn 'il in Job 38:7-8); mpḫrt bn 'il - "the assembly of the gods" (DULAT 2:566; KTU 1.65:3); 'dt 'ilm – "assembly of El/the gods" (DULAT 1:152; KTU 1.15.II:7, 11); dr 'il – "assembly (circle) of El" (DULAT 1:279-80; KTU 1.15.II:19; 1.39:7; 1.162:16; 1.87:18); dr bn 'il – "assembly (circle) of the sons of El" (DULAT 1:279-80; KTU 1.40:25, 33-34); dr dt šmm – "assembly (circle) of

those of heaven" (DULAT 1:279-80; KTU 1.10.I:3, 5); dr 'il wpḫr bʻl – "assembly (circle) of El and the assembly of Baal" (DULAT 1:279-80; KTU 1.39:7; 1.62:16; 1.87:18).

[44] On the "seventy" sons at Ugarit see *KTU* 1.4 VI.46; *CTA* 4.6.38-59.

[45] Most notably in Psalm 82:1 where God takes his seat in the "assembly of El" (NET), which is correctly interpreted as the "divine council" by the ESV. See the important article from Michael Heiser in note 41 (above).

[46] In Exodus 15:27 you have the "seventy palm trees" of *Elim* (*elim* means "gods"). Targum Pseudo-Jonathan Deut 32:8 reads, "When the Most High made allotment of the world unto the nations which proceeded from the sons of Noah, in the separation of the writings and languages of the children of men at the time of the division, He cast the lot among the *seventy angels*, the princes of the nations with whom is the revelation to oversee the city, even at that time He established the limits of the nations according to the sum of the number of the *seventy souls* of Israel who went down into Mizraim [Egypt]." See also 1 Enoch 89:59-77; 90:22-27. See the discussions in Margaret Barker, *The Revelation of Jesus Christ* (Edinburgh: T&T Clark, 2000), 226-31; John Day, *God's Conflict with the Dragon and the Sea* (London: Cambridge University Press, 1985), 175-75; Day, *Yahweh and the Gods and Goddesses of Canaan* (New York: Continuum, 2002), 23-24; Michael S. Heiser, "Deuteronomy 32:8 and the Sons of God." *Bibliotheca Sacra* 158:629 (Jan-Mar, 2001): 52-74.

[47] For example, "Before the gods I sing your praise" (Ps 138:1); "Worship him, all you gods!" (Ps 97:7); "God has taken his place in the divine council; in the midst of the gods he holds judgment" (Ps 82:1). In each case the word "gods" is the Hebrew *elohim.* God is not asking cartoon characters or figments of the human imagination or sticks in the mud to worship him. He is commanding the heavenly beings, created by him, to worship him.

[48] Isa 44:24; John 1:3; 1 Cor 8:5-6; Eph 3:9; Col 1:16; Heb 1:2-4. Hence he is the "God of gods" (Deut 10:17; Ps 50:1; 84:7; 136:2).

[49] LXX Job 1:6; 2:1; 38:7; Ps 29:1; 97:7; 138:1, etc.

[50] See note #46 and the "seventy palms of Elim."

[51] It is true that sometimes the ancient kings were referred to in the same way (see Kline, "Divine Kingship," 192). What Kline does not take into account, though he should know better because he talks about it in his writings, is the role of the divine council, the heavenly court of sons of God (Ps 82:1), and how this is often the context of the usage in the Bible. You can find a good primer on the divine council on Michael Heiser's website, but I will not discuss it further here, lest we get utterly bogged down and off track. Even if we run with Kline's argument, the most it shows is that humans can also be called sons of God in pagan cultures. Of course, these gods may very well have been semi-divine themselves (Nephilim). Even if the later kinds were not, their ancestors certainly could have been and the later kinds merely retained the title for themselves. Thus, some have tried to merge the angelic view and the divine kingship view together. Taken this way, there is nothing contradictory about a heavenly being or its offspring ruling over humans as tyrants and kings. I tend to think this is exactly what happened.

[52] Meredith Kline, *Kingdom Prologue* (Overland Park, KS: Two Age Press, 2000), 8.

[53] Cf. Gen 9:12; 15:16; 17:7, etc.

[54] Betty Champion, *Yes We Can Be Perfect In Our Generation* (LaGrange, GA: World Overcomer's Church Int., 2002), 119.

[55] This is the typical meaning of the phrase, "saw his father's nakedness" (Gen 9:22) in the OT. See Lev 18:8; 20:11, 17; Deut 22:30; 27:20. See John Sietze Bergsma, "Noah's Nakedness and the Curse of Canaan (Gen 9:20-27)," in *Journal of Biblical Literature* 124/1 (2005): 25-40.

[56] John Walton, *Covenant: God's Purpose, God's Plan* (Grand Rapids, MI: Zondervan, 1994), 72-73.

[57] This reference is found in the ancient Babylonian Talmud, *Sotah* 34a. The text literally says they carried it "between two." English translations supply the word "men" after "two," "between two men." But the Rabbis thought it was rather between two staffs and was so large that it took almost

all of the spies to carry it to Moses. Their purpose was to discourage the people from taking over the land by bringing back this (genetically manipulated?) cluster of grapes.

[58] Mary Douglas writes that these "purity laws" serve to keep "distinct the categories of creation." *Purity and Danger: An Analysis of the Concepts of Pollution and Taboo* (London: Routledge & Kegan Paul, 1966) 41–57; *Implicit Meanings: Essays in Anthropology* (London: Routledge & Kegan Paul, 1975) 261–73, 283–318.

[59] The work of Moshe Kline, a student of Mary Douglas (previous note), and Dr. Paul Hocking have helped us see the Torah as a woven text such that Leviticus is the central book, structured around a movement motif of entering and then leaving the ark of the covenant, which takes place in Leviticus 19, of which the hinge are the vv. 19-23. Moshe Kline, *Before Chapter and Verse* (2022) published through Amazon; Paul Hocking, *A New and Living Way*, Dissertation to the University of Chester (2021), also published in book form at Amazon.

[60] See Dante Fortson, *As The Days of Noah Were*, (self published, 2010), ch. 9.

[61] For more on this idea see Ronald S. Hendel, "Of Demigods and the Deluge: Toward an Interpretation of Genesis 6:1-4," *Journal of Biblical Literature* 106 (1987): 23-25.

[62] See Louisiana's RS 14:89.6, Arizona's S.B. 1307 – 492R; Ohio's SB 243. Each of these bills has been passed into law.

[63] Thanks to Dr. Sherri Tenpenny for contacting Dr. McCullough to get me these articles about the "vaccine." They are just the beginning. Anthony M. Kyriakopoulos, Peter A. McCullough, Greg Nigh, and Stephanie Seneff, "Potential Mechanisms for Human Genome Integration of Genetic Code from SARS-CoV-2 mRNA Vaccination: Implications for Disease," *J Neurol Disord* 10:10 (2022): 519; Markus Aldén, Francisko Olofsson Falla, Daowei Yang, Mohammad Barghouth, Cheng Luan, Magnus Rasmussen, and Yang De Marinis, "Intracellular Reverse Transcription of Pfizer BioNTech COVID-19 mRNA Vaccine BNT162b2 In Vitro in Human Liver Cell Line, *Curr Issues Mol Biol* 44 (2022): 1115-1126; Peter A. McCullough, "Reverse Transcription—Permanent Installation of mRNA Genetic Code: Unintended Consequence of Novel COVID-19 Vaccines," *Courageous Discourse* (Nov 3, 2022); Peter A. McCullough, "SARS-CoV-2 Spike Protein Found in the Human Nucleus," *Courageous Discourse*," (Nov 14, 2022). Sarah Sattar, Juraj Kabat, Kailey Jerome, Friederike Feldmann, Kristina Bailey, and Masfique Mehedi, "Nuclear translocation of spike mRNA and protein is a novel pathogenic feature of SARS-CoV-2," *bioRxiv* (Preprint Sept 27, 2022).

[64] It reads, "There were men of great strength and size on the earth in those days; and after that, when the sons of God had connection with the daughters of men, they gave birth to children: these were the great men of old days, the men of great name."

[65] The NT says that it was the serpent who tempted Eve. Christian tradition, using John (Revelation 12 and 20), has said this is a character named Satan. Jews had other names for him, such as Samael (Apocalypse of Baruch) or Azazel (Apocalypse of Abraham). Are these all the same person? Perhaps. Nevertheless, the point remains, it was certainly a heavenly being.

[66] See Douglas Phillips, "The Mystery of the Nephilim Presented and Solved: Discovering the True Giants of Paganism," in *Mysteries of the Ancient World*, an audio series (San Antonio, TX: Vision Forum, 2008).

[67] See Appendix: 2 Peter 2:4 and Jude 6.

[68] See Justo L. González, "Demythologization," in *Essential Theological Terms* (Louisville, KY: Westminster John Knox Press, 2005), 44.

NOTES FOR CHAPTER 1: PRE-FLOOD GIANTS (Pgs. 43-60)

[1] The two kingdoms doctrine was further developed by the two wings of the Protestant Reformation: Lutheran and Reformed. For a good Reformed summary of this topic see David VanDrunen, *Living in God's Two Kingdoms* (Wheaton, IL: Crossway, 2010).

2 Israel is a type of the heavenly kingdom which is inaugurated in Christ's First Coming and consummated in his Second Coming.

3 As pointed out in the Introduction, Cain cannot be viewed as the physical descendant of Satan as the so called "Serpent Seed" heresy teaches, because Cain is unequivocally said to be the son of Adam (Gen 4:1). For a good, non-technical introduction to this topic see Dante Fortson, *The Serpent Seed: Debunked* (Impact Agenda Media, 2010).

4 While the Serpent Seed doctrine teaches that Satan had relations with Eve, the curse is more broadly spoken to "the *nachash*" (the serpent). Satan is a *nachash*, but not all *nachash* are Satan. Nachash is a Hebrew term applied to Satan (Gen 3:1; Isa 27:1) as well as to other heavenly beings called *seraphim* (see Num 21:6-9; Deut 8:15; Isa 14:29; Jer 8:17 and the discussions in *DDD*, "Serpent," 744-747; Karen Joines, *Serpent Symbolism in the Old Testament: A Linguistic, Archaeological, and Literary Study* (Haddonfield House, New Jersey, 1974); and Michael S. Heiser, "Serpentine / Reptilian Divine Beings in the Hebrew Bible: A Preliminary Investigation."

5 The same idea is found in Gen 4:19 when the wicked Lamech "took" two women who bore him children and in Geñ 11:29 when Abram "took" Sarai for his wife. Might the former refer to some kind of unlawful taking? The text does not elaborate.

6 One of the most frightening contemporary expressions of women being filled with lust for the sons of God can be seen in the Katie Perry video: E.T. The lyrics and video are *extremely* disturbing in light of the Genesis 6 event and Perry's background from Christian fundamentalism.

7 For example, in the Testament of Reuben we read, "[The Watchers] were transformed into human males, and while the women were cohabiting with their husbands they appeared to them" (TReu 5:6). 1 Enoch says, "Whenever they want, they appear as men" (1 Enoch 17:1). See Kelley Coblentz Bautch, *A Study of the Geography of 1 Enoch 17-19* (Boston: Brill, 2003), 46-49. On shape shifting in Greek mythology see Homer, *Odyssey* 4.315-462; Ovid, *Metamorphosis* 11.250-263. You can also see this in the recent Hollywood production *Clash of the Titans*, when Zeus comes to the human Queen Danaë in the form of her husband King Acrisius and from this union, the *demigod* Perseus is born.

8 See Chapter 2.

9 For example, Chuck Missler argued that all of the names from Adam to Noah tell the story of the gospel in a sort of *name*rology Bible-code: Man (Adam) Appointed (Seth) Mortal (Enosh) Sorrow (Kenan) The Blessed God (Mahalalel) Shall Come Down (Jared) Teaching (Enoch) His Death Shall Bring (Methuselah) The Despairing (Lamech) Rest/Comfort (Noah). See Chuck Missler, "Meanings of the Names in Genesis 5," *Koinonia House* (Aug 1, 2000), http://www.khouse.org/articles/2000/284/#notes. While clever, this approach probably goes too far because there are other possible meanings for the names, some of the names he gives are dubious, and God doesn't need secret codes of names to give us the gospel. In my study of the names (below), I am only commenting on how those names may be used to explain the era in which the children were born. Pitterson, *Judgment of the Nephilim*, has recently looked at some of these names in helpful ways.

10 Unless otherwise noted, the meanings of Bible names throughout this book are found in Stelman Smith and Judson Cornwall, *The Exhaustive Dictionary of Bible Names* (North Brunswick, NJ: Bridge-Logos, 1998).

11 For example, "[I saw Watchers] in my vision, the dream-vision. Two (men) were fighting over me, saying . . . and holding a great contest over me. I asked them, 'Who are you, that you are thus empo[wered over me?' They answered me, 'We] [have been em]powered and rule over all mankind.' They said to me, 'Which of us do yo[u choose to rule (you)?' I raised my eyes and looked.] [One] *of them was terr[i]fying in his appearance, [like a serpent, [his] cl[oa]k many-colored yet very dark. . .* [And I looked again], and . . . *in his appearance, his visage like a viper. . .*" Test Amram, Q543 Frag vi: 9-14 (See Robert H. Eiseman and Michael Owen Wise, *The Dead Sea Scrolls Uncovered* [New York: Penguin Books, 1993], 164. Satan, likewise, is depicted not as a snake, but as something like a seraphim. "Standing (something) like a dragon in form, but having hands and feet like a man's, on his back six wings on the right and six on the left." Apocalypse of Abraham 23:7.

[12] For example, Jubilees 7:22, "And they begot sons, the Naphidim, and all of them were dissimilar. And each one ate his fellow. The giants killed the Naphil, and the Naphil killed the Elyo, and the Elyo mankind, and man his neighbor." 1 Baruch 3:26, "There were the giants famous from the beginning, that were of so great stature, and so expert in war." 3 Maccabees 2:4, "It was thou who didst destroy the former workers of unrighteousness, among whom were the giants, who trusted in their strength and hardihood, by covering them with a measureless flood."

[13] Jude quotes from 1 Enoch 1:9 and tells us that these are the words of Enoch who lived before the Flood. This section on giants is less than 20 verses away from the verse quoted by Jude.

[14] The coordinates of Hermon may play into their choosing this as their landing place. It sits at the only spot on earth where a 33^0 latitude and 33^0 longitude (taking Paris as the Prime Meridian) intersect. The late David Flynn offers detailed analysis of its importance, and while I'm skeptical of his views of a Mars connection, there is no question that whatever the reason Hermon was chosen, the whole thing is incredibly, deeply, and profoundly strange. See David Flynn, "2012 Year of Resurrection," https://www.youtube.com/watch?v=t68sCaPAgxQ&ab_channel=dawveed84, and other like lectures he gave on the subject.

[15] Derek Gilbert first told me about this. He has written about it in his books *Bad Moon Rising* (Crane, MO: Defender Publishing, 2019), ch. 2 and *The Second Coming of Saturn* (2022), ch. 15.

[16] This was extremely common after a war, as it demonstrated conquest of the foreign gods. Warren implies this when he says, "…on the southern peak there is a hole scooped out of the apex, the foot is surrounded by an oval of hewn stones, and at its south end is a Sacellum, or temple, nearly destroyed: the latter appears to be of more recent date than the stone oval, and the mouldings on its cornice appear to be Roman." Charles Warren, "Summit of Hermon," *Palestine Exploration Fund, Quarterly Statement* 5 (1870): 212.

[17] Warren, ibid.

[18] George W. E. Nickelsburg, *1 Enoch: A Commentary on the Book of 1 Enoch*, ed. Klaus Baltzer, Hermeneia—a Critical and Historical Commentary on the Bible (Minneapolis, MN: Fortress, 2001), 247.

[19] Picture in M. I. Clermont-Ganneau, "*24. Mount Hermon and its God in an inedited Greek Inscription*" [Italics original], *Palestine Exploration Fund: Quarterly Statement* (London: Harrison and Sons, 1903), 137 He translates the stone a little differently, "By the order of the god most great and holy, those who take the oath—hence!" (p. 138). (Note: They had to break the stone in two in order to carry by animal back to Lebanon).

[20] The Babylonians, some 750 miles from Hermon as the crow flies and several hundred more if you travel the Fertile Crescent, knew Hermon as the home of the Anunnaki (their name for the Watchers of Enoch). This is found in the oldest surviving piece of ancient literature that we have on earth, the Gilgamesh Epic (See *Gilgamesh Epic* C: Old Babylonian fragment, *ANET*, 504-05. Discussion in J. Day, *God's Conflict with the Dragon and the Sea* [Cambridge University Press, 1985], 117 and E. Lipinski, "El's Abode. Mythological Traditions Related to Mount Hermon," *Orientalia Lovaniensia Periodica* 2 [1971]: 15-41.

[21] Kelley Coblentz Bautch, A Study of the Geography of 1 Enoch 17-19: "No One Has Seen What I Have Seen" (Leiden: Brill, 2003): 62.

[22] For example, Michael Tellinger, "Ancient Artifacts, Mud Fossils and Giants," *African Dream* (2022), https://www.youtube.com/watch?v=wZoki697b3w&ab_channel=AfricanDream.

[23] Michael Tellinger, "Ancient Giant Footprint South Africa Jan 2012 Michael Tellinger Klaus Dona (1 or 2)," *The Truth Channel* (Jan 2012), https://www.youtube.com/watch?v=2HAcsdQGU8E&ab_channel=TheTruthChannel.

[24] George W. E. Nickelsburg and Klaus Baltzer, *1 Enoch : A Commentary on the Book of 1 Enoch* (Minneapolis, Minn.: Fortress, 2001), 182.

[25] Jubilees and 1 Enoch also refer to a group that were apparently the children of the Nephilim (Naphidim). They are called the Eljo or Elioud. "... and the Giants slew the Naphil, and the Naphil

slew the Eljo, and the Eljo mankind, and one man another." The word is extremely corrupt but possible meanings of it could be "against God" or "arrogant ones." Nickelsburg, *1 Enoch*, 185.

[26] For more on the giants and cannibalism see Matthew Goff, "Monstrous Appetites: Giants, Cannibalism, and Insatiable Eating in Enochic Literature," *JAJ* 1 (2010): 19-42.

[27] For instance, Judd H. Burton, *Interview With The Giant: Ethnohistorical Notes on the Nephilim* (Burton Beyond Press, 2009), 24-33.

[28] See Burton, *Interview*, 27; Raymond T. McNally, *In Search of Dracula: The History of Dracula and Vampires Completely Revised* (Boston: Mifflin, 1994), 117-118. Burton also has a bibliography for these ancient vampiric creatures.

[29] See R. Campbell Thompson, The Devils and Evil Spirits of Babylonia: Being Babylonian and Assyrian Incantations Against the Demons, Ghouls, Vampires, Hobgoblins, Ghosts, and Kindred Evil Spirits, Which Attack Mankind (reprinted by Forgotten Books at Google Books, originally published around 1903), p. 71.

[30] See also Exodus 22:19 and Deuteronomy 27:21.

[31] Francis Brown, Samuel Rolles Driver and Charles Augustus Briggs, *Enhanced Brown-Driver-Briggs Hebrew and English Lexicon*, electronic ed. (Oak Harbor, WA: Logos Research Systems, 2000), 117.

[32] William Lee Holladay, Ludwig Köhler and Ludwig Köhler, *A Concise Hebrew and Aramaic Lexicon of the Old Testament*. (Leiden: Brill, 1971), 386.

[33] See note 57 in Introduction.

[34] Charlesworth's commentary on 1 Enoch 8:1 n. d reads, "A [an early manuscript of 1 Enoch] adds *tawaleṭo 'alam*, 'transmutation of the world.' I render it as 'alchemy.' ... Ethiopian commentators [those who recopied the book over its forgotten centuries] explain this phrase as 'changing a man into a horse or mule or vice versa, or transferring an embryo from one womb to another.'" See Charlesworth, *OT Pseudepigrapha* vol. 1, p. 16.

[35] A. L. Frothingham, "Babylonian Origin of Hermes, the Snake-God, and of the Caduceus," *American Journal of Archaeology* 20: 2nd series, 1916.

[36] Gerald D. Hart, "The Earliest Medical Use of the Caduceus," *C.M.A. Journal* 107 (Dec 9, 1972): 1107.

[37] See Burton, *Interview*, 78-88.

[38] See Hedwige Rouillard, "Rephaim," in *DDD*, 692-700.

[39] Hart, 1107-08.

NOTES FOR CHAPTER 2: THE GIANT OF BABEL (Pgs. 61-84)

[1] A good summary of this can be found in James M. Boice, *Genesis Vol. 1* (Grand Rapids, MI: Baker Books, 1998), 353-59.

[2] See Introduction note 54 (Betty Champion).

[3] For instance, Leviticus 20:11 speaks directly to this, "If a man lies with his father's wife, he has uncovered his father's nakedness." To "see" the nakedness is akin to uncovering it. Leviticus 20:17, "If a man takes his sister, a daughter of his father or daughter of his mother, and sees her nakedness, and she sees his nakedness, it is a disgrace." "Seeing" and being "uncovered" are both in the Genesis 9 narrative. Also Lev 18:8, 20:11; Deut 22:30; 27:20; Hab 2:15; Ezek 22:10. See John Sietze Bergsma, "Noah's Nakedness and the Curse of Canaan (Gen 9:20-27)," in *Journal of Biblical Literature* 124/1 (2005): 25-40.

[4] Bible scholars are perplexed as to how Nimrod could be in Babylon when his ancestor Cush is identified with Ethiopia. The answer is simple. The Ethiopian Cushites were either a separate group or late arrivals to Africa, having migrated here long after Nimrod because of war or natural disaster. The later is probably the case. Greek historians consistently reported that the Cushites originally settled the coast of the Persian Gulf (south of Mesopotamia) along with their Canaanite brothers.

See François Lenormant, *A Manual of the Ancient History of the East to the Commencement of the Median Wars*, trans. E. Chavallier (Philadelphia: Lippincott & Co., 1870-71), 144ff.

[5] Cf. Victor P. Hamilton, *The Book of Genesis: Chapters 1-17*, The New International Commentary on the Old Testament (Grand Rapids, MI: Wm. B. Eerdmans Publishing Co., 1990), 339; or the TNK Bible "Like Nimrod a mighty hunter by the grace of the LORD."

[6] K. van der Toorn and P. W. van der Horst, "Nimrod Before And After The Bible," *Harvard Theological Review* 83:1 (1990), 14.

[7] On these comparisons see van der Toorn, "Nimrod," 10-11. See also J. van Dijk, *LUGAL UD ME-LÁM-bi NIR-GÁL Le récit épique et didactique des Travaux de Ninurta, du Déluge et de la Nouvelle Création* (2 vols.; Leiden: Brill, 1983), 17-18; the translation by Thorkild Jacobsen, *The Harps That Once ... Sumerian Poetry in Translation* (New Haven/London: Yale University Press, 1987), 233-72; W. Burkert, *The Orientalizing Revolution: Near Eastern Influence on Greek Culture in the Early Archaic Age* (Cambridge, 1987), 14-19, and in C. Bonnet and C. Jourdain-Annequin (eds.), *Héraclès. D'une rive á l'autre de la Méditerranée. Bilan et perspectives* (Brussels & Rome, 1992), pp.121-124; F.E. Brenk, *Relighting the Souls: Studies in Plutarch, in Greek Literature, Religion, and Philosophy, and in the New Testament Background* (Stuttgart, 1999), 5-7-26.

[8] Viticulturalists have been doing this to modern grapes for several decades now. It doesn't take a god to make a giant grape, but it does take some specialized knowledge of breeding and genetics. See for example, H. P. Olmo, "Giant-Berry Grapes: Principles of Genetics Employed to Propagate Varieties Producing Berries of Larger Size," *California Agriculture* Vol. 4 No. 6 (1950): 5-13.

[9] Genesis 10:8 actually uses the same troubling word (*chalal*) that we discussed in Genesis 4:26 (see Introduction pgs. 13-14). It literally reads, "Now Cush begat Nimrod; he began (*chalal*) to be (*lihyot*) a *gibbor*."

[10] See for example, Markus Alden (et al.), "Intracellular Reverse Transcription of Pfizer BioNTech COVID-19 mRNA Vaccine BNT162b2 In Vitro in Human Liver Cell Line," *Mol Biol* 44.3 (2022): 1115-1126. This paper was cited by Dr. Peter McCollough, the world's most published cardiologist and a growing chorus of doctors are recognizing this fact. For more, see *Covid19Reporter* (Dec 27, 2022), https://covid19reporter.com/pfizers-covid-19-vaccine-goes-into-liver-cells-and-is-converted-to-dna/. Thanks to Dr. Sherri Tenpenny for the link.

[11] van der Toorn, "Nimrod," 14.

[12] Christoph Uehlinger, "Nimrod," in *Dictionary of Deities and Demons in the Bible: DDD*, 2nd extensively rev. ed., K. van der Toorn, Bob Becking and Pieter Willem van der Horst (eds) (Leiden; Boston; Grand Rapids, Mich.: Brill; Eerdmans, 1999), 628. The idea is to take the two words without English vowels *Nmrd* (נמרד) and *Nsrk* (נסרך) (Hebrew has no vowels). ם becomes ס, and ד becomes ך. Even if you can't read ancient Hebrew, you can see the similarity in the letters, and how easy it could be to confuse them.

[13] Larry Zalcman, "Orion," *DDD*, 649.

[14] Karl Preisendanz, "Nimrod," *Pauly, Wissowa and Kroll, Real-Encyclopädie* 17 (1936): 624-27.

[15] See S. R. Driver & G. B. Gray, *The Book of Job* (ICC; Edinburgh 1921), 86.

[16] Michael M. Alouf, *History of Baalbek* (Escondido, CA: Book Tree, 1999), 29.

[17] Readers Digest Association, *The World's Last Mysteries* (Montreal: Reader's Digest, 1978), 308.

[18] Jean-Pierre Adam, "A propos du trilithon de Baalbek. Le transport et la mise en oeuvre des megaliths," *SYRIA* 54:1-2 (1977): 31-63. This paper also proposes a plausible explanation for how the stones were moved and set into place by very common, ordinary, yet ingenious techniques.

[19] It has been noted at both Ebla and Ugarit that some proper names combine an animal and a deity. The Ugaritic *ni-mi-ri-ya* translates "panther of Yah," so the idea is that Nimrod means "panther of Hadd" (i.e. Baal), analogous to *nqmd* ("victory of Hadd"). See M. J. Dahood, "Ebla, Ugarit, and the Old Testament," *TD* 27 (1979): 129; idem, "Ebla, Ugarit, and the Bible," in G. Pettinato, *The Archives of Ebla: An Empire Inscribed in Clay* (Garden City, NY: Doubleday, 1981), p. 277 cited in Victor P.

Hamilton, *The Book of Genesis: Chapters 1-17*, The New International Commentary on the Old Testament (Grand Rapids, MI: Wm. B. Eerdmans Publishing Co., 1990), 338.

[20] Van der Toorn and van der Horst give an interesting history of these legends among the Jews in their article (see reference n. 5 this chapter), pp. 16-29.

[21] The Hebrew *lipne* is a compound meaning literally "to the face." In 2 Chron 20:12 and Est 9:2 the ESV translates it "against." The Greek *enantoin* is translated "against" in places like Job 15:13, cf. Augustine, *City of God* 16.4.

[22] Eusebius, Praeparatio Evangelica 9.17.2.

[23] Josephus, *Antiquities* 1.4.118.

[24] In the LXX "titan" occurs as a synonym for Rephaim (2 Sam 23:13; 1 Chr 11:15) and as "giant" in the Apocryphal Judith 16:6.

[25] See Introduction notes #44, 46 and Chapter 3 note #1.

[26] Sibylline Oracle 3.105-158 (cf. SibOr 1.283-323). See the discussion in Gerard Mussies, "Titans," *DDD*, 874.

[27] James George Frazer, *Folk-Lore in the Old Testament: Studies in Comparative Religion, Legend, and Law*, vol. 1 (London: MacMillan and CO., 1919), 380.

[28] Peter Tompkins (*Mysteries of the Mexican Pyramids* [New York: Harper Collins, 1987], 57) suggests that the following story is about the same Cholula pyramid, but Frazer does not think so.

[29] Frazer, p. 382. See also Hubert Howe Bancroft et al., *The Native Races of the Pacific States of North America*, vol. 5: Primitive History (New York: D Appleton and Co., 1874-76), 17-18, n. 40.

[30] Frazer, ibid.

[31] Frazer, 383.

[32] William Joseph Wilkins, *Hindu Mythology, Vedic and Purānic* (London: Thacker & Co., 1882), 364.

[33] See *Satapatha Brahmana* 2.1, 2, 13-16.

[34] John Walton, "The Mesopotamian Background of the Tower of Babel Account and Its Implications," *Bulletin for Biblical Research* 5 (1995): 157.

[35] Ibid., 156.

[36] The Table is a partial list of ziggurats mentioned in Walton, 159-60.

[37] Anne Birrell, *Chinese Mythology: An Introduction* (Baltimore, MD: Johns Hopkins University Press, 1993), 234.

[38] Patricia Turner and Charles Russell Coulter, "Kun-Lun," in *Dictionary of Ancient Deities* (New York: Oxford University Press, 2001), 279.

[39] Cf. George Hart, "Ptah of Memphis," in *Egyptian Myths* (Austin, TX: University of Texas Press, 1990), 18-19.

[40] The word *"devā"* is from an older Proto-Indo-European Sanskrit word *deiwos*, which was an adjective meaning "celestial" or "shining."

[41] Cf. Prose Edda: *Gylfaginning*, 27.

[42] Lewis Spence, *The Myths of the North American Indians* (New York: Dover, 1989), 108.

[43] The scholarly paper which first proposed the Pyramids-Orion connection (Robert Bauval, "A Master Plan for the Three Pyramids of Giza Based on the Configuration of the Three Stars of the Belt of Orion," *Discussions in Egyptology* 13 [1989]: 7-18), was popularized in Bauval, *The Orion Mystery* (New York: Three Rivers Press, 1994); Graham Hancock, *Fingerprints of the Gods* (New York: Three Rivers Press, 1995) and *Heaven's Mirror: Quest for the Lost Civilization* (New York: Crown Publishers, 1998); Thomas G. Brophy, *The Origin Map* (New York: Writers Club Press, 2002); Bauval, *The Egypt Code* (New York: Disinformation Co., Ltd., 2008) and others. The theory is not without its detractors. Since then, suggestions that other ancient cites emulate Orion have also been made (see attending picture).

1. Orion's Belt. 2. Tenochtitlan (Mexico) 3. Pyramids of Giza. 4. Pyramids, Xian (China). 5. Thornborough Henges, England

Fig. FN1. Cross-Cultural Orion Connection

[44] On the Hopi hypothesis, see Gary A. David, *The Orion Zone: Ancient Star Cities of the American Southwest* (Kempton, IL: Adventures Unlimited Press, 2006). David's images are copyrighted, but have been reproduced by the History Channel. The Mesoamerican Orion connection maybe related to the complex at Tenochtitlan, Mexico (above). Sadly, many of these speculative researchers are into this stuff because of the New Age implications they believe they have "re-discovered," which only fits with the wickedness God saw in such things in the first place.

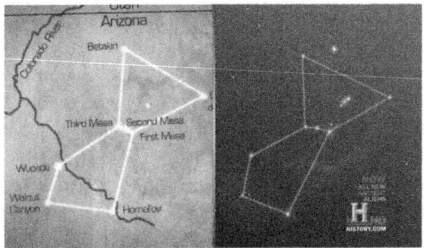

Courtesy, the History Channel

Fig. FN2. Orion Complex of Northwest Arizona

[45] Cited in Gregory K. Beale, *The Temple and the Church's Mission: A Biblical Theology of the Dwelling Place of God* (Downers Grove, IL: InterVarsity Press, 2004), 51-52.

[46] Walton, 161.

[47] See John H. Walton, *Genesis-Deuteronomy*, Zondervan Illustrated Bible Backgrounds Commentary (Old Testament) Vol. 1 (Grand Rapids, MI: Zondervan, 2009), 106.

[48] Actually, it says, "Let us go down" (Gen 11:7). As with Genesis 1:26, the plural "us" here refers to the divine council. But just like Gen 1:26, it is God alone who does the action. The council here is powerless to give the people what they want. Instead, the Only Creator curses them and disperses them.

NOTES FOR CHAPTER 3: ABRAHAM AND THE GIANT WARS (Pgs. 85-96)

[1] The number is disputed, but good defenses of a total of "70" are found in Umberto Cassuto, *A Commentary on the Book of Genesis: From Noah to Abraham* (Jerusalem: Magnes Press, 1964), 177–180; Allen P. Ross, "Studies in the Book of Genesis - Part 2: The Table of Nations in Genesis 10 - its Structure," *Bibliotheca Sacra* 137:548 (Oct-Dec 1980): 342.

[2] You can identify most of these groups by the Hebrew plural ending *–im*, such as Ludim, Anamim etc., or by the English plural ending *–ites*, such as Jebusites, Amorites etc.

[3] See François Lenormant, *A Manual of the Ancient History of the East to the Commencement of the Median Wars*, trans. E. Chavallier (Philadelphia: Lippincott & Co., 1870-71), 144ff.

[4] For this and all the names which follow see Note #9, Ch. 1.

[5] Gen 15:20-21 (which substitutes Rephaim for Hivite); Ex 3:8, 17; 13:5, 23:23; 33:2; 34:11; Num 13:29; Deut 20:17; Josh 9:1; 12:8; Jdg 3:5; 1 Kgs 9:20; 2 Chron 8:7; Ezra 9:1 (leave out the Girgashites).

[6] For instance, Genesis 48:23 refers to a "portion" or "mountain slope" that Jacob took from an Amorite. The word for a portion here is *shekem* and the incident probably refers to the events at Shechem with (Gen 33:19) Hamor the Hivite. Thus, a Hivite can be called an Amorite. Another time, the Amorites came and defeated Israel at Hormah (Deut 1:44). But in Num 14:45, we learn that it was the Amalekites and Canaanites who attacked Israel here.

[7] One scholar has suggested that they are a mixture of Hittite and Amorite per the old name for Jerusalem ("Jebus"; Jdg 19:10). A. H. Sayce, "The White Race of Palestine," in *Nature* 38:979 (Aug 2, 1888): 322.

[8] T. K. Cheyne, J. Sutherland Black, *Encyclopaedia Biblica* (London: Adam and Charles Black, 1899-1902), 2:2100.

[9] For a discussion of this see K. van der Toorn and P. W. van der Horst, "Nimrod Before And After The Bible," *Harvard Theological Review* 83:1 (1990): 23-25; also Babylonian Talmud (b.) *'Erubin* 53a.

[10] Bob Becking, "Lagamar," *DDD*, 498-99.

[11] This association was seen by the French orientalist Armand-Pierre Caussin de Perceval (1795-1871) in his Essays on the History of the Arabs before Islamism, during the Time of Mohammed, and down to the Reduction of all the Tribes under his Dominion (1847), i.26. It also comports with the Arabian historian Al-Masudi (896 – 956 A.D.) who reported that the ancient prophet Saleh (presumed to be post-diluvian but pre-Abrahamic) came to the rescue of a group called the Thamudites (a group of Canaanites, see J. W. De Forest, "The Great Deluge," in Edward Everett Hale [ed.], Old and New, Vol. 6, July 1872-Jan 1873 [Boston: Lee & Shepard, 1872]: 437), who were being threatened by a descendant of Ham (see Masudi, Prairies, c. 38, 3:90 as cited in Lina Eckenstein, A History of Sinai (New York, Macmillian Co, 1921), 50.

[12] *'Amar pil* = "He said, 'Throw.'"

[13] Amraphel may also derive from the name of the Amorite storm god Amurru. See van der Toorn, "Amurru," *DDD*, 32-33.

[14] Victor P. Hamilton, *The Book of Genesis: Chapters 1-17*, The New International Commentary on the Old Testament (Grand Rapids, MI: Wm. B. Eerdmans Publishing Co., 1990), 400.

[15] Ernest G. Clark; *Targum and Scripture: Studies in Aramaic Translations and Interpretation* (Boston: Brill, 2002), 26; Roswell D. Hitchcock, "Arioch," "An Interpreting Dictionary of Scripture Proper Names," in *Hitchcock's Complete Analysis of the Holy Bible* (New York: A. J. Johnson, 1874), 1105.

[16] Hitchcock, 1112.

[17] Of course, he does not call this episode "absurd." Here is what he writes, " ... so God avenged, with more severe punishment, the shameful lust of the others; who, while endeavoring to do violence to angels, were not only injurious towards men; but, to the utmost of their power, dishonored the celestial glory of God, by their sacrilegious fury." Calvin, *Commentary on Genesis 19:5*.

[18] Hamilton, *Genesis 1-17*, 401.

[19] Here are some examples from New England. In Middleboro, Massachusetts an infamous and mysterious "settler" named "Mr. Richmond" lived prior to 1675 and became an enemy of the native Indians living there. They managed to kill him, but many years later his (supposedly his) skeleton was found and exhumed in the presence of one "Dr. Morrill Robinson" who measured his skeleton as having been "at least seven feet and eight inches." The man also had "a double row of teeth in each jaw." Thomas Weston, *History of the Town of Middleboro, Massachusetts* (Boston: Houghton, Mifflin and Company, 1906), 400. In Deerfield, MA we read, "One of these skeletons was described to me by Henry Mather who saw it as being of monstrous size- 'the head as big as a peck basket with double teeth all round.' The skeleton was examined by Dr. Stephen Williams, who said the owner must have been nearly 8 feet high." George Sheldon, *History of Deerfield*, vol. 1 (MA: Pioneer Valley Memorial Museum, 1895), 78. In Rockingham, VT a "remarkable human skeleton" has a jawbone "of such size that a large man could easily slip it over his face, and the teeth, which were all double, were perfect." Lyman Simpson Hayes, *History of the Town of Rockingham, Vermont* (Bellow Falls, VT: The Town, 1907), 338. At Martha's Vineyard of all places, "a man easily six feet and a half, possibly

seven feet, high" had "an unusual feature … a complete double row of teeth on both upper and lower jaws." Charles Gilbert Hine, *The Story of Martha's Vineyard* (New York: Hine Brothers, 1908), 137. One skeleton from Concord, New Hampshire, a 6'3" person with a "very thick" skull and a full head of double teeth was preserved by Dr. William Prescott in his cabinet. This was reported, not in *UFO Magazine* (as one person has quipped), but in the *Boston Medical and Surgical Journal*. See J. V. C. Smith, M.D., W. W. Morland, M.D., and Francis Minot, M.D., *Boston Medical and Surgical Journal*, vol. LIII (Boston: David Clapp, 1856), 456. There are also reports from Lompock Rancho, Santa Rosa Island, and the Catalina Islands, CA; Clearwater, MN (though this one appears to be a conflation of a double-teeth finding from nearby Delano, MN [see Franklyn Curtiss-Wedge, *History of Wright County Minnesota*, vol. 1 (Chicago: H. C. Cooper, Jr., & Co., 1915), 34]; Adams County, Ohio; Jefferson County, New York; Mason County, Virginia, and other places. Compilations from these can be found in Frank Edwards, *Stranger Than Science* (New York: Lyle Stuart, 1959), 129; Henry Howe, *The Historical Collections of Ohio* (Cincinnati, OH: Pub by the state of Ohio, 1902), 350-51. Stephen Quayle, *Genesis 6 Giants: Master Builders of Prehistoric and Ancient Civilizations* (Bozeman, MT: End Time Thunder Publishers, 2002), 260.

[20] Hamilton, Ibid.

NOTES FOR CHAPTER 4: PATRIARCHAL GIANTS (Pgs. 97-102)

[1] It is common for commentaries to say that the spies exaggerated *the height* of the inhabitants of Canaan. In other words, they were not really tall (not more than seven feet). Given that we know that these people were taller than seven feet from other biblical and extra-biblical sources, it is better—if there is exaggeration at all—to think that they exaggerated *how many* of them were tall. It is not necessary to posit exaggeration in the story, however, because the spies were in trouble for their faithlessness, not for exaggeration.

[2] Eliezer D. Orenin, "Gerar," in David Noel Freedman, vol. 2, *The Anchor Yale Bible Dictionary* (New York: Doubleday, 1996), 989.

[3] The verb "to take" (*laqach*) is the same Hebrew word in all three stories.

[4] Matthew J. Goff, "Ben Sira and the Giants of the Land: A Note on Ben Sira 16:7," *JBL* 129.4 (Winter 2010): 645-55. For the reason it at the very least alludes to Genesis 6, see Appendix 2.

NOTES FOR CHAPTER 5: MOSES MEETS AMALEK (Pgs. 103-108)

[1] On the time spent in Egypt see H. W. Hoehner, "The Duration of the Egyptian Bondage," *Bibliotheca Sacra Volume* 126:504 (1969): 306-16, who sees the count beginning in Genesis 35:9-15 and J. R. Riggs, "The Length of Israel's Sojourn in Egypt," *Grace Theological Journal* 12 (1971): 18-35, who sees it beginning in Genesis 46.

[2] John Garnier, *The Worship of the Dead: The Origin and Nature of Pagan Idolatry* (London: Chapman & Hall, 1904), 74ff; Phillip J. Budd, *Numbers*, Word Biblical Commentary (Dallas: Word, Incorporated, 2002), p. 270.

[3] An example of an older dictionary that makes the proper distinction between the two Amaleks is William G. Smith, *A Dictionary of the Bible: Comprising Its Antiquities, Biography, and Natural History* in 3 Vols. (Boston: Little Brown, 1863), 1:56.

[4] "*Imlāq* is an Arabic term derived from the biblical Hebrew "Amaleq," the hereditary enemies of the Israelites (Deut 35:17), whose name appears in Arab tradition as ʿ*Amāliq* or ʿ*Amāliqa*, Amalekites, and also in Arab folklore telling of the evil king ʿAmlūq. See *Encyclopaedia of Islam*, new ed. [Leiden: E. J. Brill, 1978], 1:429." See Raphael Patai, *Arab Folktales from Palestine and Israel* (Detroit, MI: Wayne State University Press, 1998), 201, n 5.

[5] "In the Arabic colloquial, '*Imlāq* means both Amalekite and 'giant.'" Ibid.

[6] On the relation of Amalek and Ad see Augustin Calmet, *Dictionary of the Holy Bible* (Boston: Crocker and Brewster, 1832), 50.

[7] Ahmad Ibn 'Ali al-Maqrīzī, *Description Topographique et Historique de l'Egypte* (vol. 1), trans. M. U. Bouriant, ed. Ernest Lerous (Paris: Rue Bonaparte, 1895), 89-90. See the translation by Jason Colavito, "Al-Maorizi on the Pyramids of Egypt," *Jason Colavito* (2012-15). Note: In the first publication, I did not credit Colavito. He took umbrage against me on his blog, saying that I plagiarized him. I recall having run across this from another source, used *Google Translate*, and smoothed over the bad English myself. While the two are very similar, I spell certain words differently, which tells me I did not have his translation in front of me. However, it is certainly possible that I ran across it from his blog, as part of his translation predates my own publication. I usually make a note of these things and had no such note. I offer an apology to Jason if I have my history incorrect. It was certainly never my intent to do such a thing. His work here is certainly worth check out, even if he does mock me incessantly in his review of my book.

[8] Garnier, 74.

[9] Samuel G. Goodrich, *A History of All Nations, From the Earliest Periods to the Present Time* (New York: Miller, Orton, and Mulligan, 1855), 315; al-Tabarī, *The History of al-Tabarī* (vol. 2): *Prophets and Patriarchs*, trans. William M. Brinner (Albany, NY: State University of New York Press, 1987), 18.

[10] J. W. De Forest, "The Great Deluge," in Edward Everett Hale (ed.), *Old and New*, Vol. 6, July 1872-Jan 1873 (Boston: Lee & Shepard, 1872), 438ff.

[11] Sibylline Oracle 8:251-53 says, "Moses prefigured him [Christ], stretching out his holy arms, conquering Amalek by faith so that the people might know that he is elect and precious with God his father." Barnabas 12:9 says, "The son of God shall destroy by the roots the whole house of Amalek in the end of days" (taking "end of days" from the Fragment Targum Num 24:20). Also Justin Martyr, *Dialogue* 90; Chrysostom, *Homilies on the Gospel of John* 14; Maximus of Turin, *Sermon* 45.3.

NOTES FOR CHAPTER 6: SPYING OUT THE LAND (Pgs. 109-114)

[1] R. Dennis Cole, vol. 3B, *Numbers*, electronic ed., Logos Library System; The New American Commentary (Nashville: Broadman & Holman Publishers, 2001), 220.

[2] Josias Porter writes of his first-hand experience, "The houses of Bashan are not ordinary houses. Their walls are from five to eight feet thick, built of large squared blocks of basalt; their roofs are formed of slabs of the same material, hewn like planks, and reaching from wall to wall; the very doors and window-shutters are of stone, hung upon pivots projecting above and below... The houses of Kerioth and other towns in Bashan appear to be just such dwellings as a race of giants would build. The walls, the roofs, but especially the ponderous gates, doors, and bars, are in every way characteristic of a period when architecture was in its infancy, when giants were masons, and when strength and security were the grand requisites. I measured a door in Kerioth: it was nine feet high, four and a half feet wide, and ten inches thick,–one solid slab of stone. I saw the folding gates of another town in the mountains still larger and heavier. Time produces little effect on such buildings as these. The heavy stone slabs of the roofs resting on the massive walls make the structure as firm as if built of solid masonry; and the black basalt used is almost as hard as iron. There can scarcely be a doubt, therefore, that these are the very cities erected and inhabited by the Rephaim, the aboriginal occupants of Bashan." Josias Leslie Porter, *The Giant Cities of Bashan; and Syria's Holy Places* (New York: Thomas Nelson, 1884), 20, 84.

[3] Arba can also mean something like "Foursquare." Kiriath-Arba is literally "city of four" and may have been named after Arba and his three giant sons (see below) or to the four cities of Aner, Eschol, Mamre and Hebron.

[4] "Anak," *Anchor Yale Bible Dictionary* (New York: Doubleday, 1996), 222. A good study of the major giant clan names can be found in Kenneth C. Way, "Giants in the Land: A Textual and Semantic

Study of Giants in the Bible and the Ancient Near East," a Master of Arts thesis, Deerfield, IL: Trinity International University, 2000, 33-78.

[5] Nephilim is actually spelled in two different ways in this verse. Scholars suggest that the first spelling is an Aramaic spelling of an Aramaic word for "giant." Aramaic is the language spoken after the captivity in Babylon. The second spelling is the same as that of Genesis 6:4, thus the gloss (the parenthetical in the verse) is an addition (after the writing of the LXX, perhaps as new as the NT era) showing Aramaic readers that the word "giant" and the older world *nephilim* are the one and the same thing. See Introduction, note #30.

[6] For instance, "The Ruler of Iy-'anaq, *'Erum*, and all the *retainers* who are with him; the Ruler of Iy-'anaq, Abi-*yamimu*, and all the *retainers* who are with him; the Ruler of Iy-'anaq, 'Akirum, and all the *retainers* who are with him" (*Execration* Text e1 in *The Ancient Near East an Anthology of Texts and Pictures.*, ed. James Bennett Pritchard [Princeton: Princeton University Press, 1958], 328). This is found on an Egyptian Execration text (ca. 1850) which are broken pottery figurines (see picture to right). The Egyptians would make a clay model of a dreaded enemy and bind its arms behind its back. It is sort of like the practice of voodoo.

Fig. FN 3. Execration Text

[7] Shasu is a general term for the inhabitants of Edom (Horites), Amorites, Amalekites, and the Anakim (*Iy'anaq*). See Clyde E. Billington, "Goliath and The Exodus Giants: How Tall Were They"? *JETS* 50.3 (2007): 500-505.

[8] *Craft of the Scribe* 23.7 (Papyrus Anastasi I); in William W. Hallo and K. Lawson Younger, *Context of Scripture* (Leiden; Boston: Brill, 2003), 3:13.

[9] Pritchard, 477, n. 43.

[10] "Two seven-foot female skeletons were found in a twelfth-century-BC cemetery at Tell *es-Sa 'idiyeh* on the east bank of the Jordan" (Jeffrey H. Tigay, *Deuteronomy* [Philadelphia: Jewish Publication Society, 1996], 17).

[11] Generically, "Skeletons of large size have been excavated in Palestine," and more specifically, "Skeletons 3.2 m. tall [10.5 ft.] have been found elsewhere in Syro-Palestine" (Donald J. Wiseman, "Medicine in the Old Testament World," in *Medicine and the Bible*, ed. B. Palmer [Exeter: Paternoster Press, 1986], 23, 244 n. 58). For other finds consult A. T. Sandison and C. Wells, "Endocrine Diseases," in *Diseases in Antiquity*, eds. D. Brothwell and A. T. Sandison (Springfield, IL: Charles C. Thomas, 1967), 522-25; Theodore H. Gaster, *Myth, Legend and Custom in the Old Testament* (New York: Harper and Row, 1969), 311, 402-3; C. J. S. Thomson, *The Mystery and Lore of Monsters* (New York: Bell, 1968), 133.

[12] See Appendix: Giants in the Americas.

[13] Babylonian Talmud, Sota 34B.

[14] J. Jeremias, *Heiligengräber in Jesu Umwelt* (Göttingen, 1958), 82-86; cited in Charlesworth, OT Pseudepigrapha vol. 2, 391.

[15] See Introduction, note #57.

NOTES FOR CHAPTER 7: THE "LAW" OF CANAAN (Pgs. 115-120)

[1] For instance the Code of Ur-Nammu, king of Ur (ca. 2050 BC, making it contemporary with Abraham); the Laws of Eshunna (ca. 1930 BC); the codex of Lipit-Ishtar of Isin (ca. 1870 BC); and of course the famed Code of Hammurabi (1700 BC).

[2] Nesilim is how the Hittites referred to themselves.

[3] Leonard Woolley, *The Sumerians* (New York: W.W. Norton, 1965), 95.

[4] "If a man charge a man with sorcery, and cannot prove it, he who is charged with sorcery shall go to the river, into the river he shall throw himself and if the river overcome him, his accuser shall take

to himself his house. If the river show that man to be innocent and he come forth unharmed, he who charged him with sorcery shall be put to death. He who threw himself into the river shall take to himself the house of his accuser." (HC 2).

⁵ "If a man is accused of sorcery he must undergo ordeal by water; if he is proven innocent, his accuser must pay 2 shekels."

⁶ Idolatry and having other gods are not the same sin. The former is the second commandment, the latter is the first. We will discuss this more in later chapters.

NOTES FOR CHAPTER 8: ON THE WAY TO CANAAN (Pgs. 121-140)

¹ Richard Dawkins, *The God Delusion* (Boston: Houghton Mifflin Co., 2006), 51.

² This is found in Louis Ginzberg, *Legends of the Jews Vol 5: Notes to Volumes 1 and 2: From the Creation to the Exodus* (Baltimore: Johns Hopkins University Press, 1998), 53-54.

³ Shemhazai is mentioned as one of the leaders of the Watchers, the fallen angels who came upon Mt. Hermon in the days of Jared and who was bound up by the archangel Michael afterwards. 1 Enoch 6:3; 9:7; 10:11.

⁴ Louis Ginzberg, "Sihon, The King of the Amorites," in *Legends of the Jews* (ForgottenBooks, 1909, 2008), 3:219 and note 668 found in vol. 6 of the same series.

⁵ Babylonian Talmud *Rosh ha-Shanah* 3a. See Ginzberg, note 669.

⁶ For instance, "The Egyptian monuments inform us that the Amorites of Palestine were white-skinned, blue-eyed, fair-haired, and dolicho-cephalic (long-headed), and that the race was still predominant in Judah in the age of Shishak, while traces of it are still to be met with in Palestine." A. H. Sayce, "The White Race of Ancient Palestine," in *Academy* vol. 34 (1888): 55. "In the sculptures of Ramses II at Abu-Simbel 'the Shasu of Kanana' were depicted with blue eyes, and red hair, eyebrows, and beard, and the Amaur with 'the eyes blue, the eyebrows and beard red.' As 'the Shasu of Kanana' lived a little to the south of Hebron, while the Amaur are the Amorites of the Old Testament, it was clear that a population existed in Palestine in the fourteenth century before our era which had all the characteristics of the white race." A.H. Sayce, "The White Race of Palestine," in *Nature* vol. 38:979 (Aug 2, 1888): 321-22.

⁷ An interesting compilation of some of these finds can be found in Josiah Priest, *American Antiquities and Discoveries in the West* (Albany, NY: Hoffman & White, 1833).

⁸ Roy Norvill, *Giants: The Vanished Race* (Wellingborough, UK: Aquarian Press, 1979), 84.

⁹ Adam Rodgers, "Early Nevada History is Traced in Lovelock, Cave, Tomb of the Forgotten Race," in *Ancient American* 13:81 (Dec 2008): 32-35.

¹⁰ See for example Sarah Winnemucca Hopkins, *Life Among the Paiutes* (Boston: Cupples, Upham & CO., 1883), 26.

¹¹ On the idea that Og survived the Flood see Targum Pseudo-Jonathan Gen 14:13, Deut 3:11; Babylonian Talmud *Niddah* 61a; *Zebahim* 113b; *Pirke de Rabbi Eliezer* 23.2.

¹² A unicorn? On unicorns (*re'em*) in the Bible see Num 23:22; 24:8; Deut 33:17; Job 39:9-10; Ps 22:21; 29:6; 92:10; Isa 34:7 all KJV). The LXX translates the word as *monokerōs* (lit: one horn) and the Latin translates it as *unicornis*. Modern English translations opt for something like "wild ox." Perhaps this creature is purely fictional. Perhaps we have simply not found its remains. Perhaps it is based upon a now extinct form of rhinoceros, a dinosaur, or something else?

¹³ Pseudo-Jonathan Gen 14:13. A lengthy fairy-tale version of Og and Noah for reading to a child on a cold winter night is "The Giant of the Flood," in Gertrude Landa, *Jewish Fairy Tales and Legends* (New York: Bloch, 1919), 9-14.

¹⁴ See Maria Lindquist, "King Og's Iron Bed," *CBQ* 73 no. 3 (July 2011): 477-492. This is an extremely skeptical view of Og and the giants, but presents an interesting case for it being a bed.

¹⁵ Many sources and some translations opt for this idea in light of the large basalt sarcophagi and dolmens found in the area. See A. R. Millard, "King Og's Bed and Other Ancient Ironmongery," in

Ascribe to the Lord. Biblical and other studies in memory of Peter C. Craigie (ed. L. Eslinger & G. Taylor), JSOT Sup 67; Sheffield 1988): 481–492. I like how the *Jewish Encyclopedia* puts it, "The fact that the black basalt bed or sarcophagus of Og was shown at Rabbah, the chief city of the Ammonites (Deut 3:11), confirms rather than confutes the legendary nature of the giant stories." See Emil G. Hirsch, "Giants," in *Jewish Encyclopedia*.

[16] This coffin parallels a report recited by the Greek historian Herodotus (484 – 425 B.C.) in Book One (Clio) of his *Histories*. He talks about a certain blacksmith from the city Tegea who had dug up the courtyard there. He relates, "In my digging I hit upon a coffin twelve feet long. I could not believe that there had ever been men taller than now, so I opened it and saw that the corpse was just as long as the coffin. I measured it and then reburied it" (*Histories* 1.68.3). The curious thing about this story is its context. A Spartan named Lichas (no relation to the servant of Hercules) was told by an oracle to look for the bones of Orestes, the son of Agamemnon who famously fought in the mythical battle of Troy. Though the story of Troy is told as "myth," in the nineteenth century it was discovered to be a real city. Herodotus places the battle of Troy around 1,200 B.C. (a possible timeframe for Joshua's conquest of Canaan). After much debate, Lichas persuaded the smith to lease him the land and "he dug up the grave and collected the bones, then hurried off to Sparta with them" (1.68.6). Thus, we have a similar size coffin in a similar timeframe mentioned by two different cultures. Both purport to be telling actual history.

[17] See John Day, *God's Conflict with the Dragon and the Sea* (London: Cambridge University Press, 1985), 117. The *Anunnaki* were made famous by Zechariah Sitchin who believed they were aliens from another planet. Sitchin is simply mistaken. It is much better to see them as identical to the sons of God who came down in the days of Jared.

[18] The Ugaritic word is *btn*, the Akkadian is *bašmu*, and the Arabic equivalent is *baṭan*. See G. Del Olmo Lete, "Bashan," *DDD*, 161. For instance, it is paired with the Ugaritic equivalent of Leviathan, "When you killed Litan, the Fleeing Serpent, Annihilated the Twisty Serpent" (KTU 1.5.I.1-2). Heiser has a fascinating discussion of this in *The Myth That Is True* (unpublished), 170-71.

[19] Gen 30:27; 44:5; Lev 19:26; 2 Kgs 21:6. Heiser has an informative article on this as well. Heiser, "The Nachash and his Seed: Some Explanatory Notes on Why the 'Serpent' in Genesis 3 Wasn't a Serpent."

[20] For examples, see Chapter 1, n. 10.

[21] So T. K. Cheyne, J. Sutherland Black, *Encyclopaedia Biblica* (London: Adam and Charles Black, 1899-1902), 2:2101. The word is *chavvah* and is perhaps related to the Aramaic word *hewyā*, which means serpent. *Chavvah* also happens to be the name of Eve in Hebrew. Some have tried to connect Eve's name to the serpent, but recent scholarship has deemed this speculative, not to mention it flies in the face of Genesis 3:20 which says that she was called Eve because she was the mother of *all living*. See Scott C. Layton, "Remarks on the Cannanite Origin of Eve," *Catholic Biblical Quarterly* 59 (1997): 29-30.

[22] This summary is found in John Bathurst Deane, *Worship of the Serpent: Traced Throughout the World* (London: J. G. & F. Rivington, 1883, republished by Forgotten Books, 2008), 58-60. This is a fascinating book written by a Christian scholar who taught at Cambridge, a good source for serpent worship throughout the world.

[23] Aveni, Anthony, and Yonathan Mizrachi. "The Geometry and Astronomy of Rujm El-Hiri, a Megalithic Site in the Southern Levant." *Journal of Field Archaeology* 25.4 (1998): 484.

[24] Israel Ministry of Foreign Affairs, "Rogem Hiri – Ancient, Mysterious Construction," Feb 2, 1999.

[25] Og's name, like Anak, can also mean "long-necked."

[26] This picture depicts the image before Ezekiel in Ezekiel 1, upon which Daniel 7 has many parallels. For more examples of what Ezekiel and Daniel saw in the context of their ancient Persian setting see Michael Heiser, "Notes on Ezekiel's Vision," *Sitchin Is Wrong*.

[27] For multiple sites and pictures see Zvi Koenigsberg, "Gilgal: YHWH's Footprints in the Land of Israel," *TheTorah.com*.

NOTES FOR CHAPTER 9: GIANT WARS, THE SEQUEL (Pgs. 141-148)

[1] Ronald Hendel writes, "They exist in order to be wiped out: by the flood, by Moses, by David, and others." Their function is "to die" (Ronald S. Hendel, "Of Demigods and the Deluge: Toward an Interpretation of Genesis 6:1–4," *Journal of Biblical Literature* 106 [1987]: 21. Similarly, the *Dictionary of Biblical Imagery* says, "Giants are a negative image in the Bible ... God always instructs his people to destroy them ... It is hardly too much to say that in the Bible giants are towering physical specimens on the verge of being toppled" ("Giants," in *Dictionary of Biblical Imagery*, eds. L. Ryken, J. C. Wilhoit and T. Longman III [Downers Grove: InterVarsity Press, 1998], 328.

[2] See Douglas Van Dorn and Matt Foreman, *The Angel of the LORD: A Biblical, Historical, and Theological Study* (Dacono, CO: Waters of Creation Pub., 2020).

[3] Leon Wood, *A Survey of Israel's History* (Grand Rapids, MI: Zondervan Publishing House, 1970), p. 174.

[4] This circumambulation of 360° x 7 = 2,160°. This happens to be the same number miles in the diameter of the moon. Jericho means "City of the Moon." God is mocking the moon god.

[5] Emil G. Hirsch, "Giants," in *Jewish Encyclopedia* Vol. 5, ed. Isidore Singer, Cyrus Adler (New York: Funk and Wagnalls, 1912), 659. See also Ronald S. Hendel, "Biblical Views: Giants at Jericho," *Biblical Archeological Research* 35:02 (Mar/Apr 2009).

[6] Sabine Baring-Gould, Legends of Old Testament Characters from the Talmud and Other Sources (London: Macmillan, 1871), 302.

[7] *The Wycliffe Bible Encyclopedia* vol. 1, ed. Charles F. Pfeiffer, Howard Frederic Vos, and John Rea (Chicago: Moody Press, 1972), 709.

[8] Harry Emerson Fosdick, *A Pilgrimage to Palestine* (New York: Macmillan Publishing Co., 1949), 33.

[9] Georgette Corcos, *The Glory of the Old Testament* (New York: Villard Books, 1984), 108; cited in Charles DeLoach, "Ashdod's Giants," in *Giants*, 18. The term is found in execration texts.

[10] Palestine Pilgrims' Text Society, *The Library of the Palestine Pilgrims' Text Society* (London: Committee of the Palestine Exploration Fund, 1885), 425.

[11] Some, like the German bishop and poet Walter of Speyer (967 – 1027 AD, *The life and the suffering of St. Christopher the Martyr 75*) took "Canaan" and turned it into Chanaenean or the land of dogs where the inhabitants ate human flesh and barked.

[12] Jacobus de Voragine, *The Golden Legend: Readings on the Saints*, trans. William Granger Ryan (Princeton, NJ: Princeton University Press, 1993), 11.

[13] See R. D. Fulk, "The Passion of St. Christopher," in *The Beowulf Manuscript: Complete Texts and the Fight at Finnsburg* (Cambridge, MA: Harvard University Press, 2010), 1-14.

[14] E. A. Wallis Budge, *The Contendings of the Apostles* (London: H. Frowde, 1899), 206-08. Some see Abominable as the predecessor of some Christopher legends. See Andy Orchard, *Pride and Prodigies: Studies in the Monsters of the Beowulf-manuscript* (Rochester, NY: D.S. Brewer, 1995), 14-15.

[15] An interesting, more sober historical survey of the life of St. Christopher can be found in David Woods, "The Origin of the Cult of St. Christopher," 1999.

NOTES FOR CHAPTER 10: GOLIATH AND HIS BROTHERS (Pgs. 149-160)

[1] This section on Samson leans heavily on the paper Dr. Naphtali Meshel, "Samson the Demigod," TheTorah.com.

[2] For more see Gregory Mobley, *Samson and the Liminal Hero in the Ancient Near East* (New York: T&T Clark, 2006), 21-22.

[3] This shard depicts two names etymologically similar to Goliath, to which its discoverers say lends support to what we already know: Goliath was a real person. See A. M. Maeir, S. J. Wimmer, A. Zukerman, and A. Demsky, "A Late Iron Age I/early Iron Age IIA Old Canaanite Inscription from

Tell es-Sâfi/Gath, Israel: Palaeography, Dating, and Historical-Cultural Significance," *Bulletin of the American Schools of Oriental Research* 351 (Aug 2008): 39–71. It was reported, for example, in "Scientists Find 'Goliath' Inscribed on Pottery," *Associated Press* (11/10/2005).

[4] The earliest Hebrew attestation is the second century Greek Symmachus as recorded by Origen.

[5] See Clyde E. Billington, "Goliath And The Exodus Giants: How Tall Were They"? *JETS* 50.3 (2007): 489-508. Billington argues that Goliath was as tall as 8'7".

[6] See J. Daniel Hays, "Reconsidering The Height Of Goliath," *JETS* 48.4 (2005): 701-714; Hays, "The Height Of Goliath: A Response To Clyde Billington," *JETS* 50.3 (2007): 509-16.

[7] For the average height of an Israelite in David's time see G. Ernest Wright, "Troglodytes and Giants in Palestine," *Journal of Biblical Literature* 57:3 (Sept 1938): 305-309. Others suggest a slightly shorter average of between 5'0" and 5'3". See Billington, 493; Hays, "Reconsidering," 708-710.

[8] Hays claims that Goliath is never referred to as a giant (*JETS* 50.3: 516). This is simply not true. 1 Chron 20:8 LXX refers to him and three others as *gigantes*. . . GIANTS! But Saul is never referred to this way. You could argue that the LXX is simply translating *Rephaim*, and since Saul was not one of these, it wouldn't be fitting to call him that. But the word *gigantes* also translates other words that definitely mean "giants." Besides that, it is quite clear that the Rephaim were viewed as giants by people in the Bible.

[9] See Billington, 496.

[10] Gigantic tools and weapons have been discovered reminiscent of Goliath's spear's size. For example, while not weapons *per se*, in Llandudno, Wales, 50 lb. (some reports as high as 64 lb.) stone hammers were discovered in ancient (3,500 year-old) copper mines (see John Hicklin, *Llandudno and Its Vicinity* [London: Hamilton, Adams and Co., 1856], 67). For comparison, modern sledge hammers are only between 10-20 lbs. While much less certain that they were literal tools/weapons, on the island of Crete (well known for its relation to giants) in a place called Nirou Háni, several gigantic bronze double ax heads (along with ceremonial tripods) dating between 1700-1300 BC were discovered, and are now on display in the Museum of Herakleion. Similar smaller axes were discovered in what is described as a "military sanctuary" (D. Rumpel, "The Arkalokhori Axe Inscription in Relation to the Diskos of Phaistos Text," *Anistoriton Journal*, vol. 11 (2008-2009): 1-6).

Fig. FN 4. Giant Double-Axes

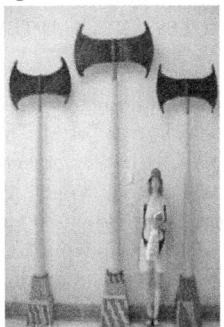

Museum of Herakleion, Crete

[11] This is Billington's argument (pgs. 506-07), and I find it persuasive. We do the same thing in translations today, converting a biblical measure to our own, when we say Goliath was 9 "feet" 9 "inches" tall. If, by chance, we happened to call our "foot" a "cubit" as the Egyptians did, then someone, many centuries later, comparing the two texts, might easily assume that we had "changed the height" of Goliath.

[12] Josephus, *Antiquities* 18.103.

[13] The LXX gives the impression that it was the whole spear that weighed this, but that isn't very impressive at all, so why mention it in the first place? A parallel idea in 1 Sam 17:7 has the tip separate from the shaft. If just the tip weighed that much, it would have been quite the spear to throw. Furthermore, this spear-tip is less than half the weight of Goliath's. If Ishbi-benob is said to be a giant, and his spear is so much lighter than Goliath's, is it really plausible that Goliath was less than seven feet tall? Or, maybe Ishbi-benob was actually a "giant" of around 5-6 ft.

[14] There is a rather glaring discrepancy between 2 Sam 21:19 which says that Elhanan killed Goliath and 1 Sam 17:50 which says that David killed him. Though I disagree with this assessment of Goliath's height, Michael Heiser has an excellent article dealing with the problem. The short answer is, Elhanan killed Lahmi, Goliath's brother. See Michael Heiser, "Clash of the Manuscripts: Goliath & the Hebrew Text of the Old Testament," *Bible Study Magazine* 1:4 (May-June, 2009): 33-35.

[15] Brian Godawa, *David Ascendant: Chronicles of the Nephilim Book Seven, special limited hardback edition* (Los Angeles: Embedded Pictures, 2014), 468. As Brian thanked me in that book for finding Dan, I thought it was only fitting that I in turn thank him for his thoughtfulness on this story and this topic.

NOTES FOR CHAPTER 11: AGAG THE AMALEKITE (Pgs. 161-166)

[1] There are six references to Amalekites in Judges. Three put them near the Midianites (Jdg 6:3; 33; 7:12), another near the Moabites and Ammonites (Jdg 3:13), one near the Sidonians (along the Sea? Jdg 10:12), and the other in the land of Ephraim in the very place where David fought Goliath (Jdg 12:15).

[2] A. van Hoonacker, "Eléments sumériens dans le livre d'Ezéchiel?," *Zeitschrift für Assyriologie* 28 (1914): 336.

[3] Michael Heiser, "The Divine Council in the New Testament: The Archons," in *Behind the Façade* Vol. 3, No. 9 (Feb 2005): 33.

[4] The manuscript is P 967.

[5] Josephus, Antiquities of the Jews 6.7.2.

[6] The OT is laid out in three sections: history (17 books), poetry (5 books), and prophecy (17 books).

NOTES FOR CHAPTER 12: DEMONS AND THE GIANTS (Pgs. 167-174)

[1] For the discussion see L. R. Wickham, "The Sons of God and the Daughters of Men: Genesis VI 2 in Early Christian Exegesis," in *Language and Meaning: Studies in Hebrew Language and Biblical Exegesis*, ed. James Barr (Leiden: Brill, 1974), 135-36.

[2] See Greg J. Riley, "Demons," *DDD*, 238-39.

[3] See Archie T. Wright, *The Origin of Evil Spirits: The Reception of Genesis 6:1-4 in Early Jewish Literature*, A Dissertation at Durham University (Tübingen: Mohr Siebeck, 2004).

[4] See the exhaustive list in Jacob J. T. Doedens, "The Sons of God in Genesis 6:1-4," Ph.D. Dissertation Theologische Universiteit Kampen (2013), 89-167. On the provenance of the Sethite origins see Jacob J. T. Doedens, "The Indecent Descent of the Sethites: The Provenance of the Sethites-Interpretation of Genesis 6:1-4." *Sárospataki Füzetek* 16:3–4 (2012): 47–57.

[5] Socrates (Plato, *Apology* 15) suggests that they are the bastard children of gods and nymphs or other women. Hesiod (*Works and Days* 110-27) says they came from the men of the golden age (i.e. prior to the Flood). Josephus makes this connection with the Greeks saying, "Many angels of God accompanied with women, and begat sons that proved unjust, and despisers of all that was good, on account of the confidence they had in their own strength; for the tradition is, that these men did what resembled the acts of those whom the Grecians call giants" (Josephus, *Antiquities* 1.3.1).

[6] John E. Hartley, *The Book of Job*, The New International Commentary on the Old Testament (Grand Rapids, MI: Wm. B. Eerdmans Publishing Co., 1988), 365.

[7] When you read up on the meaning of *rephaim*, you will quickly discover that the word does not always mean "giant," especially in neighboring Ugarit (which has the same word) where it (apparently) never means giant. For this reason, some will argue that *rephaim* in these biblical verses only refers to dead kings of long ago. We should keep in mind, however, that this does not need to be an either/or (the logical fallacy of a false dilemma). Given what we have seen in this book, it is plausible that the Rephaim giants were also the famed heroes and kings of very ancient times.

[8] For example, "There is probably here an allusion to the destruction of the earth by the general deluge. Moses, speaking concerning the state of the earth before the flood, says, Genesis 6:4, 'There were giants (*nephilim*), in the earth in those days.' Now it is likely that Job means the same by rephaim as Moses does by the nephilim; and that both refer to the antediluvians, who were all, for their exceeding great iniquities, overwhelmed by the waters of the deluge. Can those mighty men

and their neighbors, all the sinners who have been gathered to them since, be rejected from under the waters, by which they were judicially overwhelmed"? Adam Clarke, *Commentary on the Bible*, Job 26:5.

[9] CREATION: Job refers to the *tohu* in Job 26:7, "He stretches out the north over the void (*tohu*) and hangs the earth on nothing." *Tohu* was the original condition that we find the earth in Genesis 1:2 ("formless and void"). Binding up the waters in thick clouds (vs. 8) could be viewed against the backdrop of Genesis 1, as the gathering together and separating of water from land as could the boundary between light and darkness in vs. 10. THE FLOOD: He uses a verb first seen in Genesis 7:11 of the "bursting open" of the great deep (Job 26:8). He refers to the "covering of the face of the full moon" (vs. 9) where "moon" can also read "throne." In Psalm 29:10 for instance, God's throne is associated with the flood, "The LORD sits enthroned over the flood; the LORD sits enthroned as king forever."

[10] In some cases, Rahab refers to Egypt which is the personification of the sea monster.

[11] Compare the serpent/*nachash*: Gen 3:1 and Job 26:13; dragon/*tannin*: Isa 51:9 and Rev 20:2 Hebrew translation. Isaiah 27:1 also parallels the *tannin, nachash*, and *leviathan*.

[12] *Enuma Elish* 1.134-143.

[13] *KTU* 2 1.3 iii:38ff. *Yam* is also the Hebrew word for "sea."

[14] *TUAT* II/3, 317.

[15] *Enuma Elish* 4:105-108.

[16] Klaas Spronk writes, "This last word (lie/*kazab*) is used in Isa 28:15 to describe a 'covenant with death' and in Amos 2:4 it denotes the false gods. All this makes it likely that Ps 40:[4] refers. . . to the forbidden attempt to obtain help from divine forces in the netherworld." See K. Spronk, "Rahab," DDD, 685-86.

[17] Further demonstration of this idea may be found in Ezek 32:21 where the *gibborim* (Gen 6:4) greet newcomers in Sheol, and possibly vs. 27 where some have argued that the same gibborim are also called here *nephilim* (usually translated as "fallen"). See Walther Zimmerli, *Ezekiel 2: A Commentary on the Book of Ezekiel, Chapters 25-48*, Hermeneia (Philadelphia: Fortress Press, 1983), 176.

[18] This is Jubilees ("the little Genesis") explanation for the problem of how the giants' spirits could be both in Sheol and wandering the earth. After the Flood, when the spirits began to lead the sons of Noah into sin (Jub 7:26-28; 10:1-2), Noah begs God to imprison them, but Mastema—the chief prince of the spirits—strikes a bargain with God that one-tenth be allowed to stay upon the earth and continue their activity (10:8-11).

[19] As we read in 1 Enoch (above), the spirits of the giants must remain on earth because they were born on earth, and thus they roam about haunting and tormenting the children of men and women.

[20] We will deal with the fascinating verse in 1 Peter 3:19 where Christ preaches "to the spirits in prison" in Chapter 15.

[21] Perhaps also Amos 2:1, "Because he burns the bones ... to a demon." Mitchell J. Dahood, *Psalms III (101-150)*, in Anchor Yale Bible (Garden City, NY: Doubleday, 1970), 74.

[22] In light of Deut 32:8-9 where the sons of God are allotted to the nations, but Israel is the Lord's "portion" (*chalaq*), see Deut 4:19-20 where the "stars" are allotted (*chalaq*) to all the peoples; Deut 17:2-3 where they are called the "host of heaven;" and Deut 29:26 where they are called "gods" (*elohim*) who were not allotted (*chalaq*) to Israel but to the nations.

[23] "Demon" (*daimōn*) was sometimes used as a synonym for a god (*theói*) in ancient Greece, although this usage came to be obsolete later. See Bonn Manfred Hutter, "Demons and Benevolent Spirits in the Ancient New East: A Phenomenological Overview," *Angels: The Concept of Celestial Beings – Origins, Development and Reception*, Yearbook 2007, ed. Friedrich V. Reiterer, Tobias Nicklas, Karin Schöpflin (New York, de Gruyter, 2007), 21. Most Enochian scholars believes that the demons of 1En 19:1, which alludes to Deut 32:17, refers to the sons of God. Curiously, later rabbinical reflection found in the Mishnah and Talmud on the *shedu* classifies them as one of three kinds of demons (along with *mazziḳîm* and *rûḥot*). They are terribly frightening and inhabit the air, trees, plants,

rocks, niches, and waste areas. These are clearly not the fallen sons of God. See D. E. Aune, "Demonology," in *The International Standard Bible Encyclopedia, Revised*, ed. Geoffrey W. Bromiley (Wm. B. Eerdmans, 1979–1988), 922.

[24] "While gods in many cases are described in a human form, sometimes also with wings and to be differentiated from humans by their attributes, 'Demons' are described having a mixed body – they can have an animal's head with a human body, sometimes their body is composed of parts of humans, four-legged animals and birds, or to a human body a tail or horns or claws are added … Some typical 'demonic' features can be expressed by the lion's or bull's strength or by the serpent's or dragon's venom." Hutter, 25-26.

[25] Eugene E. Carpenter, "Deuteronomy," in John H Walton, Zondervan Illustrated Bible Backgrounds Commentary (Old Testament): Genesis, Exodus, Leviticus, Numbers, Deuteronomy, vol. 1 (Grand Rapids, MI: Zondervan, 2009), 518.

[26] Ludwig Koehler et al., *The Hebrew and Aramaic Lexicon of the Old Testament* (Leiden: E.J. Brill, 1994–2000), 1417.

[27] See John Skinner 1851-1925, *A Critical and Exegetical Commentary on Genesis*, International Critical Commentary (New York: Scribner, 1910), 261.

[28] Cited in Hutter, 26.

[29] Paul himself rarely uses the word. It is only found elsewhere in 1Tim 4:1 where he describes the "teachings of demons." This may refer to the tradition that the sons of God taught mankind in days gone by, but it may not. Apparently, some kind of demonic entities will do the same in the future.

[30] See Ronn Johnson, "The Old Testament Background for Paul's Use of 'Principalities and Powers,'" A Dissertation to Dallas Theological Seminary, 2004.

[31] Riley, "Demons," *DDD*, 235.

[32] For a study on this see Dale Basil Martin, "When Did Angels Become Demons," *JBL* 129.4 (Winter 2010): 657-77.

NOTES FOR CHAPTER 13: CHIMERAS (Pgs. 175-194)

[1] Cf. G.K. Beale, "Revelation," in *Commentary on the New Testament Use of the Old Testament*, G. K. Beale and D. A. Carson eds., (Grand Rapids, MI; Nottingham, UK: Baker Academic; Apollos, 2007), 1140; Robert H. Mounce, *The Book of Revelation*, The New International Commentary on the New Testament (Grand Rapids, MI: Wm. B. Eerdmans Publishing Co., 1997), 325-26; Grant R. Osborne, *Revelation*, Baker Exegetical Commentary on the New Testament (Grand Rapids, Mich.: Baker Academic, 2002), 635-36.

[2] This is the translation of the verse as found in Charlesworth's pseudepigrapha. See also the R. H. Charles edition which substitutes "shedim" for "demons." For other Jewish sources see Targum Isaiah 13:21; Midrash Rabbah Lev 5:1; 22:8; Midr Rab Gen 65:15; Sibylline Oracle 8:40-49, Babylonian Talmud Shabbat 151B.

[3] One of these birds is actually translated as an animal by the ESV ("porcupine"). Other translations read anything from a bittern to an owl (see JPS, TNK). This shows how obscure some of these terms are and how we need to be open to alternative ideas of what they might mean.

[4] H. G. Liddell, *A Lexicon : Abridged from Liddell and Scott's Greek-English Lexicon* (Oak Harbor, WA: Logos Research Systems, Inc., 1996), 725.

[5] B. Janowski, "Wild Beasts," *DDD*, 898.

[6] We have different copies of the Vulgate and they differ from one another here. Here are some lists for Isa 34:14. *Biblia Sacra Vulgata* 3rd ed. (1969): (3) *bestiae, draconibus, pilosi* (satyr); *Biblia Sacra Luxta Vulgatam* 5th ed. (2007): (4) *daimonia, onocentauris, pilosus, lamia* (vampire). *Nova Vulgata Bibliorum Sacrorum* (1986): (3 and house) *bestiae, domus* (houses), *struthiones* (ostrich), *pilosi*.

[7] Johan Lust, Erik Eynikel and Katrin Hauspie, *A Greek-English Lexicon of the Septuagint : Revised Edition* (Deutsche Bibelgesellschaft: Stuttgart, 2003).

[8] In Isa 13:22 it renders the term as *onokentauros* (see below).

[9] B. Janowski, "Jackal," *DDD*, 459.

[10] *Gilgamesh Epic*, Tablet II.36-41.

[11] Though not a world-wide treatment, see Gregory Mobley, "The Wild Man in the Bible and the Ancient Near East," *Journal of Biblical Literature* 116 (1997): 217-33. Mobley is not advocating the reality of such legends, but rather sees them as a motif picked up on in several biblical stories.

[12] Stefan Münger, "Ariel," in *Dictionary of Deities and Demons in the Bible DDD*, 2nd extensively rev. ed., ed. K. van der Toorn, Bob Becking and Pieter Willem van der Horst (Leiden; Boston; Grand Rapids, Mich.: Brill; Eerdmans, 1999), 89.

[13] Lust, Greek-English Lexicon of the Septuagint.

[14] Wilhelm Gesenius and Samuel Prideaux Tregelles, *Gesenius' Hebrew and Chaldee Lexicon to the Old Testament Scriptures* (Bellingham, WA: Logos Research Systems, Inc, 2003), 792.

[15] 1 Enoch 6:3-6.

[16] Judd Burton, *Interview With The Giant* (Burton Beyond Press, 2009), 15-23.

[17] See Josephus, *Wars of the Jews* 1.404-406.

[18] LXX Lev 4:28, 29; 5:6.

[19] Liddell, 888.

[20] 1 Enoch 55:4.

[21] 1 Enoch 54:5-6.

[22] 1 Enoch 10:4.

[23] See Burton, *Interview*, 17.

[24] See Robert Hayward, "The Priestly Blessing in Targum Pseudo-Jonathan," *Journal for the Study of the Pseudepigrapha* 10 (April 1999): 85-87.

[25] John D. W. Watts, vol. 25, *Word Biblical Commentary : Isaiah 34-66*, Word Biblical Commentary (Dallas: Word, Incorporated, 2002), 13-14.

[26] Babylonian Talmud *Shabbat* 151B.

[27] See M. Hutter, "Lilith," *DDD*, 520.

[28] Following the *Online Etymology Dictionary* (http://www.etymonline.com/), we see that "genetics" derives from *genesis* ("origin" or "generation"), from which we get the word for the first book of the Bible. "Genesis" is also said to come from *gignesthai* ("to be born") and *genos* ("race, birth, descent"). Our word "genome" comes from *gen* ("gene"). As you can see, the prefix "–gen" comes from *genes* ("born of, produced by"), so that all of these words are related *gene*alogically in the same linguistic family tree.

English	Greek Root	Translation
-gen	*genes*	"born of, produced by"
Gigantes	*gegenes*	"born from earth"
genetics	*genesis*	"origin, generation"
Genesis	*gignesthai*	"to be born"
	genos	"race, birth"
genome	*genes*	"born of, produced by"
genealogy	*genea*	"generation, descent"

[29] "Transplanted Head," *Time* LXV.3 (Jan 17, 1955).

[30] "Frankenstein Fears after Head Transplant," *BBC News* (Friday April 6, 2001).

[31] Hui Zhen Sheng, et al., "Embryonic stem cells generated by nuclear transfer of human somatic nuclei into rabbit oocytes," *Cell Research* (2003): 13, 251–26.

[32] Maryann Mott, "Animal-Human Hybrids Spark Controversy," *National Geographic*, Jan 25, 2005.

[33] Dr. Julio Antonio del Marmol, PhD in Animal Genetics. The fuller story is related in *The Lightning and Montauk: Reality vs. Fiction* (Cuban Lightning Publications Int, 2021). Thanks to Stephen Van Dorn for getting this this gem.

[34] For example, see Louisiana's "S.1435 – Human-Animal Hybrid Prohibition Act" of 2009; Arizona's "Senate Bill SB 1307" (2010); "H.R.3542 – Human-Animal Chimera Prohibition Act of 2021 (117th Congress)."

[35] These are easily tracked down, but for a short 25 minute presentation on transhumanism from a few years ago see Thomas R. Horn, "Transhumanism & the Human Enhancement revolution," *ISN* (Mar 7, 2020). Note, I'm not a super fan of Horn's eschatology and predictions that the Antichrist is right around the corner. He certainly could be, but I'm deliberately staying away from such speculations in this book because I do not find them helpful, even if there might be legitimacy in linking the unprecedented technological revolutionary times we are living in to the return of Christ. Clearly, such things do make us wonder.

[36] See for instance the burial mound at Sayre, Bradford County, Pennsylvania in the 1880s. An article ("Chemung's Predecessors Huge Giants Were Seven Feet Tall and Had Horns") appeared in the *Moorehead Expedition* on Wed, July 12, 1916 claiming a find of a horned giant human skull. Another article ("Aboriginal Sites in and Near 'TEAOGA,' now Athens, Pennsylvania") appeared in the *American Anthropologist* (Vol. 23, No. 2, April-June 1921) claiming that the horned skull was mistaken identity. I've also been told that you can artificially create "horns" on a skull without any need for hybridization.

NOTES FOR CHAPTER 14: JESUS VS. THE DEMONS (Pgs. 195-204)

[1] Compare 1 Cor 15:40-41 with Dan 8:10; Rev 12:4 etc. On stars as referring to angelic beings see Heinrich A. W. Meyer, *Critical and Exegetical Handbook to the Epistles to the Corinthians* (Edinburgh: T. & T. Clark, 1892): 2:87-88; G. G. Findlay, "St. Paul's First Epistle to the Corinthians," in W. R. Nicoll (ed.), *The Expositor's Greek Testament* (Grand Rapids, Eerdmans, 1961): 2:935-36; Anthony C. Thiselton, *The First Epistle to the Corinthians : A Commentary on the Greek Text* (Grand Rapids, Mich.: W.B. Eerdmans, 2000), 1268-69. For an interesting discussion on the relationship between stars and angelic beings see John Joseph Collins, Frank Moore Cross and Adela Yarbro Collins, *Daniel : A Commentary on the Book of Daniel*, Hermeneia (Minneapolis: Fortress Press, 1993), 331-33. Finally, all angelic *appearances* as men differ qualitatively from Christ—the Angel of the LORD in the OT—who came down out of heaven (John 6:33-58; Rev 20:1), added human flesh to his own nature (John 1:14), was born in the likeness of men (Php 2:7-8), and shares in our flesh and blood (Heb 2:14).

[2] For example, see the fascinating book detailing five exorcisms, Malachi Martin, *Hostage to the Devil* (San Francisco: Harper Collins, 1992).

[3] This pool is said in a textual gloss to have healed the first person who came into the waters after a supernatural being would come down from time to time and "stir up the waters." It this light, it makes Jesus' miracle all the more incredible (and suspicious to the people in Galilee).

[4] Rouillard, "Rephaim," *DDD*, 699.

[5] All of Galilee and synagogues (Matt 4:23-24; Mark 1:23-27; 39-41; Luke 4:33-36; 11:14-22; 13:11-17), houses (Matt 8:14-17; Mark 1:32-34; 6:10-15; 7:24-30; 9:33, 39; Luke 4:38-41) the seashore (Matt 28-33; Mark 3:9-15; 5:2-20; Luke 8:26-39), the coasts (Matt 15:22-28; 16:13-19); the plains (Luke 6:17-19); by mountains (Luke 9:37-42); outside (Matt 9:32-33), everywhere (Matt 10:7-8; Luke 8:1-3), around multitudes (Matt 12:15, 22; 17:14-21; Mark 9:14-27), you get the idea.

[6] Note that the previous three paragraphs have several references to Mark's Gospel. Mark may in fact have the Watcher tradition in mind as he writes. See the fascinating article by Rick Strelan, "The Fallen Watchers and the Disciples in Mark," *Journal for the Study of the Pseudepigrapha* 10 (Oct 1999): 73-92.

[7] Cf. Rainer Riesner, "Bethany Beyond The Jordan (John 1:28): Topography, Theology And History In The Fourth Gospel," *Tyndale Bulletin* 38 (1987): 29–63; also D. A. Carson, *The Gospel According to John* (Leicester, England; Grand Rapids, MI: InterVarsity Press; W.B. Eerdmans, 1991), 146-47; C. S. Keener, *The Gospel of John*. 2 vols. Peabody, Mass: Hendrickson, 450; Andreas J.

Köstenberger, *John*, Baker Exegetical Commentary on the New Testament (Grand Rapids, Mich.: Baker Academic, 2004), 65.

[8] Some manuscripts read seventy-two. "Seventy" is significant in light of the seventy sons of God in Jewish and Canaanite tradition as well as the seventy elders of Israel that eventually became the Sanhedrin.

[9] H. J. W. Drijvers, *Iconography of Religions* (Leiden, Netherlands: Brill, 1976), p. 18

[10] 2 Enoch 42:1.

[11] See Burton, *Interview with the Giant*, 57-58, 78-87; Strelan, 83.

[12] Mark does not record Jesus' words to Peter about the church, but he does record the Transfiguration, which occurs immediately after this in Matthew. The story of healing the boy occurs immediately after the Transfiguration in Mark's Gospel.

NOTES FOR CHAPTER 15: VICTORY (Pgs. 205-224)

[1] Ps 22:1 quoted in Matt 27:46; Ps 22:2 in Matt 27:39; Ps 22:7 in Matt 27:39; Ps 22:8 in Matt 27:43; Ps 22:12 in Matt 27:27; Ps 22:14 in Matt 27:26; Ps 22:16 in Matt 27:35; 22:18 in Matt 27:35; Ps 22:19-21 in Matt 28:6.

[2] For instance, Samuel L. Terrien, *The Psalms: Strophic Structure and Theological Commentary* (Grand Rapids, MI: Eerdmans, 2003), 232. This is also Heiser's view. If we are permitted to read into an allegory, it appears to be the idea in C. S. Lewis' *Lion, Witch and the Wardrobe* when Aslan dies on the stone table.

[3] Quoted in Thomas Aquinas, *Catena Aurea: Commentary on the Four Gospels, Collected out of the Works of the Fathers: St. Matthew*, ed. John Henry Newman, vol. 1 (Oxford: John Henry Parker, 1841), 948.

[4] See W. F. Birch, "Golgotha on Mount Zion," *The Palestine Exploration Fund* (Jan 1907): 140-47.

[5] Warren Austin Gage, *There Is No Greater Love: How Jesus Is Greater than All Who Came before Him* (Fort Lauderdale: St. Andrews House, 2013), 65–66.

[6] Ramsey J. Michaels, *1 Peter*, Word Biblical Commentary (Dallas: Word, 2002), 205-12.

[7] An excellent historical treatment of this focusing on the Reformation view is Samuel D. Renihan, *Crux, Mors, Inferi: A Primer and Reader on the Descent of Christ*, Independently Published, 2021.

[8] Frank S. Thielman, "Ephesians," *Commentary on the New Testament Use of the Old Testament*, G. K. Beale and D. A. Carson eds., (Grand Rapids, MI; Nottingham, UK: Baker Academic; Apollos, 2007), 819-20.

[9] To see my full treatment of this psalm, see Douglas Van Dorn, "God is Our Salvation: The Rider of the Clouds and the Freeing of the Captives at the Gates of Hell," *RBCNC.com* (7-9-2017).

[10] Chiasmusxchange.com has it. So does Thielman, 820.

[11] J. H. Eaton, *Psalms*, Torch Bible Commentaries (London: SCM, 1967), 172-73.

[12] On this history see William J. Dalton, *Christ's Proclamation to the Spirits: A Study of 1 Peter 3:18-4:6* (Rome: Editrice Pontifico Istituto Biblico, 1989), 27ff.

[13] More technically, it is "a region of northern Europe bounded by the Rhone River on the east, the Alps on the south-east, the Mediterranean on the south, the Pyrenees on the south-west, the Atlantic on the west, and the English Channel on the north-west." John T. Koch, "Gaul," in *Celtic Culture: A Historical Encyclopedia* vol. 1 (Santa Barbara, CA, 2006), 793.

[14] See Helmut Birkhan, *The Celts* (Vienna, 1997), 48.

[15] Paul Pezron, *The Antiquities of Nations; More Particularly of the Celtae or Gauls*, trans. Mr. D. Jones (London: R. Janeway, 1706), 276.

[16] Pezron, 48.

[17] Florus, *The Epitome of Roman History*, 1.38.3.

[18] Cited in Gerhard Herm, *The Celts* (New York: St. Martin's Press, 1975), 19. A particularly vivid and short history of the Roman wars with the giants of Gaul and neighboring Germany can be found

in Charles DeLoach, *Giants: A Reference Guide from History, the Bible, and Recorded Legend* (Metuchen, N.J.: Scarecrow Press, 1995), see especially the sections "Celtic Giants," "German Giant's Annihilation," and "Giants Who Became Gods." This includes history from the likes of Julius Caesar, Plutarch, and Diodorus among others. http://www.stevequayle.com/Giants/index2.html

[19] Hegesippus, *Histories* 2.9. This book is a compilation of Josephus' *Wars*, and is usually thought to be pseudepigraphal (that is, attributed to Hegesippus, but probably not actually written by him).

[20] These sources are cited in Johann Georg Keyssler, *Travels through Germany, Bohemia, Hungary, Switzerland, Italy, and Lorrain* Vol. 1 (London, G. Keith, 1760), 42 (footnote).

[21] Cited in Cornelius Tacitus (56 – 117 A.D.), "Treatise on the Situations, Manners, and People of Germany," in *Works* 4 (Philadelphia: Thomas Wardle, 1838), note 9.

[22] Augustine, *City of God* 15.23.2.

[23] Keyssler, 31.

[24] Ibid., 52.

[25] Caesar, *Commentary* 1.39.

[26] You can read a good brief account of the history of giants in ancient warfare in, Adrienne Mayor, "Giants in Ancient Warfare," *MHQ: The Quarterly Journal of Military History* 2.2 (Winter 1999): 98-105.

[27] Josephus, *Antiquities* 1:123.

[28] Ibid.

[29] See Frank Joseph, *Advanced Civilizations of Prehistoric America* (Rochester, VT: Bear & Company, 2010), 10-84. 19th century scholarship made this identification of the Mound-Builders with very tall Caucasians. Present scholarship tends to disagree; see Jon Muller, *Archaeology of the Lower Ohio River Valley* (Orlando: Academic Press, 1986; republished by Walnut Creek, CA: Left Coast Press, 2009), 8.

[30] Pezron, 41-42. Pezron's 18th century study of the Gaulish migrations is similar to a recent study of the Kurgan migrations, the proto-European culture (see Marija Gimbutas, "The Kurgan Culture and the Indo-Europeanization of Europe: Selected Articles from 1952 to 1993," ed. Miriam Robbins Dexter and Karlene Jones-Bley. *Journal of Indo-European Studies Monograph No. 18* [Washington, D.C.: Institute for the Study of Man, 1997]: xix + 404 pages). For more on the Kurgan, see note #28.

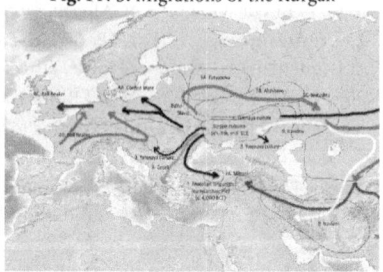

Fig. FN 5. Migrations of the Kurgan

[31] The Kurgan (note #27) have been connected to the Amorites and to the Adena "Mound Builders" of North America. http://www.mysterious-world.com/Journal/2003/Summer/Giants/. In fact, "Kurgan" means "Burial Mound." Said to be very tall in legend (see "Kurgan Horsemen" to the right), the Kurgan were popularized in the first *Highlander* movie. At one point, Sean Connery's Ramirez character tells MacLeod, "The Kurgan is the strongest of all immortals. He is the perfect warrior. He cares about nothing or no-one. He is completely evil." Curiously, the Persians depicted their kings as giants, receiving the kingdom from the demigods.

Fig. FN 6. Kurgan Horsemen

Left: 4th century B.C. Scythian horseman. Found at the Kul' Oba kurgan near Kerch (northern Black Sea). Located now in The State Hermitage Museum. Saint Petersburg, Russia. **Right:** Ardashir Coronation from Ahura Mazda, Naqsh-e Rustam, 3rd c. AD. **Note** how the legs of the riders go *all the way to the ground*! These were either very small horses, or very tall men.

[32] For this and much more supernatural strangeness in Galatia, see Douglas Van Dorn, Galatians: A Supernatural Justification (Erie, CO: Waters of Creation Pub., 2015).

[33] L. J. Alderink, "Stoicheia", in *Dictionary of Deities and Demons in the Bible*, ed. Karel van der Toorn, Bob Becking and Pieter W. van der Horst, 2nd extensively rev. ed. (Leiden; Boston; Grand Rapids, Mich.: Brill; Eerdmans, 1999), 815-18.

[34] Michaels, 207.

[35] Ibid., 208.

[36] The LXX uses the word three times: Job 40:20; 41:24; Prov 30:16. In the first instance, the behemoth is in view. In the second, it is Leviathan. This means that the term is always used in the Scripture with reference to spiritual-heavenly beings.

[37] Giants of incredible strength and ferocity, even superior to that of the Titans.

[38] Ramsey, 208.

[39] For more on the ambiguity, see Brian Godawa, *Jesus Triumphant*, Chronicles of the Nephilim Book 8 (Los Angeles: Embedded Pictures Publishing, 2015), Appendix: Jesus and the Cosmic War. Brian does a great job summarizing the ambiguity and giving other sources for further reading.

NOTES FOR CHAPTER 16: CONQUEST (Pgs. 225-234)

[1] See James M. Hamilton Jr., *God's Indwelling Presence: The Holy Spirit in the Old & New Testaments* (Nashville, TN: B&H Academic, 2006).

[2] Phillip Michael Sherman, *Babel's Tower Translated: Genesis 11 and Ancient Jewish Interpretation* (Boston: Brill, 2013), 107-08.

[3] Yuliya Minets, *The Slow Fall of Babel: Languages and Identities in Late Antique Christianity* (Alabama: Cambridge University Press, 2022), 315. She also comments on Theodoret's *Religious History* 21 as another example.

[4] Ibid., 316.

[5] James Gardner, *The War With Babylon* (Xulon Press, 2004), 108.

[6] Russell Hemati, "Demons, Idols, and Faith," *The Good, the True, the Beautiful: A Multidisciplinary Tribute to David K. Naugle*, ed. Mark J. Boone et al (Eugene, OR: Pickwick, 2021), 143-44.

[7] For more, see the fascinating charts by Roy Atwood, "The Structure of Luke's Two Volumes," ascendedking.com.

NOTES FOR CHAPTER 17: RETURN OF THE NEPHILIM? (Pgs. 235-256)

[1] I have written a sermon on this in my Revelation series preached from Dec 2020-Nov 2022. See Douglas Van Dorn, "An Introduction to the Millennium," *RBCNC.com* (8-29-2021), https://www.rbcnc.com/revelation. Obviously, there are other books out there that do the same.

[2] Cf. Chuck Missler, "The Return of the Nephilim? 'And Also After That'," *khouse.org* (Sept 1, 1997). You can find an overview of this at Tom Horn (overview of Missler at), "PART 18 — Forbidden Gates: How Genetics, Robotics, Artificial Intelligence3, Synthetic Biology, Nanotechnology, & Human Enhancement Herald the Dawn of Techno-Dimensional Spiritual Warfare," *DefenderPublishing* (Oct 5, 2010).

[3] The Old Greek reads, "They will be commixed into lines (races?) of humans." Theodotion reads, "There will be commingling among the seed of humanity."

[4] You can see this in my sermon on this passage in the series on Daniel at www.rbcnc.com/Daniel.

[5] A couple of interesting articles on this whole question are Paradox Brown, "No Nephilim in Bible Prophecy Part 2 – Dan 2:43," Nephilim Hybrids; Paradox Brown, "No Nephilim in Bible Prophecy Part 3 – Dan 2:43 not even if 'they' were fallen angels," *Nephilim Hybrids*.

[6] I'm following here the excellent study from R. T. France, *The Gospel of Matthew*, The New International Commentary on the New Testament (Grand Rapids, MI: Wm. B. Eerdmans Publication Co., 2007), 886ff.

[7] A brief study of this is Anthony A. Hoekema, "Amillennialism," in *The Meaning of the Millennium: Four Views*, ed. Robert G. Clouse (Downers Grove, IL: InterVarsity, 1977): 156-59. See also my introductory sermon at www.rbcnc.com/revelation.

[8] It was under this literary view of the book that I endeavored to preach Revelation. I recommend you consult the sermons to be found at www.rbcnc.com/revelation and the accompanying work by the scholars, especially in the John/Revelation parallels, from Dr. Warren Gage. Especially, Warren Austin Gage. *John's Gospel: A Neglected Key to Revelation?* Fort Lauderdale, FL: Warren A. Gage, 2001.

[9] H. J. W. Drijvers, *Iconography of Religions* (Leiden, Netherlands: Brill, 1976), 18.

[10] For example, Tom Horn, *Zenith 2016: The Revised & Expanded Edition of Apollyon Rising 2012* (Crane, MO: Defender, 2013); Thomas Horn, and Josh Peck, *Abaddon Ascending: The Ancient Conspiracy at the Center of CERN's Most Secretive Mission* (Crane, MO: Defender, 2016). These are rather pop-eschatology examples. In a quick search, I didn't find any more scholarly work making this connection.

[11] Some scholars suggest that there were mythological figures. See Stefan Münger, "Ariel," in *Dictionary of Deities and Demons in the Bible DDD*, 2nd extensively rev. ed., ed. K. van der Toorn, Bob Becking and Pieter Willem van der Horst (Leiden; Boston; Grand Rapids, Mich.: Brill; Eerdmans, 1999), 89. But we've already mentioned the Book of Jasher on this.

[12] Hal Lindsey, *There's a New World Coming: 'A Prophetic Odyssey'* (Santa Ana, CA: Vision House Publishers, 1973), 138-39.

[13] Test. Dan 5:6-7; cf. Irenaeus, *Against Heresies* 5.30.2.

[14] "This limitation is due to the fact noticed by Bochart (*Hieroz*. iii. 339), that the natural locust is born in the spring and dies at the end of the summer, and thus lives about five months in all." R. H. Charles, *A Critical and Exegetical Commentary on the Revelation of St John*, vol. 1, International Critical Commentary (Edinburgh: T&T Clark International, 1920), 243.

[15] Kenneth L. Gentry Jr., *The Divorce of Israel: A Redemptive-Historical Interpretation of Revelation* (Dallas, GE: Tolle Lege Press, forthcoming), 733.

[16] Vern Poythress, *The Returning King* (Phillipsburg, NJ: P&R, 2000), 28.

[17] William Hendriksen, *More Than Conquerors* (Grand Rapids: Baker, 1961), 147.

[18] For numerous literary reasons (see my sermon "The Final Battle: Gog and Magog" at www.rbcnc.com/revelation) too many to enumerate here, this battle is identical with the battles in Rev 19:19-21; 16:16-21; and 14:19-20, 10-11).

[19] Heiser, *Hermon*, 172, n. 278; Tooman, 140.

[20] Gressman, 129, n. 1; Zimmerli, 300.

[21] Seder Zeraim, Talmud – Mas. Berachoth 58a.

[22] Table in Sverre Bøe, *Gog and Magog: Ezekiel 38-39 as Pre-text for Revelation 19,17-21 and 20:7-10*, Wissenschaftliche Untersuchungen zum Neuen Testament 2. Reihe 135 (Tübingen: Mohr Siebeck, 2001), 310.

[23] Heiser, *Hermon*, 170. Heiser did a long podcast on this as well. See Michael. Heiser, "Naked Bible Podcast 152, 153 – The Gog Magog Invasion | Ezekiel 38-39," *Youtube* (May 12, 2018), https://www.youtube.com/watch?v=k3YnPvBwQxk. Transcript: https://nakedbiblepodcast.com/wp-content/uploads/2017/04/NB-152-Transcript.pdf. Heiser cites the following article as a good introduction for where the whole Russia thing originated (hint: Cold War exegesis). J. Paul Tanner, "Daniel's 'King of the North': Do We Owe Russia an Apology?" *JETS* 35.3 (Sept 1992): 315-28. Also Edwin Yamauchi, *Foes From the Northern Frontier* (Eugene, OR: Wipf & Stock, 2003), 19-27.

[24] See n. 23 for Heiser's fascinating discussion.

[25] Gentry notes that to "come up" often refers to a military attack (Jdg 12:3; 1Sa 7:7; 11:1; 2Sa 5:22; 1Ki 20:1; 2Ki 16:5; 18:17; 19:23; 24:10; 2Ch 12:2, 9; 24:23; Isa 36:1; 37:24; Jer 35:11). Gentry, *Revelation* II.705.

[26] Phillip G. Kayser, "The Last Rebellion: Revelation 20:7-10," *Biblical Blueprints* (8-26-2018), https://kaysercommentary.com/Sermons/New%20Testament/Revelation/Revelation%2020/Revelation%2020_7-10.md#fnref7, has a discussion as well as others who have taken this view.

[27] Bøe discusses this on 305, n. 255; 316ff.

[28] On the Plague of Frogs in Rev 16:13-14 (Armageddon) This is another way of talking about 20:8 where Satan deceives the nations and gathers together those from the four corners of the earth, Gog and Magog, for battle. Johnson writes, "It is a visual representation of the subtle demonic process by which the dragon, released at last from the restraint that kept him from deceiving the nations, will gather them for war." Dennis Johnson, *Triumph of the* Lamb: A Commentary on Revelation (Phillipsburg, NJ: P&R, 2001), 233.

[29] Gerhard A. Krodel, *Revelation*, Augsburg Commentary on the New Testament (Minneapolis, MN: Augsburg Publishing House, 1989), 337.

[30] Mathias Rissi, *The Future of the World: An Exegetical Study of Revelation 19.11-22.15*, Studies in Biblical Theology, Second Series 23 (Napierville, IL: Allenson, 1972), 35-36. Quoted in Bøe, 316.

[31] my changes to the usual translation are based upon word studies given in the *Dictionary of Deities and Demons in the Bible*.

APPENDIX: EXTRA-BIBLICAL LITERATURE (Pgs. 259-262)

[1] Barnabas 16:5-6 ("Scripture"); Justin Martyr (inspired but maybe not "scripture"); Irenaeus (Holy Spirit inspired), Tertullian ("Scripture"), Origen (back and forth). See the discussion in Michael Heiser, *Reversing Hermon* (Crane, MO: Defender Pub, 2017), 183-92.

[2] Jude 14-15 = 1 Enoch 1:9. Allusions to 1 Enoch in the NT include Matt 22:13; 25:31; 26:24; Col 2:3; 1Th 5:3; 1Ti 1:17; Heb 4:13; 12:23; James 3:6; 1 Peter 1:12; 3:19; 2Pet 2:4; Jude 6, 13, 16; Rev 8:8; 15:3; 19:20; 20:3; and many, many more. See Heiser, *Reversing Hermon*, 204-21; also Steve Delamarter, *A Scripture Index to Charlesworth's The Old Testament Pseudepigrapha* (Sheffield: Sheffield Academic Press, 2002).

[3] Here are just a few. 1. As Augustine reported, the book is too *old* to trust it (*City of God* 15:23). His point is that the actual words of Enoch were preserved only in oral tradition. How do we know where Enoch's words end and some Jewish writers' begin? 2. It has historical anachronisms. We do not find such things in Scripture. A good example is the first chapter which has Enoch—who lived long before the Flood—referring to Mt. Sinai (1 En 1:4). That is obviously historically inappropriate. 3. We have little to no evidence that Jews—even at Qumran who held the book in very high esteem— regarded it as Scripture (See Richard Bauckham, *Jude and the Relatives of Jesus in the Early Church* (London; New York: T&T Clark, 2004), 226-33. 4. 1 Enoch is actually five distinct books: *The Book of Watchers* (1-36); *The Book of Similitudes* (37-71); *The Book of Astronomical Writings* (72-82); *The Book of Dream Visions* (83-90); *The Book of the Epistle of Enoch* (91-107). These in turn include fragments from other books, such as *The Book of Noah* (6-11; 5:7-55:2; 60; 65-69:25; 106-108). (See E. Isaac, "1 Enoch," in *The Old Testament Pseudepigrapha* Vol. 1, ed. James H. Charlesworth [New York: Doubleday, 1983], 7). As such, it cannot be trusted as fully the words of Enoch, though it undoubtedly (as Jude explains) contains many of his actual words.

[4] D. A. Carson reports that he had private correspondence with an important Enochian scholar who suggests that Jude is citing 1 Enoch 1:9 ironically rather than positively. Carson says, "I have not seen that view defended anywhere in print, convincingly or otherwise, so at this juncture the claim still strikes me as odd." D. A. Carson, "Jude," in G. K. Beale and D. A. Carson, *Commentary on the New Testament Use of the Old Testament* (Grand Rapids, MI; Nottingham, UK: Baker Academic; Apollos, 2007), 1078.

[5] Consult any of the Commentaries cited in note 19 in the Introduction.

[6] More on Jude and other NT allusions to Enoch, see George W. E. Nickelsburg and Klaus Baltzer, *1 Enoch : A Commentary on the Book of 1 Enoch* (Minneapolis, Minn.: Fortress, 2001), 83-86; 123-24.

APPENDIX: 2 PETER 2:4 AND JUDE 6 (Pgs. 263-266)

[1] Cf. Thomas R. Schreiner, *1, 2 Peter, Jude*, New American Commentary (Nashville, TN: Broadman & Holman, 2003), 447-51.

[2] So John Gill, Matthew Henry, even John Milton, *Paradise Lost* I. 48; II. 169, 183 196; III. 82.

[3] For a list of those who agree with this see Introduction note #19.

[4] Not the word *'adam*, which the first human was named, but *'ish*.

[5] That angels have "flesh" and "bodies" and that this differs from humanity see 1Co 15:39-41.

[6] It is curious that the LXX uses the word three times: Job 40:20; 41:24; Prov 30:16. In the first instance, the behemoth is in view. In the second, it is Leviathan. This means that the term is always used in the Scripture with reference to spiritual-heavenly beings.

[7] *"Tartaroō," A Greek-English Lexicon of the New Testament*, ed. Joseph Henry Thayer (International Bible Translators, 2000).

[8] See also Appendix I - Extra-Biblical Literature.

[9] Amar Annus, "On the Origin of Watchers: A Comparative Study of the Antediluvian Wisdom in Mesopotamian and Jewish Traditions," *Journal for the Study of the Pseudepigrapha* 19.4 (2010): 277-320. This demonstration of the conceptual parallels alone blows the non-Enochian interpretation out of the water as simply failing to confront the Jews' religious beliefs in their time and place. For an evangelical, the only reason I can see to discount the traditional Enochian view is non-textual and non-grammatical-historical—i.e., Western incredulity.

[10] See Schreiner, *1, 2 Peter, Jude*, 448.

[11] Richard J. Bauckham, *Jude, 2 Peter*, Word Biblical Commentary (Waco, TX: Word Books, 1983), 46.

[12] Notice how the Watchers and/or the giants are referred to in *every* list except the most recently written—the Mishnah (*m. Sanh.*)—which dates no earlier than the second century A.D. This is no surprise, since the Jews after the rise of Christianity began to eliminate supernatural ideas of the Watchers from their theology *and Scripture*.

APPENDIX: THE STORIES OF THE GREEKS (Pgs. 267-272)

[1] See Hesiod, *Theogony* 2.453-491. Also Theophilus of Antioch, *Theophilus to Autolycus* 1.10. In Ante-Nicene Fathers, Vol. 2.

[2] One interesting attempt to do this from a Christian perspective is Robert Bowie Johnson Jr., *Athena and Eden* (2002), *Athena and Cain* (2003), *The Parthenon Code* (2004), *and Noah in Ancient Greek Art* (2007), (Annapolis, MD: Solving Light Books). On tracing the etymology and origin of fundamental Greek myths back to the ANE, see the important paper Amar Annus, "Are There Greek Rephaim? On the Etymology of Greek *Meropes* and *Titanes*," UF 31 (1999): 13-30.

APPENDIX: GIANTS IN THE AMERICAS (Pgs. 273-286)

[1] "Fragment: Niagara Falls [c. September 25-30, 1848]," in *Collected Works of Abraham Lincoln*, ed. Roy P. Basler (Ann Arbor, NI: University of Michigan Digital Library Production Services, 2001), 2:10.

[2] Timothy Green Beckley, *Giants on the Earth* (New Brunswick, NK: Global Communications, 2009); Charles DeLoach, *Giants: A Reference Guide from History, the bible, and Recorded Legend* (Metuchen, NJ: Scarecrow Press, 1995); Jonathan Gray, *Lost World of the Giants* (Brushton, NY: TEACH Services, Inc. 2006); Stephen Quayle, *Genesis 6 Giants* (Bozeman, MT: End Time Thunder Publishers, 2002). Timothy Green Beckley, *Giants on the Earth* (New Brunswick, NK: Global Communications, 2009), which adds some fresh material.

[3] Several people have compiled excellent lists of giant reports. One of the best is found on *Instagram* by Travis Roy at giants_of_ancientamerica. You can hear Travis talk about this on Blurry Creatures

Podcast, Episodes #5, 6. See also "Greater Ancestors World Museum," Greaterancestors.com; "Newspaper Accounts of Giants," JasonColavito.com. Or, one can go to the *New York Times* and search its archives for the old articles (I'm told they are much harder to find than they used to be). In case any of these sites go down, here is a very brief list of some of those articles, so that they can be entered into a search engine and found on another site: (from the *Post*) "An Indian Giants tomb" [Nov 18, 1883], "A Race of Giants" [Mar 16, 1884], "The Bones of a Giant" [Dec 9, 1887], etc; (from the *Times*) "Skeleton of Giant Found" [Nov 21, 1856], Reported Discovery of a Huge Skeleton [Dec 25, 1868], "The Early American Giant" [Feb 8, 1876], etc.

[4] A seven foot tall skeleton found by a miner named James L. Perkinson on his Yellow Jacket claim in the Atlin district. "Skeletons of Giants in Alaska," *San Francisco call* [Nov 18, 1900].

[5] There is a legend from 1833 where a group of Mexican soldiers were digging a pit and struck a 12' tall skeleton with double rows of teeth. Told for example in Jerome Clark and John Clark, *Unnatural Phenomena* (Santa Barbara, CA: ABC-CLIO, 2005), 15. Giants with double rows of teeth were also said to have been discovered on Santa Rosa Island, California, Clearwater, Minnesota and other places (see Chapter 3, n. 19).

[6] In Bridgeport, Connecticut there was an eight foot skeleton near the house of one Daniel Buckingham, Esq. Edward Rodolphus Lambert, The History of the Colony of New Haven (New Haven, CT: Hitchcock & Stafford, 1838), 126.

[7] In 1879, a 9'8" skeleton was retrieved from a stone burial mound in Brewersville, IN. *The Indianapolis News*, November 10, 1975; cited in Richard Marshall, *Mysteries of the Unexplained* (Pleasantville, N.Y.: Reader's Digest Association, 1982), 41.

[8] One example is a 7'8" skeleton with double rows of teeth. Thomas Weston, *History of the Town of Middleboro, Massachusetts* (Boston: Houghton, Mifflin and Company, 1906), 400.

[9] For example, in Monmouth a 7'6" skeleton with the head the size of a common iron tea-kettle was discovered and played with for two or three years by local boys who were "shooting Injuns!" Harry Hayman Cochrane, History of Monmouth and Wales Maine, vol. 1 (East Winthrop: Banner Company, 1894), 9-10.

[10] Among which were a 7'7", 8'0", and nearly 10' skeleton found in the Humbolt Lake bed and nearby Friedman Ranch. Lovelock *Review Miner*, June 19, 1931; September, 29, 1939; cited in Joe Oesterle and Tim Cridland, *Weird Las Vegas and Nevada* (New York: Sterling Publishing Co., 2007), 35.

[11] Around 1820 a seven foot body was discovered in Moultonborough. *Guide to the White Mountains and Lakes of New Hampshire* (Concord, NH: Tripp & Osgood, 1851), 19.

[12] Here is an example of someone clearly within this range, without specific height given (typical of many of these stories). "Mr. Peleg Sweet, who was a man of large size and full features … in digging, came upon a skull and jaw which were of such size that the skull would cover his head and the jaw could be easily slipped over his face, as though the head of a giant were enveloping his." Stephen D. Peet, "The Mound-Builders," in *History of Astabula Co., Ohio*, ed. William W. Williams (Philadelphia: Williams Bros., 1878), 19.

[13] Near Braden, OK the femur of a nine foot giant was found among skeletons of average sized people in a "huge" mound. "Oklahoma Indian Relics Unearthed," *The Washington Post* [Aug 26, 1934].

[14] Near Gastersville, PA, scientists from the Smithsonian discovered a 7'2" skeleton with coarse black hair. *American Antiquarian and Oriental Journal*, ed. Stephen D. Peet, 7:1 (January 1885): 52.

[15] A thigh bone "three or four inches longer" than the thigh bone of the seven feet man named James McGlaughlin. John Haywood, *The Natural and Aboriginal History of Tennessee: Up to the First Settlement Therein by the White People in the Year 1768* (Kingsport, TN: F.M. Hill-Books, 1973), 133.

[16] In Kanawha county in a 540 ft x 85 ft mound were at least three skeletons, one of which was 7'6". They were covered in copper jewelry. *American Antiquarian and Oriental Journal*, ed. Stephen D. Peet, 6:2 (March 1884): 133-34. *The New York Times* ran a piece on a 10'9" skeleton, "Its jaws and teeth were almost as large as a horse" found Wheeling, WV [Nov 21, 1856].

[17] Maple Creek, Wisconsin yielded a skeleton over nine feet tall as reported in the local newspaper and then in the *New York Times*, December 20, 1897.

[18] You can read about these and many more finds in many places on the Internet, but my personal warning is to be cautious and meticulous in doing your research. Don't believe everything you read. Check and recheck facts, and by all means seek out original sources. That said, an interesting compilation of some of these finds can be found in the sometimes less than trustworthy Josiah Priest, *American Antiquities and Discoveries in the West* (Albany, NY: Hoffman & White, 1833). At least some of his stories have sources and they fit in both what is reported and how they are reported with the more trustworthy sources. See also the *New York Times* articles posted at the website at the end of the last table in this chapter.

[19] Reported in the *St. Paul Daily Pioneer Press*, May 23, 1882 as summarized in N. H. Winchell and Jacob V. Brower, *1906-1911 The Aborigines of Minnesota: A Report based on the Collections of Jacob V. Brower, and on the Field Surveys and Notes of Alfred J. Hill and Theodore H. Lewis* (Minnesota Historical Society, 1911), 363. I have found five different newspaper clippings of this excavation. It was a widely publicized story.

[20] The Dresbach mound group (Dresbach, Minnesota) yielded an *eight foot skeleton* and another of similar length along with strange artifacts like shell beaded necklaces, hematite celts (a stone axe-like instrument with a beveled edge), copper chisels, copper rings, and copper hatchets, all typical finds in Adena burial mounds (Winchell, 89-90). A mound in Corrinna, MN (near Clearwater) gave up seven skeletons from *seven to eight feet* high, though a few days later it was reported that the skeletons were "not of unusual size;" yet the "prehistoric" skull did have marked facial differences compared to Indian skulls (Ibid. 217). Mounds near Moose Island lakes gave up *seven ft.* skeletons (ibid. 301). A very large mound dubbed "Grand Mound" in (old) Itasca county on the US/Canadian border was found to hold at least one skeleton "estimated at over *10 feet*." (ibid. 372). Other discoveries included a *"huge man"* found in a mound near Lake Koronis ("Giants Lived There," *The Saint Paul Globe*, Thursday, August 12, 1897, p. 4), *"human remains of men of large stature"* in various mounds in La Crescent (Winchell, 80), *"large human bones"* near Rushford (Ibid. 91), and two skeletons "the size of which indicated the sons of Amalek" with a *thigh-bone of 20 inches and double rows of teeth* (Franklyn Curtiss-Wedge, *History of Wright County Minnesota*, vol. 1 [Chicago: H. C. Cooper, Jr., & Co., 1915]). And that's just Minnesota; and that's just what I've been able to find in Minnesota.

[21] Some 10 ft. giant reports seem plausible (see note 20); others seem less so. In Oct. 1869, the most famous giant hoax in early U.S. history began. The famous 10 ft. "petrified" Cardiff Giant (New York) was "discovered" when some men were digging a well. However, it was later uncovered that the giant was sculpted and hidden there by George Hull, a rich atheist who had a fight with a Methodist pastor over Genesis 6:4. P.T. Barnum got into the act and later created his own version, decrying the other giant a hoax. From this was born the phrase "a sucker is born every minute." Two months after the Cardiff giant appeared, a story came out of Sauk Rapids (MN) that a 10 ft. petrified giant had been recovered from a quarry near the Mississippi River. This story has hallmarks of a fake. Though no one made any direct money from it, it certainly put the little town on the map. For a

Fig. FN 7.
Fake Cardiff Giant

fascinating recap of this amazing hoax see Timothy Green Beckley (ed.), *The American Goliah and other Fantastic Reports of Unknown Giants and Humongous Creatures* (New Brunswick, NJ: Global Communications, 2010).

[22] Cf. Roy Norvill, *Giants: The Vanished Race* (Wellingborough, UK: Aquarian Press, 1979), 84.

[23] Adam Rodgers, "Early Nevada History is Traced in Lovelock, Cave, Tomb of the Forgotten Race," in *Ancient American* Vol. 13, no. 81, 32-35.

[24] See Chapter 3, n. 19.

[25] Mac Rutherford, *Historic Haunts of Winchester* (Charleston, SC: Haunted America, 2007), 29.

[26] Sarah Winnemucca Hopkins, *Life Among the Paiutes* (Boston: Cupples, Upham & CO., 1883), 26.

[27] Rodgers, ibid.

[28] *Nevada Review-Miner* newspaper, June 19, 1931.

[29] William F. Cody, *An Autobiography of Buffalo Bill* (Aurora, CO: Bibliographical Center for Research, 2009), 196-97.

[30] Pedro de Cieza de Léon; *The Travels of Pedro de Cieza de Leon, A.D. 1532-50*, translated by Clements R. Markham, (London: Hakluyt Society, 1864), 189-91.

[31] See Adrienne Mayor, *Fossil Legends of the First Americans* (Princeton, NJ: Princeton University Press, 2005), 80.

[32] Genesis 14:10; 19:1-25.

[33] See the Markham translation of de Léon, 190-91, note 1; also Mayer, 82.

[34] Markham, ibid.

[35] Cf. Garcilaso de la Vega, *The Florida of the Inca*, ed. John and Jeanette Varner (Austin, TX: University of Texas Pres, 1951), 349; See Bernal Diaz, *The Conquest of New Spain*, trans. J. M. Cohen (New York: Penguin, 1963), 181; Antonio Pigafetta, *The Voyage of Magellan* (London: Yale University Press, 1969); John Smith, *Captain John Smith's America; selections from his writings*, ed. John Lankford (New York: Harper & Row, 1967), 9; George Parker Winship (Trans.), *The Coronado Expedition: 1540-1542* (Washington: Government Printing Office, 1896), 484-85.

[36] "Old Eskimo Legend Proves True – People Nine Feet Tall Visit Coast," *New York Times*, Dec. 19, 1904.

[37] *Coast to Coast*, hosted by George Noory (12-3-08).

[38] Stephen Quayle and Duncan Long, *Longwalkers* (Bozeman, MT: End Times Thunder Publishers, 2008), 274-79.

[39] The original note read, "Scientists have Found a Settlement in the Borjomi Gorge Mysterious Mythical Creature," and gave a link to a video that is now difficult to find. (the link works, but does not take you to the specific airing). A transcript with screen shots is still online. See "Breaktrough: TV-report shows the giant bones of Borjomi!"

[40] See note 21.

[41] See for example, Adrienne Mayor, *The First Fossil Hunters: Paleontology in Greek and Roman Times* (Princeton, NJ: Princeton University Press, 2001), 104-57.

[42] In fact, there are small museums and castles said to hold such artifacts to this day. There are Indiana Jones like treasure seekers that claim to have bones and have tested the bones. One of the more fascinating is the story of Father Carlos Vaca. In 1964 in Ecuador the locals discovered the bones of a 7.6 meter (nearly 25 ft., the approximate size of the giants of Peru, see note 30) giant after a particularly bad storm exposed them from under an ancient monument. They told Father Carlos who collected them. Two of these bones, a heel-bone and the os occipitale (bone under the skull) were taken by Klaus Dona to Germany where he says it was confirmed that they were both human bones, but no DNA could be recovered because of their extreme antiquity. He shows these bones in his public lectures. A huckster? Truth? Whatever it is, it is an interesting claim.

[43] Strangely, there are reports of giant skeletons with horns. However, this is not an impossible physical trait relegated only to myth. "Cutaneous horns" are well documented conical projections above the surface of the skin that can often grow quite large. See Eray Copcu, Nazan Sivrioglu, and Nil Culhaci, "Cutaneous Horns: Are These Lesions as Innocent as They Seem to Be"?, *World Journal of Surgical Oncology* 2 (2004): 1-18.

APPENDIX: GIANTS OF MONUMENT AND MYTH (Pgs. 287-306)

[1] Cited Philip Coppens, "America's Nazca Lines," *Eye of the Psychic*, https://www.eyeofthepsychic.com/intaglios/.

[2] For instance, the Blythe Intaglios which include several human-like figures, the largest of which is 167 ft. long (see Frank M. Setzler, and George C. Marshall, "Giant Effigies of the Southwest," *National Geographic* [Sept. 1952]: 389-404).

[3] Oliver Gille, "Cerne Abbas Giant May Have Held Severed Head," *The Independent* (London, England, Saturday, May 21, 1994).

[4] Carol Rose, "Cern Abbas Giant," in *Giants, Monsters, and Dragons: An Encyclopedia of Folklore, Legend, and Myth* (New York: W.W. Norton & Company Inc. 2000), 73.

[5] John Philipps Emslie and C. S. Burne, "Scraps of Folklore Collected," *Folklore* 26:2 (June 30, 1915): 153-170.

[6] Pictures and article can be found in Paul Mullis, "The Ravens Warband: The Adventure of the Dancing Men," *millennia.f2s.com*.

[7] Frank Joseph, Atlantis in Wisconsin: New Revelations About The Lost Sunken City (St. Paul, MN, Galde Press, 1995), 29.

[8] Vincent H. Gaddis, *Native American Myths and Mysteries* (Garberville, CA: Borderland Sciences, 1991), 48.

[9] Taylor L. Hansen, *The Ancient Atlantic* (Wisconsin, Amherst Press, 1969), 127.

[10] Several newspaper clippings and snippets of books (such as the journal of John Smith) can be found at: https://web.archive.org/web/20110905013828/http://www.spanishhill.com/skeletons/aboriginal_sites.shtml.

[11] The actual news article can be read online at "Horned Human Skull," puppstheories.com. This article is followed by another article claiming that it was a case of mistaken identity of deer antlers buried with the remains, implying that somehow they had gotten stuck to a human skull. There is a picture of a horned skull circulating on the internet, but I have no way of confirming if it is real or a hoax.

[12] Richard Marshall, *Mysteries of the Unexplained* (Pleasantville, NY: The Reader's Digest Association, 1983), 40.

[13] Homer, *Odyssey* 11:315-316; see also Ovid, *Metamorphoses* 1:151-176.

[14] For instance, Elwood Worchester, *The Book of Genesis in Light of Modern Knowledge* (New York: McClure, Phillips & Co., 1901), 502.

[15] Ovid, *Metamorphoses* 1:177-198.

[16] *Ibid.* 1:244-273.

[17] Poetic Edda: *Vafthruthnismol* 21.

[18] Völuspá 38.

[19] Völuspá 2.

[20] George Catlin, *The Okipa Ceremony* (Norman, OK: University of Oklahoma, 1958), 39.

[21] Don W. Dragoo, Mounds for the Dead: An Analysis of the Adena Culture (Carnegie Museum, 1963), 249.

[22] Frank Joseph, "Shawnee Deluge Story," *The Atlantis Encyclopedia* (Franklin Lakes, NJ: The Career Press, 2005), 248.

[23] Frank Joseph, *Advanced Civilizations of Prehistoric America* (Rochester, VT: Bear & Company, 2010), 73, 78, 80.

[24] Pedro Sarmiento De Gamboa, *History of the Incas*, trans. Clements Markham (Cambridge: The Hakluyt Society, 1907), 28-58.

[25] Peter Tompkins, *Mysteries of the Mexican Pyramids* (New York: Harper Collins, 1987), 57.

[26] Hubert Howe Bancroft et al., *The Native Races of the Pacific States of North America*, vol. 5: Primitive History (New York: D Appleton and Co., 1874-76), 17-18. Quote is from n. 40.

[27] Ibid, "Bochica," 75.

[28] Michael M. Alouf, *History of Baalbek* (Escondido, CA: Book Tree, 1999), 54.

[29] Readers Digest Association, *The World's Last Mysteries* (Montreal: Reader's Digest, 1978), 308.

[30] William Joseph Wilkins, *Hindu Mythology, Vedic and Purānic* (London: Thacker & Co., 1882), 364.

[31] See *Satapatha Brahmana* 2.1, 2, 13-16.

[32] Robert D. Craig, *Dictionary of Polynesian Mythology* (New York: Greenwood Press, 1989), 43.

[33] Hon. Sir Maui Pomare and James Cowan, *Legends of the Maori* (Christchurch, NZ: Kiwi Publishers, 1987), 238-39.

[34] On the Fomorians as giants and/or sea peoples see Duald Mac Firbis, *On the Fomorians and the Norsemen* (Christiania: J.C. Gundersens Bogtrykkeri, 1905), vii; as demons see John Arnott MacCulloch, *The Religion of the Ancient Celts*, (New York: Dover Publications, 2003), 51-52.

[35] Hibbert Trust, *The Hibbert Lectures*, (Cambridge: Cambridge University Press, 1896-1929), 582-83.

[36] Evans Lansing Smith and Nathan Robert Brown, *The Complete Idiot's Guide to World Mythology* (Indianapolis, IN: Alpha Books, 2008), 77.

[37] Frank Joseph, *The Destruction of Atlantis* (Rochester, VT: Bear and Company, 2002), 146-47.

[38] David Livingstone, *Missionary Travels*, cited in Elwood Worcester, *Book of Genesis* (New York: McClure, Phillips & Co., 1901), 498.

GLOSSARY

Akkadian – An extinct Semitic language that was spoken in ancient Mesopotamia.

Anunnaki – Meaning "royal blood" or "princely offspring" (i.e. "sons of God"), in the *Atra-Hasis* flood myth they burden the Igigi (a group sometimes synonymous with the Anunnaki) who rebel after 40 days and there follows the creation of mankind.

Anachronism – A logical fallacy. Inconsistency in a chronological arrangement.

Cerynean Hind – An enormous golden antlered, bronze hoofed deer (hind) that was so fast it could outrun an arrow.

Chimera – A beast possessing the attributes of more than one creature.

Cretan Bull – Zeus in the form of the bull that carried away the goddess Europa (after which Europe gets its name), or the bull Pasiphaë (goddess daughter of Helios, the Sun) fell in love with, giving birth to the *Minotaur*.

Demigod – A half heavenly, half earthly creature.

Demythologization – Ridding the Bible of "mythological" or supernatural events in order to get at the "real" meaning of a text.

Divine Council – "The heavenly host, the pantheon of divine beings who administer the affairs of the cosmos. All ancient Mediterranean cultures had some conception of a divine council. The divine council of Israelite religion, known primarily through the psalms, was distinct in important ways." (From Michael S. Heiser, "The Divine Council," in *Dictionary of the Old Testament: Wisdom, Poetry, & Writings*, ed. Tremper Longman and Peter Enns, InterVarsity Press, 2008).

Eisegesis – Reading "into" (Gk: *eis* = "in") a text whatever you want it to say with little regard as to authorial intent. It is the opposite of *exegesis*.

Equivocation – A logical fallacy. The misleading use of a term with more than one meaning or sense.

Exegesis – Explaining and interpreting "out of" (Gk: *ex* = "out") a text the meaning of the original author. It is the opposite of *eisegesis*, which only wants to explain what a passage means "to me."

Gyes - Giants of incredible strength and ferocity, even superior to that of the Titans.

Hydra – A guardian of the Underworld, it was a multi-headed sea-serpent so invincible that if one head was cut off, two more would grow in its place.

Manifest Destiny – The 19th century belief that the United States was destined to expand across the continent. It was used to justify the Mexican-American war and, according to the more left-leaning political crowd today, to perpetuate the belief and treatment of native Indians as savages, and that the white man was superior.

Marduk – The patron deity of Babylon; around the time of Hammurabi and Abraham he began to rise to the head position of the Babylonian pantheon. In the Babylonian equivalent of the sons of God, the *Anunnaki* seek a god who can defeat the gods rising against them. Marduk ends up killing Tiamat, the sea dragon, in the Babylonian creation epic: *Enuma Elish*.

Midrash – A form of Jewish interpretation resembling a modern paraphrase translation of the Bible, although midrash also feels free to add ideas not even found in the text, if it is based upon something substantial the Jews felt they could derive from it (such as oral traditions).

Minish – To make or become less; to diminish.

Minotaur – A creature with the head of a bull and the body of a man, he dwelt at the center of the Cretan Labyrinth, built for King Minos on the island of Crete.

Mishnah – The first major written composition of Jewish oral traditions called the "Oral Torah."

Nemean Lion – A vicious golden furred monster at Nemea, impervious to mortal weapons, with claws sharper than mortal swords.

Protoevangelium – Literally "the first gospel." It is a word used to describe Genesis 3:15.

Reëm – Found in Num 23:22; 24:8; Deut 33:17; Job 39:9-10, Ps 22:22; 29:6; 92:11; Isa 34:7; Zech 14:10, it is translated as "unicorn" by the KJV. It is appears to be a mythological creature, but its exact identity is a guess.

Septuagint – (abbreviated: LXX, the Roman numeral "70", for the seventy Jewish scribes who worked on it). The Greek translation of the Hebrew Bible (the Christian Old Testament) undertaken between the 3rd and 2nd centuries B.C. The LXX is invaluable because 1. It is the Scripture most often quoted by the NT and 2. We have copies of it that date to nearly 1,000 years before our oldest Hebrew manuscripts.

Stymphalian Bird – Man eating, bronze beaked, metallic feathered birds that fled from a pack of wolves loosed by Arabs; they migrated to Lake Stymphalia in Arcadia and quickly overtook the countryside and townspeople.

Sybil – From the Latin *sibylla*, meaning "prophetess;" the sibyls were said to have prophesied at certain holy sites throughout the ancient world.

Targum – An Aramaic paraphrase of the Hebrew Old Testament. Aramaic is a cousin language of Hebrew.

Torah – Hebrew for "Instruction," it is the name given by Jews to the first five books of the Old Testament known as the Books of Moses.

Two Kingdoms – The idea that God has made all things, all things are corrupted by sin, Christians should be active in human culture (Augustine's "city of man") because sin is not only "out there" but also "inside" me (i.e. I can't get away from it), all lawful vocations are honorable, Christians should live out their faith in their daily vocation, *but* human culture is distinct from the culture of heaven (Augustine's "city of God") so that we should view the Christian life in this world as a pilgrim's life, where we are simultaneously citizens of two kingdoms, one temporary and passing away, the other permanent and lasting forever.

Ugarit – An ancient Canaanite city-state in modern Syria along the coast of the Mediterranean Sea. It famously gave up a host of important religious documents used in comparative religion by Hebrew scholars.

Uniformitarianism – A scientific theory that the earth is billions of years old and only sees tiny changes upon its surface through natural processes like erosion.

Ziggurat – Ancient temples made to look like mountains. They were thought to be "stairways to heaven" and replicas of the cosmic mountain—the place where the gods met for deliberation over the affairs of earth.

Zoroaster – From unknown antiquity, the Persian prophet and founder of Zoroastrianism.

BIBLIOGRAPHY

Adam, Jean-Pierre. "A propos du trilithon de Baalbek. Le transport et la mise en oeuvre des megaliths." SYRIA 54:1-2 (1977): 31-63.

al-Maqrīzī, Ahmad Ibn 'Ali. *Description Topographique et Historique de l'Egypte* (vol. 1), trans. From the Arabic into French by M. U. Bouriant, ed. Ernest Lerous (Paris: Rue Bonaparte, 1895.

al-Tabarī. *Prophets and Patriarchs: The History of al-Tabarī* (vol. 2). Trans. William M. Brinner. Albany, NY: State University of New York Press, 1987.

Alouf, Michael M. *History of Baalbek*. Escondido, CA: Book Tree, 1999.

Alden, Markus (et al.). "Intracellular Reverse Transcription of Pfizer BioNTech COVID-19 mRNA Vaccine BNT162b2 In Vitro in Human Liver Cell Line," *Mol Biol* 44.3 (2022): 1115-1126, https://www.mdpi.com/1467-3045/44/3/73/htm.

Ambrose. *Noah and the Ark*.

The Anchor Yale Bible Dictionary. Ed. David Noel Freedman. New York: Doubleday, 1996.

The Ancient Near East an Anthology of Texts and Pictures. Ed. James Bennett Pritchard. Princeton: Princeton University Press, 1958.

Annus, Amar. "Are There Greek Rephaim? On the Etymology of Greek *Meropes* and *Titanes*." *Ugarit Forschungen* 31 (1999): 13-30.

_____. "On the Origin of Watchers: A Comparative Study of the Antediluvian Wisdom in Mesopotamian and Jewish Traditions." *Journal for the Study of the Pseudepigrapha* 19.4 (2010): 277-320.

Aquinas, Thomas. *Catena Aurea: Commentary on the Four Gospels, Collected out of the Works of the Fathers: St. Matthew*. Ed. John Henry Newman, vol. 1. Oxford: John Henry Parker, 1841.

Arnold, Clinton E. *Zondervan Illustrated Bible Backgrounds Commentary Volume 4: Hebrews to Revelation*. Grand Rapids, MI: Zondervan, 2002.

Athenagoras. *A Plea for the Christians*.

Atwood, Roy. "The Structure of Luke's Two Volumes." *ascendedking.com*.

Aune, D. E. "Demonology." *The International Standard Bible Encyclopedia, Revised*. Ed. Geoffrey W. Bromiley. Grand Rapids, MI: Wm. B. Eerdmans, 1979–1988.

Aveni, Anthony, and Yonathan Mizrachi. "The Geometry and Astronomy of Rujm El-Hiri, a Megalithic Site in the Southern Levant." *Journal of Field Archaeology* 25.4 (1998): 475-96.

Bancroft, Hubert Howe et al., *The Native Races of the Pacific States of North America*, vol. 5. New York: D Appleton and Co., 1874-76.

Baring-Gould, Sabine. *Legends of Old Testament Characters from the Talmud and Other Sources*. London: Macmillan, 1871.

Barker, Margaret, *The Revelation of Jesus Christ*. Edinburgh: T&T Clark, 2000.

Bauckham, Richard J. *Jude 2 Peter*. Word Biblical Commentary. Waco, TX: Word Books, 1983.

Bautch, Kelley Coblentz. *A Study of the Geography of 1 Enoch 17-19*. Boston: Brill, 2003.

Beale, Gregory K. *The Temple and the Church's Mission: A Biblical Theology of the Dwelling Place of God*. Downers Grove, IL: InterVarsity Press, 2004.

Beckley, Timothy Green. *Giants on the Earth*. New Brunswick, NJ: Global Communications/Conspiracy Journal, 2009.

_____. *The American Goliah and other Fantastic Reports of Unknown Giants and Humongous Creatures*. New Brunswick, NJ: Global Communications, 2010.

Bergsma, John Sietze. "Noah's Nakedness and the Curse of Canaan (Gen 9:20-27)." *Journal of Biblical Literature* 124/1 (2005): 25-40.

Billington, Clyde E. "Goliath and The Exodus Giants: How Tall Were They"? *JETS* 50.3 (2007): 489-508.

Birch, W. F. "Golgotha on Mount Zion." *The Palestine Exploration Fund* (Jan 1907): 140-47.

Birrell, Anne. *Chinese Mythology: An Introduction*. Baltimore, MD: Johns Hopkins University Press, 1993.

Blum, Edwin A. *Jude*. The Expositors Bible Commentary Vol. 12. Grand Rapids, MI: Zondervan, 1981.

Bøe, Sverre. *Gog and Magog: Ezekiel 38-39 as Pre-text for Revelation 19,17-21 and 20:7-10*. Wissenschaftliche Untersuchungen zum Neuen Testament 2. Reihe 135. Tübingen: Mohr Siebeck, 2001.

Boice, James M. *Foundations of the Christian Faith*. Downers Grove, IL: InterVarsity, 1986.

_____. *Genesis Vol. 1*. Grand Rapids, MI: Baker Books, 1998.

Brenk, F. E. *Relighting the Souls: Studies in Plutarch, in Greek Literature, Religion, and Philosophy, and in the New Testament Background*. Stuttgart, 1999.

Brenton, Sir Lancelot C. L. *The Septuagint with Apocrypha*. London: Samuel Bagster & Sons, 1851.

Brophy, Thomas G. *The Origin Map*. New York: Writers Club Press, 2002.

Enhanced Brown-Driver-Briggs Hebrew and English Lexicon, electronic edition. Edited by Francis Brown, Samuel Rolles Driver and Charles Augustus Briggs. Oak Harbor, WA: Logos Research Systems, 2000.

Budd, Phillip J. *Numbers*. Word Biblical Commentary. Dallas: Word, Incorporated, 2002.

Budge, E. A. Wallis. *The Contendings of the Apostles*. London: H. Frowde, 1899.

Burke, Edmund. *The Annual Register: A View of the History, Politicks, and Literature for the Year 1764*. London: J. Dodsley, 1765.

Burkert, W. *The Orientalizing Revolution: Near Eastern Influence on Greek Culture in the Early Archaic Age.* Cambridge, 1987.

Burton, Judd H. *Interview With The Giant: Ethnohistorical Notes on the Nephilim.* Burton Beyond Press, 2009.

Calmet, Augustin. *Dictionary of the Holy Bible.* Boston: Crocker and Brewster, 1832.

Calvin John. *Commentary on the First Book of Moses Called Genesis.* Bellingham, WA: Logos Research Systems, Inc., 2010.

Carpenter, Eugene E. "Deuteronomy." Zondervan Illustrated Bible Backgrounds Commentary (Old Testament): Genesis, Exodus, Leviticus, Numbers, Deuteronomy, vol. 1. Ed. John H Walton. Grand Rapids, MI: Zondervan, 2009.

Carson, D. A. *The Gospel According to John.* Pillar New Testament Commentary. Leicester, England; Grand Rapids, Mich.: Inter-Varsity Press; W.B. Eerdmans, 1991.

_____. "Jude." In *Commentary on the New Testament Use of the Old Testament.* G. K. Beale and D. A. Carson (eds). Grand Rapids, MI; Nottingham, UK: Baker Academic; Apollos, 2007.

Cassuto, Umberto. *A Commentary on the Book of Genesis: From Noah to Abraham.* Jerusalem: Magnes Press, 1964.

Catholic University of America. *Fathers of the Church: A New Translation.* Washington, D.C.: Catholic University of America Press, 1947.

Catlin, George. *The Okipa Ceremony.* Norman, OK: University of Oklahoma, 1958.

Champion, Betty. *Yes We Can Be Perfect Inn Our Generation.* LaGrange, GA: World Overcomer's Church Int., 2002.

Charles, R. H. *A Critical and Exegetical Commentary on the Revelation of St John,* vol. 1. International Critical Commentary. Edinburgh: T&T Clark International, 1920.

Chrysostom. *Homilies on Genesis.*

Clark; Ernest G. *Targum and Scripture: Studies in Aramaic Translations and Interpretation.* Boston: Brill, 2002.

Clarke, Adam. *Commentary on the Bible.* Nashville: Abingdon, 1977.

Clement of Alexandria. Miscellanies.

Clermont-Ganneau, M. I., "24. *Mount Hermon and its God in an inedited Greek Inscription*" [Italics original]. *Palestine Exploration Fund: Quarterly Statement* (London: Harrison and Sons, 1903: 135-40.

Clines, D. J. A. "The Significance of the 'Sons of God' Episode (Genesis 6:1–4) in the Context of the 'Primeval History' (Genesis 1–11)." *Journal for the Study of the Old Testament* 13 (1979): 33-46.

Cody, William F. *An Autobiography of Buffalo Bill.* Aurora, CO: Bibliographical Center for Research, 2009.

Colavito, Jason. "Al-Maorizi on the Pyramids of Egypt." *Jason Colavito* (2012-15).

Cole, R. Dennis. *Numbers.* New American Commentary (Nashville: Broadman & Holman Publishers, 2001.

Collins, John Joseph; Cross, Frank Moore; and Collins, Adela Yarbro. *Daniel : A Commentary on the Book of Daniel.* Hermeneia. Minneapolis: Fortress Press, 1993.

Commentary on the New Testament Use of the Old Testament. Ed. G. K. Beale and D. A. Carson. Grand Rapids, MI; Nottingham, UK: Baker Academic; Apollos, 2007.

Commodian. *The Instructions.*

A Concise Hebrew and Aramaic Lexicon of the Old Testament. Edited by William Lee Holladay, Ludwig Köhler, and Ludwig Köhler. Leiden: Brill, 1971.

Cooper, Lamar Eugene Sr. *Ezekiel.* New American Commentary. Nashville: Broadman and Holman, 1994.

Corcos, Georgette. *The Glory of the Old Testament.* New York: Villard Books, 1984.

Cornwall, Judson. *The Exhaustive Dictionary of Bible Names* (North Brunswick, NJ: Bridge-Logos, 1998.

Craig, Robert D. *Dictionary of Polynesian Mythology.* New York: Greenwood Press, 1989.

Culver, Robert Duncan. *Systematic Theology.* Great Britain: Mentor, 2005.

Curtiss-Wedge, Franklyn. *History of Wright County Minnesota*, vol. 1. Chicago: H. C. Cooper, Jr., & Co., 1915.

Dahood, Mitchell J. "Ebla, Ugarit, and the Bible." In *The Archives of Ebla: An Empire Inscribed in Clay,* ed. G. Pettinato. Garden City, NY: Doubleday, 1981.

———. *Psalms III (101-150).* Anchor Yale Bible. Garden City, NY: Doubleday, 1970.

———. "Ebla, Ugarit, and the Old Testament." *Theology Digest* 27 (1979): 127-31.

Dalton, William J. *Christ's Proclamation to the Spirits: A Study of 1 Peter 3:18-4:6.* Rome: Editrice Pontifico Istituto Biblico, 1989.

David, Gary A. *The Orion Zone: Ancient Star Cities of the American Southwest.* Kempton, IL: Adventures Unlimited Press, 2006.

Davids, Peter H. *The Letters of 2 Peter and Jude*, Pillar New Testament Commentary. Grand Rapids, MI: Eerdmans, 2006.

Dawkins, Richard. *The God Delusion.* Boston: Houghton Mifflin Co., 2006.

Day, John. *God's Conflict with the Dragon and the Sea.* London: Cambridge University Press, 1985.

———. *Yahweh and the Gods and Goddesses of Canaan.* New York: Continuum, 2002.

De Forest, J. W. "The Great Deluge." *Old and New* 6 (July 1872-Jan 1873): 437-48.

de la Vega, Garcilaso. *The Florida of the Inca.* Ed. John and Jeanette Varner. Austin, TX: University of Texas Pres, 1951.

de León, Pedro de Cieza. *The Travels of Pedro de Cieza de Leon, A.D. 1532-50.* Translated by Clements R. Markham. London: Hakluyt Society, 1864.

de Perceval, Caussin. *Essays on the History of the Arabs before Islamism, during the Time of Mohammed, and down to the Reduction of all the Tribes under his Dominion.* 1847.

de Voragine, Jacobus. *The Golden Legend: Readings on the Saints.* Trans. William Granger Ryan. Princeton, NJ: Princeton University Press, 1993.

Deane, John Bathurst. *Worship of the Serpent: Traced Throughout the World.* London: J. G. & F. Rivington, 1883, republished by Forgotten Books, 2008.

Delamarter, Steve. *A Scripture Index to Charlesworth's The Old Testament Pseudepigrapha.* Sheffield: Sheffield Academic Press, 2002.

DeLoach, Charles. *Giants: A Reference Guide from History, the bible, and Recorded Legend.* Metuchen, NJ: Scarecrow Press, 1995.

Diaz, Bernal. *The Conquest of New Spain.* Trans. J. M. Cohen. New York: Penguin, 1963.

Dictionary of Ancient Deities. Eds. Turner, Patricia and Coulter, Charles Russell. New York: Oxford University Press, 2001.

Dictionary of Biblical Imagery. Eds. Ryken, L., Wilhoit, J. C., and Longman III, T. Downers Grove: InterVarsity Press, 1998.

Dictionary of Deities and Demons in the Bible, 2nd extensively revised edition. Eds. van der Toorn, K., Becking, Bob, and van der Horst, Pieter Willem. Boston: Eerdmans, 1999.

A Dictionary of the Ugaritic Language in the Alphabetic Tradition (DULAT). Eds. del Olmo Lete, Gregorio and Sanmartín, Joaquín. Boston: Brill, 2003.

Doedens, Jacob J. T. "The Indecent Descent of the Sethites: The Provenance of the Sethites-Interpretation of Genesis 6:1-4." *Sárospataki Füzetek* 16:3–4 (2012): 47–57. https://www.academia.edu/17793988/The_Indecent_Descent_of_the_Sethites_The_Provenance_of_the_Sethites_Interpretation_of_Genesis_6_1_4.

_____. "The Sons of God in Genesis 6:1-4." Ph.D. Dissertation Theologische Universiteit Kampen (2013). http://theoluniv.ub.rug.nl/32/7/2013Doedens%20Dissertation.pdf.

Douglas, Mary. *Implicit Meanings: Essays in Anthropology.* London: Routledge & Kegan Paul, 1975.

_____. *Purity and Danger: An Analysis of the Concepts of Pollution and Taboo/* London: Routledge & Kegan Paul, 1966.

Dragoo, Don W. *Mounds for the Dead: An Analysis of the Adena Culture.* Carnegie Museum, 1963.

Driver, S. R. & Gray, G. B. *The Book of Job.* ICC; Edinburgh 1921.

Drijvers, H. J. W. *Iconography of Religions.* Leiden, Netherlands: Brill, 1976.

Eaton, J. H. *Psalms.* Torch Bible Commentaries. London: SCM, 1967.

Eckenstein, Lina. *A History of Sinai.* New York, Macmillian Co, 1921.

Edwards, Frank. *Stranger Than Science.* New York: Lyle Stuart, 1959.

Eiseman, Robert H. and Wise, Michael Owen. *The Dead Sea Scrolls Uncovered.* New York: Penguin Books, 1993.

Encyclopaedia Biblica. Eds. Cheyne, T. K. And Black, J. Sutherland. London: Adam and Charles Black, 1899-1902.

Encyclopedia Britannica, vol. 9. Edinburgh: Archibald Constable and Company, 1823.

Erickson, Millard. *Christian Theology.* Grand Rapids, MI: Baker, 1998.

Emslie, John Philipps and Burne, C. S. "Scraps of Folklore Collected." *Folklore* 26:2 (June 30, 1915): 153-170.

Eusebius. *Preparation for the Gospel.*

Fulk, R. D. "The Passion of St. Christopher." In *The Beowulf Manuscript: Complete Texts and the Fight at Finnsburg.* Cambridge, MA: Harvard University Press, 2010.

Feinberg, Charles. *The Prophecy of Ezekiel.* Chicago: Moody Press, 1969.

Findlay, G. G. "St. Paul's First Epistle to the Corinthians." in *The Expositor's Greek Testament.* Ed. W. R. Nicoll. Grand Rapids, Eerdmans, 1961.

Flynn, David. "2012 Year of Resurrection." (2005). https://www.youtube.com/watch?v=t68sCaPAgxQ&ab_channel=dawveed84.

Fortson, Dante. *As The Days of Noah Were.* Impact Agenda Media, 2010.

_____. *The Serpent Seed: Debunked.* Impact Agenda Media, 2010.

Fosdick, Harry Emerson. *A Pilgrimage to Palestine.* New York: Macmillan Publishing Co., 1949.

Frazer, James George. *Folk-Lore in the Old Testament: Studies in Comparative Religion, Legend, and Law,* vol. 1. London: MacMillan and CO., 1919. https://archive.org/stream/folkloreinoldte00frazgoog#page/n398/mode/2up/search/chapter+v.

Frothingham, A. L. "Babylonian Origin of Hermes, the Snake-God, and of the Caduceus." *American Journal of Archaeology* 20: 2nd series, (1916).

Gaddis, Vincent H. *Native American Myths and Mysteries.* Garberville, CA: Borderland Sciences, 1991.

Gage, Warren Austin. *John's Gospel: A Neglected Key to Revelation?* Fort Lauderdale. FL: Warren A. Gage, 2001.

_____. "Revelation Class with Dr. Warren Gage: Lecture 4." *Preterism.org* (March 4, 2020). https://preterism.org/2020/05/26/revelation-warren-gage-gcc-class-04/.

_____. *There Is No Greater Love: How Jesus Is Greater than All Who Came before Him.* Fort Lauderdale: St. Andrews House, 2013.

Gardner, James. *The War With Babylon.* Xulon Press, 2004.

Garnier, John. *The Worship of the Dead: The Origin and Nature of Pagan Idolatry.* London: Chapman & Hall, 1904.

Gaster, Theodore H. *Myth, Legend and Custom in the Old Testament.* New York: Harper and Row, 1969.

Gentry, Kenneth L. Jr. *The Divorce of Israel: A Redemptive-Historical Interpretation of Revelation.* Dallas, GE: Tolle Lege Press, forthcoming.

Gesenius' Hebrew and Chaldee Lexicon to the Old Testament Scriptures. Eds. Wilhelm Gesenius and Samuel Prideaux Tregelles. Bellingham, WA: Logos Research Systems, Inc, 2003.

Gilgamesh Epic.

Gimbutas, Marija. "The Kurgan Culture and the Indo-Europeanization of Europe: Selected Articles from 1952 to 1993." Edited by Miriam Robbins Dexter and Karlene

Jones-Bley. *Journal of Indo-European Studies Monograph No. 18.* Washington, D.C.: Institute for the Study of Man, 1997: xix + 404 pages.

Gille, Oliver. "Cerne Abbas Giant May Have Held Severed Head." *The Independent.* London, England, Saturday, May 21, 1994.

Ginzberg, Louis. *Legends of the Jews.* ForgottenBooks, 1909, 2008.

Godawa, Brian. *David Ascendant: Chronicles of the Nephilim Book Seven, special limited hardback edition.* Los Angeles: Embedded Pictures, 2014.

_____. *Jesus Triumphant.* Chronicles of the Nephilim Book 8. Los Angeles: Embedded Pictures Publishing, 2015.

_____. *When Giants Were Upon the Earth: The Watchers, the Nephilim, and the Biblical Cosmic War of the Seed.* TX: Warrior Poet Publishing, 2014, 2021.

Goff, Matthew J. "Ben Sira and the Giants of the Land: A Note on Ben Sira 16:7." *Journal of Biblical Literature* 129.4 (Winter 2010): 645-55.

_____. "Monstrous Appetites: Giants, Cannibalism, and Insatiable Eating in Enochic Literature," *Journal of Ancient Judaism* 1 (2010): 19-42.

González, Justo L. "Demythologization," in *Essential Theological Terms* (Louisville, KY: Westminster John Knox Press, 2005.

Goodrich, Samuel G. *A History of All Nations, From the Earliest Periods to the Present Time.* New York: Miller, Orton, and Mulligan, 1855.

Gordon, Cyrus. "אלהים (Elohim) in Its Reputed Meaning of *Rulers, Judges.*" *Journal of Biblical Literature* 54 (1935): 139–144.

Gould, George Milbry and Pyle, Walter Lytle. *Anomalies and Curiosities of Medicine.* Philadelphia: W.B. Saunders, 1901.

Gray, Jonathan. *Lost World of the Giants.* Brushton, NY: TEACH Services, Inc. 2006.

Gilbert, Derek P. *Bad Moon Rising.* Crane, MO: Defender Publishing, 2019.

_____. *The Second Coming of Saturn.* Crane, MO: Defender Publishing, 2022.

Green, Gene L. *Jude & 2 Peter.* Baker Exegetical Commentary on the New Testament. Grand Rapids, MI: Baker Academic, 2008.

Green, Michael. *2 Peter and Jude,* Tyndale New Testament Commentaries. Downers Grove, IL: InterVarsity, 1987.

A Greek-English Lexicon of the Septuagint : Revised Edition. Eds. Johan Lust, Erik Eynikel and Katrin Hauspie. Deutsche Bibelgesellschaft: Stuttgart, 2003.

Gressmann, H. *Der Messias.* FRLANT 6. Göttingen: Vandenhoeck & Ruprecht, 1929.

Gunkel, H. *Genesis.* Göttingen, 1910.

Hallo William W. and Younger, K. Lawson. *Context of Scripture.* Leiden; Boston: Brill, 2003.

Hamilton Jr., James M. *God's Indwelling Presence: The Holy Spirit in the Old & New Testaments.* Nashville, TN: B&H Academic, 2006.

Hamilton, Victor P. *The Book of Genesis: Chapters 1-17.* The New International Commentary on the Old Testament. Grand Rapids, MI: Wm. B. Eerdmans Publishing Co., 1990.

Hancock, Graham. *Fingerprints of the Gods*. New York: Three Rivers Press, 1995.

_____, *Heaven's Mirror: Quest for the Lost Civilization*. New York: Crown Publishers, 1998.

Hansen, Taylor L. *The Ancient Atlantic*. Wisconsin, Amherst Press, 1969.

Hart, George. *Egyptian Myths*. Austin, TX: University of Texas Press, 1990.

Hart, Gerald D. "The Earliest Medical Use of the Caduceus." *C.M.A. Journal* 107 (Dec 9, 1972): 1107-1110.

Hartley, John E. *The Book of Job*. The New International Commentary on the Old Testament. Grand Rapids, MI: Wm. B. Eerdmans Publishing Co., 1988.

Hayes, Lyman Simpson. *History of the Town of Rockingham, Vermont*. Bellow Falls, VT: The Town, 1907.

Hayward, Robert. "The Priestly Blessing in Targum Pseudo-Jonathan." *Journal for the Study of the Pseudepigrapha* 10 (April 1999): 81-101.

Haywood, John. *The Natural and Aboriginal History of Tennessee: Up to the First Settlement Therein by the White People in the Year 1768*. Kingsport, TN: F.M. Hill-Books, 1973.

Hays, J. Daniel "Reconsidering The Height Of Goliath." *JETS* 48.4 (2005): 701-714.

_____, "The Height Of Goliath: A Response To Clyde Billington." *JETS* 50.3 (2007): 509-16.

The Hebrew and Aramaic Lexicon of the Old Testament. Ed. Ludwig Koehler et al. Leiden: E.J. Brill, 1994–2000.

Heiser, Michael S. *The Bible Code Myth*. Acid Test Press, 2001.

_____, "Clash of the Manuscripts: Goliath & the Hebrew Text of the Old Testament." *Bible Study Magazine* 1:4 (May-June, 2009): 33-35: http://www.biblestudymagazine.com/interactive/goliath/.

_____. "Deuteronomy 32:8 and the Sons of God." *Bibliotheca Sacra* 158:629 (Jan-Mar, 2001): 52-74.

_____. "The Divine Council in Late Canonical and Non-Canonical Second Temple Jewish Literature." A Dissertation at the University of Wisconsin-Madison, 2004.

_____, "The Divine Council in the New Testament: The Archons." *Behind the Façade* 3:9 (Feb 2005): 32-34.

_____,*The Myth That Is True*. Unpublished. Available to purchase at: http://www.michaelsheiser.com/

_____, "The Nachash and his Seed: Some Explanatory Notes on Why the 'Serpent' in Genesis 3 Wasn't a Serpent." http://www.thedivinecouncil.com/nachashnotes.pdf.

_____. "Naked Bible Podcast 152, 153 – The Gog Magog Invasion | Ezekiel 38-39," *Youtube* (May 12, 2018). Also with Transcript. https://nakedbiblepodcast.com/wp-content/uploads/2017/04/NB-152-Transcript.pdf.

_____. *Reversing Hermon*. Crane, MO: Defender Pub, 2017.

_____. "Serpentine / Reptilian Divine Beings in the Hebrew Bible: A Preliminary Investigation." http://www.scribd.com/doc/63497725/Michael-s-Heiser-Serpentine.

_____. *The Unseen Realm: Recovering the Supernatural Worldview of the Bible*. Bellingham, WA: Lexham Press, 2015.

_____. "You've Seen One Elohim, You've Seen Them All? A Critique of Mormonism's Use of Psalm 82," *FARMS Review* 19/1 (2007): 221–266.

Hemati, Russell. "Demons, Idols, and Faith." *The Good, the True, the Beautiful: A Multidisciplinary Tribute to David K. Naugle*. Ed. Mark J. Boone et al. Eugene, OR: Pickwick, 2021.

Hendel, Ronald S. "Biblical Views: Giants at Jericho." *Biblical Archaeological Research* 35:02 (Mar/Apr 2009).

_____. "Of Demigods and the Deluge: Toward an Interpretation of Genesis 6:1–4." *Journal of Biblical Literature* 106 (1987): 13-26.

Hendriksen, William. *More Than Conquerors*. Grand Rapids: Baker, 1961.

Herm, Gerhard. *The Celts*. New York: St. Martin's Press, 1975.

Heron, Patrick. *The Nephilim and the Pyramid of the Apocalypse*. New York, NY: Citadel Press, 2004.

Hesiod. *The Works and Days*. Trans. Richmond Lattimore. Ann Arbor: University of Michigan, 1959.

Hibbert Trust. *The Hibbert Lectures*. Cambridge: Cambridge University Press, 1896-1929.

Hine, Charles Gilbert. *The Story of Martha's Vineyard*. New York: Hine Brothers, 1908.

Hitchcock, Roswell D. *Hitchcock's Complete Analysis of the Holy Bible*. New York: A. J. Johnson, 1874.

Hocking, Paul. *A New and Living Way*. Dissertation to the University of Chester. Amazon, 2021..

Hoehner, H. W. "The Duration of the Egyptian Bondage." *Bibliotheca Sacra Volume* 126:504 (1969): 306-16.

Hoekema, Anthony A. "Amillennialism." *The Meaning of the Millennium: Four Views*. Ed. Robert G. Clouse. Downers Grove, IL: InterVarsity, 1977: 155-87.

Homer. *The Odyssey*.

Horn, Thomas R. "PART 18 — Forbidden Gates: How Genetics, Robotics, Artificial Intelligence3, Synthetic Biology, Nanotechnology, & Human Enhancement Herald the Dawn of Techno-Dimensional Spiritual Warfare." *Defender Publishing* (Oct 5, 2010).

_____. "Transhumanism & the Human Enhancement revolution." *ISN* (Mar 7, 2020).

_____. *Zenith 2016: The Revised & Expanded Edition of Apollyon Rising 2012*. Crane, MO: Defender, 2013.

Horn, Thomas and Peck, Josh. *Abaddon Ascending: The Ancient Conspiracy at the Center of CERN's Most Secretive Mission*. Crane, MO: Defender, 2016.

Howe, Henry. *The Historical Collections of Ohio*. Cincinnati, OH: Pub by the state of Ohio, 1902.

Hutter, Bonn Manfred. "Demons and Benevolent Spirits in the Ancient New East: A Phenomenological Overview." *Angels: The Concept of Celestial Beings – Origins*,

Development and Reception, Yearbook 2007. Ed. Friedrich V. Reiterer, Tobias Nicklas, Karin Schöpflin. New York, de Gruyter, 2007: 23-34.

Irenaeus. *Demonstration of the Apostolic Preaching.*

_____. *Against Heresies.*

Jacobsen, Thorkild. *The Harps That Once ... Sumerian Poetry in Translation.* New Haven/London: Yale University Press, 1987.

Jeremias, J. *Heiligengräber in Jesu Umwelt.* Göttingen, 1958.

Jerome. *Hebrew Questions on Genesis.*

Jewish Encyclopedia. Ed. Isidore Singer and Cyrus Adler. New York: Funk and Wagnalls, 1912.

Johnson, Dennis. *Triumph of the* Lamb: *A Commentary on Revelation.* Phillipsburg, NJ: P&R, 2001.

Johnson, Robert Bowie Jr. *Athena and Eden.* Annapolis, MD: Solving Light Books, 2002.

_____. *Athena and Cain.* Annapolis, MD: Solving Light Books, 2003.

_____. *The Parthenon Code.* Annapolis, MD: Solving Light Books, 2004.

_____. *Noah in Ancient Greek Art.* Annapolis, MD: Solving Light Books, 2007.

Johnson, Ronn. "The Old Testament Background for Paul's Use of 'Principalities and Powers.'" A Dissertation to Dallas Theological Seminary, 2004.

Joines, Karen. *Serpent Symbolism in the Old Testament: A Linguistic, Archaeological, and Literary Study.* Haddonfield House, New Jersey, 1974.

Joseph, Frank. *Advanced Civilizations of Prehistoric America.* Rochester, VT: Bear & Company, 2010.

_____. *The Atlantis Encyclopedia.* Franklin Lakes, NJ: The Career Press, 205.

_____.*Atlantis in Wisconsin: New Revelations About The Lost Sunken City.* St. Paul, MN, Galde Press, 1995.

_____.*The Destruction of Atlantis* (Rochester, VT: Bear & Company, 2002.

Josephus. *Antiquities of the Jews.*

Justin Martyr. *First Apology.*

Kayser, Phillip G. "The Last Rebellion: Revelation 20:7-10." *Biblical Blueprints* (8-26-2018). https://kaysercommentary.com/Sermons/New%20Testament/Revelation/Revelation%2020/Revelation%2020_7-10.md#fnref7.

Keener, C. S. *The Gospel of John* 2 vols. Peabody, Mass: Hendrickson.

Keil, Carl Friedrich and Delitzsch, Franz. *Commentary on the Old Testament.* Peabody, MA: Hendrickson, 2002.

Keyssler, Johann Georg. *Travels through Germany, Bohemia, Hungary, Switzerland, Italy, and Lorrain.* London, G. Keith, 1760.

Kline, Meredith G. "Divine Kingship and Genesis 6:1-4." *Westminster Theological Journal* 24.2 (1962): 187-204.

_____. *Kingdom Prologue.* Overland Park, KS: Two Age Press, 2000.

Kline, Moshe. *Before Chapter and Verse.* (2022).

Koch, John T. *Celtic Culture: A Historical Encyclopedia.* Santa Barbara, CA, 2006.

Koenigsberg, Zvi. "Gilgal: YHWH's Footprints in the Land of Israel." *TheTorah.com*.

Köstenberger, Andreas J. *John*. Baker exegetical commentary on the New Testament. Grand Rapids, Mich.: Baker Academic, 2004.

Kraeling, E. "The Significance and Origin of Gen. 6:1-4." *Journal of Near Eastern Studies* 6 (1947): 193-208.

Krodel, Gerhard A. *Revelation*. Augsburg Commentary on the New Testament. Minneapolis, MN: Augsburg Publishing House, 1989.

Lactantius. *Divine Institutes*.

Landa, Gertrude. *Jewish Fairy Tales and Legends*. New York: Bloch, 1919.

Lipinski, E. "El's Abode. Mythological Traditions Related to Mount Hermon." *Orientalia Lovaniensia Periodica* 2 (1971): 15-41.

Layton, Scott C. "Remarks on the Canaanite Origin of Eve." *Catholic Biblical Quarterly* 59 (1997): 22-32.

Lenormant, François. *A Manual of the Ancient History of the East to the Commencement of the Median Wars*. Trans. E. Chavallier. Philadelphia: Lippincott & Co., 1870-71.

Lewis, C. S. "Autobiography: The Letters of C.S. Lewis to Arthur Greeves." In *The Essential C.S. Lewis*. Ed. Lyle W. Dorsett. New York: Touchstone, 1996.

A Lexicon : Abridged from Liddell and Scott's Greek-English Lexicon. Ed. H. G. Liddell. Oak Harbor, WA: Logos Research Systems, Inc., 1996.

Life of Adam and Eve.

Lindquist, Maria. "King Og's Iron Bed." *Catholic Biblical Quarterly* 73:3 (July 2011): 477-492.

Livingstone, David. *Missionary Travels*. London: Ward Lock, 1910.

Luther, Martin. *Luther's Works*. Ed. Jaroslav Jan Pelikan, Hilton C. Oswald and Helmut T. Lehmann. Saint Louis: Concordia Publishing House, 1999.

Mac Firbis, Duald. *On the Fomorians and the Norsemen*. Christiania: J.C. Gundersens Bogtrykkeri, 1905.

MacCulloch, John Arnott. *The Religion of the Ancient Celts*. New York: Dover Publications, 2003.

Maeir, A. M., Wimmer, S. J., Zukerman, A., and Demsky, A., "A Late Iron Age I/early Iron Age IIA Old Canaanite Inscription from Tell es-Sâfi/Gath, Israel: Palaeography, Dating, and Historical-Cultural Significance." BULLETIN OF THE AMERICAN SCHOOLS OF ORIENTAL RESEARCH 351 (Aug 2008): 39–71.

Marshall, Richard. *Mysteries of the Unexplained*. Pleasantville, NY: The Reader's Digest Association, 1983.

Martin, Dale Basil. "When Did Angels Become Demons." *Journal of Biblical Literature* 129.4 (Winter 2010): 657-77.

Mathews, K. A. *Genesis 1-11:26*. The New American Commentary. Nashville: Broadman & Holman Publishers, 2001.

Martínez, Florentino García and Tigchelaar, Eibert J. C. *The Dead Sea Scrolls Study Edition (Transcriptions and Translations)*. Leiden; New York: Brill, 1997-1998.

Mayor, Adrienne. *Fossil Legends of the First Americans.* Princeton, NJ: Princeton University Press, 2005.

___. "Giants in Ancient Warfare." *MHQ: The Quarterly Journal of Military History* 2.2 (Winter 1999): 98-105.

_____. *The First Fossil Hunters: Paleontology in Greek and Roman Times.* Princeton, NJ: Princeton University Press, 2001.

McNally, Raymond T. *In Search of Dracula: The History of Dracula and Vampires Completely Revised.* Boston: Mifflin, 1994.

Meyer, A. W. *Critical and Exegetical Handbook to the Epistles to the Corinthians.* Edinburgh: T. & T. Clark, 1892.

Michaels, Ramsey J. *1 Peter.* Word Biblical Commentary. Dallas: Word, 2002.

Millard, A. R. "A New Babylonian 'Genesis' Story." *Tyndale Bulletin* 18 (1967): 3-18.

_____. "King Og's Bed and Other Ancient Ironmongery." In *Ascribe to the Lord. Biblical and other studies in memory of Peter C. Craigie.* Eds. L. Eslinger & G. Taylor). JSOT Sup 67; Sheffield 1988: 481–492.

Minets, Yuliya. *The Slow Fall of Babel: Languages and Identities in Late Antique Christianity.* Alabama: Cambridge University Press, 2022.

Missler, Chuck. "Meanings of the Names in Genesis 5." *Koinonia House* (Aug 1, 2000).

Chuck Missler, "The Return of the Nephilim? 'And Also After That'." *Koinonia House* (Sept 1, 1997).

Mobley, Gregory. "The Wild Man in the Bible and the Ancient Near East." *Journal of Biblical Literature* 116 (1997): 217-33.

_____. *Samson and the Liminal Hero in the Ancient Near East.* New York: T&T Clark, 2006.

Moo, Douglas J. *2 Peter, Jude.* NIV Application Commentary. Grand Rapids, MI: Zondervan, 1996.

Mott, Maryann. "Animal-Human Hybrids Spark Controversy." *National Geographic* (Jan 25, 2005).

Mounce, Robert H. *The Book of Revelation.* The New International Commentary on the New Testament. Grand Rapids, MI: Wm. B. Eerdmans Publishing Co., 1997.

Muller, Jon. *Archaeology of the Lower Ohio River Valley.* Walnut Creek, CA: Left Coast Press, 2009.

Murray, John. *Principles of Conduct.* Grand Rapids: Wm. B. Eerdmans, 1957.

Newman, Robert C. "The Ancient Exegesis of Genesis 6:2, 4." *Grace Theological Journal* 5.1 (1984): 13-36.

Nickelsburg George W. E., and Baltzer, Klaus. *1 Enoch : A Commentary on the Book of 1 Enoch.* Minneapolis, Minn.: Fortress, 2001.

Norvill, Roy. *Giants: The Vanished Race.* Wellingborough, UK: Aquarian Press, 1979.

Oesterle, Joe and Cridland, Tim. *Weird Las Vegas and Nevada.* New York: Sterling Publishing Co., 2007.

Old Testament Pseudepigrapha (2 vols). Ed. James H. Charlesworth. New York: Yale University Press, 1983.

Olmo, H. P. "Giant-Berry Grapes: Principles of Genetics Employed to Propagate Varieties Producing Berries of Larger Size." *California Agriculture* Vol. 4 No. 6 (1950): 5-13.

Orchard, Andy. *Pride and Prodigies: Studies in the Monsters of the Beowulf-manuscript*. Rochester, NY: D.S. Brewer, 1995.

Osborne, Grant R. *Revelation*. Baker Exegetical Commentary on the New Testament. Grand Rapids, Mich.: Baker Academic, 2002.

Palestine Pilgrims' Text Society. *The Library of the Palestine Pilgrims' Text Society*. London: Committee of the Palestine Exploration Fund, 1885.

Patai, Raphael. *Arab Folktales from Palestine and Israel*. Detroit, MI: Wayne State University Press, 1998.

Peet, Stephen D. (ed). *American Antiquarian and Oriental Journal* 6:2 (March 1884): 133-34.

_____. "The Mound-Builders," in *History of Astabula Co., Ohio*. Ed. William W. Williams. Philadelphia: Williams Bros., 1878): 16-20.

Pezron, Paul. *The Antiquities of Nations; More Particularly of the Celte or Gauls*. Trans. Mr. D. Jones. London: R. Janeway, 1706.

Pink, Arthur W. *Gleanings in Genesis*. Bellingham, WA: Logos Research Systems, Inc., 2005.

Phillips, Douglas. "The Mystery of the Nephilim Presented and Solved: Discovering the True Giants of Paganism." In *Mysteries of the Ancient World*, an audio series. San Antonio, TX: Vision Forum, 2008.

Pigafetta, Antonio *The Voyage of Magellan*. London: Yale University Press, 1969.

Pitterson, Ryan. *Judgment of the Nephilim*. NY: Days of Noe Publishing, 2017.

Porter, Josias Leslie. *The Giant Cities of Bashan; and Syria's Holy Places*. New York: Thomas Nelson, 1884.

Poythress, Vern. *The Returning King*. Phillipsburg, NJ: P&R, 2000.

Preisendanz, Karl. "Nimrod." In *Pauly, Wissowa and Kroll, Real-Encyclopädie* 17 (1936): 624-27.

Priest, Josiah. *American Antiquities and Discoveries in the West*. Albany, NY: Hoffman & White, 1833.

Pseudo Clement. *Homilies*.

_____. *Recognitions*.

Quayle, Stephen. *Genesis 6 Giants*. Bozeman, MT: End Time Thunder Publishers, 2002.

Quayle, Stephen and Long, Duncan. *Longwalkers*. Bozeman, MT: End Times Thunder Publishers, 2008.

Readers Digest Association. *The World's Last Mysteries*. Montreal: Reader's Digest, 1978.

Reeves, John C. *Jewish Lore in Manichaean Cosmogony: Studies in the Book of Giants Traditions*. Cincinnati: Hebrew Union College Press, 1992.

Renihan, Samuel D. Crux, *Mors, Inferi: A Primer and Reader on the Descent of Christ*. Independently Published, 2021.

Reymond, Robert L. *A New Systematic Theology of the Christian Faith*. Nashville: Thomas Nelson, 1998.

Riesner, Rainer. "Bethany Beyond The Jordan (John 1:28) Topography, Theology And History In The Fourth Gospel." *Tyndale Bulletin* 38 (1987): 29–63.

Riggs, J. R. "The Length of Israel's Sojourn in Egypt." *Grace Theological Journal* 12 (1971): 18-35.

Rissi, Mathias. *The Future of the World: An Exegetical Study of Revelation 19.11-22.15*. Studies in Biblical Theology, Second Series 23. Napierville, IL: Allenson, 1972.

Roberts, A., Donaldson, J., Coxe, A. C., and Menzies, A. *The Ante-Nicene Fathers* in 10 volumes. Buffalo: Christian Literature, 1886.

Rodgers, Adam. "Early Nevada History is Traced in Lovelock, Cave, Tomb of the Forgotten Race." *Ancient American* 13:81 (Dec 2008): 32-35.

Rose, Carol. *Giants, Monsters, and Dragons: An Encyclopedia of Folklore, Legend, and Myth*. New York: W.W. Norton & Company Inc. 2000.

Ross, Allen P. "Studies in the Book of Genesis - Part 2: The Table of Nations in Genesis 10 - its Structure." *BibSac* 137:548 (Oct-Dec 1980): 340-50.

Rutherford, Mac. *Historic Haunts of Winchester*. Charleston, SC: Haunted America, 2007.

Sandison, A. T., and Wells, C. "Endocrine Diseases." In *Diseases in Antiquity*, eds. Don Brothwell and A. T. Sandison, 521-31. Springfield, IL: Charles C. Thomas, 1967.

Sanger, Laura. *The Roots of the Federal Reserve: Tracing the Nephilim from Noah to the US Dollar*. Dallas, TX: Relentlessly Creative Books, 2020.

Sarna, Nahum M. *Genesis*. The JPS Torah Commentary. Philadelphia: Jewish Publication Society, 1989.

Sayce, A. H. "The White Race of Palestine." *Nature* 38:979 (Aug 2, 1888): 321-23.

Schaeffer, Francis. "Genesis in Space and Time." In *The Complete Works of Francis A. Schaeffer: A Christian Worldview*. Westchester, IL: Crossway Books, 1996.

Schaff, Philip *The Nicene and Post-Nicene Fathers Vol. II*. Oak Harbor: Logos Research Systems, 1997).

Schreiner, Thomas R. *1, 2 Peter, Jude*. New American Commentary. Nashville, TN: Broadman & Holman, 2003.

Segal, Alan. *Two Powers in Heaven: Early Rabbinic Reports about Christianity and Gnosticism*. Boston, Brill Academic Pub, 2002.

Sulpicius Severus. History.

Setzler, Frank M. and Marshall, George C. "Giant Effigies of the Southwest." *National Geographic* (Sept. 1952): 389-404.

Sheldon, George. *History of Deerfield*, vol. 1. MA: Pioneer Valley Memorial Museum, 1895.

Sherman, Phillip Michael. *Babel's Tower Translated: Genesis 11 and Ancient Jewish Interpretation*. Boston: Brill, 2013.

Skinner, John. *A Critical and Exegetical Commentary on Genesis*, International Critical Commentary. New York: Scribner, 1910.

Smith, Evans Lansing and Brown, Nathan Robert. *The Complete Idiot's Guide to World Mythology*. Indianapolis, IN: Alpha Books, 2008.

Smith, J. V. C. (M.D.), Morland, W. W. (M.D.), and Minot, Francis (M.D.). *Boston Medical and Surgical Journal*. Volume LIII. Boston: David Clapp, 1856.

Smith, John. *Captain John Smith's America; selections from his writings*. Ed. John Lankford. New York: Harper & Row, 1967.

Smith, William G. *A Dictionary of the Bible: Comprising Its Antiquities, Biography, and Natural History in 3 Vols*. Boston: Little Brown, 1863.

Spence, Lewis. *The Myths of the North American Indians*. New York: Dover, 1989.

Stigers, Harold G. *A Commentary on Genesis*. Grand Rapids: Zondervan, 1967.

Strelan, Rick. "The Fallen Watchers and the Disciples in Mark." *Journal for the Study of the Pseudepigrapha* 10 (Oct 1999): 73-92.

Tanner, J. Paul. "Daniel's 'King of the North': Do We Owe Russia an Apology?" *Journal of the Evangelical Theological Society* 35.3 (Sept 1992): 315-28.

Tellinger, Michael. "Ancient Artifacts, Mud Fossils and Giants." *African Dream* (2022), https://www.youtube.com/watch?v=wZoki697b3w&ab_channel=AfricanDream.

_____. "Ancient Giant Footprint South Africa Jan 2012 Michael Tellinger Klaus Dona (1 or 2)," *The Truth Channel* (Jan 2012), https://www.youtube.com/watch?v=2HAcsdQGU8E&ab_channel=TheTruth-Channel.

Terrien, Samuel L. *The Psalms: Strophic Structure and Theological Commentary*. Grand Rapids, MI: Eerdmans, 2003.

Tertullian. *Against Marcion*.

_____. *On Idolatry*.

_____. *The Veiling of Virgins*.

Theodoret. *Questions on Genesis*.

Thielman, Frank S. "Ephesians." Commentary *on the New Testament Use of the Old Testament*. Ed. G. K. Beale and D. A. Carson. Grand Rapids, MI; Nottingham, UK: Baker Academic; Apollos, 2007.

Thiselton, Anthony C. *The First Epistle to the Corinthians : A Commentary on the Greek Text*. Grand Rapids, Mich.: W.B. Eerdmans, 2000.

Tompkins, Peter. *Mysteries of the Mexican Pyramids*. New York: Harper Collins, 1987.

Thompson, R. Campbell. *The Devils and Evil Spirits of Babylonia: Being Babylonian and Assyrian Incantations Against the Demons, Ghouls, Vampires, Hobgoblins, Ghosts, and Kindred Evil Spirits, Which Attach Mankind*. Forgotten Books, originally published 1903.

Thomson, C. J. S. *The Mystery and Lore of Monsters*. New York: Bell, 1968.

Tigay, Jeffrey H. *Deuteronomy*. Philadelphia: Jewish Publication Society, 1996.

Tompkins, Peter. *Mysteries of the Mexican Pyramids*. New York: Harper Collins, 1987.

Tolkien, J. R. R. "A Letter to Milton Waldman." Reprinted in *The Simarillion*. New York: Houghton Mifflin Co, 2001.

———. *The Tolkien Reader* (New York: Del Rey, 1968)

Tooman, William A. *Gog of Magog*. Forschungen zum Alten Testament 2. Reihe 52. Tübingen: Mohr Siebeck, 2011.

Unger, Merrill F. "The Old Testament Revelation Concerning Eternity Past." *Bibliotheca Sacra* 114:454 (Apr '57): 135-41.

van Binsbergen, Wim. "The Heroes in Flood Myths Worldwide." Leiden: Erasmus University Rotterdam, 2010. http://www.shikanda.net/topicalities/binsbergen_flood_heroes.pdf

van der Kooij, Arie. "Peshitta Genesis 6: 'Sons of God' – Angels of Judges?'. *Journal of Northwest Semitic Languages* 23/1 (1997): 43-51.

van der Toorn, K. and van der Horst, P. W. "Nimrod Before And After The Bible." *Harvard Theological Review* 83:1 (1990): 1-29.

van Dijk, J. *LUGAL UD ME-LÁM-bi NIR-GÁL Le récit épique et didactique des Travaux de Ninurta, du Déluge et de la Nouvelle Création in 2* vols. Leiden: Brill, 1983.

Van Dorn, Douglas. "An Introduction to the Millennium," *RBCNC.com* (8-29-2021), https://www.rbcnc.com/revelation.

———. *Daniel Series*. RBCNC.com/Daniel.

———. "God is Our Salvation: The Rider of the Clouds and the Freeing of the Captives at the Gates of Hell." *RBCNC.com* (7-9-2017).

———. *Revelation Series*. RBCNC.com/Revelation.

Van Dorn, Douglas and Foreman, Matt. T*he Angel of the LORD: A Biblical, Historical, and Theological Study*. Dacono, CO: Waters of Creation Pub., 2020.

van Gemeren, W. A. "The Sons of God in Genesis 6:1–4 (An Example of Evangelical Demythologization?)." *Westminster Theological Journal* 43 (1981): 320-348.

van Hoonacker, A. "Eléments sumériens dans le livre d'Ezéchiel"? *Zeitschrift für Assyriologie* 28 (1914): 333-36.

VanDrunen, David. *Living in God's Two Kingdoms*. Wheaton, IL: Crossway, 2010.

Walton, John. *Covenant: God's Purpose, God's Plan*. Grand Rapids, MI: Zondervan, 1994.

———. "The Mesopotamian Background of the Tower of Babel Account and Its Implications." *Bulletin for Biblical Research* 5 (1995): 155-75.

Warren, Charles. "Summit of Hermon." *Palestine Exploration Fund, Quarterly Statement* 5 (1870): 210-44. https://biblicalstudies.org.uk/pdf/pefqs/1869-71_210.pdf.

Watts, John D. W. *Isaiah 34-66*. Word Biblical Commentary. Dallas: Word, Incorporated, 2002.

Way, Kenneth C. "Giants in the Land: A Textual and Semantic Study of Giants in the Bible and the Ancient Near East." A Thesis. Deerfield, IL: Trinity International University, 2000.

Webb, Robert L. "The Use of 'Story' in the Letter of Jude: Rhetorical Strategies of Jude's Narrative Episodes." *Journal for the Study of the New Testament* 31 (2008): 53-87.

Weston, Thomas. *History of the Town of Middleboro, Massachusetts*. Boston: Houghton, Mifflin and Company, 1906.

Wevers, John William. *Genesis*. Vetus Testamentum Graecum. Auctoritate Academiae Scientiarum Gottingensis Editum. Göttingen: Vandenhoeck & Ruprecht, 1974.

Wenham, Gordon J. *Genesis 1-15*. Word Biblical Commentary. Dallas: Word, Incorporated, 2002.

Wickham, L. R. "The Sons of God and the Daughters of Men: Genesis VI 2 in Early Christian Exegesis." In *Language and Meaning: Studies in Hebrew Language and Biblical Exegesis*. Ed. James Barr, 135-47. Leiden: Brill, 1974.

Wilkins, William Joseph. *Hindu Mythology, Vedic and Purānic*. London: Thacker & Co., 1882.

Winchell, N. H. and Brower, Jacob V. *1906-1911 The Aborigines of Minnesota: A Report based on the Collections of Jacob V. Brower, and on the Field Surveys and Notes of Alfred J. Hill and Theodore H. Lewis*. Minnesota Historical Society, 1911.

Winnemucca Hopkins, Sarah. *Life Among the Paiutes*. Boston: Cupples, Upham & CO., 1883.

Winship, George Parker (translator). *The Coronado Expedition: 1540-1542*. Washington: Government Printing Office, 1896.

Wiseman, Donald J. "Medicine in the Old Testament World." In *Medicine and the Bible*, ed. B. Palmer, 13-42. Exeter: Paternoster Press, 1986.

Wood, Edward J. *Giants and Dwarfs*. London: Bentley, 1868.

Wood, Leon. *A Survey of Israel's History*. Grand Rapids, MI: Zondervan Publishing House, 1970.

Woolley, Leonard. *The Sumerians*. New York: W.W. Norton, 1965.

Worcester, Elwood. *The Book of Genesis in Light of Modern Knowledge*. New York: McClure, Phillips & Co., 1901.

Wright, Archie T. *The Origin of Evil Spirits: The Reception of Genesis 6:1-4 in Early Jewish Literature*. Tübingen: Mohr Siebeck, 2004.

Wright, G. Ernest. "Troglodytes and Giants in Palestine." *Journal of Biblical Literature* 57:3 (Sept 1938): 305-309.

Wyatt, N. *Religious Texts from Ugarit*, 2nd ed., Biblical seminar, 53. New York: Sheffield Academic Press, 2002.

The Wycliffe Bible Encyclopedia. Eds. Charles F. Pfeiffer, Howard Frederic Vos, and John Rea. Chicago: Moody Press, 1972.

Yamauchi, Edwin. *Foes From the Northern Frontier*. Eugene, OR: Wipf & Stock, 2003.

Young, Gordon Douglas. *Ugarit in Retrospect*. Winona Lake, IN: Eisenbrauns, 1981.

Zimmerli, Walther. *Ezekiel 2: A Commentary on the Book of Ezekiel, Chapters 25-48*. Hermeneia. Philadelphia: Fortress Press, 1983.

Zondervan Illustrated Bible Backgrounds Commentary (Old Testament) Vol. 1: Genesis-Deuteronomy. Ed. John H. Walton. Grand Rapids, MI: Zondervan, 2009.

ABOUT DOUG VAN DORN

Doug Van Dorn has pastored the Reformed Baptist Church of Northern Colorado since 2001. He graduated from Bethel College in 1992, majoring in Marketing and minoring in Bible. He was a youth pastor for four years in Denver. He holds the Master of Divinity degree from Denver Seminary (2001).

Doug has served on councils and boards for two Baptist Associations, the current one which he helped found in 2016. The Reformed Baptist Network seeks to glorify God through fellowship and cooperation in fulfilling the Great Commission to the ends of the earth. There are currently 55 churches in this international association of churches.

Doug has co-hosted the radio show *Journey's End*, the *Peeranormal* and *Iron and Myth* podcasts, started the Waters of Creation Publishing Company, owned two other small businesses, and has appeared on numerous podcasts, radio, and television shows.

Married since 1994, he and Janelle are the proud parents of four beautiful young girls. Born and raised in Colorado, he has climbed all 54 of Colorado's 14,000 ft. mountains and also Mt. Rainier (WA) and Mt. Shasta (CA).

To find out more about any of these things go to:
https://www.douglasvandorn.com/

The Church website is
https://rbcnc.com

Books in the Christ In All Scripture Series

(the supplement series to this book)

John Owen's treatment is perfect for those wanting to ground their theology of the Angel in the high orthodoxy of the Reformation. The quotations from the Fathers bolster his thesis.

Peter Allix's work is comprehensive and is especially helpful for those familiar with modern scholarship wishing to root their theology in conservative Protestant/Reformed orthodoxy.

Gerard De Gols' study, especially the second half, is imminently practical and would help anyone wanting to learn more about why it matters that Christ is present in the Old Testament.

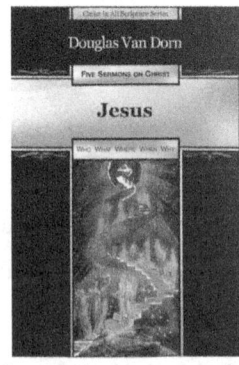

Owen, Allix, & De Gols. The full texts together in one volume, minus quotations from the Fathers and Reformers.

The Second Edition of *From the Shadows to the Savior*, it explores even more of the titles given to Christ in the OT than Allix goes into.

Practical sermons are for the further exploration of the fullness of Christ, especially as he is found in the New Testament. (forthcoming)

Other Books by Doug Van Dorn

Giants: Sons of the gods (2013)

The bestselling non-fiction book on
Genesis 6 and the Nephilim.
350 reviews. 4.5+++ stars on Amazon.

Goliath. You know the story. But why is it in the Bible? Is it just to give us a little moral pick-me-up as we seek to emulate a small shepherd boy who defeated a giant? Have you ever wondered where Goliath came from? Did you know he had brothers, one with 24 fingers and toes? Did you know their ancestry is steeped in unimaginable horror? Genesis 6. The Nephilim. The first few verses of this chapter have long been the speculation of supernatural events that produced demigods and a flood that God used to destroy the whole world. The whole world remembers them. Once upon a time, all Christians knew them. But for many centuries this view was mocked, though it was the only known view at the time of the writing of the New Testament. Today, it is making a resurgence among Bible-believing scholars, and for good reason. The Nephilim were on the earth in those days, and also afterward...

This book delves deep into the dark and ancient recesses of our past to bring you rich treasures long buried. It is a carefully researched, heavily footnoted, and selectively illustrated story of the giants of the Bible. There is more here than meets the eye, much more. Here you will learn the invisible, supernatural storyline of the Bible that is always just beneath the surface, lurking like the spawn of the ancient leviathan. It is a storyline no person can afford to ignore any longer. Unlike other more sensational books on the topic, there is no undue speculation to be found here. The author is a Bible-believing Christian who refuses to use such ideas to tell you the end of the world is drawing nigh. Once you discover the truth about these fantastic creatures, you will come to see the ministry and work of Jesus Christ in a very new and exalting light. Come. Learn the fascinating, sobering, yet true story of real giants who played a significant role in the bible ... and still do so today.

Available in Paperback or Kindle at Amazon.com

The Unseen Realm: Q & A Companion
(2016)

Edited by Michael Heiser.
Published by Lexham Press.

In *The Unseen Realm*, Dr. Michael S. Heiser unpacked 15 years of research while exploring what the Bible really says about the supernatural world. That book has nearly 900 reviews and a five-star rating. It is a game-changer.

Doug helps you further explore *The Unseen Realm* with a fresh perspective and an easy-to-follow format. The book summarizes key concepts and themes from Heiser's book and includes questions aimed at helping you gain a deeper understanding of the biblical author's supernatural worldview.

The format is that of a catechism: A Question followed by the Answer. There are 95 Questions (nod to Martin Luther) divided into 12 Parts:

Chapters:
Part I—God
Part II—The Lesser Gods
Part III—The Sons of God
Part IV—Divine Council
Part V—Sin, Rebellion, and the Fall
Part VI—Rebellion before the flood
Part VII—Rebellion after the flood
Part VIII—The Promise Anticipated
Part IX—The Promise Fulfilled
Part X—The Good News

**Available in Paperback or Kindle at Amazon.com
or on the Bible-software platform Logos at Logos.com**

From the Shadows to the Savior:

Christ in the Old Testament
(2015)

Few subjects are as important—yet ignored or misapplied--as the one addressed in this book. Jesus Christ is the absolute center and focus of the totality of God's word. Many people confess this belief, since Jesus himself taught it (Luke 24:27; John 5:39). Christians have done well to see this on one or two levels, yet truly understanding just how primary he is as an actor—even in the Old Testament—is something few have considered.

In this book (the first edition of *Patterned, Promised, Present* in the Christ in All Scripture Series), adapted from a series of blog posts for the Decablog, Doug helps us see the light of Christ that emerges from the dark hallways of Scriptures that so many find outdated, unintelligible, and irrelevant for today's Church.

Learn how Christ is found in such things as prophecy, typology, and the law. Then, come in for a deeper study of how the Person himself is actually present, walking, speaking, and acting, beginning in the very first book of the Bible. Learn how words such as "Word," "Name," "Glory," and "Wisdom" are all ideas that the Scripture itself attaches to Christ who in the OT is called The Angel of the LORD. Then see if such ideas don't radically change the way you think about all of God's word in this truly life-changing summary of Christ in the Old Testament.

Chapters:
NT Passages and Reflections
Christ in Prophecy
Christ in Typology
Christ and the Law
Christ: The Angel of the LORD
Christ: The Word of God
Christ: The Name of the LORD
Christ: The Wisdom of God
Christ: The Son of God
Christ: The Glory of God
Christ: The Right Arm of God

Available in Paperback or Kindle at Amazon.com

Waters of Creation:
A Biblical-Theological Study of Baptism
(2009)

This is the one book on baptism that you must read. It was seven years in the making. Doug believes that until a new approach is taken, separations over the meaning, mode, and recipients of baptism will never be bridged.

This new approach traces the roots of baptism deep into the OT Scriptures. When understood properly, we discover that baptism is always the sign that God has used to initiate his people into a new creation. Baptism in the NT is not "new." Rather, it derives its origin from OT predecessors. It has a direct, sacramental counterpart, and it isn't circumcision. It is baptism. When we understand that baptism comes from baptism, especially in its sacramental expression in the priestly covenant, reasons for the NT practice begin to make perfect sense.

Now Baptists have an argument that infant Baptists can finally understand, because we are beginning our argument in the same place. This is an Old Testament covenantal approach to the Baptist position with baptistic conclusions as to the mode and recipients of baptism. That's what happens when we root baptism in baptism rather than circumcision.

Chapters:
The Baptism of Jesus
Baptism and the Sanctuary
Baptism and the Priesthood
Baptism and the Covenant
Implications for Christian Baptism

Available in Paperback or Kindle at Amazon.com

Covenant Theology:
A Reformed Baptist Primer
(2014)

Covenant theology is often said to be the domain of infant Baptists alone. But there really are such things as Reformed Baptists who believe in covenant theology as a basic system for approaching Scripture.

This primer sets out to give the basics of a Reformed Baptist covenant theology and to do so in a way that is understandable to the uninitiated. It was originally a series we did on Sunday nights at our church. It agrees with classical formulations of covenant theology in that there is a Covenant of Redemption, a Covenant of Works, and a Covenant of Grace in the Bible.

The book takes a multi-perspective approach to the Covenant of Redemption in that this covenant is the basis for the classic formula that Christ's death is sufficient for all, but efficient for the elect. It sees the Covenant of Works for Adam in a broader context of a covenant made with all of creation, a covenant where laws establish the parameters for creation's existence.

It differs from Paedobaptist covenant theology in that it sees the Covenant of Grace as only properly coming through Jesus Christ. OT gracious covenants are typological of the Covenant of Grace but save people on the basis of the coming work of Christ through faith alone. This is the traditional way Reformed Baptists have articulated the Covenant of Grace.

Finally, it sees an entire covenant in the Old Testament as often (but not always) missing from formulations of covenant theology. In the opinion of the author, this "priestly covenant" is vital to a proper understanding of 1. The continuity of the practice of baptism from OT to NT, 2. The answer to why we never find infants being baptized in the NT, and 3. A more precise way to parse the legal aspects of the OT economy, thereby helping us understand why the moral law continues today. This volume works from the basic presupposition that continuity in God's word is more basic than discontinuity. In this, it differs from dispensationalism and new covenant theology. The book suggests that this is the greatest strength of covenant theology, which does also recognize discontinuity.

Available in Paperback or Kindle at Amazon.com

Galatians:
A Supernatural Justification
(2012)

A play on words, the subtitle of this book gives you the two main points it tries to get across. Galatians central message teaches how a person is *justified* before a holy God. This once precious and central teaching of Protestant theology is often misunderstood or relegated the pile of irrelevant, stale doctrine.

Perhaps that is why the Apostle Paul supercharges his teaching with an oft-overlooked side of this letter - the *supernatural* beings who tempt us and teach us to give up the only truth that will save us. Galatian Christians would have been familiar with these supernatural beings; their culture was steeped in it. Thus, they mistake Paul for the messenger-healer god Hermes, and Barnabas for Zeus. Paul's warning: "Even if we or an angel from heaven should preach to you a gospel contrary to the one we preached to you, let him be accursed." This is Paul's fatherly way of showing his children in the faith that the gospel is paramount; it alone is able to save. Such a warning like this can have new power, as people are returning with reckless abandon to the worship of the old gods.

This book is from a series of sermons preached at the Reformed Baptist Church of Northern Colorado in 2011.

Available in Paperback or Kindle at Amazon.com

The Five Solas
of the Reformation
(2019)
100+reviews. 4.5+++ stars on Amazon

The 500th anniversary of the Reformation occurred in 2017. It was October 31, 1517 that Martin Luther nailed his 95 Thesis to the door of the great cathedral at Wittenberg, Germany. He had no idea what that simple act would do. His bold proclamation and challenge to for Rome to reform her ways and beliefs was met with hostility from some and great sympathy from others. Out of this sympathy arose Protestantism, a movement deeply concerned with grounding all things on Holy Scripture, giving glory to God alone, and recovering for that generation the biblical gospel of Jesus Christ. In five chapters, Doug Van Dorn takes us back to these ancient catch-phrases that once moved a continent. Scripture Alone, Grace Alone, Faith Alone, Christ Alone, and To God Be the Glory Alone became the rallying cry of all who longed to see men and women, boys and girls saved and set free from sin, death, and the devil. The end of the book contains four helpful Appendices on songs, Church Fathers on the solas, a bibliography for further research, and a letter from Martin Luther.

Available in Paperback or Kindle at Amazon.com

Conspiracy Theory
A Christian Evaluation of a Taboo Subject
(2020)

These days, when you throw "conspiracy theory" at someone, it is for one purpose—to be a thought-stopper and a discussion killer. But having this discussion grows more important by the day. People are engaging in "conspiracy theories" whether some want to admit it or not. Frankly, it is a discussion that needs to happen. This book is not about specific conspiracies, but rather is a serious look at the phrase from a definitional, historical, biblical, and Christian point of view. The main goal is to come to some helpful conclusions on how a Christian can remain sane in a world of conspiracy theories. And, we'll have some fun along the way.

Chapters
Origin of this Book
The Origin of a Phrase
A Brief History of Conspiracies
A Brief Biblical Theology of Conspiracies
A Textual conspiracy
Evaluating Conspiracy Theories
Remaining Sane in a World of Conspiracies

Available in Paperback or Kindle at Amazon.com

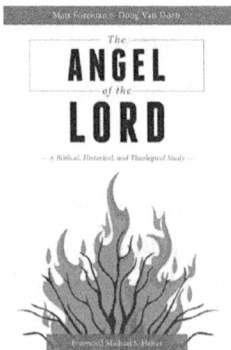

The Angel of the LORD
A Biblical, Historical, & Theological Study
(2020)
100+ reviews. 5 full star rating on Amazon.

In the early books of the Old Testament, the mysterious "Angel of the Lord" repeatedly appears—visibly, audibly, even physically—to the Patriarchs, to Moses, to the Prophets. Who is this Angel? Exploring the biblical texts, the testimony of church history, and the insights of Systematic Theology, Matt Foreman and Doug Van Dorn argue that the answer is beyond doubt: the Angel of the Lord is a manifestation of God the Son. Even more, they argue that this Angel appears more often than people realize, because he appears under different titles, including: the Word, the Name, the Glory, the Face, the Right Hand, even the Son. They show that even some of the ancient Jews spoke of a Second Yahweh in the Old Testament. Christian theologians throughout history have taught this same understanding. Christians today need to be taught again how the Person of Jesus appears throughout the Bible and how he speaks to us today.

Foreword by Michael S. Heiser

"The *Angel of the Lord* is a masterful work of not only biblical and pastoral theology, it is also a much-needed apologetic. Rare is the book that would fit well on the shelf of both the professional scholar and the armchair theologian. *Angel of the Lord* is precisely that kind of book."
~ *Voddie Baucham (D.Min., D.D.), Dean of the Seminary at African Christian University*

Available in Paperback or Kindle at Amazon.com

The Creeds
Christian Faith Essentials
(2023)

The old saying goes, "In essentials unity, in non-essentials liberty, and in all things charity [or love]." There is no better way to define what is essential to the Christian Faith or to stand firm in what we believe ("creed" comes from the Latin for "I believe") than in knowing and cherishing the short teachings of Scripture that were encapsulated in the ecumenical creeds of the early church.

For nearly 2,000 years, the creeds (our "one faith") have been lighthouses, guiding and protecting the church through dark and dangerous storms that batter her people with waves of doubt and unbelief, and through howling winds of human cunning, craftiness, and deceitful doctrines, blow her off-course, carrying her dangerously close to rocky shoals.

The Creeds is a collection of five sermons (along with several helpful appendices) adapted to book form on four creeds of the early church: the Old Roman Symbol (2nd cent.), the Apostles' Creed (4th-7th cent.), and the Nicene Creeds (325 and 381). After an important grounding introductory chapter, it looks at the four parts of the creeds (God the Father, God the Son, God the Holy Spirit, and the Kingdom) in harmony with one another, making this a unique and devotional contribution to this subject.

Available in Paperback or Kindle at Amazon.com

Made in United States
Orlando, FL
24 June 2024

48250804R10235